Real Estate
Principles and Practices
A Contemporary Approach

Fourth Edition

Real Estate

Principles and Practices

A Contemporary Approach

Fourth Edition

Arlyne Geschwender
Randall School of Real Estate

GSP

Gorsuch Scarisbrick, Publishers
Scottsdale, Arizona

To all who are interested in learning more about real estate, with special thanks to the many students who have encouraged me along the way.

The publisher makes every reasonable best effort to ensure the accuracy and completeness of the information and answers contained in this book. Due to the ever changing nature of applicable laws and practices, the reader is cautioned and advised to always consult with the instructor when questions arise. Test questions have been checked for correct correlation with the question answered. If the reader encounters a questionable answer, the reader should always consult the text or the instructor for a more complete answer and analysis of the answer. Should the reader believe that an alternative interpretation of the information contained in this book is possible, he or she is encouraged to consult with the instructor.

Publisher   John W. Gorsuch
Editor   Sandra E. Byrd
Developmental Editor   Gay L. Pauley
Production Editor   Mary B. Cullen
Cover Design   Kevin Kall
Typesetting   Ash Street Typecrafters

Gorsuch Scarisbrick, Publishers
8233 Via Paseo del Norte, F400
Scottsdale, Arizona 85258

10 9 8 7 6 5 4 3 2 1

ISBN 0-89787-932-5

Printed in the United States of America.

Contents

PART FIVE   BASIC TOOLS   301

Illustrations

Preface

At some point in life every person is involved with real estate. Since the time when early beings sought refuge in caves, the need for shelter has been a fact of life. In much more recent times, with the great housing boom of the late 1970s and early 1980s, people began to realize that real property ownership could be a hedge against rising inflation. Although dramatic increases in real estate values came to a halt during the 1980s, real estate is still considered a solid investment.

After many years of teaching real estate classes, I felt strongly that there was a need for a principles and practices textbook written in a clear and concise manner—one that would be understandable to the novice entering the world of real estate. Furthermore, it seemed only logical to organize the textbook around the natural sequence of events in a real estate transaction. This text is divided into five parts: an introduction to real estate, the process of a sale, other aspects of ownership, fair housing and license laws, and basic tools for the salesperson, broker, or investor.

Part One begins by giving the reader a brief overview of real estate, and Chapter 2 discusses property rights and ownership interests and introduces readers to the concepts of real estate ownership. Chapter 3 covers land descriptions and survey systems, acquainting the reader with legal descriptions. Chapter 4 explains estates, deeds, and the various methods by which title to real property can be taken.

Part Two follows the process of a real estate transaction. In Chapter 5, readers are introduced to the important role that contracts play in the process of listing, selling, leasing, and optioning real property. Using the sale of a single property as an example, Chapters 6 through 10 illustrate the natural sequence of the process, beginning with the listing contract and concluding with the closing of the sale. Chapter 6 covers the function and purpose of the brokerage firm and explains the listing contract. The offer to purchase the property follows in Chapter 7. Lending sources (Chapter 8) and financing the purchase (Chapter 9) are the next steps in the process. Chapter 10 discusses closing procedures from both the lender's and the broker's viewpoint and includes settlement statements for the seller and the buyer.

Part Three deals with other aspects of real estate ownership. Other forms of residence, such as condominiums, cooperatives, and time-sharing units, are covered in Chapter 11; leases are explained in Chapter 12; and a discussion of property management is offered in Chapter 13. Investments and tax aspects of real estate ownership are covered in Chapter 14. A discussion of appraisals (Chapter 15) is followed by material on land use controls and regulations, along with environmental issues that affect our land (Chapter 16).

Part Four covers the federal fair housing laws as they apply to sales and rentals of real property (Chapter 17). A brief overview of the license laws act, which mandates the licensing of persons engaging in the real estate business, is offered in Chapter 18.

Finally, Part Five considers the various math applications encountered in real estate transactions (Chapter 19). Problems on computing interest, profit and loss, taxes and commission, ratio and proportion, and loan amortization are provided as examples of basic real estate arithmetic. A practice examination consisting of 100 multiple choice questions covers material presented in the 19 chapters. An in-depth glossary of real estate terms and an answer key to the chapter review questions conclude the text.

Never before has real estate been so complex or challenging. It is my hope that this textbook will provide students with the foundation of knowledge they need to enter the field of real estate.

Acknowledgments

I would like to give special thanks to Joyce D. Remsburg of Trident Technical College and Jack Kelley of Jack Kelley's Northeastern College of Real Estate for their valuable and perceptive critiques of the fourth edition manuscript and for the suggestions they made toward improving the book. My thanks also to Kent Geschwender for his assistance with current loan information.

Thank you to the staff of Gorsuch Scarisbrick, Publishers, especially to Sandra Byrd, for her support and encouragement, and to Mary Cullen, for her assistance during the production process.

Finally, sincere thanks to my staff at the Randall School of Real Estate for understanding my need to spend long hours at the computer.

To the Student

This text has been written especially for the person who is taking a first course in real estate. It provides an easily understood introduction into this many-faceted subject. Whether the reader plans to pursue a career in real estate or is interested in learning for the purpose of buying, selling, leasing, or managing real estate, the text covers the fundamentals of real estate principles and practices.

To assist you in using this text, I recommend the following:

1. Review the key words that begin each chapter, watch for **boldfaced** key words as they are used within the chapter, and review the glossary when necessary. Once you have learned the vocabulary of real estate, you will be surprised at how quickly the concepts become clear.

2. Read the chapters in sequence. It may help you to better understand the strange new language of real estate if you also reread portions of some chapters. The wide margins are for your use in making notes and jotting down any questions you have. By placing your questions in these margins, you will have them available to ask in class.

3. Answer the discussion questions at the end of each chapter. These questions will help you consider what you have learned and put ideas into your own words. Your instructor may use these questions to stimulate class discussions.

4. Answer the review questions at the end of each chapter and check your answers with the answer key at the end of the book. If you miss a question, reread the pages on which the material appears.

5. When you finish the text, take the practice examination offered at the end of the book and then review your answers. Use your score on this test to evaluate your progress and indicate problem areas that will need review.

While text headings outline the contents of the book, the special phrases placed in the margins bring out important topics and ideas. As you review the material, these marginal notes will help you identify and locate the main concepts in each chapter.

Since Part Two of the text follows the natural sequence of events in a real estate transaction, it will help you put the process in perspective. Legal documents are introduced as they are used in the listing and sale of real estate, and each instrument is explained in detail. Understanding these documents and the part they play in a real estate transaction will enhance your ability to become a true professional in the field.

There will always be more people,
but there will never be more land.

Real Property

Chapter 1 of this text introduces the reader to how economic conditions in a region will affect real estate and conversely how real estate contributes to the prosperity of a community.

Chapter 2 explains property rights and ownership interests and familiarizes the reader with a basic knowledge of real estate ownership.

Chapter 3 covers land descriptions and the survey systems to acquaint the reader with the premise of surveying. The legal description that defines ownership is covered.

Chapter 4 introduces how title to real property is held, explaining estates, the various types of deeds, and methods of holding title.

PART ONE

Real Estate and the Economy

KEY WORDS

business cycles
economic base
free enterprise

gross national product (GNP)
ownership cycle

OVERVIEW

Each of us at some time in our lives becomes involved with real estate. Since we all need shelter, we either rent or purchase a place in which to live. Moreover, as one of the largest industries in the United States, real estate has a direct impact on our economy, community, and society. Thus, it seems appropriate to begin this text by exploring the role and contribution of real estate.

As homeownership became available to the average man and woman, real estate became a vehicle by which individuals could prosper and the nation could grow. Often, the largest portion of the estate the average person accumulates in a lifetime is the equity built up through homeownership. Thus, homeownership can serve as a forced savings plan.

More immediately, real estate provides us with a sense of community in an otherwise very mobile society. With advanced modes of transportation to facilitate our mobility, Americans have been on the move throughout this country's history. To own a home signifies establishing roots. Better housed than people in any other nation, Americans in all age groups and economic levels take pride in their homes. Homeownership in the United States is the underpinning of the ideal of the American way of life and assists in promoting pride in citizenship.

This chapter explains how real estate helps to support a community and, conversely, how the **economic base** of a community impacts the value of real estate. In addition, the chapter discusses how housing changes to meet public needs as demographics change in a region. A look to the future concludes the chapter.

HOUSING NEEDS

In 1980 the Census Bureau counted 226.5 million people in the United States. The 1990 census report swelled that number to 249.5 million people. Recent studies indicate that the total may reach 260 to 280 million people by the year 2000, and

Housing for the senior citizen

increasing immigration numbers may push that figure even higher. This anticipated growth in population accentuates the importance of land and housing as a marketable commodity. The population increase can in part be contributed to the "graying" of America—citizens are living longer and more productive lives. Some indicators estimate this increase will rise by 20 percent. In the last 25 years, the age 65 and older population has been escalating at a rate double that of the rest of the population, and for the first time in our country's history, we have more senior citizens than teenagers. We will see an increase in housing built strictly for the retiree and the elderly. Housing provisions for this aging segment of the population have been springing up in all parts of the country, with special emphasis in the sunbelt areas of Arizona, Texas, Florida, and California. Currently, the population growth in these sunbelt states is triple the rate of the rest of the country. However, much of this active, older generation will elect to remain near family or where their working lives were spent. Realizing this, communities all over America are gearing up to meet this trend and to produce housing for this segment of the population.

Population characteristics

Changes in population distribution patterns are continually monitored by real estate analysts. Population demographics experience change slowly. Consequently, this change needs to be analyzed over a period of decades. Any rapid growth in a particular area of the country will require additional housing units. Conversely, if statistics reveal a decline in population, housing needs will be lessened. Tracking these changes includes determining the population's characteristics, since this will affect not only the number but the type of housing units needed. For example, provisions for the single student in college cities are evidenced by dormitories and apartments surrounding the campuses.

Changing family definition

The greatest apparent sociological change relevant to real estate in the last decade has appeared in the composition of the family structure. Single parent status has increased, as has the number of singles living alone, resulting in a trend toward single households. Many unmarried young people are opting for ownership rather than renting. At an early age young adults are beginning to accumulate equity through homeownership, and condominiums are now popular since they provide ownership without the care and maintenance required by a single-family home. (See Chapter 11 on condominiums.)

An increase in "mingles" (unrelated singles) purchasing real estate together is also prevalent with young adults. Another market is the first-time buyers who later decide to upgrade their investment, moving up to a larger home. For many of these young adults the size and location of one's home is an important aspect of social mobility.

We have determined that age plays a factor in the distribution of housing needs. Also of importance is inflation. In the 1970s and 1980s inflated values made housing increasingly unaffordable to much of the population. Housing costs escalated the highest in the northeast and western sections of the United States. In some areas of the country the entry-level buyer had been virtually priced out of the market. Two major contributing factors were rising land costs and financing rates. Land costs increase when the supply becomes scarce in areas where housing is needed. Naturally this need is greater near employment centers. Financing rates fluctuate according to the availability of funds to the housing market and play a major role in determining who can afford housing. In addition to these factors, as our country grows and prospers, the cost of all commodities increases. Housing is no exception. Vast changes have occurred as the humble beginnings of the simple shelter which afforded few amenities has been transformed into the home with many creature comforts we enjoy today.

CONTRIBUTION TO THE ECONOMY

The rights and benefits inherent in real property ownership contribute to the economy of our country. Through taxation, real estate provides the monetary basis upon which schools, parks, recreation areas, public transportation, utility services, and roads are built and maintained. Large corporations establish factories and businesses in areas where employees can live well. The community that can offer a favorable and attractive economic environment will prosper and grow.

In some communities, blighted areas are reclaimed and restored or redeveloped by concerned community members, ultimately adding to the tax roles of the area. Buildings with historic significance are renovated and become prized landmarks. The social impact that real estate has upon the economy of an area is immense.

REAL ESTATE CREATES EMPLOYMENT

On the national level, real estate accounts for a substantial share of the **gross national product (GNP)**. The gross national product is the sum (value) of all goods and services produced and used in the country. Dividing the GNP by the total population gives us a means of measuring the flow of income for that particular year, indicating our standard of living (although inflation changes the impact of these figures to a degree).

Contribution of real estate to GNP

Through the study of economics we become aware of the resources people use to produce goods to satisfy the needs and desires of purchasers. Our natural resources are used in developing the products that are produced by the labor of our people. The buyers ultimately dictate how much will be produced of any given product. If the supply is greater than the demand, the supplier is left with inventory that may need to be reduced in price or withheld from the market until the present supply is consumed.

Our economic system has changed greatly since the first settlers came to these shores. Each settler filled many roles, since it was necessary to produce everything they needed. The pioneers made their own soap and candles, wove their own cloth, cut trees and built their log cabins, tilled the soil, and hunted wild game for food. Today a great many people produce these needs in an assortment of factories and production centers, resulting in specialization. As an example, electrical power dispelled the need for candles, so today we find specialty shops selling candles which are purchased for aesthetic reasons. Commercial farmers produce our food, and it is packaged in a variety of ways: fresh, canned, dried, and frozen in an attempt to meet everyone's desires.

Consider the tremendous number of people who are either directly or indirectly involved with housing. Begin with the plotting of a subdivision, which requires the services of engineers and surveyors. Operators of heavy equipment construct the roads, and workers install public utilities in preparation for the homes. The construction of the house itself requires a general contractor, subcontractors, and builders and suppliers of all the materials that compose the structure, from the foundation, siding, drywall, windows, doors, and cabinetry to the plumbing, electrical, and gas connections. Appliances and furnishings that ultimately go into the house must be supplied and installed.

The services performed include the savings and loan institutions financing the sale, the title companies insuring the title, the insurance companies insuring the premises, and the appraisers placing a value on the property. Attorneys oversee the closing, city offices record the documents, and nurseries provide the lawn and plantings. Local, state, and federal government have departments devoted entirely to real estate issues.

Local government interests include land use planning and zoning laws. The U.S. Department of Housing and Urban Development (HUD) was established solely to monitor and administrate housing needs. Finally, approximately 2.1 million licensed real estate agents service the public in the listing, selling, renting, and managing of real property.

As we can see, the numbers of people added to the employment rolls through transactions in real estate are indeed large, adding to the prosperity of the community. Clearly, real estate is big business.

PURCHASING THE HOME

At an individual level, the decision to purchase a home is one of the most important decisions made by the average person. That first home is a most meaningful step and is looked upon by the owner as much more than mere shelter. It represents pride, accomplishment, and security. In making a selection, the considerations faced by the purchaser include deciding upon the location, the style, the condition, and the size of the home and its proximity to public transportation, schools, shopping, and employment. Buyers' needs vary; what is perfect for the young family with school-age children may not meet the needs of the childless couple.

New homeowners become involved in their new neighborhood and contribute to the socioeconomic existence of the community, participating in the school system, churches, and neighborhood associations. Some become involved in the local political arena, taking an active part not only with their votes, but also by campaigning for their choice of candidate or being a candidate themselves. They make purchases at the nearby shopping centers, contributing to the success of the business community.

THE OWNERSHIP CYCLE

The **ownership cycle** of real estate in an average person's experience in real estate usually begins with renting, creating a need for apartment units. The first move into a home allows the individual to begin building an equity that will supply the basis for the next move into a larger home. Often moves are necessitated by employment transfers to other parts of the country. As an owner's equity builds and salary increases, a place must be sought to put the savings to work. For many, investment takes the form of the purchase of additional real estate. Whether the purchase is residential income property or an office building or a commercial structure, the investor adds to the prosperity of the area, since each individual property affects the community. After the family is raised and people grow older and retire, their needs change, and they choose smaller homes with less maintenance. Some of this senior citizen group may return to renting. (See Figure 1.1.)

HOW ECONOMIC CONDITIONS AFFECT REAL ESTATE

Our **free enterprise** system is based on the premise that the more you produce, the more you receive. The open market system allows consumers to decide what they want and the producers to compete to supply those needs. Extremely successful in encouraging economic progress, the open market system forces suppliers to be competitive in offering goods for consumption, giving both buyers and sellers choices. When a product is in great demand, more people become involved in its production in the hopes of making money to have the purchasing power to buy other commodities. Competition results in improved products, thus elevating our standard of living. Currently, great competition in the field of electronics and especially in the

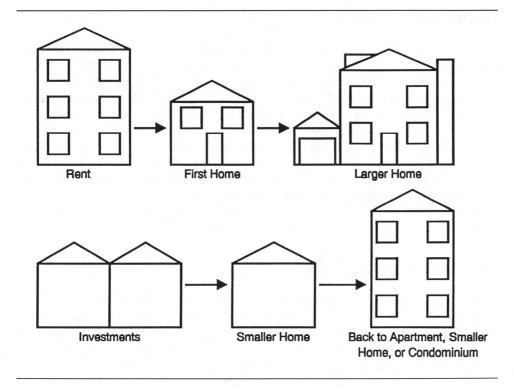

FIGURE 1.1
The ownership cycle.

advancement of the computer has benefited the consumer in the form of better equipment at lower prices. Buyers are the decision makers and have many choices in today's market, whether it is food, electronics, automobiles, or housing.

Business cycles create problems for the economy in general and especially for the real estate industry. The economic conditions of the country play a great part in the real estate cycle. We can track the fluctuations of real estate values to the conditions in the marketplace. When interest rates rose to an all-time high of 17.5 percent in 1982, sales of housing slowed dramatically in most areas of the country. As interest rates fell, buyers once again began the home search, and the marketplace hummed with sales.

Effect of business cycles on real estate

However, each region experiences "buyer's" and "seller's" markets, depending on what is happening locally. In 1985–1986 a sluggish land market was in effect in the farm belt. When farmers with overextended credit failed to meet their loan obligations, the farms were foreclosed and auctioned off to the highest bidder. During this same time, astronomical prices were being paid for homes in the northeastern section of the country. A reversal of these conditions occurred in the late 1980s when a drastic slowdown occurred in the northeast and values in the farm belt began rising. Unlike most other commodities, real estate relates to the economy of the particular area in which it is located, with supply and demand a strong force in the market value of the property.

Real estate is exciting, not only because it is a needed commodity, but also because "owning a piece of the earth" has long been a dream of the American people. Many early immigrants came to our land for personal freedom, including the right to own real property. Today, the desire to own our own piece of land and the promise that it is possible to do so are a large part of our American dream. Thus, real estate has implications far beyond the exchange of money and land.

ECONOMIC BASE

To the economist, land is the supreme substance from which all our nation's goods are produced. The farmers use land to produce crops, the lumber mills cut trees to supply wood for houses and furniture and to provide the pulp for the paper upon which this book is printed, and so on. To have an economically sound base, each community must produce commodities (goods or services) that it can sell and in turn use the funds earned to purchase what the community does not produce. Cities like to maintain a broad economic base rather than relying on one industry because if that industry should collapse and the city's residents were without jobs it could mean the decline of property values and tax bases. The ghost towns near the abandoned mines that ran out of ore are examples of communities that died out because they were dependent solely upon one commodity. In modern times, similar problems arose in Detroit when the automobile industry encountered financial difficulties.

THE 1980s TO THE 1990s

Market conditions for a decade

Sharp changes in market conditions influence the eventual success of a real estate project, so investors and real estate salespersons must be aware of the trends that produce these cycles. If we review the status of the economy in the 1980s, we see that it fluctuated up and down, having a seesaw effect upon the national and local real estate markets. The crisis during the decade of the 1980s, which began in mild recession, included the unequaled deficit of the federal government and the collapse of savings and loans nationwide. We witnessed bankruptcies in the farm communities and a halt to inflation. The Tax Reform Act of 1986 greatly affected real estate investments, we experienced a shocking stock market plunge in 1987, and fluctuating interest rates prevailed. While other factors played a role in the condition of the economy, the volatile factors listed above can be justifiably blamed for the up and down swings the real estate market endured. We eased out of the 1980s intact, with a slowed growth in some parts of the country that began to climb as we entered the 1990s. When buyers spend, the GNP experiences growth.

In the early 1990s lower interest rates spurred a recessionary economy. As inflated property values recorrected due to market pressures, mortgage interest rates fell to 7 percent and even lower, a rate unheard of for decades. Real estate practitioners and the rest of the country waited to see if the U.S. would climb out of its ongoing recession.

SUMMARY

In summary, some of the factors that determine the market demand for real estate are:

1. Relocation of families. Our mobile society has families on the move, largely because of employment opportunities and a desire for environmental change.
2. Formation of non-traditional households. Young singles have become more interested in owning property and, in addition to married couples, create a demand for a first home.
3. Cost of housing. High prices can eliminate the first-time buyer.
4. Financing. When interest rates rise, the demand for loans declines, causing many buyers to be priced out of the market.
5. Changing life-styles. Our cycle of ownership illustrated that as individuals age, they tend to downsize their housing needs. Also to be considered are the new innovations in appliances and labor-saving devices and the house styles themselves that prompt people to move up as their income increases.

DISCUSSION QUESTIONS

1. Why can we say that real estate creates employment?
2. Are housing needs constant in a given area? Explain.
3. Explain business cycles as they relate to real estate.
4. How do economic conditions affect the real estate market?

Land: Its Characteristics and Acquisition

2

KEY WORDS

accretion
ad valorem tax
adverse possession
allodial system
avulsion
bundle of rights
chattel
codicil
color of title
descent
devise
doctrine of prior appropriation
durability
easement by prescription
eminent domain
escheat
feudal system

fixtures
immobility
indestructible
intestate
littoral rights
mill
nonhomogeneous
personal property
police power
profit a prendre
quiet title action
real estate
real property
riparian rights
scarcity
situs
testate

OVERVIEW

Historically, land acquisition has been the crux of major battles throughout the world. Landownership has played a part in everything from the rise of great political powers to the development of individual self-worth. We have learned a great deal from the past. Many of today's fundamental ideas concerning ownership and transfer of real property have been handed down relatively unchanged from medieval times.

The evolution of landownership began when tribes of nomads stopped roaming to settle and form communities. Staying in one area, they began to cultivate crops and build shelters. Tribal chiefs controlled the village, allocating areas of land to individual families to use. The tribe often found it necessary to fight off aggressors who sought to infringe on their possessionary rights. As time passed, the feudal concept developed.

Evolution of landownership

The **feudal system** prevailed in Europe during the Middle Ages and gave the king control of all the land. Feudalism formed the political, economic, and social

Feudal system

organization of medieval Europe. Under the feudal system, social position was determined by the amount of land held. The king maintained ownership of the land, distributing it among lords and nobles who in return pledged to support the king with taxes and their allegiance. The lords supervised serfs who worked the land. In the early Middle Ages the lords did not own property as we do today; they merely had the right to use or administer the land.

Our nation was developed from a vast wilderness just a few hundred years ago by the British, the first to colonize North America in large numbers. The king of England granted charters to private enterprises as joint stock companies, vesting them with authority to found and govern chartered colonies. The governors appointed by the king were to rule these colonies. Many people coming to our shores were seeking religious freedom and an opportunity to prosper. Independent-thinking colonists united against Britain when they felt that trade and taxes were unfair—declaring their independence July 4, 1776. The doors to this new world, with opportunity of private ownership of land, were then opened to all people.

Allodial system Our system of landownership is the **allodial system**, which gives individuals the right to own land. We can acquire real estate without government interference and then buy, sell, exchange, option, lease, or will the real estate we own.

Perhaps the most exciting chapter in the history of land acquisition occurred during America's westward expansion. Pioneers explored and settled a wilderness, carving out homesites for their families and for generations to come. Promises of individual landownership through grants by the United States government prompted thousands of early Americans to forsake the comforts of established cities for the spartan life of the western frontier. To encourage the settlement of public lands, Congress gave land to all settlers who complied with the homestead laws. There was little exchange of properties in those early days, but as the territories and states became more settled, the need for land to supply food and shelter for new arrivals became apparent, and people began to sell off portions of their holdings.

Land remains the most prized possession of the average individual in the United States. The pioneers of a century ago would view with amazement the concrete empires that have replaced their sod houses. As the United States population grows and shifts, land development continues and land use changes. Determination of whether such growth and change are positive or negative usually depends upon who is making the determination.

This chapter defines the physical and economic characteristics of land and explains how they affect the value of land. It defines and differentiates among real and personal property, explains real property rights, and discusses government rights and/or powers regarding private property. Finally, the chapter concludes with explanations of how one acquires real property and how one can lose that ownership.

CHARACTERISTICS OF LAND

The distinct characteristics of land can be classified into two general categories: physical and economic (see Figure 2.1). These characteristics determine its utility and value.

Physical Characteristics

The physical characteristics of land are its immobility, its indestructibility, and its non-homogeneity.

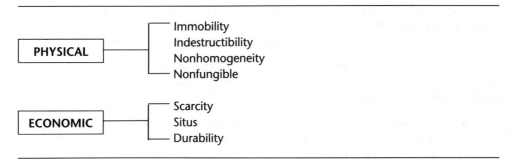

FIGURE 2.1
Characteristics of land.

Land consists of various types of soil, rocks, and minerals. It contains valleys and plains, lakes and rivers, mountains and canyons. Whatever the makeup of the land, it is fixed; that is, it is not movable. It remains permanently in a fixed geographical location. This **immobility** of land determines its value. That a parcel of land will always be exactly where it lies does not, however, guarantee that its value will remain constant.

Immobility

Since land remains in a permanent location, except for erosion and depletion, it never wears out. Hills have been leveled in the construction of highways and building sites, rivers have changed channels, minerals have been taken from the soil, but the land is still there; it is literally **indestructible**. We are living on the same land as our ancestors and the natives before them. When improvements (buildings, utilities, and so on) are added to the land, they too are of a permanent nature, though unlike the land they will depreciate and need to be replaced over a period of time. Land's durability makes it an ideal commodity for investors, though the economic climate of an area can have an impact on its value.

Indestructibility

Since there are no two identical parcels of land, land is **nonhomogeneous**. Unlike manufactured goods that are duplicated many times, any two parcels of land will vary. The fact that the location of each parcel is different creates a variance in itself.

Nonhomogeneity

Recognizing that land is nonhomogeneous has resulted in its being legally referred to as *nonfungible* (not substitutable). One property cannot be substituted for another. While the same house plan may be followed on several sites, differences in material and craftsmanship will occur in the construction. The parcels of land, though similar to the eye, will also vary.

Because of the differences in the physical characteristics of land, it is divided into agricultural, residential, commercial, industrial, and recreational uses. The use to which land is designated is determined to a great degree by what it is best suited for.

Agriculture began with the early settlers who farmed the valleys and plains and cleared forestlands that lent themselves to cultivation. Some agricultural land is best suited for raising wheat, as in the central plains states. In warmer climates, the temperature and soil are ideal for orange groves. Irrigation can supplement the lack of rainfall, but northern temperatures would freeze many fruit crops.

Agricultural

As cities develop and their populations grow, they encroach onto neighboring farmland. Although the land is physically suited to raising crops, it is put to a new use. Desire by workers to live near employment creates a demand for housing in close proximity to the job centers. Homesites must be adaptable to construction. While hilly land is suitable for homesites, extremely steep hills are undesirable, particularly in areas of the country where snow and rain could create travel problems. Known flood zones and areas with the possibility of mud slides are also to be avoided as possible homesites.

Residential

Commercial   Commercial property is located where business is generated for merchants. The busy streets along which traffic flows beckon to the builders of restaurants and shopping centers. Their properties should be easily accessible for the shopper.

Industrial   Industrial land is generally located near transportation facilities, such as railways, trucking, airlines, and waterways. In order to attract industrial users, tracts are developed around these services.

Recreational   Land unsuitable for other uses may be perfect for recreational purposes. The mountains of Colorado abound with ski lodges and nature trails. Rivers and lakes are used for boating, fishing, and water sports. Resort areas are developed near ocean beaches, especially in warmer climates. Stated briefly, the physical characteristics of land determine to a great extent its use.

Economic Characteristics

While its physical and economic characteristics overlap to some degree, land has some distinct economic characteristics, including *scarcity, situs* (location), and *durability* (permanence). To determine value, think of the acronym DUST (demand, utility, scarcity, and transferability).

Economic conditions in an area dictate if its worth will rise or fall. Demand and scarcity are the greatest influences on its value. Land's fixity makes it vulnerable for the collection of debt. Liens may be placed against the property and a sale ordered so that payment to the creditor is made.

Scarcity   Land acquires value when it is desired. Since we cannot develop or manufacture more land, the supply is *fixed*. If there is a **scarcity** of usable land for homesites in a given area, the value of the land tends to rise. Creativity has resulted in more high-rise construction in congested areas where the supply of open land is limited. The air about us is absolutely essential to us, but because of its abundance, we do not have to purchase it; it is free. Likewise, when too many homes in a similar price range are placed on the market in a given area, the abundance may cause a decrease in value and a buyer's market will occur. That is, a large selection may lead the prospective buyer to offer less than the asking price. If, on the other hand, few homes are available, the buyer who needs housing may be willing to pay more. Demand for a commodity is created in part by its scarcity. The law of supply and demand dictates that scarcity influences supply, and desire influences demand.

Situs   The **situs**, or location, of the land also determines its value. You may have heard the phrase, "location, location, location," a prime factor in establishing value. Travel 20 miles out of the city, and the land is not as costly because it is farther from the center of employment. We are not in short supply of land across the United States, but the available sites near heavily populated areas are limited. In large part, the availability of utilities determines the direction of growth. Near large metropolitan cities such as Chicago and New York, many workers spend hours commuting daily to and from their employment. Homes by the sea will command a higher price than similar homes situated two blocks from the shore. Lots with views or with trees are considered more valuable than those without these amenities, and weather is still another important factor to some.

Value is further determined by what the soil contains. Land rich in oil and gold will be far more valuable than arid desert void of minerals. Fertile agricultural land will be more productive, and hence more valuable, than dry, rocky, grazing land.

Durability   While land is considered indestructible, the **durability** of the improvements that have been made to it must be considered. Although, unlike land, such improvements are vulnerable to natural disasters such as earthquakes, tornadoes, or fire, with proper maintenance they can have an indefinite economic life. However, the use for which a structure may have originally been intended may change. For example, obsolete warehouses in downtown areas of large cities are being renovated and converted into residential apartments, condominiums, and specialty shops. Houses more than 100 years old have been updated and modernized and continue to be used as residences. Many cities have historic preservation committees that bestow landmark designations on old, architecturally aesthetic buildings to preserve our heritage. A move back to urban city areas, especially by young professionals, has been due in part to the aesthetic value of these older homes.

Land is indeed where it all begins: it produces food for animals and humans, it provides water and minerals, and it provides for recreation.

REAL PROPERTY RIGHTS

Private ownership of real property gives the owner the right to possess and use the land to the exclusion of all others. All legal rights attached to the property are the owner's, including the right to possess, exclude, sell, lease, mortgage, give away, exchange, and will (Figure 2.2). This combination of privileges is often referred to as a **bundle of rights**. It gives the owner the *surface rights*, the *subsurface rights*, and the *air rights* above the land as well. For example, an owner may diminish his bundle of rights by selling or leasing these privileges to another. He may lease the subsurface rights to one party, lease the air rights to a second person, and retain the surface rights for his use. A landowner may lease or sell the surface rights to farm the land to one party and the subsurface rights to explore for oil to another. When real property is sold, a purchaser receives no more rights than the seller's real property interest.

Bundle of rights

Surface rights are the most readily visible. These rights include buildings erected on the land or fences of various materials and heights built to designate boundaries and provide security and privacy. The land itself may be cultivated to produce crops or planted in trees. The *subsurface rights* give the holder the right to drill for oil or gas, to dig for gravel and sand, and to extract other minerals. While the owner may own either specific or unlimited minerals, the right of exploration or removal of both of

Surface and subsurface rights

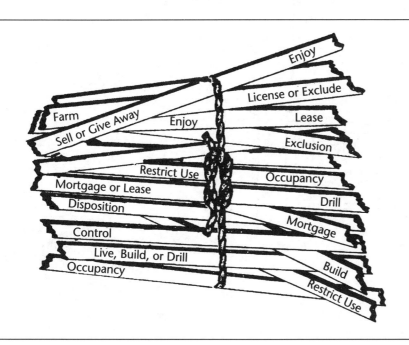

FIGURE 2.2
Bundle of rights.

these minerals may be severely restricted due to deed restriction or environmental laws.

The right to extract minerals such as oil and gas may be sold by one landowner to another. Commonly referred to as oil and gas leases with the right to capture, it permits the holder to drill beneath the surface and to remove the mineral. This is a **profit a prendre**, which is the right to use and extract from the land of another. There will be a royalty clause which gives the lessor (landowner) a percentage of the profits. It may also include a statement that allows the owner to collect rent if there is no production activity. (See Figure 2.3.)

Air rights   The owner of land also possesses the air rights over the property (see Figure 2.4). *Air rights* may be leased or sold and allow the holder to occupy the open space above the designated space of another. This can be in the form of a walkway over a busy street or between buildings. A restaurant may be built over a freeway, or a building may be erected over railroad tracks. The original concept of landownership was that

FIGURE 2.3
Rights in land.

FIGURE 2.4
Air rights.

not only did one own the surface rights, but also the rights from the core of the earth to the heavens above. With emergence of air travel, the courts decreed that it is reasonable that air flights over one's property are not considered trespassing.

One's air rights may also be converged upon by factory smoke and fumes from automobiles. When this becomes hazardous to health, environmental laws are passed, such as the emission control placed on automobiles.

Water is one of our most valuable natural resources, essential to our very existence. Since rainfall is distributed unevenly across the United States, most areas have a water problem of some kind. Considering this, the appropriation of water rights is of prime importance in some states. *Water rights* are established by either the doctrine of **riparian** and **littoral rights** or by the **doctrine of prior appropriation**. The lakes and flowing streams are surface waters available for use under these doctrines (see Figure 2.5).

Water rights

If an owner's land borders a moving body of water, such as a stream or a waterway, under *riparian rights* the landowner is entitled to share in the use of the water. These rights do not extend to damming the water and depriving a neighbor downstream of the use of the water, nor do they extend to actual ownership of the water, but merely to the main characteristics of riparian rights, equality of rights, and reasonable use. If the water is nonnavigable, the landowner has rights out to the middle of the stream. However, if the sides of the lot have designated lengths (150'), the designated length prevails over the wording that indicates ownership to the middle of the stream. Under riparian rights, if a shortage of water develops, first priority is given to necessary household use. When that need is filled, agricultural use will be served, followed by commercial and industrial uses. Most states east of the Mississippi employ this method of water rights.

Riparian rights

If the property borders water, such as rivers, lakes, or oceans, the landowner abutting the water has littoral rights. *Littoral* is a Latin word referring to shore; this water does not have the characteristics of a watercourse. Ordinarily holding title only to the high-water mark, the owners may use and enjoy the water bordering their land but cannot divert the water. In some states, however, this right has been reduced by the *doctrine of prior appropriation*. Adopted in the arid western states, this principle was originally based upon custom and necessity, and finally established in law. Colorado adheres strictly to this doctrine. Simply said, the first owner is privileged with the first claim on the water. This law allows the first user to channel the water for use, depriving other landowners along the watercourse of their equal share. This right established by the appropriator stays with the landowner. The prior appropriator must have an

Littoral rights

Doctrine of prior appropriation

FIGURE 2.5
Water rights.

intent to use the water and actually divert the water from the source of supply. However, this use must be of benefit to the owner and not diverted by the owner for another's use, and the water must actually be diverted by an artificial structure. At least 10 states subscribe to a combination of the riparian and the prior appropriation doctrine.

Groundwater refers to that water in the earth beneath the saturation point. The water passes beneath the land's surface and does not flow in an underground stream, nor is it supplied by streams flowing on the earth's surface. Ownership of land includes the right to drill below the surface, whether near the surface or hundreds of feet below. *Percolating water* is the water found underground and is that tapped by the farmer for a well. The farmer may not drill an excessive number of wells and sell the water, thus draining this percolating water from the adjoining landowner. In agricultural areas, heavy irrigation uses could create a water shortage.

Floodwaters are the waters that overflow the channels of a stream or body of water. In such instances the abutting landowner can erect a dike to guard against this overflow. *Tidelands* refers to the shorelines that are affected by the tides. The landowner that adjoins these shores owns to the high-water mark.

Gaining and losing land

An owner whose land borders a body of water may actually gain land due to the slow build-up of soil caused by natural forces such as wind and waves. This process is referred to as **accretion**, and the land gained by accretion is the alluvion deposit (soil deposited). The sudden and rapid washing away of land is known as **avulsion**. Boundary lines remain the same regardless of how much land is swept downstream. *Reliction* (or dereliction) occurs when the body of water recedes, exposing dry land.

The opposite of accretion, *erosion* results in the gradual loss of land. The erosion of soil is a gradual process created by the action of the natural elements. Rain, wind, water, and extreme weather changes erode the earth's surface. Terracing cultivated land and planting trees helps to absorb water and preserve fertile topsoil from being washed or blown away. Some types of erosion can also be controlled by building dams. The Grand Canyon in Arizona is an example of thousands of years of erosion by the Colorado River.

RIGHTS OF GOVERNMENT

The rights of the government over an individual's real estate include the right of taxation, special assessments, eminent domain, escheat, and police power. A memory tool for recalling these rights is PETE:

The right to **P**olice powers
The right to **E**minent domain
The right to **T**ax
The right to **E**scheat

Taxation

Private ownership of land is subject to government rule, "for the common good." Thus, laws controlling the land are among the government's basic functions. Ever since feudal times when land was controlled by the king, it has been necessary for governments to protect their citizens in time of war. In the Middle Ages, taxes were collected and allegiance was pledged to the king in return for this protection. So it is today. The Constitution of the United States provides for the collection of taxes for the general welfare and common defense of the nation. Consequently, taxes are collected on all real property according to its value. On new property, the cost of construction determines to a great extent the real value of the property. In many cities buyers are required by law to disclose the purchase price on a tax assessment form that must accompany the deed when it is recorded. The property is then placed on the tax roles at the new sale price. To unify tax on property in the area, the assessor's office may periodically call for a reappraisal of all property values. This enables the assessor to keep the values that have risen due to inflation current with the marketplace.

Property taxes will vary greatly between cities because of the different needs and services a community may offer. If a city offers schools, libraries, public transportation, parks and community centers, public utilities, trash hauling, and well-maintained streets and parks, the cost of these services must be borne in part by property taxes. On the other hand, the property's value is indirectly enhanced by these services. The more properties on the tax roll, the greater number of people there are to contribute to the cost of the services.

Location will also determine the cost of property taxes. The costs of road maintenance will be higher in areas of the country where snow removal and subsequent additional street repairs are necessary. If a community is basically a retirement city, services such as schools and playgrounds may not be in the tax budget.

Other revenue generated by the city from sources, such as taxes placed on gambling casinos and lotteries or oil royalties received from property owned by the city, will assist in offsetting high property taxes.

An equal charge of taxes is made on all real property according to value and is known as an **ad valorem tax**. The assessor appraises the property for taxation purposes, and the assessed value is provided by the law of the municipality. The city, county, or state then sets the *rate* or *levy* (the **mill**, or the tax expressed in dollars) according to the amount of money needed to meet the budget and expenses of the government. The amount needed is divided by the total assessed value of a property in the taxing body to determine the rate. One mill equals one-tenth of one cent.

Ad valorem tax

To determine the amount of taxes on a property, the assessed value is multiplied by the rate:

$80,000   *appraised value*
$\times$ .35   *percentage of taxation*
$28,000   *assessed value*
$\times$ .080   *mill levy*
$ 2,240   *taxes*

Taxes are sometimes expressed in dollars, for example, $2.75 per $100 of appraised value:

$80,000   *appraised value*
$\times$.0275   *per $100 of value*
$ 2,200   *taxes*

Special Assessments

To pay for the cost of improvements, such as pavement, sidewalks, curbs, streetlights, and public utilities, an assessment is levied against property adjacent to the improvements. For example, if a street is paved, each of the abutting homeowners will pay their proportionate share, which is usually based on the front footage of each property. If a sewer line is being extended into a specific neighborhood, ordinarily each of the property owners in that area will be equally assessed since it will benefit the entire area.

Eminent Domain

The right of **eminent domain** permits the government to take private property for public use with "just compensation" to the owners. The act of taking the property is accomplished through *condemnation proceedings*. The United States Constitution prohibits the confiscation of private property without just compensation.

Government's right to condemn property

A series of events takes place when a unit of government finds it necessary to take private property. The condemnor (city, county, state, or federal agency) negotiates with the condemnee (the owner) as to the purchase price. If an agreement can be reached, the condemnor purchases the property for the agreed-upon price, and no condemnation action is necessary. However, if an agreement cannot be reached, legal proceedings are in order. A petition is filed in the county court to condemn the property. Appraisers (usually three) are appointed by the judge of the county court to appraise the property. Market value is established by these fee appraisers who may be called upon as witnesses to validate their appraisal. After a hearing is held, during which evidence from both the condemnee and the condemnor is given, a determination of price is made. If either of the parties feels the award is not just, an appeal may be made to the district court, and a trial by jury will be held.

Many times only a partial segment of a property is taken, and the appraisers must determine what the value of the portion taken was and what the remaining value is. This is referred to as the *before and after value*.

Examples of eminent domain proceedings can include the need for public recreation areas, the widening of streets, a water company needing to lay a water line, or the expansion needs of a university.

Escheat

The term **escheat** means reverting or lapsing of property back to the sovereign state through legal procedures. The doctrine of escheat dates from feudal days when all land was ultimately owned by the king.

Today, the state (or in some cases the county) acquires the property of an **intestate** person (one who dies without leaving a will) who has no heirs.

Each state's statutes set the parameters and the judicial process for establishing the right to acquire the property. Many states cannot claim the property until the court so orders; others acquire title immediately upon the death of an intestate. In the latter situation, the state must go to probate court to establish ownership. If no heirs come forth, the sovereign state succeeds to the property according to statute (law). In some states, this means that property goes to the county where the parcel is located. The majority of decedents have either made wills or have heirs, so escheat is not an ordinary means for the state to acquire property.

The right of escheat also extends to abandoned property. If property owners desert and abandon their property, the law of escheat allows the government to acquire ownership.

Police Power

The governmental powers within a local municipality may impose additional restrictions and controls upon land. These imposed limitations over the private use of land are necessary for an orderly growth pattern within the community. This power of the government to regulate land use is referred to as **police power** and must be in the interest of the public welfare. Zoning laws, building codes, taxation, eminent domain, escheat, and planning laws are all examples of police power.

PERSONAL PROPERTY VS. REAL PROPERTY

If something can be owned, it is property, either real or personal. Ownership of land gives us the right to use and possess it to the exclusion of all others. **Real estate** refers to the land and anything that is permanently affixed to the land by nature or by humans, such as a house. **Real property** is the interest held in the real estate. **Personal property** is referred to as **chattel**, or *personalty*, and is any kind of property that is movable in nature, such as a chair or a table, and is therefore not *real property*. A tree is real property until you fell it, and then it becomes personal in nature. Build a bookcase from this wood, and it would be considered personal property; but attach it to the wall in the library of the house, and it becomes real property once again. If there is a question as to whether a particular piece of property is real or personal, intention of the owners is considered. If the owners intended to take the object in question with them when they conveyed the property, then it is considered personal property.

A memory device for whether an object should be considered real or personal is MARIA:

Manner of attachment
Appropriateness to use intended
Relationship of parties
Intent of parties
Agreement to the contrary

The manner in which the item was attached to the real property determines if it should remain real property. The drapery rods are nailed to the wall and are considered real property, but the draperies that hang on the rods are easily slipped off and are therefore personal property. A mailbox is permanently affixed to the house or to a post beside the driveway and thus becomes real property. The gas line that is run to the pole on which the gas grill sits is for the sole purpose of supplying gas to the grill. While the grill could be easily removed, the "appropriateness to use intended" dictates that the grill is real property. The water heater, a necessary item in any dwelling, is installed with piping in a very permanent manner. While it could be removed, it is essential to the property and therefore considered a part of the real property. Clearly the intention of the parties who had the water heater installed was that it remain with the property.

Manner of attachment

Appropriateness to use intended

To be positive that no unpleasant circumstances arise from a misunderstanding on the part of either party upon the transfer of real property, it is prudent to list articles that are to be included with the sale in the purchase contract. Certain questionable items that are to be considered real property should be clearly stated as being transferred in the sale. Built-in bookcases, television antennas, gas grills, and built-in appliances are a few examples of articles that could trigger misunderstanding. If the sellers state that they are taking the gas grill or the mailbox, this should be stipulated in the contract.

Relationship and intent of parties

Common examples of real property:
land
buildings
carpeting, tacked down
trees and shrubs
furnace
built-in appliances

Common examples of personal property:
furniture
annual crops
farm machinery
jewelry

Things attached to real estate by roots, such as trees and produce growing on the land, are classified in two groups:

1. *Fructus naturales* are the trees, bushes, and grass and are considered real property.
2. *Fructus industriales*, or *emblements*, are the annual crops which include vegetables, fruits, and grains (corn, wheat, and oats) and are not referred to as real property. When selling farmland, the crops are normally considered personal property since they are replanted annually. This allows the tenant farmer the right to harvest the crops since they are considered personal property of the tenant.

Fixtures are items of personal property that become real once they are affixed to real estate; for example, light fixtures, cabinets, bookcases, plumbing fixtures, carpeting, and shrubbery. Once attached they are considered a part of the real estate.

Trade fixtures

Items that have been affixed to real estate by a tenant to be used in the tenant's business or trade are *trade fixtures*. The tenant clearly needs the items to conduct business, but when the lease expires will expect to remove the fixtures. Most states require that the trade fixtures be removed before expiration of the lease. If left beyond, the real estate owner acquires the fixtures through accession. Examples of trade fixtures include:

- coolers, stoves, and ovens in a restaurant
- shelving and display cases in a retail store
- printing presses in a print shop
- a dentist chair and equipment

If a fixture is purchased on a payment plan, the supplier can secure her interest by fixture filing (recording the chattel mortgage) before the goods become fixtures or within 10 days after the item is affixed. Refer to your particular state law. If the business should fail, the supplier would have a right to remove the fixture. Many times fixtures are used as collateral for a loan, and if it is recorded prior to the fixture filing, the loan would take precedence.

Domestic fixtures placed in a dwelling for a tenant's use and pleasure, such as bookcases or a special light fixture, may be removed upon expiration of the lease. If damage occurs upon its removal, any repairs would be the responsibility of the tenant.

ACQUIRING OWNERSHIP

By purchase

While the government can acquire property through its right of eminent domain and by escheat, there are many avenues by which an individual may assume title to real estate. Real estate can be obtained *by purchase*. The owner sells it voluntarily (voluntary alienation) to the purchaser.

By will

Ownership of real estate also can be obtained through *a will*, a formal written document that permits the distribution of an owner's property after death. To be legal, a will must be in writing, signed, witnessed, and attested. The maker of a will has died **testate** and is said to have left her last will and testament. The person who made the will is the *testator* (masculine) or *testatrix* (feminine). The will states who is to inherit the property. Willed real estate is known as a **devise**, and the receiver is the *devisee*. An *executor* (masculine) or *executrix* (feminine) should be named in the will to carry out the terms of the deceased. If no executor is named, an *administrator* (personal representative) is appointed by the court. If personal property is being willed, it is referred to as a *legacy* or *bequest*, and the receiver is the *legatee*.

The parties named in the will have no rights until the death of the owner. Most state laws mandate that the will be filed for probate with the court prior to distribution to the devisee. The validity of the will is determined at a hearing held by the court, and the terms of the will are carried out by the executor or the administrator.

The laws of each state must be adhered to for the will to be legal. If the will provides for less than this statutory right, the surviving spouse can renounce the will and request the minimum rights as stated under the law. The right to renounce a will is usually reserved by law to only the spouse and not to any other heir.

The person who dies without leaving a will has died intestate, and his property passes to heirs by **descent**. The laws of inheritance are statutory and vary from state to state. The premise of these laws is that intestate decedents would undoubtedly desire their property to succeed to their heirs. In the majority of the states, the surviving spouse receives one-half or one-third of the estate. The children receive the estate if there is no surviving spouse. Any claims and debts against the estate will be satisfied first.

By descent

Twenty-seven states* recognize the holographic will, which is a handwritten will, dated, written, and signed entirely in the maker's handwriting. It is important not to have any printed words in or on the holographic will, or it becomes invalid.

A written amendment to an existing will is a **codicil**. The codicil changes some conditions of the will without the need for rewriting the entire document. Just as with the original will, the codicil must be signed, dated, and witnessed. The amendment by a codicil to a will is the only way to change the terms of the will since to alter the will by penciling in notations or deletions is not acceptable under the law.

Codicil to will

LOSING OWNERSHIP RIGHTS

Under certain conditions property may be taken from the rightful owner. A true owner may lose ownership if another person occupies the property for a prescribed statutory period in a hostile, continuous, distinct, visible, and actual way. This is known as **adverse possession**. Do not confuse adverse possession with squatter's rights. The latter pertains to the right to occupy land by undisturbed and lengthy use but not with legal title. In acquiring land by adverse possession, the adverse claimant must make an actual claim of ownership to the occupied property. This claimant brings a **quiet title action** suit in a local court against anyone who may have any claim to the property. If the claim is valid, the court will award title to the claimant. If the adverse claimant has been paying taxes on the land, it reveals some appearance of ownership and is referred to as **color of title**. Many states will permit one adverse claimant to tack his possession onto a previous adverse occupant if the first occupant is a relative or if the tacking is done by contract. For example, a mother may occupy a property for three years, after which her son takes possession of the premises and tacks on to the previous possession of his mother. An example of taking property by contract would be "A" sells his rights to "B," and "B" could take possession, continue to occupy the property, and file claim to the property when the statutory term has been met. The adverse claimant must follow the procedure in filing the claim as outlined in the state's statutes. States vary in the occupancy requirements of an adverse claimant from 5 years to 25 years. The adverse possession law encourages true owners not to abandon their property.

Adverse possession

Adverse possession by tacking

Adverse possession by contract

The statute of limitations determines the adverse claimant's rights. Possession must be open and notorious, exclusive, and uninterrupted. The owner must commence

*The following states recognize holographic wills: Alaska, Arizona, Arkansas, California, Colorado, Idaho, Kentucky, Louisiana, Maryland, Mississippi, Montana, Nebraska, Nevada, New Jersey, New York, North Carolina, North Dakota, Oklahoma, Pennsylvania, Rhode Island, South Dakota, Tennessee, Texas, Utah, Virginia, West Virginia, and Wyoming.

legal action from the wrongful occupant within the period of time stated in the state's statutes or is subject to losing the property. Most states with Torrens registration recognize that those registered cannot be lost through adverse possession (see Chapter 10 for further discussion of Torrens registration).

Easement by prescription

Prescription is an easement one acquires in the land of another through continuous use for a statutory period. It is sometimes referred to as an **easement by prescription**. An example would be a privately owned road used continuously by the public. The owner should permanently post a sign stating that the road is private property or barricade the road once a year, indicating it is indeed privately owned, to avoid losing rights of ownership through prescription. The owner does not lose title; the trespasser has only acquired the right to go over the land.

PUBLIC ACQUISITION OF PROPERTY

Ownership by dedication

Title to property may be obtained by private grant, such as a gift by dedication in which real estate is transferred by an individual to the public and accepted by someone on behalf of the public. An example of a gift by dedication would be a street dedicated to the city when a new subdivision is formed. The developer must lay the streets in the subdivision, but by dedicating them to the city, any maintenance responsibility would be transferred to the city. Acceptance must be made by a public official.

SUMMARY

This chapter began with a short comparison of land rights under the feudal system in contrast to the allodial system of today. The physical characteristics of land have a great effect on its value. The use to which the land can be put largely determines that value. Therefore, a farmer would value a valley rather than a mountain, since to cultivate a mountainside would not be sensible when the valley below lends itself far better to agricultural pursuits. Similarly, the mountain would have more value to a ski resort owner.

The economic characteristics of land involve the location, the scarcity, and the demand for land. Value depends on where the property is and how much is available. The last lots in a subdivision usually are more expensive since the supply is scarce. The obvious fixity of land makes it permanent and unmovable in nature.

Ownership of real property gives the owner a bundle of rights (possession, quiet enjoyment, use, disposition) that are determined by the ownership rights of the past owner. These rights may include surface, subsurface, and air rights or all three. While owning real property allows for exclusive doctrine over the property, the government does exercise certain controls. If the property is needed for public use, the government can condemn it under the right of eminent domain. Property taxes must be paid on all real estate to support some of the costs of the local government.

The methods of acquiring ownership in land include purchase, will, and descent. Ownership can be lost through adverse possession, and certain rights can be acquired by another under an easement prescription. Finally, the public can obtain land through dedication, such as a gift of land for a park or school.

DISCUSSION QUESTIONS

1. How can property owners provide for the disposition of their property after death?
2. Under what circumstances can personal property become real property?

3. What rights, if any, does the government have over privately owned property?

4. What are the two methods of acquiring ownership of land by adverse possession?

5. Explain why police power is advantageous to the property owner.

6. When is real property considered abandoned?

7. An individual can acquire title to real property by several methods. By which means would you prefer to obtain title? Give reasons for your answer.

REVIEW QUESTIONS

Answers to these questions are found in the Answer Key section at the back of the book.

1. Possession of property through the removal of the true owner's rights is called:

   a. adverse possession
   b. codicil
   c. dedication
   d. reliction

2. Title to real property may be obtained by means of:

   a. adverse possession
   b. inheritance
   c. devise
   d. all of the above

3. When a person dies intestate and no heirs can be located for intestate succession, the real property of the deceased will revert to the state through a process known as:

   a. reconveyance
   b. escheat
   c. reversion
   d. condemnation

4. Land can be taken by adverse possession:

   a. if adverse claimant cultivates crops
   b. if it is possessed in a manner hostile to owner
   c. if possessed with owner's knowledge and consent
   d. if owner receives rent

5. When property is transferred by adverse possession:

   a. it is involuntary
   b. it is governed by statute
   c. both of the above
   d. neither of the above

6. Abandoned private property redeemed by local government is an example of:

   a. police power
   b. eminent domain
   c. taxation
   d. escheat

7. If a person dies testate, any real estate owned by the deceased will:

   a. come under the laws of escheat
   b. go into a life estate
   c. pass to the heirs
   d. be titled to the devisee

8. The act of the state exercising its right of eminent domain is:

   a. escheat
   b. police power
   c. both of the above
   d. neither of the above

9. All of the following are governmental rights, EXCEPT:

   a. taxation
   b. police power
   c. eminent domain
   d. adverse possession

10. The physical characteristics of land include all of the following, EXCEPT:

    a. scarcity
    b. fixity
    c. permanence
    d. nonhomogeneity

11. The legal rights attached to real estate are referred to as:

    a. situs
    b. bundle of rights
    c. severance rights

d. reliction rights

12. Which of the following does NOT include a right in real property?

    a. surface rights
    b. subsurface rights
    c. water rights
    d. avulsion rights

13. Which of the following is NOT real property?

    a. garage
    b. television antenna
    c. tractor
    d. trees

14. The doctrine of prior appropriation of water rights provides for:

    a. the first owner to have first claim on water
    b. the water rights to be held by the state
    c. water rights to be leased from the local government
    d. the prevention of erosion

15. A tax levied against a property because it will benefit from the improvement is a (an):

    a. escheat
    b. special assessment
    c. ad valorem tax
    d. percentage tax

16. The most prominent economic characteristics of land include:

    a. scarcity, durability, nonhomogeneity
    b. scarcity, situs, durability
    c. situs, permanence, immobility
    d. permanence, immobility, indestructibility

17. Because no two parcels of land are identical, land is referred to as:

    a. permanent
    b. durable
    c. quaint
    d. nonhomogeneous

18. Common examples of personal property include all of the following, EXCEPT:

    a. farm machinery
    b. trade fixtures
    c. a furnace
    d. annual crops

19. A right acquired in another's real property through continuous use is:

    a. eminent domain
    b. descent
    c. easement by prescription
    d. easement by color of title

20. Taxation of real property provides in part for all of the following services, EXCEPT:

    a. schools
    b. street maintenance
    c. libraries
    d. airline transportation

Land Descriptions

3

OVERVIEW

The surveying of land dates from early times. No one knows for certain when the surveying of land first began but historians believe that it was practiced by the Chinese and Egyptians thousands of years ago. All legal descriptions are founded upon **surveys**, so some historical background in the development of land surveying may be of interest to the novice in real estate. Surveying is important because it is necessary to have a sufficient description of the property to correctly identify and locate it. Every parcel of land that is sold or mortgaged must have a legal description. While a street address is the commonly used means of identifying the location of a property, legal documents require the legal description since street addresses may be changed. For example, when a city annexes a nearby subdivision or village, it is not unusual to extend the streets of that city into the newly annexed area.

To arrive at an accurate description of a particular parcel of land, several methods are followed. This chapter explains how a survey is conducted and discusses the metes and bounds system of measurement, the government rectangular survey system, and the final platting of a subdivision using the lot and block system.

THE ART OF SURVEYING

Surveying is the technique of measuring the size and shape of a parcel of land and thus fixing its boundaries. The surveyor uses a transit, which is a telescope set on a tripod. Attached are a compass and horizontal and vertical arcs used to measure angles. The surveyor adjusts the lens to meet the marks on a sight pole held by another surveyor (the rodman), thus measuring distances. For precise measurements, a surveyor may use an invor tape made of nickel and steel. Unlike a steel tape, it is less affected by temperature changes.

Surveying is based on geometry, so surveyors must know mathematics and must also be capable of using the sensitive instruments that are tools of the surveyor's trade.

METES AND BOUNDS

Monuments

The **metes and bounds** method of measuring land is the oldest known method used in the United States. The original 13 colonies were surveyed by this method, but precise directions and measurements were not used. A selected **monument** served as the reference point, or point of beginning (POB), and the particular piece of land was described in terms of other natural and artificial monuments. Natural boundaries are created by nature, such as trees, rivers, and lakes. Artificial monuments are highways, section corners, and roads. Because of the vagueness involved, descriptions using monuments usually are concluded by referring to the area as being "xx acres, more or less." A typical description is shown in Figure 3.1.

Because of the possible destruction of natural boundaries, the description lacks the permanence needed to correctly identify the property in later years. The old oak tree died, rivers changed channels, and artificial monuments were removed. Surveyors did not always record their surveys, causing disputes and subsequent legal ramifications. Today metes and bounds descriptions usually make reference to government survey lines as the place of beginning. If an owner sells off a portion of land that is irregular in shape or if it cannot be identified except by using courses and distances, the surveyor will elect to use the metes and bounds in combination with the **rectangular survey system**, the government method of surveying.

Metes refers to the measurement of length or distance from one point to another. *Bounds* pertains to the direction of the course. In the metes and bounds description in Figure 3.2, the metes (distance) are shown in feet, and the bounds (direction) are in degrees, minutes, and seconds. Two important factors must be present in this survey:

1. The description must begin at some known point, which is referred to as the point of beginning, usually a monument.

Beginning at a point at the southeast corner of Fish Lake; thence south to the burr oak tree; thence west along the northern boundary of the Blake farm to the fence at the corner of the Masterson farm and the Blake farm; thence north to Fish Lake Road and east to a large boulder; thence north to Fish Lake and easterly along the shoreline back to the point of beginning.

FIGURE 3.1
Monument description.

A metes and bounds description of this area: Beginning at a point 80′ South and 40′ West of the NE corner of the NE¼ of Section 1, thence south 250′, thence SW 30°12′10″ for a distance of 500′, thence North 330′, thence 45° Northeast 320′, thence East 220′ to the point of beginning.

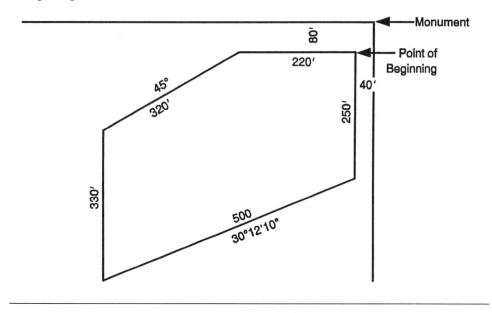

FIGURE 3.2
Metes and bounds description.

2. The description must close, that is, the survey needs to come back to the point of beginning.

As time passed, problems arose with the metes and bounds system because the natural boundaries would disappear. This all resulted in a lack of permanence. With the rapid expansion toward the western part of the United States, it soon became apparent that a system with more uniformity needed to be adopted.

In Figure 3.2 note that the description begins with a permanent marker called a monument. This monument is used as the reference point, and the surveyor will go to the nearest corner of the property being surveyed. In Figure 3.2 the surveyor traveled 80 feet south and 40 feet west to the point of beginning. Reading through the legal description and traveling clockwise, we come back to the true point of beginning. The surveyors place iron pins or stakes into the land at the corners of the boundaries.

The metes and bounds land description (see Figure 3.3) contains

1. a point of beginning
2. the corners, usually defined by the placement of iron pins
3. definite measurements and distances
4. a close, or return to the point of beginning

In the metes and bounds description, the course will usually not run due east and west or due north and south, but will be angular, such as south 40 degrees east. In this instance, it is necessary to measure the angles by the units of degrees, minutes, and seconds. A degree is 1/360 of a circle and is divided into 60 minutes; each minute has 60 seconds (see Figure 3.4). Measuring angles in a **plat** (detailed plan) is done by using an instrument called a protractor.

Bench marks are permanent reference marks placed by United States government surveyors to designate locations and elevations. Surveyors use them as references

Bench marks

FIGURE 3.3
Metes and bounds description.

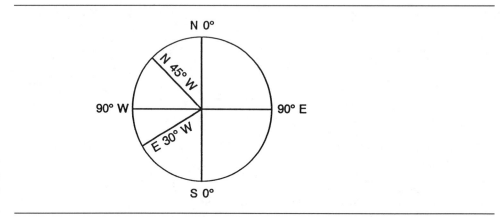

FIGURE 3.4
There are 360 degrees in a circle; each quarter contains 90 degrees.

when locating boundaries of a particular parcel of land. Bench marks may also be the brass markers surveyors place into a concrete drive or sidewalk. The bench mark is more permanent than a natural monument, such as a tree or a large rock, and if it is destroyed, its position is easier to relocate, since it is mutually dependent with other reference points of the survey.

THE GOVERNMENT RECTANGULAR SYSTEM

The rectangular survey system of land description was adopted by the federal government in 1787. It was used by most of the United States except for the original 13 colonies and the Atlantic Coast states, with the exception of Florida. Upon admission to the Union, the states of West Virginia, Tennessee, Texas, Kentucky, and Hawaii retained regulation over surveys of land within their borders, and they have not conformed to the rectangular system. A total of 30 of the 50 states use the rectangular system of survey.

When traveling by air over the country, it is interesting to note that the land far below appears as an orderly series of squares and rectangles, a result of the rectangular survey system.

Meridians and Base Lines

In the rectangular system of survey there are 36 principal meridians and 32 base lines in the country. Latitude and longitude lines provide these base lines and meridians. A **meridian** is a line that runs directly north and south, and a **base line** is a line that runs east and west. These imaginary lines grid the surface of the earth. Starting from some tangible **landmark**, the surveyors ran a line due north through the area to be surveyed. This line running north and south was designated as the meridian for that particular state or area. In some states, these lines were called the first or second meridian. In others, they were actually given names, such as the Indian Meridian in Oklahoma. A base line was fixed at right angles to the meridian, to run due east and west, and this line was designated as the base line for that area. The surveyors would use the point where the meridian and base line intersected as their point of beginning (see Figure 3.5).

Surveying by latitude and longitude

Correction Lines

Because of the curvature of the earth, it was necessary to place **correction lines** at 24-mile intervals along the meridians to the north and south of the base lines. While the eye cannot see this curvature, it is very real. The north line of a township is many feet shorter than its south line. At every fourth township north of the base line, the difference could be 200 feet.

The correction lines, combined with guide meridians, enable the surveyors to divide the territory into squares approximately 24 miles on each side. The 24-four miles square is known as a **check**.

Checks

Townships

The check was divided by **township** lines into smaller tracts of land. These lines run parallel to the base lines at six-mile intervals, resulting in a grid of squares approximately six miles wide on each side of the township lines. These grids and ranges are thus described as being east and west of the principal meridians.

To facilitate locating a township in the grid, the townships have both a township number and a range number. The first townships adjacent to and parallel to the base line are numbered one north or south, the next is numbered two north or south, proceeding on until reaching the next base line.

Likewise, a range number was given to each township running parallel to the principal meridian, commencing with number one east if it were directly east of the meridian or range one west if it were west (see Figure 3.6).

Range

Sections

The townships were further subdivided into 36 sections each, with a **section** containing 640 acres. These sections were numbered 1 to 36, beginning with 1 in the northeast corner of the township and proceeding west and east alternately, ending in the southeast corner with section 36 (see Figure 3.7).

Townships

By using the section number, the township number north or south of the base line, and the range number east or west of the controlling principal meridian, a parcel of land can be easily identified. The description may read: Section 8 of Township 3 North, Range 3 West of the 6th Principal Meridian. By looking at Figure 3.6, we can locate the section.

Let us take it a step further. A legal description reads: The NE¼ of the SE¼ of Section 5 in T5N, R11W of the 6th PM. Legal descriptions are always read starting

Figure 3.5   The meridian and base line system of surveying.

A check is 24 miles square and is divided into 16 townships, each of which is 6 miles square. Townships and ranges are signified by a code; for example, township 1 north and range 4 west is T1N, R4W.

FIGURE 3.6
Subdivision of a check.

FIGURE 3.7
A township containing 36 sections. Section 16 has been set aside as a school section.

backward, thus we would locate the range and township and then the section. The SE¼ would be identified and then proceed on to locate the NE¼ of said SE¼, which contains 40 acres (see Figure 3.8).

Fractional sections

Not all sections form an exact square because of the convergence of the meridians or due to bordering areas of water. To make allowances for this, the government added or deducted from one row of sections—from sections 1 through 6 (the north row) of the township if the difference occurred when measuring from south to north, and from the west row (sections 6, 7, 18, 19, 30, and 31) if the excess or deficiency occurred in the east or west measurements. These sections bordering on the north and west sides of a township are referred to as fractional sections (see Figure 3.9).

Government lots

The law further provided for any portions of land that could not be divided into equal fractional portions to be termed *government lots*. Fractional parcels were also created by bodies of water converging into a particular area (see Figure 3.9).

Existing Indian reservations were excluded by law from the rectangular system, as were military posts and land privately owned. As time passed and reserves were abandoned, the surveyors were unable to establish exact lines with the original survey, thus fractional sections resulted.

THE LOT AND BLOCK SYSTEM

The **lot and block number system** of land description is used by subdividers in the platting of subdivisions of land. This can usually be considered the final platting of an area. A careful survey is made by a surveyor before any development of the land can begin. The tract of land is divided into blocks, which are separated by streets. The

FIGURE 3.8 A section.

FIGURE 3.9 The shaded lots and the lots bordering the lake are fractional sections. The lots bordering the lake are called *government* lots.

blocks are platted into lots for single-family dwellings, and the lots are numbered in sequence for easy identification. Usually the subdivision is given a name to further identify the area. Once the subdivider decides the manner in which the area is to be laid out, a surveyor prepares a survey sketch establishing the boundaries and legal descriptions of the area. The plat will be certified by the surveyor and signed by the developer. Upon approval by the planning board of the local municipality, the plat is recorded and placed in a *map book*, which contains plats of all the subdivisions in the county. The book is indexed and may be inspected by anyone. The lots in the subdivision may be readily recognized in the deed when the lot and block number, the subdivision name, and the section, township, and range are recorded in the map book (see Figure 3.10).

The plat

Assessors Map Book

In many areas of the country assessors attach a number to every registered parcel of land in their county. This method assists the assessor in preparing the tax roll. The *assessors map book* is prepared from the plats submitted by the developer of the subdivision. Each page has the assigned parcel number, book and page, and the lot and block number of the parcel. The book is generally available for purchase, and many real estate offices find it convenient to have a copy for reference.

VERTICAL LAND DESCRIPTIONS

Chapter 11 relates how condominium and townhouse ownership divides the single lot even further. In a high-rise condominium, the owner owns an air lot plus an interest in the common elements of the property. The master deed permits individual fee simple ownership within a larger estate. This horizontal property law has permitted owners of apartment houses to sell individual units and give fee simple ownership to the purchasers.

Air lot

In preparing a survey of an air lot, a surveyor describes each unit by reference to the elevation above the lot and the land beneath it. The point from which the lot is

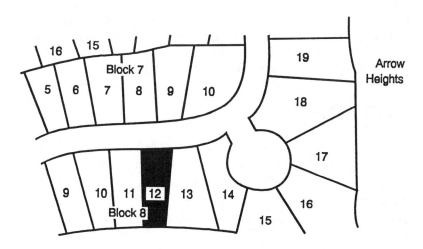

Lot twelve (12), block eight (8) in Arrow Heights, a subdivision in Kent County, as surveyed, platted, and recorded.

FIGURE 3.10
Subdivision plat.

Datum measured is referred to as a datum. The **datum** is a level surface from which heights are measured. It may be mean sea level (zero feet), or the city may have established its own datum. The surveyor will start from this datum when measuring air lots.

Land Measurements

Measurements used in land surveying include:

1. *Rod*: 16.5 feet.
2. *Chain*: 4 rods, 100 links, or 66 feet. Chain measurements were made by actual metallic chain constructed in early days of iron and later of heavy steel links. Accuracy was difficult because the links tended to stretch and the chain would twist and knot. In the 1900s surveyors started using steel ribbon tapes.
3. *Link*: 7.92 inches. A link originally referred to one loop of the chain that surveyors formerly used.
4. *Mile*: 5,280 feet, or 320 rods.
5. *Acre*: 43,560 square feet, 4,840 square yards, or 160 square rods.
6. *Section*: 640 acres, or 1 square mile.
7. *Township*: 36 sections, or 6 miles square (36 square miles).
8. *Check*: 24 miles square (576 square miles), or 16 townships.

SUMMARY

Early in American history, Congress recognized the need for dividing land so that an area could be easily identified. While the metes and bounds method was used in surveying the original 13 colonies and some of the eastern coastal states, by the late 1700s the federal government had developed the rectangular survey system.

Your home most likely has a street address if you live in a town or city and has a route and box number if it is a rural address. The property also has a legal description. Legal descriptions are used to describe each individual parcel of real estate so that title can be transferred with complete assurance that the property is correctly identified.

Today the three main methods of describing real estate are metes and bounds, rectangular survey, and the lot and block number. When title to real estate is transferred, the title company insuring the title will point out that it does not insure against loss or damage due to discrepancies, conflicts in boundary lines, shortage in areas, encroachments, or any other facts that a correct survey and inspection of the premises would disclose and that are not shown by the public record. If there is any doubt as to the exact boundaries of a property, a surveyor will prepare a certified survey.

DISCUSSION QUESTIONS

1. Does your state use the rectangular survey system of land description? If so, what principal meridian and base line is used? Refer to Figure 3.5 in this chapter.
2. Explain why surveyors rely on the use of bench marks.
3. Give the legal description of your school location.
4. Explain how surveyors compensate for the curvature of the earth.
5. Why isn't a street address a sufficient means of identifying a property?

REVIEW QUESTIONS

Answers to these questions are found in the Answer Key section at the back of the book.

1. To simplify and improve the system of determining individual parcels of land, the federal government adopted which type of land description?

   a. metes and bounds
   b. lot and block number
   c. monuments
   d. rectangular survey

2. Section 36 of a township can be found at the:

   a. northeast corner of the township
   b. northwest corner of the township
   c. southeast corner of the township
   d. southwest corner of the township

3. An acre contains:

   a. 3,840 square feet
   b. 6,490 square feet
   c. 4,356 square feet
   d. 43,560 square feet

4. Which of the following is true of a section of land?

   a. it contains 640 acres
   b. a half section is a quarter-mile square
   c. it contains 320 acres
   d. it contains 3,860 square feet

5. The NW¼ of the SE¼ of the SW¼ of section 9 contains:

   a. 160 acres
   b. 80 acres
   c. 40 acres
   d. 10 acres

6. Section 9 of a township is directly below:

   a. section 5
   b. section 3
   c. section 4
   d. section 16

7. The length of the north side of the NE¼ of the SE¼ of a section is how many feet?

   a. 660 feet
   b. 2,640 feet
   c. 1,320 feet
   d. 5,280 feet

8. Because of the curvature of the earth, it is necessary to compensate for shortages in the rectangular survey system through:

   a. correction lines
   b. fractional lots
   c. bench marks
   d. principal meridians

9. The legal description of the shaded area in the diagram is:

   a. NW¼ of the SW¼
   b. SW¼ of the NE¼
   c. SW¼ of the NW¼
   d. SW¼ of the SW¼ of the NW¼

10. Give the township and range for the four areas surrounding township 9 north and range 1 west of the 6th principal meridian:

    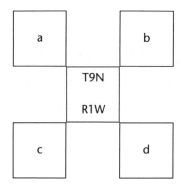

    a.
    b.
    c.
    d.

11. Establish the number of acres in the following description of a section of land: Beginning at the NE corner of the N½, thence in a diagonal line to the

SW corner of the NE¼, thence in a diagonal line to the SE corner of the SE¼, thence north to the point of beginning:

a. 80 acres

b. 160 acres

c. 320 acres

d. 40 acres

12. Special provisions in the rectangular survey system were made for all of the following, EXCEPT:

a. Indian reservations

b. fractional lots

c. schools

d. churches

13. Below is a diagram of a section of land. Establish the following parcels and the number of acres in each:

a. SE¼ of the SW¼

b. SE¼ of the SE¼ of the NW¼

c. S½ of the SW¼ of the NE¼

d. W½ of the SE¼

14. A land developer is going to subdivide the N½ of the SW¼ of the NW¼ of a section of land into residential lots 70 feet × 110 feet. He is allowing 420,450 square feet for streets. How many lots will be realized?

a. 5

b. 58

c. 59

d. 100

15. Identification objects used by surveyors to establish description points are referred to as:

a. metes and bounds

b. correction lines

c. monuments

d. meridians

16. Which surveying method uses boundaries and measurements of length in distances from one point to the other?

a. monuments

b. metes and bounds

c. rectangular survey

d. lot and block

17. Fractional sections that contain more or less than 640 acres are referred to as:

a. government lots

b. irregular plots

c. lots and blocks

d. school sections

18. Which of the following would NOT be included as part of the legal description of a parcel of land?

a. metes and bounds

b. street address

c. lot and block

d. rectangular survey

Estates, Interests, Deeds, and Title

KEY WORDS

acknowledgment	habendum clause
community property	homestead
consideration	joint tenancy
co-ownership	legal life estate
curtesy	life estate
deed	nonfreehold estate
dower	recordation
estate	remainderman
fee simple	reversioner
fee simple defeasible	severalty ownership
fee simple to a condition subsequent	tenancy in common
freehold estate	tenancy by the entireties
grantee	title
grantor	warranty deed

OVERVIEW

An **estate** in land determines the legally recognized interest the person has in the real property. There are two main types of estates in real estate—freehold and nonfreehold, also referred to as less than freehold.

This chapter covers the quantity and the quality of estates the holder may possess. The contents of a deed and conveying of title by various types of deeds are explained. Alternate means of holding title and legal life estates complete the chapter.

FREEHOLD ESTATES

A **freehold estate** is ownership for an indefinite duration. The term *freehold*, passed down from English common law, means that any interest held in land is uncertain; thus, the length of time a freehold estate will exist cannot be predetermined. Freehold estates include *fee simple, fee simple defeasible*, and *life estates*. The freehold estates may be an *estate of inheritance*, giving the holder the right to pass the real property on to the owner's heirs; or a *not of inheritance freehold estate*, which does not carry the right to will property but is only for the duration of the owner's life.

Fee simple absolute

Fee simple absolute is the most complete type of estate, giving the estate holder complete rights to the land with absolute ownership. The owner of an estate in **fee simple** title can sell it, will it, give it away, or retain possession for as long as the person desires. While the estate is subject to governmental and land use restrictions, the owner has the most power over the land that may be acquired in real estate.

Fee simple determinable

There are two types of **fee simple defeasible** (qualified fee) estates. The *fee simple determinable*, or conditional, limits the estate holder to the terms set forth by the grantor. A parent may deed property to a child with the stipulation that it can never be sold, but must be passed down to the next generation (a fee tail). Land may be given to the city for a park on the condition that it never be used for any other purpose. The deed will specifically make reference to the fact that the estate is conditional "as long as" the land is used for the purpose stated and the grantor has "qualified" the estate being granted. If the city vacates the property as a park, deciding instead to use it for a parking lot, the land will revert to the original grantor, the grantor's heirs, or a **reversioner** named by the grantor. That person holds a future or contingent interest in the property. While the holder of a fee simple determinable has fee simple title, the holder is limited by the conditions set forth by the grantor.

Fee simple to a condition subsequent

The **fee simple to a condition subsequent** gives the same possession and use rights as the fee simple determinable. However, when the fee simple is subject to a condition subsequent, the original grantor must take action to reenter the property and gain possession if the condition has been broken, as in the city abandoning the property as a park. If the grantor does not take action to regain the property, the fee simple subject to a condition subsequent will continue even though the terms have been broken. To summarize, the basic variance of the condition subsequent is that the violation of the conveyance must have occurred, and the original owners must go to court and demand return of the property, whereas the fee simple determinable terminates ownership, and the property automatically reverts to the remainderman (see below).

Life estate

A **life estate** is granted by an owner through a will or deed or by operation of law without the owner's consent. A **legal life estate** that is created by law, such as dower, curtesy, and homestead, is not recognized in all states. Two forms of a life estate may be granted by the holder of the estate: an ordinary life estate measured by the life of the recipient (life tenant) or a life estate measured by the life of another (*pur autre vie*). In this type of life estate, the estate held by A would be determined by the life of B.

The estate holder, referred to as a life tenant, loses all rights to the estate upon death. During his life, while the estate is in effect, the life tenant has the right of use, possession, enjoyment, and income. The life tenant is responsible to maintain the property in reasonable repair and to pay property taxes. The life tenant can do nothing to diminish the value of the real estate, which is referred to as laying waste to the property. Nor can the life tenant change the use of the property; a farm could not be subdivided into housing lots or dug up for a gravel pit. While the life tenant may lease the property, all leases will automatically be canceled upon the death of the life tenant. Similarly, while the property may be mortgaged, the mortgage would terminate upon the life tenant's death. The mortgagee would thus want the protection of being named beneficiary of a term life insurance policy on the property or the cosignature of the remainderman on the mortgage note. The life tenant may sell the property, the grantee receiving only the rights of the holder. The remainderman could also sell his interest, which would be subject to the life tenant's interest. The purchaser would not come into possession until the life tenant's death. If the remainderman and the life tenant both convey their interests, the grantee would receive fee simple title. Since the life estate ceases to exist upon the death of a named party or parties, it cannot be bequeathed. (See Figure 4.1.)

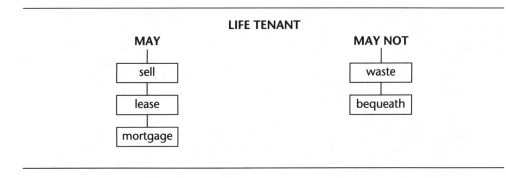

FIGURE 4.1
Life tenant.

FUTURE INTERESTS IN LIFE ESTATES

Remainderman

Future interest consists of two basic types: **remainderman** and reversion. The grantor of the life estate makes provisions for the property upon the life tenant's death by either naming a remainderman or creating a reversionary interest. The remainderman is the person named in the establishment of the life estate to succeed to the property. For example, Jones gives an estate to his wife for her life and upon her death, to his brother. Jones has given a life estate to his wife and to his brother a future interest, a remainder or nonpossessory estate.

Reversionary interest

A reversionary interest would revert at some future time to the grantor or the grantor's heirs. If Jones does not name his brother (or anyone else) as remainderman, upon the death of his wife, the estate will revert to Jones. If Jones is not living, it will pass to his devisee as stated in his will or to his heirs if no will is left. This is referred to as a reversionary interest.

NONFREEHOLD (LESS THAN FREEHOLD) ESTATES

Leasehold interests

A **nonfreehold estate**, or less than freehold estate, gives a possessory interest in real property for a definite period of time. These estates, often referred to as *leasehold interests*, encompass the rights a tenant has in the property of an owner. Generally conveyed by contract, they include an *estate for years, periodic estate, estate at will*, and a *tenancy at sufferance*. Less than freehold estates will be covered in detail in Chapter 12.

THE DEED

After becoming aware of the estate that is granted in real property, it is important to understand the document that transfers title to that estate.

Conveying title

Title (evidence of ownership) is acquired by transferring the property to the new owner with a written instrument known as a **deed**. The deed conveys the grantor's interest in the real property to the grantee. Thus:

1. The deed gives tangible proof of title conveying the property from the grantor to the grantee.
2. Title declares the quality of the estate as defined in the deed. Title is actually an intangible thing.
3. Estate defines the quantity and refers to the amount the grantor is deeding to the grantee.

Livery of seizin

This means of conveying ownership of land has been in existence for many years. Prior to this, it was customary to merely go out on the land and pass a handful of soil or break a twig and shake hands. By this basic ritualistic action the land was transferred. This act was referred to as *livery of seizin*, which simply means "transfer of possession." Today, the **grantor**, the seller of real property, conveys title to the **grantee**, the purchaser, by means of a written document that is the deed.

A deed must be properly executed, delivered, and accepted for title to pass. According to statutes in most states, the deed must be in writing. The deed is *executed* (signed) only by the grantor(s). If a corporation is selling real property, the deed must contain the signature of a designated officer who signs on behalf of the corporation. In many states the corporate seal is required to be placed on the deed.

Acknowledgment

Signatures are notarized

Most states require that the grantor's signature be **acknowledged** (sworn to under oath) for it to be recorded. In many states the grantor is required to sign the deed in the presence of a witness and the notary public, agreeing that this is a voluntary act and deed. The notary public attests to the fact that the signatures are genuine by placing his seal and signature on the deed. Note that the notary is attesting to the *validity* of the signatures, not the document. The public official should request identification from the person signing the document. The notary public has been appointed by the secretary of state to administer oaths and witness signatures. Others authorized to validate signatures may include judges, justices of the peace, and all officers in the military service. Many real estate brokers and salespersons obtain a notary commission so that they can witness documents as a service to their clients and customers.

Delivery and Acceptance

It is necessary to establish that the deed has been *delivered and accepted* for title to pass. This delivery must be made by the grantor. For an owner to place a deed in a safety deposit box with the intention that title pass after the owner's death is not allowable; the deed must be delivered within the grantor's lifetime. A third party, such as a real estate agent, an escrow agent, or an attorney who represents the grantee, may accept the deed, and delivery is presumed. In most states, delivery to a third party must be acceptable to the grantee.

Recordation

Constructive notice

Chain of title

The purpose of recording any instrument is to give constructive notice to the world of the transaction. State laws require mandatory **recordation** of liens against a property and assessments against real property for public improvements, divorce decrees, and unpaid taxes. However, recording a deed or any document that affects ownership in land is not compulsory in most states, but is a right of the holder. If such documents are recorded, the "chain of title" continues on record. Normally, purchasers will want the deed recorded to protect their interests in the event the deed is misplaced. Prompt recording protects the owner if someone later tries to claim title.

Recording is usually performed at the county office in which the property is located. A fee based upon the nature of the document and the number of pages, is collected on every instrument recorded. The document must be the original. The recorder will endorse in the instrument the correct filing number and the exact time at which the document was filed, including the year, month, day, hour, and minute that it was received. The contents of the document are then transferred in writing to the appropriate book of records, and the original instrument is returned to the person who left it to be recorded. Thus, anyone desiring to look up information regarding a particular piece of property may do so by visiting the county courthouse where the document was recorded. If the deed is lost or burned in a fire, its destruction will not affect the owner's title since it is now recorded in the public records.

Actual notice refers to having actual knowledge of who holds ownership of a property. If a deed was not recorded but a second buyer had knowledge that a sale took place, the party would not have a valid claim to the property. While possession of the property gives actual notice, a prudent buyer will give constructive notice by recording the deed, since it affords the owner absolute protection from anyone else claiming ownership.

Actual notice

Contents

A deed must contain certain elements, including the following:

1. competent parties, usually identified with names and addresses
2. consideration (something of value)
3. words of conveyance (granting clause)
4. description of the real estate
5. restrictions
6. the quantities or quality of the interest being conveyed (**habendum clause**)
7. signatures of the grantors

As in any legal contract, the parties involved must be *competent* and capable of entering into a contract. Minors or persons adjudged insane are considered legally incompetent, and the deed could be voided by the incompetent. If a grantee is determined to be mentally incapable of decision making, the deed may be revoked by the grantee. If it appears that a grantor is under undue influence of another, the courts will request the grantee to correct the situation as it exists. Such a situation may occur between a child and an elderly parent. However, legal capacity can exist regardless of age or eccentric behavior.

Competent parties

The **consideration**, or the price paid for the property, must be recited on all deeds (see Figure 4.2, number 2). Even a token amount may be stated, such as, "One dollar ($1.00) and other valuable consideration." If the property is being conveyed as a gift, the simple phrase, "for love and affection," may be used in some states. The full consideration must be stated if the transfer is by order of the court or if the deed is from a trustee or a corporation.

Consideration

The *words of conveyance* are the words that expressly grant the title to the grantee. Various kinds of deeds will state the granting clause differently, but all must express the grantor's intention to convey the property (see Figure 4.2, number 3). The grantee(s) name(s) will follow the granting clause and will spell out their relationship. In the **warranty deed** (see Figure 4.2, number 4) Kurt and Susan Kindly, husband and wife, are taking title. If Kurt Kindly was taking title by himself, the deed would state: Kurt Kindly, a married man.

Words of conveyance

The specific rights of the grantees are recited after their names. In the example shown, the Kindlys are taking title as joint tenants, vesting their entire rights in the survivor. This is a very important phrase in any deed since it determines the rights of the survivor should one of the parties die.

The *description* of the property must be sufficient to identify the real estate. In most states the legal description, citing the lot, block, and subdivision is preferred (see Figure 4.2, number 5).

Description

Restrictions may be written into the deed such as, "subject to real estate taxes and subsequent assessments (see Figure 4.2, number 7)." If the grantee is assuming an

Restrictions

WARRANTY DEED, VESTING ENTIRE TITLE IN SURVIVOR

OMAHA PRINTING COMPANY

KNOW ALL MEN BY THESE PRESENTS, That

Harvey J. Wender and Della J. Wender, husband and wife, **1**

in consideration of Eighty Four Thousand and no/100 ($84,000.00)-----**2**----------- DOLLARS
in hand paid, do hereby grant, bargain, sell, convey and confirm unto **3**

Kurt K. Kindly and Susan A. Kindly, husband and wife **4**

as **JOINT TENANTS,** and not as tenants in common; the following described real estate, situate in the County of
Kent   and State of   to-wit:

Lot Eight (8), Block One (1), in Confusion Hill
subdivision, an Addition to Any City, Kent
County, USA, as surveyed, platted and recorded. **5**

STATE
DOCUMENTARY **6**
STAMPS
$126.00

together with all the tenements, hereditaments, and appurtenances to the same belonging, and all the estate, title, dower,
right of homestead, claim or demand whatsoever of the said grantors   , of, in or to the same, or any part thereof,
subject to covenants, restrictions and easements of record, all regular taxes and
subsequent taxes and assessments. **7**

   **IT BEING THE INTENTION OF ALL PARTIES HERETO, THAT IN THE EVENT OF THE DEATH OF
EITHER OF SAID GRANTEES, THE ENTIRE FEE SIMPLE TITLE TO THE REAL ESTATE DESCRIBED
HEREIN SHALL VEST IN THE SURVIVING GRANTEE. 8**
   TO HAVE AND TO HOLD the above described premises, with the appurtenances, unto the said grantees as
JOINT TENANTS, and not as tenants in common, and to their assigns, or to the heirs and assigns of the survivor of
them, forever, and we the grantors named herein for ourselves **9** and our heirs, executors, and
administrators, do covenant with the grantees named herein and with their assigns and with the heirs and assigns of
the survivor of them, that we are lawfully seized of said premises; that they are free from incumbrance except
as stated herein, and that we the said grantors have good right and lawful authority to sell the same, and
that we will and our heirs, executors and administrators shall warrant and defend the same
unto the grantees named herein and unto their assigns and unto the heirs and assigns of the survivor of them, forever,
against the lawful claims of all persons whomsoever, excluding the exceptions named herein.

   IN WITNESS WHEREOF we have hereunto set our hands this 14th day of
May   A. D., 1994   *Harvey J. Wender*
                                          (Harvey J. Wender)
In presence of   *Della J. Wender*   **10**
Judy M. Selling   **11**   (Della J. Wender)

STATE OF   }
County of Kent   } ss.   On this 14th day of May
A. D. 1994   , before me, a Notary Public in and for said County, personally came the above named
Harvey J. Wender and Della J. Wender, husband and wife

12   who are personally known to me to be the identical persons whose names
affixed to the above instrument as grantors , and they have
acknowledged said instrument to be their voluntary act and deed.
WITNESS my hand and Notarial Seal the date last aforesaid.

SEAL

Judy M. Selling Notary Public.
My commission expires on the 8th day of July A. D., 1996

FIGURE 4.2
General warranty deed.

existing mortgage, it would also be recited in the "subject to" section of the deed. Generally, the phrase "subject to easements and restrictions of record" does not recite what these easements and restrictions may be. The subdivider filed the covenants and restrictions that relate to the subdivision, and so the deed merely refers to this fact. The grantor may place further restrictions in the deed limiting the use of the property.

The *qualities and quantity of the interest* being conveyed by the grantor will be shown in the deed. In the warranty deed, the grantors warrant the title through themselves, their heirs, and even their predecessors. The clause specifies that there are no liens on the property except as shown in section 7 and that upon signing the deed the grantors give up any present or future claim to the property (see Figure 4.2, number 9). However, when a grantor conveys title with a quitclaim deed, no warranties are given. *Quality and quantity of interest*

The *signatures of the grantors* (see Figure 4.2, number 10) must also appear on all deeds. All the owners of the property must execute the instrument. In most states if a married person holds title alone, the spouse must still sign the deed to extinguish any rights to the property. If a grantor cannot write, the grantor must place an "X" for his mark in the presence of witnesses. If the property is owned by a corporation, the deed is signed by its authorized officer(s), and the corporate seal is placed on the deed. *Signatures*

The deed illustrated in Figure 4.2 is a warranty deed, vesting entire title to the grantee. This deed is for joint tenancy ownership, which will be explained under deeds in this chapter. The numbers on the deed designate the following:

1. The sellers' names appear conveying the property. Their names must be exactly as they appeared when they took title. The marital status of the grantors is stated as well.
2. The amount the real estate is selling for. While we have used the actual amount, in some states it is legal to merely put a token amount such as, "$1.00 and other valuable consideration."
3. The clause of conveyance must be present in all deeds. This deed states that the seller will "grant, bargain, sell, convey and confirm" the property to the buyer.
4. The buyers' names, along with their marital status.
5. The complete legal description of the property.
6. Tax stamps affixed or evidence of payment made (in states where a transfer fee is required).
7. This paragraph enumerates any limitations that exist in the conveyance of the property and includes the loan assumption clause if a loan is being assumed.
8. This is the joint tenancy clause, vesting entire rights in the survivor.
9. The habendum clause defines the quantity of the estate being granted to the grantees and is referred to as the "to have and to hold" clause.
10. Signatures of the grantors—exactly as shown at number 1.
11. Signature of witness (not needed in all states).
12. The acknowledgment of the document by the notary public. In this instance, the real estate agent was a notary public, and so she witnessed the owners' signatures to the deed. Some people feel that it is best to have some other disinterested party do this.

Conveyance Fee (Real Estate Transfer Tax)

When title to real property is transferred, the state may collect a sales tax on the transfer of the property. The cost of this transfer tax varies from state to state, with some states charging no revenue upon the sale of real estate. Generally, this transfer fee is paid by the grantor, and the amount is stamped on the deed by the registrar of deeds at the time the instrument is recorded. For example, if the tax is based on the rate of *Title transfer tax*

$1.50 per $1,000 or any part thereof and a property sells for $100,000, the state would collect $150. If a property sold for $105,000, it would be necessary to add another $7.50 to the $150.00. In the deed shown in Figure 4.2, the purchase price of the property was $84,000. At the rate of $1.50 per $1,000, the grantors would pay a sales tax of $126 (see number 6).

Types of Deeds

The following deeds are the most commonly used:

Warranty deed

- The *general warranty deed* conveys the highest and most complete ownership in real estate. The grantors of a general warranty deed guarantee the title against the whole world. They are telling the grantee that it is free and clear of all liens and that they are relinquishing all rights through themselves, their heirs, and even their predecessors. A sample of a warranty deed is shown in Figure 4.2. The warranties that a grantor conveys in a general warranty deed include:

  1. *Covenant of seizin*: The grantors declare they are in full possession of the interests granted.
  2. *Quiet enjoyment*: No one will evict the grantee with a prior title.
  3. *Freedom from encumbrances*: There will be no liens, physical encumbrances, or unpaid taxes on the interest deeded unless specifically noted in the deed. (For example, a grantee might agree to assume an existing mortgage.) Title defects warranted against in addition to liens and unpaid taxes include mortgages, assessments, dower rights, and leases. Physical defects would include easements, building restrictions, fences, and encroachments.
  4. *Further assurances*: Insures good title and should any faults be found in the deed, the grantor will correct them.
  5. *Right to convey*: Guarantees possession and title; states the grantor has the authority to pass title.
  6. *Covenant of warranty*: The grantor will indemnify the grantee for any loss that may occur due to a defect in the title.

Special warranty deed

- In the *special warranty deed* the grantors guarantee the title through themselves and their heirs, but not their predecessors. Basically, the grantors are giving the same guarantee as in a general warranty deed, but they are covering only the time they owned interest in the property. The period of time covered represents the only difference from a general warranty deed. This form is most used by corporations because of limitations that are placed on them. Some states use the special warranty deed in lieu of a general warranty.

Grant deed

- A *grant deed* contains warranties as in a warranty deed, but they are created by the grantors themselves. The grantors imply that they own title and that they have not previously conveyed the real property to another. The warranty includes encumbrances made while the grantors owned it, but not those made during another's ownership. As in the special warranty deed, the grantors warrant only for their time of ownership.

Bargain and sale deed

- A *bargain and sale deed* is similar to the quitclaim deed in that it contains no warranties. However, in this deed the grantors do acknowledge that they have an interest in the real property. The grantees must have the title searched to be absolutely certain that they are receiving a good and marketable title.

  The words of conveyance usually will state "grant, bargain, and sell" or "grant and release," implying that the grantor holds title to the property. If the deed contains covenants against the grantor's acts (which can be added to the deed), it has the same validity as a special warranty deed.

- The *quitclaim deed* gives no warranties to the grantee. The grantors may not have clear title and may be conveying only the interest they have in the property. The grantors "quit their claim," and the grantee receives whatever interest the grantors have. This deed is often used to remove a *cloud on the title*, which is a partial interest in real property. It is also used to correct defects in a title, such as an incorrect description or an error in the spelling of a grantor's name.

    Quitclaim deed

    Special purpose deeds are used to comply with certain legal purposes. They include the deed of trust, sheriff's deed, tax deed, correction deed, executor's deed, guardian's deed, cession deed, and director's deed.

    Special purpose deeds

- A *deed of trust* is not merely a deed but is a deed to secure payment of a debt. Not only does it convey title, but it is held in trust by a third disinterested party for the benefit of the lender and is sometimes referred to as a *trust deed*. When the terms of this deed are satisfied by the repayment of the debt, title is conveyed to the borrower by a deed of reconveyance. Further explanation of this type of deed can be found in Chapter 9 on financing, since the main function of a deed of trust is to secure a note.

- The *sheriff's deed* transfers real estate sold at a public sale, usually the result of a foreclosure on a judgment or a mortgage. There are no warranties or representations with this deed, since the sheriff is acting on behalf of the public. The court will issue the order that permits the sheriff to issue the deed.

- A *tax deed* transfers real estate that has been sold by the government because taxes have not been paid. As with the sheriff's deed, there are no warranties.

- A *correction deed* (sometimes referred to as a reformation deed or a deed of confirmation) is used to correct an error, such as a mistake in the spelling of a name, an inaccuracy in the legal description of a property, or some omission. The grantors must correct the mistake if they gave a covenant of further assurances (as with a warranty deed). The correction deed must conform to the requirements of a legal document; usually a quitclaim deed is used.

- The *executor's deed* is issued by an executor of an estate upon the sale of the deceased person's real property. This is a judicial deed and is executed under court approval and carries no warranty other than against the executor's acts. Unlike other deeds, the executor's deed must state the full purchase price.

- The *guardian's deed*, issued to convey a minor's interest in real property, passes title carrying the covenant that neither the guardian nor the minor have encumbered the property.

- A *cession deed* is given by the subdivider when dedicating the streets in the subdivision to the county or city. All street rights (and the obligation of maintenance) are transferred to the appropriate unit of government.

- A *director's deed* is used when a public agency sells surplus land.

TAKING TITLE TO REAL PROPERTY

When taking title to real property, ownership may be described as joint tenancy, tenancy in common, concurrent ownership, tenancy by the entirety, severalty ownership, or multiple ownership. (See Figure 4.3 for a diagram of different types of ownership and Figure 4.4 for a list of the form of ownership allowed in each state.)

Joint Tenancy

Joint tenancy is ownership by two or more persons with the right of survivorship. This must be clearly stated in the deed, otherwise tenancy in common may be assumed in most states. Joint tenancy means that when one of the owners dies, the surviving

Right of survivorship

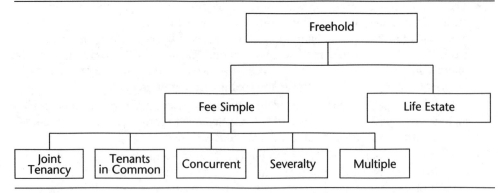

FIGURE 4.3
Types of real property ownership.

joint tenant(s) obtain the property. In joint tenancy all the joint tenants must have the same:

1. *Time*—the interest must be acquired at the same time.
2. *Title*—all joint tenants must receive their interest through a single deed.
3. *Interest*—the rights of the owners must be equal.
4. *Possession*—all owners must have equal rights of possession and may share in the occupancy, use, and profits, and each have equal responsibility for maintenance and costs of the property ownership.

Joint tenancy is generally used only by family members because of the right of survivorship, but may be used by others. If parties own property under joint tenancy, when one dies, the survivor receives the property. However, the value of the entire property would be subject to estate taxes twice. Because of possible tax consequences such as these, it has become increasingly important for people to seek counsel when taking title. In joint tenancy ownership, if one of the parties dies, the unity of ownership continues. For example, if three individuals own a property in joint tenancy and one of the parties dies, the remaining two parties still own the property in joint tenancy, receiving the deceased person's share under the right of survivorship. The decedent's share is not passed to the heirs, nor does it pass by will.

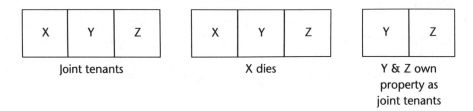

Conversely, if one of the three parties *sold* her share to another, the joint tenancy would cease to exist between the three parties. The remaining two owners would be joint tenants, but the new owner would be a tenant in common since there is no unity of time.

	Tenancy in Common	Joint Tenancy	Tenancy by the Entirety	Community Property
Alabama	X	X		
Alaska	X	X	X	
Arizona	X	X		X
Arkansas	X	X	X	
California	X	X		X
Colorado	X	X		
Connecticut	X	X		
Delaware	X	X	X	
District of Columbia	X	X	X	
Florida	X	X	X	
Georgia	X	X		
Hawaii	X	X	X	
Idaho	X	X		X
Illinois	X	X		
Indiana	X	X	X	
Iowa	X	X		
Kansas	X	X		
Kentucky	X	X	X	
Louisiana*				
Maine	X	X		
Maryland	X	X	X	
Massachusetts	X	X	X	
Michigan	X	X	X	
Minnesota	X	X		
Mississippi	X	X	X	
Missouri	X	X	X	
Montana	X	X		
Nebraska	X	X		
Nevada	X	X		X
New Hampshire	X	X		
New Jersey	X	X	X	
New Mexico	X	X		X
New York	X	X	X	
North Carolina	X	X	X	
North Dakota	X	X		
Ohio	X		X	
Oklahoma	X	X	X	
Oregon	X		X	
Pennsylvania	X	X	X	
Rhode Island	X	X	X	
South Carolina	X	X		
South Dakota	X	X		
Tennessee	X	X	X	
Texas	X	X		X
Utah	X	X	X	
Vermont	X	X	X	
Virginia	X	X	X	
Washington	X	X		X
West Virginia	X	X		
Wisconsin	X	X		
Wyoming	X	X	X	

FIGURE 4.4
Forms of ownership allowed in each state.

*Louisiana's state statutes create ownership interests that differ from joint tenancy, tenancy by the entireties, or community property.

Advantages of joint tenancy ownership:

1. Probate expenses may be eliminated.
2. The surviving joint tenant automatically succeeds to the title immediately.
3. Estate held in joint tenancy would not be subject to debts incurred by the decedent.

Disadvantages of joint tenancy ownership:

1. Other than the decedent's spouse (if the spouse is a joint tenant), the decedent's heirs will not inherit the property.
2. Joint tenants relinquish the right to will their share of the property.
3. It may create tax problems.
4. It does not replace the need for a will.

Tenancy in Common

Without survivorship

Tenancy in common is ownership by two or more persons without the right of survivorship. If one of the owners dies, that owner's interest passes to heirs or to a devisee and not to the surviving tenant in common. Each owner has an undivided interest in the whole. That is, one person cannot designate ownership of the south side of the lot and the other owner the north side; they own the whole with an undivided interest. This is true in all types of ownership. However, each person's share need not be equal; one tenant-in-common owner could own two-thirds of the value of the whole, while the other owns one-third. In addition, one owner may sell her interest without the consent of the other owner so that, unlike joint tenancy, title may be taken at different times.

Tenancy by the Entirety

Ownership by husband and wife

Tenancy by the entirety can only be held by husband and wife. As with joint tenancy, it vests entire rights in the surviving spouse. Neither the husband nor wife can convey the property without the consent of the other. Not all states recognize tenancy by the entirety. While it provides for automatic survivorship, it can establish inheritance tax problems and should not be used as a replacement for a will. In states that recognize tenancy by the entirety, the deed generally will need to specifically state this fact.

Historically, under English common law, the wife was considered a "part" of her husband with no separate rights in property. Thus, as a "single unit" the tenancy by the entireties gave him absolute control. However, the laws today recognize a wife's rights and benefits as equal to a husband's and states that use of tenancy by the entireties acknowledges this. Should the couple divorce, tenancy by the entireties automatically ceases to exist, and the parties become tenants in common.

Concurrent ownership is held by two or more persons in **co-ownership**, as in joint tenants, tenants in common, partnership, or corporations.

Severalty Ownership

Sole ownership

Severalty ownership is the sole ownership of a property by one person. Do not think of the term as implying several, but look at the first five letters, *sever*; the person's ownership is "severed" from all others. Ownership has been cut away.

While a married person may own property in severalty, most states will require the spouse to sign away any marital rights upon the sale of the property.

In law, a corporation is a legal person and as such takes title to property in severalty.

There are advantages in sole ownership of real property. The individual makes the decision when to buy or sell and on what terms. Unlike concurrent ownership, the owner has total control. Needless to say, with that control comes all responsibility of maintenance and care.

Community Property

In the seven states* that recognize community property laws, ownership of property acquired by either husband or wife during the marriage is considered **community property**. They are considered to have contributed equally to the marriage, and thus any property they purchase will be equally shared. This is true even if one of the spouses does not work outside the home.

Property held prior to the marriage does not apply and is considered separate property. Property that is acquired *after* marriage by inheritance or gift is also excluded from community property. If one of the parties purchased property with separate funds, this too would be excluded.

Community property states allow the spouse to devise by will that spouse's portion of the estate to anyone. In the states of California, Idaho, Nevada, New Mexico, and Washington, if no will is left, the deceased person's estate reverts to the surviving spouse. However, in Arizona and Texas, the heirs of the deceased would be the beneficiaries.

Partition

A co-owner of real property may *partition* a court of law to terminate the shared ownership. If the co-owners have not voluntarily agreed to the dissolving of the estate, one co-owner can sue for partition, and the courts will conduct a compulsory division of the land. If it is not feasible to actually divide the land, a sale will be ordered, and the proceeds will be split in accordance with each owner's share. A co-owner may demand partition regardless of the amount of the co-owner's share.

In addition to the individual and concurrent forms of ownership, group ownership is held by business enterprises. Partnerships, corporations, syndications, and trusts hold real estate for business purposes.

Partnership

A *partnership* is formed when two or more people join together in a business venture for the purpose of making a profit. The partnership will operate under its own name or in the name of the owners. If operating under a trade name—for example, XYZ Partnership—the property will be held in severalty since a partnership is considered by law as a single entity. If held in the names of the individual owners, title would be held as tenants in common or joint tenancy.

Legal Life Estates

As stated earlier, legal life estates are established by statute and include dower, curtesy, and homestead as a result of marriage. While many states have abolished dower and curtesy rights and have initiated statutory laws as substitutions, other states still maintain many features of old English common law. The underlying reason for curtesy and dower rights is to legally protect property rights of a surviving spouse. There is an old expression, "one to buy, two to sell," meaning both parties must release their rights.

*Arizona, California, Idaho, Nevada, New Mexico, Texas, and Washington.

Inchoate rights

Dower is the right a wife has to her husband's estate at the time of his death. Since this right does not materialize until death, it is *inchoate* or incomplete. This law guarantees the wife a minimum of a one-third interest in her husband's estate, protecting her against any creditor's claims or acts by her husband to disinherit her.

Dower rights further protect the wife since the husband cannot sell real property without her consent. The wife must relinquish her rights by signing the deed.

Curtesy represents the husband's life interest in any of his deceased wife's property. However, many states require that a child be born to the marriage in order for curtesy rights to take effect. The wife also has the option to will her property to another and defeat the curtesy rights. As with dower rights, all states require that the husband sign any deed affecting title to property held by the wife.

Homestead rights

The family's place of residence is classified as their **homestead**. Most states have enacted homestead laws to exempt the home from a forced sale due to liens and judgments by creditors. It is protection for the family in the event of a financial disaster, conceived primarily to benefit dependents.

States that have established homestead laws require that the real estate is the family's permanent residence. Additionally, the property may have to be filed as a homestead at the county courthouse. States vary in the requirements of establishing a homestead. Some states will designate a single person as fulfilling the term *family*. Each state determines the amount to be exempt. For example, if the law exempts $10,000 from debts, upon the sale and satisfaction of any taxes due, mortgages, and mechanic's liens, the owner would receive the first $10,000 with the remainder applied toward other outstanding debts.

Most homestead laws were legislated when much of the country was rural and the laws served as protection for the farmer and his family. Some states exempt a certain amount of farmland, such as 160 acres. Today the amount is often less than the farmer's debts.

While the homestead exemption benefits the owner to a degree, there are some claims that are not exempt. They include

1. real estate taxes
2. real estate special assessments
3. real estate mortgages
4. mechanic's liens

SUMMARY

This chapter discusses the ownership of real property, which includes defining the estates, interests, deeds, and title held in real property.

A freehold estate conveys the maximum interest available under the law. The owner can dispose of the property as the owner wishes, and it is inheritable by the heirs upon death. A life estate gives the holder the right of possession and use of the land for that person's lifetime. A less than freehold estate gives possessory or controlling interest in the real estate for a definite period of time as stated in the lease.

To thoroughly understand the instrument that conveys title to real property, considerable space is allotted to the explanation of the deeds. The contents of the deed are very important. If a deed lacks a description of the property, the conveyance clause or consideration, the names of the parties, or the grantors' signatures, it is invalid. Proper execution of the deed must be carried out and delivery made for title to pass.

There are several types of deeds, with different interests acquired in each. A general warranty deed (sometimes simply referred to as a warranty deed) conveys the greatest quality of interest. It clearly spells out the covenants the grantor warrants and promises. In a special warranty deed, the grantor only warrants the title since the grantor took possession. A bargain and sale deed confirms that an interest is held by the grantor, but the grantor is not warranting that interest; in a quitclaim deed no warranties are given, as signers only give whatever interest they hold. If I gave you a quitclaim deed to the Brooklyn Bridge, you would receive exactly the interest I have, which is zero.

When taking title to real property, the grantee may hold interest by means of joint tenancy, tenancy in common, severalty, tenancy by the entireties, or multiple ownership. Since laws vary from state to state, careful consideration should be given as to how a person wishes to take title. While many married couples automatically think they should hold title by joint tenancy, this may not always be wise; the property is subject to inheritance tax upon the death of the first partner and again upon the survivor's death.

Multiple ownership, sometimes in the form of a partnership, has become increasingly popular. When an inflationary economy exists, many people acquire investment property. If they are unable to finance a purchase alone, they pool their funds with others. Investments and their tax benefits are covered in Chapter 14 on investments.

DISCUSSION QUESTIONS

1. How would you prefer to hold title to real property? Give reasons for your answer.
2. Explain why a buyer would prefer to receive a warranty rather than a quitclaim deed.
3. If a married couple takes title as tenants in common, what consequences may arise if one person dies?
4. When property in your city is sold, is a tax levied upon the transfer of title? If so, compute the tax on the property in Figure 4.2 using your tax levy.
5. What would be the preferred way for two business partners to take title to a building they purchased to accommodate their business? Explain pros and cons of joint tenancy and tenancy in common ownership in this instance.
6. Explain the difference among title, deed, and estate.
7. If you were selling property you owned, what type of deed would you give the purchaser? Explain.

REVIEW QUESTIONS

Answers to these questions are found in the Answer Key section at the back of the book.

1. The essential ingredients of a deed include:

   a. the signatures of the grantees and grantors
   b. words of conveyance
   c. recordation
   d. date of birth

2. If Charlie Brown purchases a property and receives title from the grantor by a quitclaim deed:

   a. Brown does not receive clear title
   b. Brown receives whatever title the grantor had
   c. Brown can force the grantor to correct any title defects.
   d. Brown receives no title

3. The responsibility of recording a deed lies with:

   a. the state

   b. the county

   c. the grantor

   d. the grantee

4. Deed restrictions are considered:

   a. general liens

   b. escheat

   c. an encumbrance

   d. enforceable only by the property owner

5. Property held in joint tenancy, upon the death of one of the tenants, would pass to:

   a. the state

   b. the owner's heirs

   c. the spouse

   d. the surviving joint tenant

6. A life tenant can do all of the following with her interest, EXCEPT:

   a. sell

   b. lease

   c. bequeath

   d. mortgage

7. A warranty deed guarantees against all, EXCEPT:

   a. the grantor's heirs

   b. easements of record

   c. a mortgage

   d. a judgment creating a lien

8. Susan Jones lists her home with Sam Suresell and indicates that she wishes to deliver the deed that best protects her when she passes title. Ms. Jones will convey title by means of:

   a. a quitclaim deed

   b. a warranty deed

   c. a special warranty deed

   d. a grant deed

9. Henry Dudd subsequently views the Jones home and decides to make an offer to purchase the property. He informs the sales agent, Diane Dealquick, that he wants the deed that will give him the most assurance of receiving a clear title. Ms. Dealquick suggests:

   a. a quitclaim deed

   b. a warranty deed

   c. a special warranty deed

   d. a grant deed

10. After much negotiation, Jones and Dudd agree that Jones will deliver a deed that ensures good title through her time of ownership only. The deed agreed upon was:

   a. a quitclaim deed

   b. a warranty deed

   c. a special warranty deed

   d. a grant deed

11. A deed that is executed by the grantor several days before it is delivered is:

   a. invalid and not enforceable

   b. valid as long as it is recorded

   c. valid upon delivery

   d. invalid if not recorded within 10 days

12. For a deed to be recorded it must contain:

   a. the signatures of the grantors and grantees

   b. consideration

   c. grantee's social security number

   d. grantor's social security number

13. For a deed to be conveyed, it must be:

   a. signed

   b. accepted

   c. acknowledged

   d. recorded

14. One deed of conveyance an owner of real estate may use to voluntarily transfer right, title, or interest in real estate is:

   a. warranty deed

   b. sheriff's deed

   c. foreclosure deed

   d. deed of trust

15. Two friends jointly purchase a property. To protect their heirs, they should take title in:

   a. joint tenancy

   b. severalty

   c. life estate

   d. tenancy in common

16. The "to have and hold" clause in a deed is represented by the:

   a. consideration

   b. acknowledgment

   c. words of conveyance

   d. habendum clause

17. Tenancy by the entirety may exist between:

    a. family members only

    b. any two parties of legal age

    c. siblings

    d. persons married to each other

18. Joel Smith and Mark Jones lived together in a home they purchased. Joel dies in an automobile accident. Mark now owns the property in severalty. Joel and Mark had title to the property as:

    a. tenants by the entirety

    b. joint tenants

    c. tenants in common

    d. owners in severalty

19. What is the primary purpose of a deed?

    a. transfer of title

    b. quantity of ownership

    c. recordation

    d. legal evidence

20. For a deed to be considered valid, it must:

    a. contain an adequate description of the property

    b. be acknowledged

    c. be recorded

    d. be drawn on any day but Sunday

21. The covenant of quiet enjoyment refers to:

    a. occupancy

    b. ownership

    c. the prevention of interference by other parties

    d. the absence of liens on the property

22. Marcia Moore had a life estate to which her daughter was named remainderman. Ms. Moore leased the property for five years. Three years later, she passed away, and the daughter decided to cancel the lease, BUT:

    a. the lease was totally void from the beginning

    b. the terms of the lease prevailed

    c. the lease was void upon the death of the life tenant

    d. the lessee can sue for damages if evicted

23. Ownership of real property in fee simple title gives the title holder:

    a. a nonfreehold estate

    b. a freehold estate

    c. a less than freehold estate

    d. an estate in remainder

24. A fee simple determinable estate can best be described as:

    a. an unqualified estate

    b. an estate of inheritance

    c. a fee simple absolute estate

    d. limiting the estate holder to the terms set forth by the grantor

The Orderly Process
of a Sale

This section begins the explanation of the process of the sale. Chapter 5 introduces contract and business law so the reader can develop an understanding of the various contracts used in real estate transactions. Once this foundation has been laid, the rest of the chapters in this section follow the natural sequence of events in listing and selling a property. Throughout this section, a single property is used as an example to give continuity to the procedures involved in a transaction.

Chapter 6 explains the role of the real estate brokerage firm and its relationship to the seller when listing a property for sale. The listing contract is explained and the various types of listings are described.

Chapter 7 builds upon Chapter 6, dealing with locating the buyer to purchase the property. The offer to purchase is written after the buyers are given an estimate of the costs involved. A step-by-step analysis of the agreement is covered with an explanation of rejections and counteroffers. The role of the real estate agent in representing the buyer and seller is explained and defined.

Chapter 8 covers the role of financial institutions, since most real estate sales are financed, and gives a background of the lending institutions and the loans they issue.

Chapter 9 further develops an understanding of finance by explaining the mortgage and deed of trust—the financing instruments used by the lending institutions. A description of the many types of mortgages available completes the chapter.

Chapter 10 completes this section with the closing of the transaction. The responsibilities of the real estate firm (or the escrow company), the lender, and the title company are all covered. The many forms used in closing a sale are shown, concluding with the buyer's and seller's closing statements and the broker's trust account balance sheet.

Contracts and Business Law

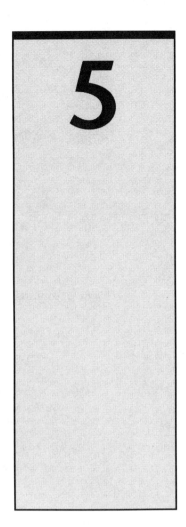

KEY WORDS

bilateral contract
consideration
contract
dual contract
executed contract
executory contract
expressed contract
fraud
implied contract
latent defect
misrepresentation
novation

offer and acceptance
option
parol evidence rule
patent defect
rescind
specific performance
unenforceable contract
unilateral contract
valid contract
void contract
voidable contract

OVERVIEW

Since contracts are an essential part of real estate transactions and we could not do business without them, it is necessary to fully understand contract law. This chapter will take you through the "making of a contract," explaining all the elements and legal requirements of a valid and binding contract.

The contracts most frequently used in real estate are the listing and purchase agreements, leases, installment contracts, options, escrow agreements, and mortgages. Their use is an everyday occurrence for the real estate agent, and subsequent chapters will cover each in detail.

CONTRACTS

A **contract** is a voluntary agreement between two or more parties to perform (or abstain from performing) a legal act on which they have had a "meeting of the minds." In other words, they agreed on the subject matter of the contract. In this legally enforceable agreement, the parties are bound to the conditions of the contract.

Contracts may be implied or expressed, oral or written. An **implied contract** is neither written nor explicitly stated orally, but is created by an act of the party. Most people enter into implied business contracts every day when they ask for a cup of coffee at a restaurant, take public transportation to work, make a purchase at a store, or have the dentist fill a cavity. No promise was exchanged, but the implication is that

Implied contract

they will pay for these services and goods. Implied contracts are not enforceable and are rarely used in real estate transactions. Real estate salespeople not only want to be sure that they are paid for their services by the seller, but as the agents which involved a third party (the buyer), they do not want to be sued if one of the parties fails to fulfill a contractual obligation. An expressed written contract removes these problems as the law provides protection on expressed contracts.

Expressed contract   An **expressed contract** may be written or oral, but all written contracts are expressed. A purchase agreement will be in writing and specifically spell out the intentions of the parties. A lease may be oral or written. Tenants taking possession of the premises show their expressed consent to occupy and pay rent. The landlord expresses consent by permitting the party to move into the premises.

Bilateral contract   A **bilateral contract** embodies the promise on the part of both parties to the contract. In a purchase contract, the offeror (buyer) promises to buy, and the offeree (seller) promises to sell. A lease is another example of a bilateral contract; the lessee (tenant) agrees to pay rent and the lessor (landlord) to give possession.

Unilateral contract   A **unilateral contract** is the promise on the part of one party to complete an act. In a listing contract the owner lists the property and agrees to pay the agent a commission upon the sale. The agent naturally hopes to sell the property and earn a commission, but the contract does not bind the salesperson to perform. Likewise, in an option contract the optionor agrees to sell the property to the optionee, but the optionee is not bound to purchase. The listing agreement and option become bilateral only if performance occurs through the sale of the property.

ELEMENTS OF A CONTRACT

A valid, legally binding contract requires certain basic elements and qualities:

1. *Offer and acceptance*: A meeting of the minds on the subject matter.
2. *Consideration*: Good or valuable exchange, something of value.
3. *Capacity of the parties*: The parties must be capable of entering into a contract.
4. *Legality of the object*: The contract must be for a legal purpose.
5. *Contract in writing and signed*: When required by law.

Upon fulfillment of these five conditions, a valid and binding agreement is "contracted" and becomes legally enforceable. These contract conditions are expanded upon below.

Offer and acceptance   The concept of **offer and acceptance** means that the parties have agreed by mutual consent to the terms of a contract. For example, in the purchase agreement the buyer (offeror) agrees to purchase the property on the terms stated. If the sellers (offerees) sign the contract, they agree to the terms offered, and both parties are obligated to abide by the contract. The terms of the contract must be precise and clearly defined. If they are not specified in detail so that each party understands the terms, mutual agreement does not exist.

Consideration   The **consideration** must be evident in all contracts, indicating a mutual exchange of promises, for the contract to be legally binding. This consideration must offer a benefit or a detriment with one party giving and the other receiving. In the example of a purchase agreement, the buyer agrees to purchase the property for a stated price, and upon acceptance by the seller, a transaction is agreed to. The earnest money deposit the buyer places with the broker shows the purchaser's good faith in wanting to perform according to the terms of the contract, and while it is "consideration," it does not represent the consideration that makes a valid contract. In real estate the word *consideration* means something of value, such as money, and something that is also necessary for the contract to be legally valid. In the event the buyer should decide not to perform, the earnest money may be dispersed to the seller as liquidated damages, which will be covered later in Chapter 7.

A promise must be accompanied by consideration from one party to another to be enforceable. You may have heard the term *good or valuable consideration*. Good consideration is recognized by law when an act is given for consideration. You hire a nursery to trim your trees on the promise that upon completion of the act you will pay the agreed-upon fee. Another example: "A" promises to sell his condominium to "B" for one-half its market value if "B" marries "A's" daughter. If "B" marries the daughter, "A" must fulfill his promise since the act was carried out. In this situation, "A's" daughter had other plans for her life so the transfer did not take place. Nevertheless, "A" wanted his daughter to have the property, so he deeded it to her for "love and affection," which meets the legal requirement of consideration in some states.

Good consideration

The vast majority of contracts carry valuable consideration in the form of money. The deed used in Chapter 4 carries the phrase, "in consideration of Eighty Four Thousand and no/100 ($84,000)—-DOLLARS in hand paid," representing the valuable consideration the buyers are giving to the sellers. One party agrees to sell property to another for a stated price; in other words, one gives money, and the other relinquishes property for the monetary consideration.

Valuable consideration

The law is emphatic in stating who is able and who is not able to enter into a contract. To be capable of entering into a contract, one must be able to understand what the contract contains and to carry out its terms.

Minors

In many states the age of majority is 18 years, while in other states it may be up to the age of 21 years. A person not of legal age may rescind a contract; however, the person who accepts the minor's contract is still bound to the terms of the contract. This law provides protection for minors since they may not be able to understand contract terms. The minor must request release from the contract while still a minor or within a reasonable time period after reaching majority. Failure to rescind the contract makes it valid. Since few minors would have the funds to purchase real estate, the problem is not prevalent. A guardian or trustee may act for a minor in the event the minor had received property (as through inheritance) and it was deemed in the best interest of the minor that the property be sold.

Capacity of the parties

Mental Incompetency

A mentally incompetent person cannot enter into a contract since the person is not responsible for his actions. Mental instability is sometimes difficult to prove. An insane or mentally handicapped person must have someone appointed by law, as a guardian or conservator, to act on the person's behalf. The elderly person may feel competent but not possess the ability to deal with the complex involvement of selling a home. The real estate salesperson should inquire if the person has a family member to assist in the decision-making process. Careful consideration must be given to anyone the salesperson feels is borderline incompetent.

Some states have extended the law to include intoxicated persons or persons high on drugs and chemically dependent. If property was sold to a person, knowing the party was intoxicated and unable to make a sound judgment, the party to the contract may ask the courts to annul the contract. This would need to be done within a reasonable time after the party becomes sober and realizes what has transpired. In West Virginia, someone entering into a contract while drunk is considered insane, and therefore the contract is void. Court action is necessary.

Lawful object

The purpose of the promise in a contract must be a lawful one. One could not enter into a legal contract with someone to burn down a house, irrespective of the consequences, as it could not be legally completed or enforced.

If one party to a contract is not at fault, the courts will intervene to avenge the injured party. As an example, Evans purchases a property and opens a delicatessen only to be closed down because zoning laws did not permit the space to be used for a commercial purpose. Evans can **rescind** (cancel) the purchase contract upon proof that the property was sold under false pretense.

Written and signed contracts

All states have enacted a statute of frauds requiring that certain contracts be in writing in order to be enforceable. These statutes of frauds protect against fraud and perjury. The document must be signed by the party or parties against whom enforcement would be sought. In lieu of a legal document, a written memorandum such as a series of letters and telegrams would suffice. The memorandum must describe the property and contain the names of the parties, conditions, terms of the sale, and signatures of the party (or parties) against whom compliance is sought.

While some state statutes do not require a lease of less than a year to be in writing, it is far wiser to have it written than to rely on oral evidence. If the oral lease were for two years, it would be unenforceable at the very beginning.

Parol Evidence Rule

The **parol evidence rule** forbids the admittance of any prior verbal or written evidence to vary or add to the terms of a written instrument. If the contract has been properly written, there is no valid reason to introduce such evidence. The parol evidence rule helps eliminate fraudulent claims. One particular point to remember is that the execution of a written contract, whether the law requires it to be written or not, supersedes all the negotiations and stipulations that preceded or accompanied the execution of the instrument. For example, if a buyer informs a broker that she wants the drapes to remain with the house, but this was not put into the purchase agreement nor transmitted to the seller, and the seller signed and accepted the contract as written expecting to remove the drapes, the buyer could not bring in the oral statement that preceded the written document. In this instance, the broker was remiss in not placing it in the contract, and the buyer was negligent in not reading the contract carefully before signing it.

Executory and Executed Contracts

A contract that has not been completed is an **executory contract**; performance has not taken place. A purchase agreement in which the seller has not yet transferred title is an example of an executory contract. Upon title passing, the contract has been **executed**; that is, the terms of the agreement have been carried out. Execution of a contract simply refers to the fact that it has been signed. When parties sign a deed, they execute the document.

Dual Contracts

When real estate is sold or purchased, it is illegal to have **dual contracts** between buyer and seller, with each contract containing a different price so that the buyer can obtain a larger loan from a lender. Such a dual contract, written for the purpose of obtaining a larger loan from the lender, would subject a sales agent to a fine or revocation of their license. Nor could the sales agent declare to the lender that the earnest deposit was greater than it truly was, or delay in depositing the earnest money so it appears that the purchaser has more assets than actually is the case.

VALIDITY OF CONTRACTS

A contract may be valid, void, voidable, or unenforceable.

The **valid contract** complies with all the requirements of contract law. It exists when all parties agree to the terms of an enforceable contract. It has been contracted with all the essential elements previously discussed in this chapter and is legally binding and enforceable.

A contract is **void** when entered into for an illegal purpose, having no legal force or validity. A void agreement is, in effect, no contract.

A contract is **voidable** when one person may cancel the promise, for example, if the party is a minor. The contract is a valid act but may be rescinded by the minor. This is also true of parties who acted under duress or undue influence.

An **unenforceable contract** appears to be valid but cannot be enforced. It may not be in writing in accordance with the statute of frauds and consequently cannot be enforced by court action. For example, a property owner may orally state to a salesperson that he may sell his property, but without a written contract, the salesperson may have trouble proving the oral agreement.

Misrepresentation and fraud can make a contract unenforceable. **Misrepresentation** is an erroneous statement made without the intention to deceive, but with an effect on the finalization of the contract. This does not include a mere expression of opinion. However, if a statement is made with the intent to induce a party to a contract, the person making the statement is liable. The defrauded party may rescind the contract or collect money damages. In the case of a sale, if the seller withholds a pertinent fact that has an effect on the property value, the buyer may retain the property but sue the seller for any difference between the actual value and the purchase price. Courts have ruled against agents who knew or should have known about a material defect and withheld the information from the purchaser.

Misrepresentation

Fraud is an outright attempt to cheat someone. If a false statement is knowingly made regarding a material fact, and if the other party relies upon that statement and suffers damages, fraud has been committed. For example, a seller shows her property, and when asked if the home is on public sewer responds affirmatively, even though this was a deliberate misstatement of fact. After the sale is consummated, the purchaser learns that the house has a septic system. The actions of the seller constitute fraud. Had the seller honestly believed the property was on sewer, it would be a mistake but the contract would still be voidable.

Fraud

A defect hidden from the view of the purchaser (for example, defective plumbing) is known as a **latent defect** and must be revealed to the intended purchaser. However, if a defect can be seen, it is a **patent defect**, and the buyer must observe it personally. A large crack on a dining room wall can be seen, and the purchaser can examine the defect. If the sales agent has any thought that the buyer would not notice the defect, it should be pointed out to the buyer.

Latent and patent defects

The contract must be entered into by the free will of all parties. To force persons to perform against their will is unlawful constraint. Any contract entered into under duress would not be valid. To threaten someone by force is referred to as menace. If a person is under undue influence when signing a contract, it is voidable by the signer.

Performance of a Contract

The contract terms should state when the performance of the contract is to transpire. Purchase contracts call for a set date upon which the closing of the sale will take place; leases state the length of the lease and the date of termination. If a contract does not contain a date, the act should be performed within a reasonable time. The type of contract will determine the defining of reasonable time.

Assignment of a Contract

Assigning holders' rights to another

Since all contracts are assignable, unless they specifically state to the contrary, the *assignor* (holder of the contract) may assign all rights to the assignee (receiver of the contract). If a purchaser assigns all rights in a purchase agreement to a third party, the *assignee* would have all the rights, privileges, and obligations that the buyer had under the contract terms. The terms of the contract must be fulfilled as they were stated. If a contract requires an obligation that is personal (as with a listing contract), it is not assignable without the consent of the seller. If a renowned artist is contracted to paint a portrait, he cannot assign another artist to complete the painting.

Novation

The terms of a contract may also be completed by **novation**. Novation requires the substitution of a new contract for the existing contract. For example, John Blair contracts with Joe Bright for the removal of snow from Blair's property for the winter months of November through March for a certain amount of money. In December, Joe Bright moves to another state, but Jim Jones is willing to carry out the contract as written. This substitution of names is novation.

Discharging of a Contract

When terms of a contract have been fulfilled, the contract is completed or discharged. If performance has not taken place, the contract has been breached unless the parties have agreed to cancel. Under the following conditions, complete performance has failed to take place:

1. *Damage to the property*: If the property is destroyed (as by fire, tornado, or a hurricane) prior to performance, the contract may be cancelled.
2. *Death*: If the contract cannot be completed by someone else equally capable of performing the act, it will be discharged. For example, a renowned portrait artist with a unique painting style dies; the party who employed the artist justifiably may cancel the contract. However, in the situation of a purchase agreement, if the buyer dies, the estate can be held responsible to complete the terms of the contract. Death of the seller may prevent completion unless the deed has been delivered into escrow.
3. *Rescission of the contract by mutual agreement*: All parties involved decide to rescind the contract. For example, the parties who contract to purchase the property learn that they are to be transferred to another city and inform the salesperson that they wish to cancel the contract. With the seller's agreement the cancellation is agreed upon. This agreement to cancel the contract should be in writing and signed by the purchasers and the seller so that the rights of both parties are protected. Commission earned by the listing broker should also be taken into account.
4. *Partial performance*: The parties agree to terminate the contract before completion. For example, a designer is contracted to redecorate a house, but after a portion is completed, decides to cancel the contract because the homeowner is displeased.

Laches

Laches is delay or negligence in asserting one's legal rights; the party has waited too long to complain. The statute of limitations sets a time limit within which one may claim a legal right. This time limit varies widely among states. If the party does not exercise this right within that time, the claim is waived. For example, a house constructed on a vacant lot may not have a wood shake roof as was stipulated in the covenants of the subdivision. The neighbors must bring action within the required time or lose their legal right to insist upon compliance.

If one of the parties to the contract has failed to carry out conditions of the agreement, a breach is committed. For example, a tenant decides to move but has six months remaining on the lease. If the tenant defaults on paying the remainder due, the contract has been breached.

SPECIFIC PERFORMANCE

Specific performance is a remedy in a court of equity compelling the defendant to carry out the terms of the contract. A decree of specific performance may be brought by the injured party, demanding that the defendant perform the promise made or pay damages for losses suffered. When a party brings such a suit, the party agrees to abide by the decree of the court. The general belief of the court is that the injured party should be compensated to the extent of the party's position prior to the breach of the contract. In real estate transactions these actual damages could include a seller's loss upon failure of the buyer to fulfill the contract, a buyer's loss if a seller defaults, a real estate agent's commission, a change in interest rates or closing costs, or the expense of making a double move.

In the purchase of a property, if the buyer does not go through with the purchase, the seller may take recourse in one of the following actions:

Sellers' recourse

1. The seller may rescind the contract and release the buyer from any obligation.
2. The seller may retain the earnest money and declare it forfeited as liquidated damages.
3. The seller may resell the property and sue the buyer for the difference if a loss occurs on the second sale.
4. The seller may sue for the balance of the purchase price.

The usual procedure is to retain the earnest money, dividing it equally between the brokerage firm and the seller (if this is written in the listing agreement). The mechanics of a legal suit are involved and lengthy, and the seller usually favors placing the property on the open market again for a sale.

If the seller refuses to transfer the property to the buyer in accordance with the contract, the buyer has a choice of the following remedies:

Buyers' recourse

1. The buyer may agree to rescind the contract and receive the return of any earnest deposit that was placed with the broker.
2. The buyer may sue for specific performance in an effort to force the seller to perform.
3. The buyer may bring action for money damages against the seller. For example, if the buyers purchase another property with the expectation of moving into the new premises and suddenly find they will not be able to take possession, this could result in the cost of two moves if they are forced to seek temporary housing until they locate and close on the purchase of a substitute house.

OPTION TO PURCHASE

An **option** is a contract granting the exclusive right to buy for a limited time. In an option, time is of the essence. The optionee (prospective purchaser) takes the option, and the optionor (owner) gives the option. Again, this contract must be in writing to be enforceable and must contain a consideration (dollar value) to be valid. If the optionee does not wish to carry out the option, the consideration is forfeited. The optionor retains all the rights of ownership during the term of the option. The optionee is not entitled to any rents or benefits, having only the exclusive right to buy. If the option expires and the parties choose to renew the option, an additional consideration is necessary. The optionee may also assign the option to another. An option is a unilateral contract since it embodies a promise on the part of only one person, the optionor. The differences between an option and a purchase contract are:

1. An option gives the right to buy to the purchaser, who may or may not choose to exercise that right.
2. A purchase contract is an offer to purchase real estate; if accepted by the seller, it becomes a binding contract.

COMMONLY USED CONTRACTS

The contracts used most frequently in real estate transactions are:

1. *Listing contract*: The employment contract between the seller and the brokerage firm (Chapter 6).
2. *Purchase agreement*: The contract between the buyer and the seller (Chapter 7).
3. *The option contract*: Used to reserve the right to purchase a property.
4. *Lease*: Between the tenant and the landlord (Chapter 12).
5. *Property management contract*: Between the property manager and the owner (Chapter 13).
6. *Mortgage*: Between the owner (mortgagor) and the lender (mortgagee) (Chapter 9).
7. *Land contract*: An installment sale contract between the vendee (buyer) and vendor (seller) (Chapter 8).

Although other contracts are used, the above will be covered in depth in the chapters mentioned. The columns below explain the position of the parties involved in contracts.

Contract	Buyer	Owner/ Seller	Lender	Third Party	Tenant
purchase agreement	grantee	grantor			
land contract	vendee	vendor			
option	optionee	optioner			
assignment	assignee	assignor			
offer to purchase	offeror	offeree			
mortgage	mortgagor		mortgagee		
deed of trust	trustor		beneficiary	trustee	
lease		lessor			lessee

The listing contract is not included in the above since the seller (grantor to be) is only granting permission to the real estate firm to sell the property. The firm is not taking title; it has merely received an employment contract to offer the property for sale.

SUMMARY

The essential elements in the making of a contract include the offer and acceptance, consideration, capacity of the parties, and legality of the object.

A contract is either implied by an act or expressed, orally or in writing. The statute of frauds requires that contracts must be in writing to be enforceable. The written contract leaves no doubt as to the intention of the parties. A written contract must be signed by the parties to the contract.

The unilateral contract obligates only one of the parties, whereas in the bilateral contract both parties must perform according to the terms of the contract.

A contract in which performance has not taken place is an executory contract, such as a purchase agreement. The contract is binding when the seller accepts the buyer's offer, but completion does not occur until later. Upon finalization of a contract, it is said to be executed; the terms have been carried out.

A valid contract meets all the requirements of law, whereas a void contract has no legal force. A contract is voidable if one of the parties can cancel, such as a minor. A contract may have the appearance of being valid but may be unenforceable.

When misrepresentation or fraud is involved, the contract may be set aside. Misrepresentation is the act of giving misinformation with no intent to commit fraud. However, the person giving the incorrect information is responsible and if the person is a licensed sales agent, may be subject to losing his license. Fraud is done deliberately in an effort to obtain someone's consent to enter into the contract.

Any defect that cannot be seen by a prospective purchaser is a latent defect and must be revealed to the buyer if it is known. A patent defect is in plain view and need not be pointed out.

Contracts are assignable unless they specifically state otherwise. All obligations pass to the assignee, and the contract must be performed as it was written. Assumable mortgages are transferred to the purchaser by novation, the new owner taking over the responsibility of paying the loan.

Sometimes contracts are not completed, either due to destruction of the property, death, or partial performance. If one of the parties defaults, there are remedies for the injured party.

DISCUSSION QUESTIONS

1. Give an example of a void, a voidable, and an unenforceable contract.
2. Why is a consideration necessary in a contract?
3. Alice Dunbar signed a contract to purchase a larger home so that she would have more storage space for the computer equipment she sells as a representative for a computer company. Before the sale closed, she received complaints from several neighbors stating that they heard she was going to run a business from the home and felt that trucks making deliveries several times weekly would be a danger to their small children. Ms. Dunbar informed the salesperson that she wanted to cancel the contract because of unpleasant confrontations she foresaw. Can she legally rescind the contract? If so, why?
4. Explain a situation in which a contract may be discharged without fulfilling the terms of a written agreement.
5. Give examples of a situation in which an option would be used.

REVIEW QUESTIONS

Answers to these questions are found in the Answer Key section at the back of the book.

1. A contract based upon which of the following would NOT be capable of being voided by the injured party?

   a. error
   b. undue influence
   c. fraud
   d. change of heart

2. A latent defect is best described as:

   a. a defect that the prudent buyer can see
   b. an old defect
   c. a defect that is hidden from view
   d. a breach of contract by the seller

3. Which of the following persons CANNOT be held to a contract?

   a. a minor
   b. an unmarried woman
   c. an elderly person
   d. a widow or widower

4. The difference between an option and a purchase agreement is:

   a. the option gives the right to buy; the purchase contract, if accepted by the seller, is a binding contract to buy
   b. the option need not be in writing, but the purchase contract must be in writing
   c. the option is always in favor of the optionee, while the purchase contract favors the grantee
   d. the option is a bilateral contract, while the purchase agreement is a unilateral contract

5. If an optionee fails to exercise his option within the stated time:

   a. he may sue the optionor for the consideration
   b. he may automatically renew the option if he puts down another consideration
   c. he forfeits the consideration
   d. the purchase is automatically confirmed

6. The important object in the offer and acceptance of a contract is:

   a. the good intent of both grantee and grantor in fulfilling the contract
   b. "meeting of the minds" on the subject matter of the contract
   c. the capability of each party entering into the contract
   d. the legality of the contract

7. Rescission of a contract most nearly means:

   a. all goes back to the way it was before the contract
   b. ratification of the contract
   c. affirmation of the contract
   d. execution of the contract

8. "Meeting of the minds" refers to:

   a. the consummation of the contract
   b. the consideration
   c. the offer and acceptance
   d. the closing of the transaction

9. The term *contractual ability* refers to:

   a. the contract containing all of the covenants needed to make it legal
   b. the attorney having the ability to draw the contract
   c. the capability of two people to enter into a written agreement
   d. the legality of the contract

10. All of the following are essential to a valid contract, EXCEPT:

    a. consideration
    b. duress
    c. offer and acceptance
    d. legality of object

11. If the purchaser assigns her interest in the property while the contract is still pending, realizing a profit:

    a. the seller receives the profit
    b. it cancels the contract
    c. the broker receives the profit
    d. the original purchaser receives the profit

12. A contract between a competent and an incompetent party can be voided by:

    a. the incompetent

b. the competent

c. no one; can't be voided

d. agreement of the parties only

13. A unilateral contract:

    a. embodies a promise on the part of both parties

    b. binds only one party to the contract terms

    c. is voidable by the maker

    d. has been executed by all parties

14. The substitution of a new contract for an existing contract is:

    a. execution

b. breach of contract

c. specific performance

d. novation

15. Upon the default of a contract, all of the following are remedies to the injured party, EXCEPT:

    a. specific performance

    b. retention of the earnest deposit as liquidated damages

    c. execution of the contract

    d. rescission of the contract

The Brokerage Firm: Listing the Property

OVERVIEW

The real estate brokerage firm lists the property, and when a prospective buyer signs the offer to purchase and it is accepted by the seller, a binding contract exists. Once the financing has been secured, the closing of the transaction takes place.

In this chapter the agency relationship between the seller and the brokerage firm is explained, along with the obligations of the parties and the actual listing of the property.

THE BROKERAGE FIRM

As in most industries and professions, specialization has emerged in the field of real estate. The most familiar of these specialized services is provided by the real estate brokerage firm. The complexity of the laws dealing with the sale and transfer of land makes it difficult for the average citizen to handle the entire operation without assistance. Real estate brokerage firms serve the public by listing and selling the property of others. To provide this service, it is necessary to have a **license** to sell real estate—a *License* privilege granted by the real estate commission or regulatory agency of each state. All 50 states have statutes governing real estate brokerage; therefore, to maintain a license, a high degree of professionalism is required.

SALESPERSON AND BROKER

Licensing the agent

Generally a state issues two types of real estate licenses: the salesperson's and the broker's. A salesperson is a licensed individual who has complied with the regulations set forth by the state real estate commission or regulatory agency and has subsequently become licensed to sell the property of others. The salesperson must always operate under the jurisdiction and supervision of a **broker**. A broker must fulfill additional qualifications before being issued a broker's license. Brokers may conduct real estate business under their own name or under a trade name, they may form a partnership with another broker, or they may be part of a corporation. In some states a broker working under the employ of another broker is referred to as an associate broker. Chapter 18 covers license law regulations in greater detail.

Generally speaking, privately owned real estate brokerage firms may be involved in the listing, selling, exchanging, optioning, leasing, managing, building, appraising, or buying of real estate (see Figure 6.1). They may sell new and existing residential properties, raw land, farms, and commercial or industrial properties. Many firms have a separate department to handle the leasing and management of clients' income property. Others subdivide and develop land to erect homes, apartments, shopping centers, and office buildings.

Some real estate agents also obtain an appraiser license and appraise on a fee basis. In August 1989, Congress adopted the Financial Institution's Reform, Recovery and Enforcement Act (FIRREA). Title XI of the act provides for the regulation of real estate appraisers when they appraise real estate in "federally related transactions" as defined in Title XI of the act. As a consequence, states are legislating the licensing of appraisers. This is discussed more fully in Chapter 15, which specifically covers appraisals. Insurance is sold in connection with some real estate offices, supplying buyers with protection on their newly purchased properties. A separate insurance license is needed.

Persons deciding to make real estate their profession can look forward to interesting and varied experiences. The large sums of money involved in the purchasing of real estate demand close supervision of each licensee by state real estate commissions.

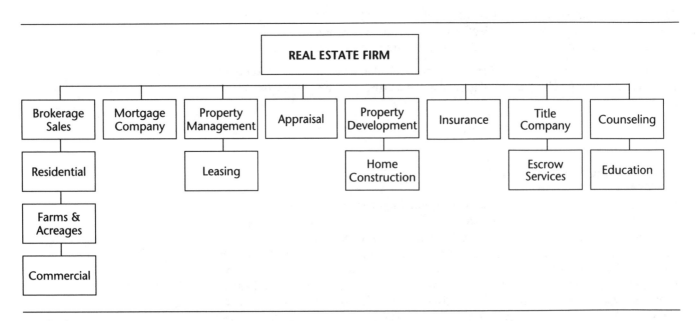

FIGURE 6.1   Possible departments in a real estate firm.

However, professionalism, experience, and knowledge are just as important as state licensing requirements. For the prospective sales representative, expertise and professionalism are essential ingredients for a successful career in real estate.

Need for a Professional

While the law permits property owners to sell their own homes, the owners will soon become aware of the many complex details that are involved in the marketing of real estate. To begin with, they must determine the value of the property. The owners' concept of the worth of the property may be influenced by sentimental attachments and by the costs of maintenance and additions made over the years, but for an accurate valuation the owners need to be familiar with the current real estate market and the trends of the buying public.

Complex real estate procedures

The owner must next attract the right sales prospects—people who are ready, willing, and able to buy, not just those who are curious to see what the interior of the home looks like. The real estate salesperson will qualify customers in advance, ensuring that only those who are definitely prospective buyers will be shown the house.

A property owner is at a disadvantage when it comes to tactfully questioning the buyer's financial status in order to qualify the buyer for the purchase of the property. Hours may be spent showing the home to prospects who cannot afford to purchase it. A vital cog in almost every real estate transaction is the financing. What types of loans are available to the buyer? What are the current interest rates? Should the purchaser buy under FHA? Can the prospect qualify for VA financing? Would a conventional loan, a fixed or an adjustable rate mortgage, or a land contract better suit the buyer's needs?

The owner must also know how to prorate such items as property taxes, the insurance (if the policy is to be assumed by the purchaser), and the interest on the existing loan if it is to be assumed. Real estate salespersons are specialists in their field since they deal in such transactions every day. Sales ability is learned and perfected through specialized practice and training.

THE AGENCY RELATIONSHIP

The creation of an **agency** occurs when one party appoints another to act on her behalf in transacting business with a third party. The agency law has evolved from common practices (common law) and from legislated law.

In the instance of a listing, the owner of the property is known as the **principal**, and the agency is created between the broker and the principal. A **fiduciary** relationship has been formed between the broker and the principal, meaning the principal has faith, trust, and confidence in the broker hired. The broker represents the owner and derives authority from the owner for the specific purpose of negotiating a sale. The principal is bound by the broker's acts, within the scope of authority granted the broker. The listing contract is a specific agency; that is, that specific broker is employed for a particular purpose. When the broker has accomplished this purpose, the broker's authority ends. In many states verbal listings are not enforceable.

Fiduciary relationships

Before discussing the specific fiduciary duties that the broker assumes, it is important to point out that an agency relationship can also be established between a *buyer* and a broker. This arrangement is referred to as **buyer brokerage** or buyer agency, and in such arrangements the buyer is the principal. Buyer brokerage is still relatively rare: the vast majority of brokers are retained to sell real estate rather than to help the buyer find a suitable property. However, buyer brokerage is becoming more common, with some brokerages being created specifically to represent buyers. And in commercial real estate it is not uncommon for real estate brokers to be retained to locate a specific type of property for a client. (Buyer brokerage will be discussed in more detail in the next chapter.)

Whether the seller or the buyer is the principal in an agency relationship, the fiduciary relationship requires that the broker fulfill certain obligations. The broker:

Responsibilities of agent

1. Cannot receive undisclosed profit from the transaction unknown to the principal.
2. Must obey all lawful requests issued by the principal and as outlined by the contract.
3. Is acting for the principal and cannot represent another without the knowledge of both parties (known as dual agency). To prevent confusion, many states now require that brokers must disclose in writing whom they represent.
4. Owes the principal loyalty and disclosure of material facts that may affect the value of the property, such as a proposed change in zoning that would increase or decrease the value of the property.
5. Must account for all money coming into the broker's possession.
6. Does not reveal information that would be detrimental to the broker's negotiating power; for example, that the seller is forced to sell for financial reasons or is willing to take less than the asking price. Or, in the case of buyer agency, that the buyer would be willing to raise his or her current offer. The broker must honor the confidentiality of the principal.

The agency relationship also places certain responsibilities upon the principal:

1. All pertinent facts or hidden (latent) defects must be disclosed to the broker.
2. The agent must not be hindered by acts of the principal in efforts to carry out a transaction.

The broker and seller also have a responsibility to purchasers: the broker must be honest and fair with the potential buyer and under no circumstances conceal any defects. Fair representation must be made.

TYPES OF AGENCIES

Specific agency

The agency created between a principal and the agent is a **specific agency**. The real estate agent is a special agent, meaning that the agent is limited to producing a buyer for the principal as stated under the terms of the listing contract. The **agent** has been given authority to perform this one act, with the terms specifically defined in the listing contract.

General agency

In a **general agency**, an agent would possess more latitude and could literally "speak" for the principal. The general agent would be given power of attorney to represent the principal, who would outline the framework under which the principal wants the agent to act, as in buying and selling investment properties. Other examples of a general agent would be the general manager of a business who has been given a great amount of decision-making authority in operating the business and the property manager who manages business properties for an absentee owner.

Universal agency

A **universal agency** is generally created by power of attorney since the principals are delegating the agent to act in their behalf for a broad range of legal matters, not for a specific purpose such as a real estate transaction.

Ostensible agency

An **ostensible agency** or *implied agency* or *agency by estoppel* occurs when third parties are led to believe that someone is their agent. For example, agent Lucy Brown of A-1 Realty tells John Windsor of Landmark Realty that she has a listing on her neighbor's house. Windsor shows the property while the neighbor is home and writes a contract with the prospect. The neighbor later refuses to pay a commission, stating that he had no listing with Lucy. An ostensible agency would exist in such a case since the neighbor (the third party) never denied that Lucy had the listing when Windsor showed the property and thus John Windsor had no reason to disbelieve Lucy Brown.

An **agency by ratification** occurs when an event takes place and is "ratified" and agreed to after the happening. In the above example, if Lucy Brown's neighbor had agreed to pay the commission, he would be ratifying the sale and agreeing that Lucy is his agent.

Agency by ratification

Contract Between Broker and Salesperson

Real estate firms generally do not hire their salespeople as employees or pay them a salary. Instead, salespeople typically work as independent contractors and are paid strictly on the basis of production; when a sale is finalized, they receive a percentage of the total commission earned. Unlike the requirements in paying salaried employees, the broker does not need to withhold social security tax and income tax on commission paid to independent contractors; the responsibility for paying these taxes belongs to the salesperson. A written contractual agreement should be entered into between the broker and the salesperson to safeguard the broker in the event of an Internal Revenue Service (IRS) investigation.

Independent contractor

Unless salespeople are employees, the broker cannot pay any of the associated expenses, such as entertainment costs, license and trade membership fees, or automobile expenses. And since these salespeople are not employees, the broker cannot make it mandatory that they attend sales meetings or require office hours.

Employee contract

Briefly:

Employee	**Independent Contractor**
1. receives a salary	1. receives no minimum salary
2. broker must withhold social security, income tax, and unemployment tax from salary	2. salesperson pays taxes
3. broker can require set hours for agent	3. sets own hours
4. broker can pay extras (as fees for agents)	4. pays for all expenses—receives no extra compensation

OBTAINING THE LISTING

It is important for the real estate firm to secure listings because listings represent the merchandise the company has to offer for sale. Salespeople will seek these listings through relatives, friends, neighbors, business associates, and acquaintances. Salespeople may also develop a "listing farm," that is, they will select a certain neighborhood of homes where a reasonable turnover in ownership is expected and actively "farm" the area. Many salespeople prepare newsletters with information on household tips, recipes, financing trends, current interest rates, and data on recent sales in the area and deliver them to homeowners in the selected neighborhood. By calling on the homeowners in person, by telephone, and by mail the salesperson will become known to the owners.

When property owners call brokerage firms to list their houses, they are naturally anxious to obtain top dollar for the property. Pricing the property at its fair market value will result in the best price in the quickest period of time and at the least inconvenience to the seller. The agent will determine the property value by comparing it to

Comparable market analysis similar properties that have recently sold, which is referred to as a **comparable market analysis**. The salesperson follows a series of steps in the preparation of the market analysis, which would typically include:

1. Measuring the house for square footage.
2. Comparing the subject property with recent sales and with competition on the market similar in square footage and style. The **multiple listing service (MLS)** is of great value in easily locating the sold properties. If the MLS is computerized and the firm has a computer, the salesperson can pull up comparable sold listings.
3. A proceeds to seller form informs the sellers what their proceeds will be from the sale (see Figure 6.2).
4. A listing contract as shown in Figure 6.3.
5. Several well-written ads to show the seller how the property would be marketed.

Name __Harvey and Della Wender__   Phone __313-0234__   Date 3-10-1994

Address __1040 Clear Street__   Legal Description __Lot 8, Block 1, Confusion Hill__

Projected Sales Price __$85,500__

PROCEEDS TO SELLER
ESTIMATED

	VA	FHA	PMI	ASSUME
1. Balance 1st Mortgage	45,320.10	45,320.10	45,320.10	45,320.10
2. Record Release	5.50	5.50	5.50	
3. Title Insurance/Abstract	159.63	159.63	159.63	159.63
4. Transfer Tax	126.00	126.00	126.00	126.00
5. Professional Fee	5,985.00	5,985.00	5,985.00	5,985.00
6. Discount Points* (2% VA, FHA)	1,710.00	1,560.00	-0-	-0-
7. Termite Inspection	50.00			
8. Prepayment Penalty			-0-	-0-
9. Prorated Interest				
10. Home Protection Plan				
11. _____				
12. Sale price	85,500.00	85,500.00	85,500.00	85,500.00
13. Less Cost	53,356.23	53,156.23	51,596.23	51,590.73
14. Balance	32,143.77	32,343.77	33,903.77	33,909.27

Existing escrow account is returned to sellers when property is refinanced. Taxes and interest are normally prorated.

Existing escrow account is retained by lender and assigned to buyers when loan is assumed. Terms of the contract will dictate whether or not escrow is reimbursed and if taxes and interest are to be prorated.

Final figures determined at closing.

*Discount points vary and are subject to change.

FIGURE 6.2
Proceeds to seller form.

LISTING CONTRACT   Date <u>March 10, 1994</u>

1 We hereby agree to list and offer for sale our property hereafter described and give you the sole and exclusive right to and including <u>June 10, 1994</u> to sell <u>1040 Clear St.</u> Legal <u>Lot 8, Block 1, Confusion Hill</u> <u>Subdivision</u> together with attached fixtures for the sum of $ <u>85,500</u>, upon the following terms: <u>loan assumption, cash, conventional</u>

2 I agree to pay you a cash commission of <u>7</u> % of the gross sales price, with minimum commission of $ <u>2000.00</u>, (whichever is greater) said commission to be payable under any of the following conditions:

A. If a sale is made, or a purchaser found, who is ready, willing and able to purchase the property before the expiration of this listing, by you, myself, or any other person, at the above price and terms or for any other price and terms I may agree to accept.

B. If you are unfairly hindered by me in the showing or attempting to sell said premises within the listed period.

C. If you are prevented in closing the sale of this property by existing liens, judgments, or suits pending against said property.

D. If I make a sale of said premises to any one due to your efforts or advertising done under this listing within <u>90</u> days after the expiration date. This property is offered without respect to race, color, national origin or religion.

3 In case of the forfeiture, by a prospective purchaser, of any earnest money payment, upon the within described property, said earnest money, after expense incurred by you has been deducted, shall be divided one-half to the owners and one-half to the agent.

4 I hereby represent that to the best of my knowledge, information and belief there are no termites in the buildings on the real estate hereinbefore described, and if termites are found in said buildings and it is known that such condition existed prior to the time of the closing of the sale thereof, I hereby agree to indemnify you and hold you harmless from any and all loss, damage or expense to which you may be subjected arising in connection therewith.

5 I agree to furnish either a complete abstract certified to date of sale showing merchantable title or a Title Insurance Policy, to complete said sale and to pay any expense incurred in perfecting the title in case it is found defective, and convey within <u>30</u> days from date of sale, the property by warranty deed, or <u>none other</u> executed by all persons having any interest therein, and clear of all encumbrances except <u>no exceptions</u>

Possession to be given <u>90 days</u> after closing.
For Sale sign and Lock Box permitted.

We hereby accept the above listing and agree to the above terms. Receipt of a copy of this agreement is hereby acknowledged.

6
<u>A-1 Real Estate Company</u>
Real Estate Company
By <u>Judy M. Selling</u>
Sales Agent

<u>Harvey J. Wender</u> Owner
Husband
<u>Della G. Wender</u> Owner
Wife

<u>1040 Clear Street</u> Address

Telephone Residence <u>313-0234</u>   Business <u>313-0003</u>

7

Address	1040 Clear St.	Legal	Lot 8, Block 1, Confusion Hill Subdivision		
Style	ranch	Occupant	owner	Age	7
Rooms	6	Possession	negotiable		
Bedrooms	3	Mtg	Ready S & L	Mtg. Bal	45,320.10
Baths	1 - 3/4	Type Mtg	FHA	Int	10 %
2 Car Garage	attached	Payment	547.68	Incl. Taxes yes	Ins yes
Lot size	85 x 110	2nd Mtg	– – – –	Taxes 19XX $	1550.00
Square Ft.	1170 Main ___ 2nd Fl ___	Fin B 420			

Living Room	20 x 15	Fireplace	one	Dishwasher	X
Dining Room	12 x 13	Exterior	wood	Disposal	X
Kitchen	10 x 12	Roof	comp.	Range/oven	X
Family Room	– – – –	Heat	FA Gas	Power Humid	X
Rec Room	28 x 15	Central Air	yes	Grade School	William Flem.
Bedroom	10 x 12	Fencing	chain link	Jr. High	Carter Jr. High
Bedroom	12 x 11	Paving	X	High School	Carter High
Bedroom	12 x 15	Water	X	Sewer	X
Bedroom		Gas	X	Elec	X

FIGURE 6.3   Exclusive right to sell listing contract.

This packet of information is presented to the sellers with the expectation of obtaining the listing. A professional approach such as this lends credence to the salesperson's ability to successfully market the home.

THE LISTING CONTRACT

Signed by all owners

The **listing contract** must be signed by all the owners of the property, as it constitutes employment of the agent. If the property is held by a partnership or by a corporation, the agent should verify that the partner or officer signing the listing agreement has the capacity to authorize the sale. Any *restrictions* on the sale should be noted in the listing agreement. Once the salesperson's broker has accepted the listing, the broker is responsible to the principal and cannot delegate this authority to another. This does not necessarily mean that the agent will not cooperate with other brokers, but the responsibility for making appointments for showing of the property, for negotiating agreements of sale with the owners, and for closing the transaction generally rests with the listing broker and salesperson.

The listing broker must ask the principal what personal property, if any, will remain with the property. These items will then be included on the listing contract. An example might be draperies custom made for a particular room; the owners may decide it will facilitate a sale to leave them.

If the owners have an attached fixture, which is rightly real estate, that they do not want to leave, they should indicate it is to be shown as excluded from the listing and sales agreement, or it should be removed and replaced prior to any showings of the property. For example, Aunt Harriet may have given the owners the crystal chandelier in the dining room as a wedding gift. Removing it will prevent the problem of a buyer seeing the chandelier and insisting it must stay if he purchases the home.

In addition, it is important that at the time the property is listed the salesperson clearly explain to the sellers all costs involved in the sale of the real property. The salesperson should never assume that the sellers understand their obligations and costs concerning the sale, but should always enumerate them clearly. The "Proceeds to Seller" form (see Figure 6.2) should be completed by the salesperson at the time of listing, giving the sellers an estimate of what they will net after all costs.

The listing contract itself allows the real estate firm to review listed properties at a glance. If a purchaser calls on a particular property, all the pertinent and accurate data are readily accessible on the contract. This eliminates errors that could arise if this information were not readily available. Listing contracts vary in different areas of the country. Some states allow verbal listings, but in many states the law requires listing contracts to be in writing to be enforceable. In these states, the contract must also be signed by the parties to be charged or held to the agreement in order to be legally enforceable.

The listing contract should contain the following basic information:

1. a description of the property
2. the amount of commission to be paid and when it will be paid
3. the expiration date
4. the signature of the party or parties to be charged

There are four types of listing contracts. Each differs in the degree of responsibility and the legal rights assigned to the broker.

Exclusive Right to Sell

The **exclusive right to sell** contract gives the real estate firm the sole right to act as agent for the sellers. Should the principals find a purchaser during the term of the listing, they are obligated by the employment contract to pay a commission to the brokerage firm. Appointments for showings of the property by other firms generally are made through the listing firm, as they are responsible to the seller. The exclusive right to sell listing is the most popular listing, since the firm that lists the property receives a commission regardless of who sells the property.

In the exclusive right to sell contract (shown in Figure 6.3), the numbered sections outline the contract terms as follows:

Contents of a listing contract

Section 1 states the expiration date of the listing and the street address and legal description of the property. It also states the offering price and the terms of sale.

Section 2 states the commission to be paid and the terms under which the sellers agree to pay the broker. These conditions include the following:

a. if an offer is made by a bona fide purchaser during the term of the listing for the listed price or any other price or terms the sellers agreed would be acceptable
b. if the sellers unfairly hinder showings of the property
c. if the sale cannot close due to liens, judgments, or suits pending against the property
d. if a sale is made due to the salesperson's efforts or advertising during the listing or within a specified number of days of the expiration date

Section 3 states that if the purchaser forfeits the earnest money deposit, it will be divided equally between owner and broker after the broker's expenses have been deducted.

Section 4 explains that if termite damage is found and was known about by the owners prior to closing a sale, the owners will carry full responsibility.

Section 5 states that the owners agree to provide either an abstract of title that has been brought to date or a title insurance policy and that the owners agree to correct any defects in the title. On this contract, the owners will give a warranty deed. The possession date is stated. The owners also agree that a "For Sale" sign and a lock box may be placed on the property.

Section 6 lists the owners' signatures and the sales agent's signature.

Section 7 gives a description of the property, room sizes, loan information, and other data pertinent to the listed property.

Exclusive Agency

Under the terms of the **exclusive agency** contract only one firm is hired to sell the property, but the owners retain possession to sell the property themselves without paying a commission to the firm. If the broker is the procuring cause in the transaction, the owner would be liable for the commission; that is, if the brokerage firm caused the sale to happen, as by introducing the buyers to the property.

Seller retains right to sell

With this type of contract, problems may arise as to whether the listing broker actually was instrumental in introducing the purchaser to the property. A buyer may see the sign in the yard, stop and visit with the owner, and subsequently purchase the home directly from the owner. In this case, the broker's "For Sale" sign was the procuring cause, and the owner would be responsible for paying the broker's fee. Under the exclusive agency listing the broker may be reluctant to spend money on advertising and promoting the property knowing that if the owner finds a buyer before the broker, the broker will not receive a commission.

If another broker sells the property as a subagent of the listing broker, the seller is committed to pay a commission.

Open Listing

Hiring more than one firm

An **open listing** is open to any number of brokers the sellers wish to employ. The sellers are obligated to pay a commission only to that broker who successfully produces a buyer ready, willing, and able to purchase the home. If the owners sell it themselves, they need not pay anyone a fee. Generally under an open listing the owners will not allow signs on the property, and salespeople will be less enthusiastic in trying to find a buyer. An agent will be reluctant to advertise a property on which there is no protection should a sale result.

Open listings are not always in writing, and while the owner may feel "everyone will be working to sell it," the opposite is usually true. The brokers are more inclined to spend their time and money on properties for which they will be ensured a return on their investment when a sale occurs.

Net Listing

In a **net listing** a property is listed at an agreed-upon net price, and the broker receives the excess over and above the net listing as the earned commission. Net listings are illegal in some states and frowned on by other real estate regulatory agencies, as they can easily lead to disputes and misunderstandings.

California real estate law requires that the broker give to the seller in writing before the seller signs the contract (1) the exact sale price and (2) broker's total earnings.

A net listing may be an exclusive right to sell, an exclusive agency, or an open listing. A net listing is not a type of listing but a way of calculating the commission.

$$\begin{array}{r} 100\% \\ -\ 7\% \\ \hline 93\% = .93 \end{array}$$

$50,000 \div .93 = 53,800$ Rounded up

The property will need to sell for $53,800 if the listing broker wishes to net a 7 percent commission.

Agent Compensation

Fee is negotiable

The rate of the professional service fee depends upon the contract, as there is no set commission. To set commission rates would be a violation of federal and state antitrust laws. The fee is negotiable between the seller and the real estate firm. The commission is payable under the following terms:

1. The broker must produce a buyer who is ready to buy now, willing (has not been forced), and financially able to buy.
2. The broker must be able to prove performance (with a signed listing).
3. The sale must be consummated.
4. If the sale is terminated by the seller's refusal to close after accepting the offer, the fee must still be paid to the broker.

Terminating the Listing

The listing will prevail until the property is sold or the listing expires, whichever occurs first. However, by mutual consent between the principal and the brokerage firm, a listing may be terminated. Upon entering into the listing contract, the seller agrees not to hinder the brokerage firm and its agents in their endeavors to show the property. If the principal simply decides to break the contract for no valid reason, the brokerage firm, under the terms of the contract, has a right to sue for damages. Conversely, the real estate firm must spend time on marketing the property and make an earnest effort to locate prospective purchasers. If no such effort is made, ample reason to terminate the listing would exist. Should either of the parties die, the listing would be canceled. If there are any economic changes in the property that would affect the property's value, such as a zoning change, the listing contract can be terminated. Certain acts over which the principal and the broker have no control will nullify the listing. If the property is destroyed by fire, tornado, hurricane, earthquake, or other act of nature, cancellation of the listing would become effective since the property listed no longer exists.

By mutual consent

At the end of the listing term, the listing expires unless the parties agree to extend the employment contract. Most states require that written listings state a specific termination date. Automatic extensions, which state that the contract will continue until either party gives written notice to terminate the listing, are generally not recognized and are considered illegal in some states. However, many times owners will relist the property with the same broker if they are satisfied with the servicing of the listing. Market conditions may have prevented a sale within the listed time frame.

Expiration of time

MULTIPLE LISTING SERVICES

A multiple listing service (MLS) is not a different type of listing, but an organized exchange of real estate listings conducted by a group of brokers, usually members of a real estate board. A standard multiple listing form is used by the members, who turn all their listings in to a central service bureau, from where they are distributed to all members.

Cooperation among brokers

On July 1, 1992, the **National Association of Realtors® (NAR)** initiated a policy change in their multiple listing service. Offer of subagency through the MLS PLUS, a new feature, is now optional rather than mandatory. When submitting listings, MLS participants are now required to offer cooperation either in the form of subagency or to buyers' agents or both. All offers must include an offer of compensation. This rule is a result of the emergence of buyer agencies in many parts of the country and allows the buyer's broker to participate in a commission split while retaining a fiduciary relationship to the buyer and not to the seller.

With an MLS, brokerage firms cooperate on the sale of the properties; a single dwelling has not only the members of one agency working on its sale, but the majority of the firms belonging to the MLS exchange, thus exposing the property to more customers. If for any reason the owner does not want her property in the MLS exchange, a signed waiver will protect the listing broker.

If a salesperson does not have a property among his own company's listing that meets the requirements of a prospect, the multiple listing service broadens the chances for making a sale. Many large MLS services publish the listings in a book form, distributing them to the members on a weekly or other basis.

Computer terminals are another service made available by MLS. Salespeople can search the computer for new listings on a daily basis and thus enhance their ability to locate properties for their prospects. Not only may the sales office have a terminal, but personal computers may be available to the individual in small carrying cases, providing instant access wherever the salesperson may be.

Some services have a broker load system where the listing is loaded into the computer from the broker's office, thus shortening the time to make the listing available to all members.

Most MLS services will require that new listings be turned in for processing within a limited time frame, such as 48 hours. A penalty may be imposed upon members who fail to comply with the time requirement for processing the listing.

ANTITRUST LAW

The Sherman Antitrust Act was enacted to maintain fair trade among competitors. Price fixing is contrary to the open market system as we know it. Real estate firms must be certain to make it clear that the commission payable is between the real estate firm and the client, not predetermined by a multiple listing service or any real estate association or group of brokers. Although it is common for rates to be uniform in a given area, brokers can charge any fee that is agreed upon between the firm and the principal. Discussion regarding commissions should never be between anyone but the broker and the principal.

Often, the market dictates the fee. If sales are brisk, the fee may be negotiated for less. If sales are slow, the property owner may offer a higher commission rate in hopes of a quicker sale. Expensive properties are frequently listed at a commission rate several percent lower than normal.

Restraint of trade and denial of multilisting services are other areas that have challenged real estate brokers.

REAL ESTATE ASSOCIATIONS

Trade organizations

A real estate board is a voluntary organization whose membership comprises persons engaged in some phase of the real estate business or who are directly or indirectly interested in real estate. Most boards maintain an affiliate classification of membership that is open to lending institutions, appraisers, title and abstracting companies, and others whose duties or interests are related to real estate.

The purpose of a real estate board is to promote good ethics among its members, promote the enactment of legislation for the protection of property rights and interests, and secure the benefits of united efforts for its members. The board upholds fair practices and generally endeavors to professionalize the industry.

Members of the local real estate board also belong to the state association. The salesperson or broker who resides in areas where no local board exists is a member-at-large of the state association. Yearly conventions are held by the members where ideas are exchanged and new concepts within the industry are discussed. Educational seminars are always an important part of the conventions.

The REALTOR®

The National Association of REALTORS® (NAR) is the parent organization of the state boards and is headquartered in Chicago, Illinois. Its membership is composed of members of local boards and state associations. All members that belong to the organization can refer to themselves as **REALTORS®**, a registered trademark that can only be used by NAR members. The NAR has set forth a strict code of ethics to which all members must adhere.

Under the umbrella of NAR are numerous affiliate organizations that offer a wide range of educational opportunities. Some of the institutes offer designations upon completion of courses and successfully passing their examinations. For example, the Institute for Real Estate Management (IREM) has specialized property management courses and the Women's Council of REALTORS® (WCR) has developed leadership training courses and relocation courses. With specialization becoming more prevalent in real estate, the availability of these courses is an important reason to belong to the National Association of REALTORS®.

A Realtist is a member of a group of brokers known as the National Association of Real Estate Brokers. The association began in 1947 and is composed of minority brokers who promote improved housing in the areas they serve.

SUMMARY

The first step in the sale of real property is to make the property available to prospective buyers. The owners can offer it for sale themselves or arrange to be represented by a real estate salesperson. If the owner hires a broker, there are four types of listings to consider. The exclusive right to sell gives the real estate firm the sole right to act as the agent of the owner, while the exclusive agency listing allows the owners an opportunity to sell it themselves. The open listing is used by the owners if they desire to list with more than one agency. The net listing sets the dollar amount that the seller wants to net from the sale with the agency receiving the excess.

Most real estate agents insist upon the exclusive right to sell contract, since they spend time and money obtaining a sale for the owner. The brokerage firm is paid only when it produces a buyer who meets the terms to which the owner agreed in the listing. It is thus understandable that the brokerage firm's services are worthy of a contract that protects its interests.

The multiple listing service is the vehicle used by real estate companies to make known to other firms the data on their listings. This method encourages cooperation among companies since all salespeople are aware of the property's availability.

The National Association of REALTORS® is the parent organization to state and local real estate boards. These voluntary trade associations help promote good ethics among their members and generally endeavor to professionalize the industry.

DISCUSSION QUESTIONS

1. Explain why a listing contract creates a specific agency.
2. What are the possible consequences of overpricing a property?
3. As a real estate salesperson, what type of listing would you prefer? Give reasons for your answer.
4. In what circumstances can a listing be canceled?
5. Give examples of specific, general, universal, and ostensible agencies.
6. Give reasons that property owners would list their property with a real estate firm in lieu of selling it "by owner."
7. If you worked for a brokerage firm, would you prefer to be an employee or an independent contractor? Give reasons for your answer.

REVIEW QUESTIONS

Answers to these questions are found in the Answer Key section at the back of the book.

1. What do general, special, and universal agencies have in common?

   a. they originate with the principal
   b. they create ongoing business for the agent
   c. they empower the agent to sign all contracts for the principal
   d. they share all of the above characteristics

2. A real estate salesperson must:

   a. always be under the employ of a broker
   b. never refuse to accept a listing
   c. hold a national real estate license
   d. belong to a multiple listing service

3. An exclusive right to sell listing contract:

   a. gives the broker a commission based on an agreed price the seller wishes to net, with the broker receiving the excess over the agreed amount
   b. makes the brokerage firm the exclusive agent for a stipulated period of time
   c. allows the owner the right to sell the property without paying a commission to the listing broker
   d. will automatically be renewed if it expires before the property is sold

4. Under the terms and conditions of an open listing:

   a. the owner may sell the property but must pay a commission to the listing broker
   b. the listing is given to any number of brokers the seller wishes to hire, with a commission going only to the selling firm
   c. one broker is given the listing, but it is "open" for other brokers to sell
   d. upon the sale, the commission is split between all the brokers who were given the listing

5. It is mandatory that a listing contract:

   a. have a termination date
   b. be signed by the purchasers
   c. have an automatic renewal clause
   d. be processed through a multiple listing service

6. Under the rules of a multiple listing service:

   a. only the firm that has the listing may show the property
   b. all members of the MLS cooperate in selling the property
   c. all the firms belonging to the MLS may place their signs on the property
   d. properties are advertised only in the MLS book

7. The term REALTOR® is a coined word:

   a. available for use only by members of the multiple listing service
   b. used only by members of the National Association of REALTORS®
   c. used by all licensed real estate agents
   d. issued for the use of real estate brokers, but not salespersons

8. The type of agency created when a broker lists a property under the exclusive right to sell is:

   a. a general agency
   b. a specific agency
   c. a universal agency
   d. an ostensible agency

9. A real estate broker is:

   a. appointed by the property owner to act for and in his stead in the sale of the owner's property
   b. not responsible for the salesperson's actions
   c. responsible to sell the property within the listed time frame
   d. always employed as a general agent to the property owner

10. The most desirable type of listing for a real estate broker is a(n):

    a. open listing
    b. net listing
    c. exclusive right to sell listing
    d. exclusive listing

11. An owner gives an open listing to firms X and Y. Firm X sells the property to a buyer to whom firm Y had previously shown the property. The commission was:

    a. earned by firm X
    b. earned by firm Y
    c. split evenly between X and Y

d. arbitrated by the Board of REALTORS®

12. If an owner sells her own home on which you have an exclusive agency:

   a. you receive no commission
   b. you receive a full commission
   c. you receive half commission
   d. you receive 40 percent

13. Which is the closest to a multiple listing?

   a. cooperative
   b. net listing
   c. exclusive agency
   d. exclusive right to sell

14. Mr. Jennings lists his house with Ms. Walls, a real estate salesperson employed by the A-1 Real Estate Company. The agency exists:

   a. between Jennings and Walls
   b. between Jennings and the A-1 Real Estate Company
   c. between A-1 Realty, the multiple listing service, and Jennings
   d. for the duration of the listing time between the salesperson and the principal

15. The least protection a broker has is with a(n):

   a. exclusive agency
   b. open listing
   c. exclusive right to sell
   d. multiple listing

16. The brokerage firm receives the excess over and above a specified sales price in a(n):

   a. net listing
   b. gross listing
   c. open listing
   d. exclusive listing

17. Broker X has an exclusive agency on a property that she learns has been sold by broker Y. Broker Y receives a full commission. Broker X should:

   a. request half commission from broker Y
   b. request full commission from broker Y
   c. request full commission from the owner
   d. realize that no commission is due her

18. A listing may be canceled for all of the following reason(s) EXCEPT:

   a. the owner of the property dies

b. the broker files bankruptcy
c. the property is destroyed by fire
d. owner changes his mind

19. A property owner is planning to travel for three months and wants to sell two of his rental properties while absent from the city. In giving the real estate broker a written power of attorney to sell these two properties, the owner would be establishing which type of agency?

   a. universal
   b. dual
   c. special
   d. general

20. The law of agency is between:

   a. principal and brokerage firm
   b. salesperson and principal
   c. broker and attorney
   d. seller and broker's attorney

21. Sally Wells obtains two listings: one is an open listing from owner A, and the other is an exclusive agency listing from owner B. After one week A and B, who had previously visited about their properties, decide to exchange their real estate. Sally Wells will obtain the following:

   a. a commission from A and B
   b. a commission from A
   c. a commission from B
   d. no commission since the owners exchanged their properties

22. What happens when a principal sells his home under an exclusive right to sell listing?

   a. the broker receives no commission
   b. the broker receives a commission on the gross sales price
   c. the broker receives half the commission ordinarily due him
   d. legal action will need to be instigated if the broker is to receive a commission

23. The only way a seller could terminate an exclusive agency is if:

   a. a buyer is introduced by a broker from another real estate firm
   b. a buyer is introduced by the seller
   c. the seller decides the broker is not advertising the property often enough

d. the seller writes a contract with a buyer who was shown the property by the listing agent

24. Which of the following listings is least likely to be defined as a percentage of the sale price?

   a. open listing
   b. net listing
   c. exclusive agency
   d. exclusive right to sell

25. A licensed broker brings a buyer and seller together. The buyer later finds out he is being transferred. The buyer goes to the seller, and they agree to rescind the contract. The broker involved:

   a. gets to keep the earnest deposit as liquidation damage
   b. gets a full commission from the seller
   c. gets no monetary compensation
   d. keeps ½ the commission

Marketing and Selling Real Estate

7

OVERVIEW

As discussed briefly in Chapter 6, in most cases the real estate agent represents the seller of real estate. However, it is certainly possible for real estate agents to represent the buyer in a transaction rather than the seller, and this arrangement is referred to as **buyer agency** or buyer brokerage. Buyer brokerage will be discussed in this chapter. Because the former arrangement, with the agent representing the seller, is far more common, the initial sections of the chapter will deal exclusively with seller agency.

Once a property has been listed for sale, the real estate firm then performs the function for which it was employed—finding a buyer. Usually the broker advertises the property in the newspaper and places a "For Sale" sign on the premises to bring responses from prospective purchasers. In addition, the sales representatives check their lists of prospects to see if the new listing will meet anyone's requirements. If the firm belongs to a multiple listing service, it immediately sends the listing information to the service for processing. Open houses (holding the house open for inspection) are another means of attracting would-be buyers.

THE PURCHASE AGREEMENT

The salesperson prequalifies buyers prior to showing them properties to determine the price range they will qualify to purchase. When a prospective buyer makes the decision to purchase a particular property, the salesperson completes an estimated buyer's figures form. These costs will vary across the country and among lenders. The form gives the buyer a clear picture of what money will be needed to close the loan and what the monthly payments will be. With the buyer's approval of the estimated costs, a **purchase agreement** is then written. In some parts of the country this document is referred to as an offer and acceptance or a deposit receipt.

Upon acceptance, the agreement is a contract and, according to the statute of frauds in most states, must be in writing to be enforceable. While the writing of the contract is generally done by the selling agent, some states require that since a contract is a legal document, the actual writing of the offer to purchase must be done by an attorney. In this instance, after the buyers have selected the property they desire to purchase, the licensee directs them to an attorney. Other states have the view that the completion of a printed purchase agreement (see Figure 7.1) does not constitute the practice of law. If the printed document contains all the essential elements and provisions for contingencies, protection for both parties is provided. Regardless of the laws of your state, the presentation of the offer to the seller will in most communities still be the listing agent's responsibility.

OFFER TO PURCHASE

The offer-to-purchase contract shown in Figure 7.1 contains the following information:

Elements of a purchase contract

Section A states the date the offer to purchase was signed, along with the street and legal address of the property. Any personal property included in the sale is written in this section of the agreement.

Section B stipulates that the owners will convey good title, free of all liens (unless the buyers are assuming an existing mortgage). The sellers further agree that any existing indebtedness against the property will be paid.

Section C sets forth the purchase price and the amount of the earnest deposit. The balance of the purchase price will be paid according to the type of financing checked in Section D.

Section D contains four choices: the buyers may either (1) pay cash, (2) assume the existing mortgage, (3) obtain a new loan, or (4) request a land contract (owner financing).

Section E contains any additional conditions of the agreement that need to be clarified.

Section F provides for proration of taxes.

Section G states that the buyers have inspected the premises and agree to accept the property in its present condition. The sellers agree to maintain all the component parts in working order. The sellers further state they will be responsible for any loss to the property until title is conveyed. If any termite damage is found, they promise to pay for repairs.

Section H states the contract is binding upon the parties and their heirs and assigns. The purchasers sign the agreement.

Section I is the statement of receipt for the earnest deposit and the time allowed for the owners to accept the offer. The real estate company's name and address are also stated.

Section J shows the date of acceptance and the signatures of the accepting owners and of the witness.

Section K is signed by the buyers to show that they received a copy of the accepted contract.

(This is a legally binding contract. If not understood, seek legal advice.)

PURCHASE AGREEMENT

_____April 9_____ 1994

A

I, the undersigned Purchaser, hereby agree to purchase the property described as follows:
Address ___1040 Clear Street_____
Legal Description _Lot 8, Block 1, Confusion Hill Subdivision_____
including all fixtures and equipment permanently attached to said premises. The only personal property included is as follows:
_____living room drapes_____
_____

B

Subject, however, and on condition that the owner thereof has good, valid and marketable title, in fee simple, and said owner
agrees to convey title to said property to me or my nominees by warranty deed or _____none other_____
free and clear of all liens, encumbrances or special taxes levied or assessed, except _____no exceptions_____
This offer subject to all building and use restrictions, utility easements not exceeding 10 feet in width abutting the boundary
of said property, and covenants now of record. Seller agrees to pay any assessments for paving, curb, sidewalk or utilities
previously constructed or now under construction but not yet assessed.

C

I agree to pay for same _____Eighty-four thousand & no/100 —___ ($ _84,000.00_____) DOLLARS, on the
following terms: $ _2000.00_____ deposited herewith as evidence by your receipt attached below. Balance to be
paid only as shown in following paragraphs ____3, 5, 6_____:

D

#1 CASH
Balance of $ _____ to be paid in cash or by certified check at time of delivery of deed, no financing
being required.

#2 LOAN ASSUMPTION
I agree to assume and pay existing mortgage balance in favor of _____
in the approximate amount of $ _____ and pay the balance in cash or by certified check at the time of
delivery of deed; it being understood that present mortgage terms call for stated interest rate of _____% per annum and payments of $ _____ per _____. Said payment includes _____.
Stated interest on existing loan to be prorated to date of closing. I agree to reimburse the Seller for the amount in the escrow reserve account which is to be assigned to me.

#3 CONDITIONAL UPON LOAN
Balance of $ _82,000_____ to be paid in cash or by certified check at time of delivery of deed, conditional
however, upon my ability to obtain a loan, to be secured by first mortgage, or deed of trust, on above described property in
the amount of $ _67,200_____. Said loan to be VA _____, FHA _____, CONVENTIONAL _X_____,
P.M.I. _____, or VA/FHA _____, with terms providing for stated interest not exceeding ___10__% per annum, and monthly
payments of approximately $ _590.02_____ plus taxes and insurance. Loan origination fee/service fee to be paid by
purchaser. I agree to make application for said loan within 10 days of acceptance of this offer. I hereby authorize you to negotiate for a loan on the above basis and I agree to sign all papers and pay all costs in connection therewith.

#4 LAND CONTRACT
Balance to be evidenced by land contract with present owner, providing for additional cash payment or certified check of
$ _____ at time of execution of the contract, and remainder $ _____ to be paid in monthly payments of
$ _____, or more, which monthly payments shall include stated interest at the rate of _____% per annum
computed monthly on the unpaid portion of the principal. All other terms and conditions of the land contract to be as mutually
agreed.

E

#5
_____possession no later than May 15, 1994_____
_____

F

#6 TAXES
All real estate taxes shall be pro-rated as of date of possession __May 15, 1994_____.

G

This offer is based upon my personal inspection or investigation of the premises and not upon any representation or warranties of condition by the Seller or his agent. Seller agrees to maintain, until delivery of possession, the heating, air conditioning, water heater, sewer, plumbing and electrical systems and any built-in appliances in working conditions.

Any risk of loss to the property shall be borne by the Seller until title has been conveyed to the Purchaser. In the event,
prior to closing, the structures on said property are materially damaged by fire, explosion or any other cause, Purchaser shall
have the right to rescind this agreement, whereupon Seller shall then refund to Purchaser the deposit made hereunder. Purchaser, except for V.A. loan, agrees to pay the cost of a termite inspection of the house and attached structures, and Seller
agrees to pay for any treatment or repair work found necessary. If repairs are found to be needed for issuance of termite warranty, upon completion of repairs, Purchaser agrees to accept said treated real estate.

FIGURE 7.1   Offer-to-purchase contract, also known as purchase agreement or purchase contract.   _(continued)_

H
This offer is binding upon both parties and the heirs and assigns of said parties.
WITNESS:

Judy M. Selling   _Kurt K. Kindly_ , Purchaser

Susan A. Kindly , Purchaser

Address ___328 Harbor Lane___ Phone ___333-0193___

I
RECEIVED FROM _____Kurt K. Kindly & Susan A. Kindly_____
the sum of _two thousand and no/100_   —   ($ _2000.00_) DOLLARS (by _check_)
to apply on the purchase price of the above described property. In the event the above offer is not accepted by the owner of said property within the time hereinafter specified, or that in the event there are any defects in the title which cannot be cured as specified above, the money hereby paid is to be refunded. If purchaser fails to consummate the purchase, the owner may, at his option, retain said money hereby paid as liquidated damages for such failure to carry out said agreement of sale, subject to the terms of the listing agreement.
This receipt is not an acceptance of the above offer, it being understood that the above proposition is taken subject to the written approval and acceptance by the owner on or before _10 p.m. on April 9, 1994_

445 Homestead Ave.   _333-3004_   _A-1 Real Estate_
OFFICE ADDRESS   PHONE #   REAL ESTATE COMPANY

J
ACCEPTANCE: _April 9_ , _1994_

We agree to the above stated terms and will deliver possession and title and perform according to this contract.
We agree to pay A-1 Real Estate Company a cash fee of 7% of the sale price.

Judy M. Selling   _Harvey J. Wender_
WITNESS   SELLER

Della J. Wender
                           SELLER

K
We are in receipt of the seller's acceptance of our contract.

Judy M. Selling   _Kurt K. Kindly_
WITNESS   BUYER

April 10, 1994   _Susan A. Kindly_
                           BUYER

FIGURE 7.1   (Continued).

Presenting the Offer

When the offer to purchase is written, a copy is given to the offeror (purchaser) as a receipt. The sales agent then takes the offer to the offeree (seller) for formal acceptance. Generally it is the listing agent who contacts the sellers to present the offer. If the sellers agree to all the conditions of the offer, they sign the acceptance. In Figure 7.1 at Section J, the sellers accepted the offer as written.

When the terms of the contract are agreed upon, a copy is left with the seller, and the agent notifies the buyer that the offer was accepted and gives the buyer a copy of the signed contract. In our sample purchase agreement at Section K, the buyers sign that they have received a copy of the seller's acceptance.

An offer may be rescinded at any time prior to the seller's acceptance, so it behooves the sales agent to deliver the contract promptly.

Counteroffers

To alter any portion of the offer nullifies the entire agreement. If the seller does not accept the terms, the seller may elect to make a **counteroffer**. Any counteroffer revokes the previous offer and is replaced with a new contract. A counteroffer is not a partial acceptance since an acceptance cannot be conditional. However, the counteroffer can be dated and signed by the owner and the time limit for acceptance of this new offer be stated. The buyer can now agree to the new terms or decide against purchasing the property.

When an offer is countered, the property is available for another offer, whether from the original offeror or from another party. If the seller counters an offer and meanwhile another offer from a second party is presented to the seller, the seller may accept the second party's offer after withdrawing the counteroffer to the first party (assuming the first party did not act upon and accept the counter). Time is of the essence, and a would-be buyer may lose the property he is attempting to purchase by negotiating terms and price. Conversely, the buyer may save money in such negotiating tactics. (See Figure 7.2.)

Earnest Deposits

The **earnest money** is the deposit that the purchaser gives to the broker at the time the written contract to purchase is offered. It binds the contract and demonstrates the good intent of the purchaser. In some states the earnest deposit is referred to as hand money or a binder. This earnest money deposit must be placed in the broker's **trust account** upon acceptance of the offer. It is credited to the buyer's total payment at the time of closing. If the offer is not accepted, the earnest money is returned to the would-be purchaser.

Seller determines amount of deposit

The amount of the earnest money is negotiable and not set by law, though in some areas it is common practice to ask for 5 or 10 percent of the purchase price as a deposit. The size of the deposit should be sufficient to show the seller that the buyer's offer is sincere. However, in the final analysis the sellers determine what they will accept. The earnest money will be forfeited if the buyer defaults on the contract because the seller took the property off the market and may have missed an opportunity to sell it to someone else.

Many states require the broker to obtain a release in writing covering the forfeiture of the funds if the buyer decides not to complete the contract. This penalty must

FIGURE 7.2
Counteroffers.

be disclosed in writing at time of acceptance by the broker and before presentation of the contract to the seller. Although the funds are entrusted to the broker's care, the broker must not make decisions as to their dispersal without written permission. In the case of the buyer defaulting, not only would the buyer agree in writing to relinquish the earnest deposit, but the seller would agree in writing to accept the deposit as liquidated damages. If the property later sells for less, the seller has been compensated, at least in part, for the difference.

Some brokers have a statement in their listing contract that in case of the forfeiture by a prospective purchaser of any earnest money deposit, after expenses incurred by the broker are deducted, the money is divided one-half to the owners and one-half to the broker. Some also have a statement that if there is a dispute as to what and who caused the breach, the funds will be turned over to a third or disinterested party called an interpleader, which is usually the circuit court.

Trust Accounts

Earnest deposit is safeguarded

In most states a broker must maintain a trust account in the firm's name in a depository located in the state where the broker is doing business. All customer or client money coming into the possession of the broker must be kept in that trust account, unless there is written agreement to the contrary, or until the transaction is consummated or terminated. Ledgers and journals must be kept by the broker showing all entries. This includes earnest deposits, down payments, and security deposits on leased property. Many states require a separate trust account for the processing of sales and another trust account for rents received from the managing of rental properties. Each deposit must be separately identified in the trust account records, and the broker shall not be entitled to any part of the money as a commission until the sale is final. Most states require the trust account to be a noninterest-bearing checking account; however, if a substantial earnest deposit is given and the closing is scheduled for a time months later, the buyer may desire his deposit to be earning interest. In such a situation, with written approval of both buyer and seller, the broker will place the deposit in an interest-bearing account.

The trust accounts are audited in most states, generally on an annual basis. If the books reveal any discrepancies, the broker's license could be in jeopardy. It is the broker's duty to safeguard the funds of others in all transactions.

LEASE OPTIONS

Option gives right to buy

Another means of purchasing property is the **lease option**, that is, leasing with an option to buy. The option permits the lessee to purchase the property within a set period of time at the price and terms defined in the lease option agreement. The lessee must execute her right to buy within the time frame stated in the lease option or the right is forfeited. If the lessee elects to perform on the option agreement, a purchase agreement will be completed as in a regular sale. If the lessee chooses not to exercise the option, either the lease will expire or be renewed or the property owner can place the property on the open market for sale.

The use of the lease option generally occurs when financing terms are not advantageous to the purchaser or when the seller is having difficulty finding a buyer for a particular property. It permits someone to lease the property and later make the decision to buy or not. In some instances the property owner may allow a portion of the rent to apply toward the down payment. If the property has not appreciated in value, the seller may be eager to apply the rent toward the purchase price. Conversely, the lessee may not be as eager to purchase it if similar properties can be bought for less.

Right of First Refusal

A tenant may wish to rent a property with the **right of first refusal** to purchase. This allows the tenant the right to match any offer that the property owner may receive. It does not obligate the renter to perform, but gives the tenant an advantage in having the first right to buy. This could prove to be a disadvantage to the owner as prospective purchasers may shy away from offering to buy when aware that the tenant holds a previous right to meet any offer presented to the owner.

Lease Purchase

Unlike an option to buy, a lease purchase binds the lessee to the terms of the lease purchase agreement. It is generally used if the lessee wants to purchase the property but does not have the funds, if financing may be difficult to obtain, or if the title needs to be cleared. Usually a portion of the rent is applied toward the purchase price. This method of buying allows the lessee to obtain possession with title transferred to the lessee at a later agreed-upon date as stated in the lease purchase agreement.

Equitable Interest

Once the offer is accepted by the owner, the buyer has an **equitable interest** in the real estate. The seller is still the title holder of record until the closing of the transaction and delivery of the deed, but the buyer has what is known as *equitable title*. The seller must perform in accordance with the signed contract and now holds title in name only.

The question may arise: Can the buyer assign the contract to another? As stated in *Assignment of contract* the chapter on contracts, unless it specifically states to the contrary, the buyer has the right to transfer the equitable interest. However, the assignee must perform according to the terms of the contract. In some instances the buyer may have been acting as a **strawman**—that is, the offer was made with the intent of transferring the contract prior to the closing. In this case, the true buyer may have wanted to remain anonymous until the seller accepted the terms of the offer.

Most contracts, including options, leases, mortgages, and land contracts, are assignable unless they specifically state to the contrary. However, if the contract is for a personal right, as in a listing contract, the assignor would need the consent of the seller.

Bill of Sale

Occasionally a purchase offer for real property will include personal property. Although a deed is used to transfer the real property, a **bill of sale** is used when chattel (personal property) is sold. The bill of sale transfers the goods.

Marketable Title

The owner is responsible to deliver good and **marketable title** to the buyer. It must be free of any defects, liens, and encumbrances. The only time an existing mortgage remains against the property would be when the purchaser is assuming the loan.

Uniform Commercial Code

The **Uniform Commercial Code (UCC)** has been mandated in varying degrees in all *Chattel sales* 50 states in an effort to make laws covering chattel (personal property) sales uniform. The law covers any conditional sales contracts and chattel mortgages, including stocks and commercial paper. It covers the sale of personal property and only relates to real estate when fixtures are involved. If a chattel is purchased and financed, the financial statement can be filed at the recorder's office. If subsequently the chattel is not paid for, the creditor can repossess it from the property.

Bulk transfers are also regulated by the Uniform Commercial Code. This act covers the transfer of a large amount of inventory or material. The merchant cannot sell out stock and keep the money, leaving creditors unpaid. Any buyer of the merchandise is required by the UCC to receive an inventory of the goods from the seller along with a list of creditors. The buyer must then give notice to any creditor that a sale is pending. The induction of bulk transfers takes place if a business is sold or if it is liquidated.

THE QUESTION OF AGENCY AND LOYALTY

As discussed earlier, in the vast majority of real estate transactions the agent represents the seller. Although buyers can enter into a relationship with a broker to represent their interests only, thus establishing buyer agency, most buyers in fact work with the seller's agent when shopping for a home. As a result of this interaction between buyers and seller's agent, the sometimes confusing question of agent loyalty needs to be addressed.

A recent Federal Trade Commission survey revealed that more than 70 percent of buyers in real estate transactions thought that when two agents were involved in a transaction, the selling sales agent was representing them; 82 percent believed that whatever they told the selling sales agent was confidential. Clearly the majority of buyers believe that real estate agents are acting on their behalf since the sales agent is showing them properties, writing and presenting offers in their behalf, and seeming to care that they purchase the property that best suits their needs. Because of the rapport that develops naturally between home buyers and the sales agent, the buyers come to believe that the sales agent is representing them at "no fee." Hence, they may confide to the sales agent that the price offered is not their final bid for the property, not realizing that the agent is obligated to work in the best interest of the principal, in this case the seller.

Such possible misinterpretation of the standard seller agency relationship has led to stricter legislation regarding disclosure of agency status. Currently, 44 states and the District of Columbia have passed laws or regulations requiring agency disclosure by real estate brokers. A few states do not require disclosure in writing, but the oral agency status must be confirmed in writing in the purchase agreement. Ideally, such notice should be presented at the first meeting because early disclosure minimizes any chance of misunderstanding.

The state of Colorado has modified an earlier requirement for verbal disclosure. Effective July 1, 1993, Colorado requires written disclosure on a form adopted by the state commission. The form, "Working with a Real Estate Broker," will ensure that the public understands from the onset who the licensees in a transaction are working for and that they receive adequate, uniform information concerning current agency law and practice. Although no time is set for giving the disclosure, it must be made prior to providing specific assistance.

West Virginia law states that the buyer is to sign a Notice of Agency Disclosure form no later than before signing the purchase agreement.

At the very least, such a statement should appear in the offer-to-purchase contract. For example, the statement in bold type above the blank for the buyer's signature might read "All parties signing the document acknowledge that they have been informed that all real estate agents involved in this transaction are agents of and are representing the seller."

While the selling agent represents the seller, the agent nonetheless owes the buyer fair treatment. While counseling and confidentiality are owed only to the principal, the buyer is entitled to true disclosure of all the facts concerning the property. In fact, new accountability for real estate agents was raised when suit was brought by the Eastons over structural problems of a home they purchased 25 miles east of San Francisco. Two months after the Eastons bought their $250,000 hillside ranch home, the land began to buckle and creep. Years of litigation followed that broadened to include not only the previous owner but also three real estate companies and two contractors. The lawsuit raised the question of whether the real estate brokers are financially liable if they sell a defective property, even if they were unaware of the problem at the time of the sale. Both the trial court and the California Supreme Court decided the selling broker was negligent and had been obligated to investigate the property. Previously it was considered sufficient that the selling agent disclose facts that the agent knew about the property. The landmark Easton case reached beyond this and stated it was the selling broker's responsibility to discover and disclose that there may be a problem on a property. The courts awarded the Eastons in excess of $200,000 in damages, which was largely covered by insurance held by one of the real estate firms.

Representing the seller

The case resulted in California legislation that requires a seller to complete a standardized **disclosure statement**. The form has a checklist of inspections of potential problem areas, such as settling, landfill areas, septic tanks, room additions that were noncode, and appliances (see Figure 7.3). The California law states that a broker's responsibility is limited to areas that are accessible for visual inspection. A real estate broker is not expected to be a specialist in areas such as engineering and architecture or land faults and soil compaction.

Seller disclosure statement

Other states are following California's action and are mandating that the seller complete a disclosure statement form. In states without such legislation, many brokers are requesting that the sellers sign a disclosure form. Some forms merely ask the seller to respond to the questions by checking the appropriate box—yes, no, or I don't know.

Because of the Easton case, other lawsuits followed, and brokers are concerned that it may result in frivolous claims. Many have purchased malpractice insurance, commonly referred to as **errors and omission insurance**. For an annual premium the broker is defended against a claim. Kentucky was the first state to enact legislation mandating such insurance. Some real estate companies are being denied errors and omission insurance if they are involved in more than listing and selling real property, since additional risks are incurred if the company is in property management, construction, or land development. While the insurance rates are high, the trend toward consumerism has propelled brokers to insure against unhappy buyers. A case in point was a problem that resulted when the purchaser of an acreage was alarmed several months after the sale by the sight of a backhoe digging a trench across his property. He learned the adjoining property owners had been given an easement by the past owner to tap into his well. The easement was never recorded so the buyer had no knowledge of its existence. The seller declared he had told the sales agent about the easement, but the sales agent had no recollection of the conversation. Fortunately, attorneys for the errors and omissions insurance company defended the broker and his sales agent.

Errors and omission insurance

Subscription to errors and omission insurance has increased as more states are mandating that all licensees carry the insurance. The states that legislate the requirement also offer the insurance through a selected provider that must insure every licensee. The annual fee is nominal, usually anywhere from $65 to $100.

NCR (No Carbon Required)   **SELLER'S PROPERTY DISCLOSURE STATEMENT**   Page 1 of 2
(Including the main structure and any outbuildings)

PROPERTY ADDRESS _____
SELLER'S NAME _____

1. TITLE AND ACCESS

a. Is the property currently leased? _____ If so, when does the lease expire? _____ Does the lessee have an option to extend the lease? _____

b. Does anyone have a first right of refusal to buy, option, or lease the property? _____ If so, who: _____

c. Do you know of any existing, pending or potential legal actions concerning the property or the Homeowners Association? _____

d. Are there any bonds, assessments, or judgements which are either liens upon the property or which limit its use? _____

e. Do you own real property adjacent to, across the street from, or in the same sub-division as the subject property? If yes, please describe: _____

f. Do you know of any encroachments, easements, licenses, boundary disputes, or third party claims affecting the property (rights of other people to interfere with the use of the property in any way)? _____ If so, explain: _____

g. Are you aware of any pending real estate development in your area (such as condominiums, planned unit developments, subdivisions, or property for commercial, educational, or religious use)? _____

h. Do you experience any excessive noises, for example airplanes, trains, trucks, freeway, etc.? _____

i. Are you aware of any other conditions that could affect the value or desirability of the property? _____

2. LAND

a. Does the property have any filled ground? _____ If so, is the house built on filled or unstable ground? _____

b. Do you know of any past or present settling or soil movement problems on the property or on adjacent properties? _____ If so, have they resulted in any structural damage? _____ What was the extent of damage? _____

c. Do you know of any past or present drainage or flooding problem on your property or adjacent properties? _____ If so, explain on separate sheet. Is there water standing on the property after rainfall? _____ Any active springs? _____

d. Is the property in a designated flood zone? _____

e. Is the property in a "Special Studies Zone" as provided by the Alquist-Priolo Geological Hazard Zones Act? _____

f. Are you aware of any past or present problems with driveways, walkways, patios, or retaining walls on your property or adjacent properties due to drainage, flooding, or soil movement (such as large cracks, potholes, raised sections)? _____ If so, please describe: _____

3. STRUCTURAL DISCLOSURES

a. Do you know of any structural additions or alterations, or the installation, alteration, repair, or replacement of significant components of the structures upon the property, completed during the term of your ownership or that of a prior owner ☐ with, ☐ without an appropriate permit or other authority for construction from a public agency having jurisdiction? _____ ☐ Explanation attached.

b. Approx. age of structure: _____ Do you know of any condition in the original or existing design or workmanship of the structure that would be considered substandard? _____ If so, please explain: _____

c. Are you aware of excessive settling, slanted floors, large cracks in walls, foundations, garage floors, driveways, chimneys, or fireplaces? _____ If so, explain: _____

d. Are you aware of any structural wood members, including mudsills, being below soil level? _____

e. Is crawlspace, if any, below soil level? _____

f. Do you know of any inspection reports, surveys, studies, notices, etc. concerning the property? _____ If so, please list each one, even if you have already made them available _____

g. Date of last structural pest control inspection? _____ By whom? _____

h. Do you prefer a pre-sale structural pest control inspection? _____

i. Date of last City/County mandatory inspection report? _____

j. Have you any Notice(s) of Violations relating to the property from any City, County or State Agencies? _____ If so, please explain: _____

k. Do you know of any violations of government regulations, ordinances, or zoning laws regarding this property? _____ If so, explain: _____

4. ROOF, GUTTERS, DOWNSPOUTS

a. Type of roof: ☐ Tar and Gravel, ☐ Asphalt Shingle, ☐ Wood Shingle, ☐ Tile, ☐ Other _____ Age of roof: _____

b. Has roof been resurfaced? _____ If so, what year? _____ Is there a guarantee on the roof? _____ For how long? _____ By whom? _____

c. Has roof ever leaked since you owned the property? _____ If so, what was done to correct the leak? _____

d. Are gutters and downspouts free of holes and excessive rust? _____

e. Do downspouts empty into drainage system or onto splash blocks? _____ Is water directed away from structure? _____

5. PLUMBING SYSTEM

a. Source of water supply: ☐ Public, ☐ Private Well. If well water, when was water sample last checked for safety? _____ Result of test: _____

b. Well water pump: _____ Date installed: _____ Condition: _____ Sufficient water during late summer? _____

c. Are water supply pipes copper or galvanized? _____

d. Are you aware of below normal water pressure in your water supply lines (normal is 50 to 70 lbs.)? _____

e. Are you aware of excessive rust stains in tubs, lavatories and sinks? _____

f. Are you aware of water standing around any of the lawn sprinkler heads? _____

g. Are there any plumbing leaks around and under sinks, toilets, showers, bathtubs, and lavatories? _____ If so, where? _____

h. Pool: Age: _____ Pool Heater: ☐ Gas, ☐ Electric, ☐ Solar. Pool Sweep? _____ Date of last inspection: _____ By whom? _____ Regular maintenance? _____

i. Hot Tub/Spa: _____ Date of last inspection: _____ By Whom: _____

j. ☐ City Sewer, ☐ Septic Tank: ☐ Concrete, ☐ Redwood. Capacity: _____ Is septic tank in good working order? _____

6. ELECTRICAL SYSTEM

a. 220 Volt? _____

b. Are there any damaged or malfunctioning receptacles? _____

c. Are you aware of any damaged or malfunctioning switches? _____

d. Are there any extension cords stapled to baseboards or underneath carpets or rugs? _____

e. Does outside TV antenna have a ground connection? _____

f. Are you aware of any defects, malfunctioning, or illegal installation of electrical equipment in or outside the house? _____

Seller's Initials [_____] [_____]   (CONTINUED ON PAGE 109.2)

FORM 109.1 (4-86)   COPYRIGHT © 1986, BY PROFESSIONAL PUBLISHING CORP. 122 PAUL DR. SAN RAFAEL, CA 94903   **PROFESSIONAL PUBLISHING**

FIGURE 7.3
Seller's property disclosure statement.

(continued)

NCR (No Carbon Required)   Page 2 of 2

7. HEATING, AIR CONDITIONING, OTHER EQUIPMENT

a. Is the house insulated? _____ _____
b. Type of Heating System: _____
c. Is furnace room or furnace closet adequately vented? _____
d. Are fuel-consuming heating devices adequately vented to the outside, directly or through a chimney? _____
e. Date of last inspection of Heating Equipment: _____ By whom: _____
f. Solar heating: _____ In working order? _____
g. Air Conditioning: _____ Date of last inspection: _____ By whom: _____
h. Does Fireplace have a damper? _____
i. Provision for outside venting of clothes dryer? _____
j. Approximate age of water heater: _____ Capacity: _____ Is your water heater equipped with temperature pressure relief valve, which is a required safety device? _____
k. Electric garage door opener: _____ Condition: _____ Number of controls: _____
l. Burglar alarm: _____ Make: _____ In working order? _____ Owned: _____ Leased: _____ Rented: _____
m. Smoke Detectors: _____ How many? _____ ☐ 110 V, ☐ Battery. In working order? _____
n. Lawn Sprinklers: _____ Automatic clock _____ In working order? _____
o. Water softener: _____ In working order? _____
p. Sump pump: _____ In working order? _____
q. Are you aware of any of the above equipment that is in need of repair or replacement or is illegally installed? _____

8. BUILT-IN APPLIANCES

a. Are you aware of any built-in appliances that are in need of repair or replacement? _____ If so, which: _____

9. PERSONAL PROPERTY INCLUDED IN THE PURCHASE PRICE

a. The following items of personal property are included in the purchase price: _____
_____
b. Are there any liens against any of these items? _____ If so, please explain: _____

10. HOME PROTECTION PROGRAM

a. Do you want to provide a Home Protection Program at your expense? _____

11. CONDOMINIUMS

a. Please check availability of copies of the following documents: ☐ CC&Rs, ☐ Condominium Declaration, ☐ Association Bylaws, ☐ Articles of Incorporation, ☐ Subdivision Report, ☐ Current Financial Statement ☐ Regulations currently in force.
b. Does the Condominium Declaration contain any resale restrictions? _____
c. Does the Homeowners Association have the first right of refusal? _____
d. Please check occupancy restrictions imposed by the association, including but not limited to: ☐ Pets, ☐ Storage of Recreational Vehicles or Boats on driveways or in common areas, ☐ Advertising or For Sale signs, ☐ Architectural or decorative alterations subject to association approval, ☐ Others: _____
e. In case of a conversion, have you an engineer's report on the condition of the building and its equipment? _____
f. Monthly/annual association dues:$ _____ What is included in the association dues? _____
g. Has your association notified you of any future dues increases or special assessments? _____ If so, please give details _____
_____
h. Are all dues, assessments, and taxes current? _____
i. Has there been a Notice of Default filed against your property? _____ If yes, please explain: _____
j. I shall provide a statement from the Condominium Homeowners Association documenting the amount of any delinquent assessments, including penalties, attorney's fees, and any other charges provided for in the management documents to be delivered to Purchaser. _____
k. Security: ☐ Inter-com, ☐ Closed circuit TV, ☐ Guards, ☐ Electric gate, ☐ Other: _____
l. Parking: Does each unit have its own designated parking spaces? _____ How close to unit? _____ Is space ample? _____ Guest parking? _____
m. Sound proofing adequate? _____ Are there noisy trash chutes? _____ Bond guaranteeing completion of common area and facilities? _____
Property Management Co. _____

12. NEWLY CONSTRUCTED RESIDENCES

a. Is deposit held in trust fund? _____
b. Bond guaranteeing completion of unit? _____
c. Is builder a member of Home Builders Association? _____ Is Home Owners Warranty (HOW) available? _____
d. Will carpets, draperies, and appliances be identical to those shown in model unit? _____
e. Please list expiration dates of warranties covering appliances and equipment: _____
Final Inspection date: _____ Occupancy Permit date: _____ Contractor: _____ License _____

13. OWNERSHIP

a. Are you a builder or developer? _____
b. Are you a licensed real estate agent? _____
c. Have all persons on the title signed the listing agreement? _____
d. Please list all persons on the title who are not U.S. citizens: _____
e. Are you aware of anything else you should disclose to a prospective purchaser? _____ If so, please explain (use addendum if necessary): _____
_____

The foregoing answers and explanations are true and complete to the best of my/our knowledge and I/we have retained a copy hereof. I/we herewith authorize _____ , the agent in this transaction, to disclose the information set forth above to other real estate brokers, real estate agents, and prospective purchasers of the property.

Dated: _____   Seller: _____   Seller: _____

I/we acknowledge receipt of this SELLER'S PROPERTY DISCLOSURE STATEMENT, including additional explanations, if any, attached hereto.

Dated: _____   Purchaser: _____   Purchaser: _____

I am satisfied with the above SELLER'S PROPERTY DISCLOSURE STATEMENT.
Dated: _____   Purchaser: _____   Purchaser: _____

I am NOT satisfied with the above SELLER'S PROPERTY DISCLOSURE STATEMENT and herewith rescind my offer to purchase above property.

Dated: _____   Purchaser: _____   Purchaser: _____

I reserve the right to have the property inspected by the following professional(s) _____
and to submit a copy of the inspection report(s) to Seller's agent on or before _____.

Dated: _____   Purchaser: _____   Purchaser: _____

FORM   109.2   (2-85)   COPYRIGHT © 1985, BY PROFESSIONAL PUBLISHING CORP. 122 PAUL DR. SAN RAFAEL, CA 94903   **PROFESSIONAL PUBLISHING**

FIGURE 7.3
(Continued).

BUYER AGENCY

Buyer hires broker

Although the discussion up to this point has focused on those situations in which the broker represents the seller, in buyer agency relationships the buyer becomes the principal in the transaction, and the agent's loyalty is owed to the buyer. The broker will give the buyer complete loyalty and work strictly for the buyer's best interest.

In the buyer agency arrangement, compensation must be addressed early in the contract process. There are several options available:

1. The buyer may agree to pay a flat fee or a percentage of the purchase price.
2. The buyer may have the agent ask the seller to pay the fee, with the buyer agent and the selling agent splitting the fee since a joint effort by both agents brings about the sale.
3. The parties may pay their agents as per their respective contracts. This can result in an overall large percentage of commission being paid. However, consider the fact that when a buyer and seller each hire an attorney to represent them, they both pay.

In the past, a buyer agency was generally used for the purchase of commercial rather than residential real estate, with agents being retained to locate a specific commercial building, for example. However, the use of buyer agency is becoming more widespread across the country. In some parts of the United States, buyers of residential properties are being exposed to advertising by real estate agents who wish to represent them. In such cases, the buyer and the buyer's agent have a very clear understanding that the agent is solely responsible to the buyer and has no other loyalties.

When the buyer's agent makes the first contact with the listing agent, it is important that the listing agent is immediately informed that either:

1. the buyer's agent is declining the usual subagency arrangement and is operating strictly as a buyer's agent and as such will be paid by the buyer, or;
2. the agent is acting as the buyer's agent and expects the normal commission split.

Counseling with the Seller

Because of the increased use of buyer agents, a discussion with the sellers should ensue at the time the sales agent takes the listing regarding the possibility that a buyer's sales agent may sell the property. The listing sales agent should explain to the seller that if this occurs the seller has a couple of avenues to pursue:

a. pay only the listing broker's commission and request the selling broker obtain a commission from the buyer
b. pay the full commission to the listing broker with the knowledge that the listing broker will give the buyer's broker the same share as the firm usually splits with a cooperating broker

It is important to inform the seller that a buyer's agent will not be representing the seller's interest. The deciding factor for the seller, however, should be that he has listed the property to get it sold, and that should remain his primary concern.

A listing agent can share a commission with a buyer broker only when he has the *expressed consent* of the principal. Informing the seller when the listing is signed permits the seller to make an informed decision so that no problems occur when it is time to close the sale.

Remember, the commission is paid when the transaction is consummated. Some agents feel that the agent should be paid only by whom he represents: the selling broker by the seller and the buyer broker by the buyer. This has little to do with negotiating and finalizing a sale, however.

DUAL AGENCY

Dual agency, under which the agent works for both the buyer and the seller, must be disclosed to both buyer and seller. In some states this disclosure must be in writing. However, since buyers and sellers have adverse interests, the agent who represents both may have a difficult time representing both effectively and fairly. Thus, dual agency is discouraged in most instances and is illegal in some states.

Representing buyer and seller

Dual agency may occur unintentionally. For instance, if subagent A shows property to a buyer, it is possible that subagent A has never even met the seller since she is not the original listing agent. Therefore, even though subagent A owes loyalty to the seller by virtue of the listing contract, she may in fact feel more loyalty to the buyer, with whom she has established a rapport. Real estate agents must be wary of such situations, since they are legally obligated to represent the seller's best interests in such cases, regardless of their relationship with the buyer.

AGENT OR FACILITATOR?

Although it would mean abandoning the legal basis on which real estate agents have conducted business since the early 1900s, some states are investigating the alternative of changing the licensee's role from "agent" to "facilitator." When problems arise the broker is usually brought into the lawsuit because the broker is representing the principal. If the licensee were to be a facilitator, the risk would be considerably diminished. The role of the "nonagent facilitator" is being given serious thought in several states. Proponents of the concept feel that the real estate practitioner is the middleperson who conducts negotiations between buyer and seller and as such should have no legal liability.

Another option being discussed is to simply refer to the licensee as what he truly is: real estate broker or real estate salesperson. Forget the agency connotation, and use the term that individuals who sell securities or stocks are known by—brokers.

The reality of the marketplace is that although an agent owes allegiance to the principal (also called the *client*), he also must be fair and honest to the third party involved in the transaction (also known as the *customer*).

BUYER'S WARRANTIES

Home Buyer's Insurance

Home buyer's insurance is available in many areas of the country for the purchaser's protection. If it is a newly constructed home, the builder may insure the house under the Home Owners Warranty Corporation, referred to as the HOW program. A 10-year warranty plan, the insurance covers defects in material, faulty workmanship, and structural problems. If a major defect should arise, the buyer is protected against costly repairs.

New construction

Home Warranty Insurance

Home warranty insurance is also available on existing homes. The policy may be purchased by the buyer or seller and covers such items as heating, air conditioning,

Existing property

electrical, plumbing, and appliances. These policies generally carry a deductible amount, and coverage on some items may be excluded.

If insurance is not available, some buyers may request an inspection on such major items as heating and air conditioning as a contingency of the purchase agreement. Preinspections by qualified service representatives or home inspection agencies assure the buyer that the items in question are in workable order.

Property Insurance

Property owners will also want to protect against financial loss in the event their investment is damaged by fire, tornado, flood, or other perils. While fire is the most common cause for concern, extended coverage is available to insure against other catastrophes. The property owner (insured) makes payments (referred to as an insurance premium) to the insurance company (insurer), and if a loss does occur, the insurance company indemnifies (pays) the insured for the loss. Insurance companies invest the premiums received from the insured, building up reserves to cover losses of their policy holders, to pay dividends to their stockholders, and to meet operating expenses. A property owner could self-insure by setting aside funds to cover a loss, but most homeowners feel that the gamble is too great. If they borrowed funds to purchase the property, they have little choice since the mortgagee will want protection for the funds advanced on the loan. Insurance is based on a large number of risks, and insurance companies are able to spread their risk by serving a large clientele over a broad section of the country. Many companies also diversify into other types of insurance, such as life, automobile, and annuities.

Any additions to the basic insurance contract (called the insurance policy) is an endorsement or rider, and it covers losses beyond those ordinarily covered. For example, if a property is located in an area where earthquakes may occur, the rider would protect the owner from such an event.

Types of policies   There are five different policies written to cover the owner of a single-family home. The basic policy is the Homeowner 1 (HO-1). Homeowner 2 (HO-2) is broader in scope, and Homeowner 5 (HO-5) covers all risks except those perils listed as exclusions.

Basic Homeowner 1 (HO-1) covers the following losses:

1. fire
2. lightning
3. windstorm or hail
4. explosion
5. loss sustained upon removal of property from an endangered premises
6. riot or civil commotion
7. aircraft
8. vehicles
9. smoke
10. theft
11. vandalism and malicious mischief
12. breaking of glass (that is part of the building)

Broad Homeowner 2 (HO-2) covers all of the above 12 perils, plus the following:

13. collapse of all or a part of building(s)
14. falling objects
15. weight of ice, snow, or sleet

16. sudden and accidental tearing asunder, cracking, burning, or bulging of a steam or hot water heating system or of appliances for heating water

17. freezing of plumbing, heating, and air conditioning systems

18. sudden and accidental damages to electrical appliances

19. sudden and accidental injury from artificially generated currents to electrical appliances, devices, fixtures, and wiring

Comprehensive Homeowner 3 (HO-3) covers all the above 19 items plus risks of physical loss to buildings.

Comprehensive Homeowner 4 (HO-4) is a tenant's policy used by renters that covers household goods and personal belongings from loss that may occur under the broad form HO-2.

Comprehensive Homeowner 5 (HO-5), in addition to the above coverage in Homeowner 1, 2, and 3, covers all perils except flood, landslide, mudflow, tidal wave, earthquakes, underground water, settling, cracking, war, and nuclear accident. Also excluded are mortgages and debts, currency, money, bonds, and manuscripts.

Policies have deductible amount clauses; if the deductible is $100, the first $100 of loss would be paid by the homeowner. Since the basic purpose is to protect owners from losses they cannot cover, the deductible prevents nuisance claims that cause the expense of having a claim adjustor inspect these small items.

To collect under an insurance policy the person must have an insurable interest such as a property owner or mortgagee holds. The insurance rates are in direct proportion to the risk involved. Brick buildings have lower rates than frame, tile roofs are rated lower than wood shingles, and the proximity to fire hydrants is considered. Insurance companies will have standard rates set so each property does not have to be analyzed and rated on an individual basis. If the insured pays a premium of $210 a year for $60,000 coverage, the annual rate is figured as:

$$\text{Rate} = \frac{\$210}{\$60,000} = .0035 \text{ or } \$3.50 \text{ per } \$1,000 \text{ of coverage}$$

Coinsurance

When loss to property occurs, it generally is not a total and complete loss. If the property was insured for less than its market value, without the coinsurance clause the owner would be entitled to collect the full amount without paying a premium that justifies the coverage. Typically the homeowner carries a policy that covers to 80 percent of the property improvement value. The formula used is:

$$\text{amount recovered} = \frac{\text{amount carried}}{\substack{\text{amt. should} \\ \text{be carried}}} \times \text{loss}$$

Thus, if the property improvements are valued at $70,000, and the owner carries insurance with an 80 percent coinsurance clause, the owner must carry $56,000 of insurance to collect 100 percent of the losses. If a $10,000 loss occurs:

$$\frac{\text{amount carried}}{\$56,000} = \$56,000 \times \$10,000 = \$10,000 \text{ amount required}$$

If the insured carried more insurance than was needed, no additional amount could be received. Since *more* was not lost, the insured would only receive the $10,000, so it would prove foolish to insure for more than one could recover. Using the $70,000 value again, assume the owner only insured the property for $49,000 (70 percent of value).

$$\frac{\text{amount carried}}{\text{amount required}} \quad \frac{\$49,000}{\$56,000} \times \$10,000 \text{ loss} = \$8,750$$

In this situation $1,250 of the owner's loss will need to be paid by the owner.

Liability

The homeowner's policy will cover personal liability in the event someone slips on an icy driveway, falls off a porch, or otherwise receives injuries. A tree limb falling on a visitor's automobile causing damage could result in a lawsuit, and the insurance protects against such events. This also protects the family if they are injured or cause injury to another even if they are off the premises. Any legal costs in defending the insured is also covered up to the amount stated on the policy.

The price of an insurance policy is a small annual fee to pay when one analyzes the broad coverage and protection it offers. Not only does it insure the real estate, but additionally any personal liability that would rise from injury to oneself or others.

SUMMARY

The procedures for carrying out the terms of a purchase contract are complicated, so the broker must take care in handling responsibility as a broker of the seller. In addition to diligence, the act of negotiating is important to the finalization of the contract. As a professional salesperson, the agent must weigh the value of each offer when presenting it to the seller. If any item in the offer is countered by the seller, it voids the entire offer, and the seller may lose a potential buyer.

To safeguard the purchaser's deposit the real estate firm is required by law to place the earnest deposit in its trust account after the offer is accepted. This must be done within the time stipulated in the license law of each state. The money is not withdrawn from the trust account until the sale is final. Most states have examiners audit trust accounts to ensure that they are maintained as the law mandates.

In recent years new emphasis has been placed on the question of whom the selling broker represents. Many buyers erroneously feel the salesperson is their agent, due in part to the relationship that is formed in the process of hunting for a suitable home. Greater responsibility for clarification rests with the salesperson, and consequently, some states are requiring a disclosure statement in the purchase agreement revealing whom the broker is representing.

A dual agency exists if the salesperson represents both the buyer and the seller. Since formalities are not required to create an agency relationship, the selling brokers must take care not to imply that they represent the buyer. A buyer's agency can be formed between the buyer and the selling agent, but this must then be disclosed to the seller and seller's sales agent.

A subagency relationship exists when a salesperson shows the property of another broker and is thus bound by the agency relationship of the listing broker.

The need for protection on the newly acquired real estate is covered in detail, with attention given to the protection offered in the various types of homeowner insurance policies. The reader should have attained a good understanding of coinsurance and how it is calculated.

DISCUSSION QUESTIONS

1. Why would a broker decide to purchase errors and omission insurance?
2. Can a broker fairly represent both buyer and seller? Give reasons for your answers.
3. Discuss who the selling broker represents.
4. What insurance protection is available to the purchaser before the sale is finalized? After the sale is closed?
5. Discuss the advantages of buyers hiring a broker to solely represent their interests.
6. When is dual agency used? Explain your answer.

REVIEW QUESTIONS

Answers to these questions are found in the Answer Key section at the back of the book.

1. A broker's trust account is used:

   a. for the deposit of earnest money only
   b. in lieu of a general account
   c. for the deposit of money, belonging to others, that comes into the broker's possession
   d. to compensate the broker for expenditures

2. Which of the following facts concerning a counteroffer is true?

   a. if the counteroffer is rejected, the original offer to purchase can be accepted
   b. counteroffers are rarely accepted
   c. the offeree and the offeror have reversed their positions
   d. the counteroffer will remain open for acceptance for 10 days

3. If a purchaser assigns her interest in the property while the contract is still pending, realizing a profit:

   a. the seller receives the profit
   b. it cancels the contract
   c. the broker receives the profit
   d. the original purchaser receives the profit

4. Ms. Jones hires A-1 Realty to sell her house and explains to agent Judy Jewel the reason she wants to sell is that the house has a faulty sewer system. Jewel does not include this information on the listing agreement. The property is sold by salesperson Paul Parker of another real estate firm, who looked only at the listing agreement. Whose license is in jeopardy?

   a. Judy Jewel
   b. Paul Parker
   c. both Judy and Paul
   d. neither Judy nor Paul

5. To whom must a copy of the accepted purchase agreement be delivered?

   a. buyer
   b. seller
   c. buyer and seller
   d. real estate commissioner

6. Funds deposited in a trust account that will ultimately belong to the broker:

   a. cannot be used by the broker until the sale is consummated or terminated
   b. may be transferred to the broker's business account if one of the parties to the contract has agreed in writing
   c. is advanced to the seller as part of the proceeds
   d. are kept in the account until the monthly audit

7. A lessee has the right as specified in the lease contract to purchase the property because of:

   a. a lease clause
   b. the right of first refusal
   c. a reversionary clause
   d. a transfer clause

8. A person who hires another to represent him is known as:

   a. a customer

b. a principal

c. a broker

d. an agent

9. An offeror may withdraw an offer until:

a. the closing date

b. the deed is recorded

c. the contract is signed

d. the offeror is notified that the offer has been accepted

10. When a contract for the sale of real estate is signed by the purchaser and the seller, the purchaser acquires:

a. equitable title to the property

b. legal title to the property

c. immediate possession

d. a nonfreehold interest

11. The amount and type of earnest deposit required is determined by the:

a. seller

b. buyer

c. law

d. broker

12. A sales agent has a listing on a property and has just written a purchase agreement. The agent could do the following:

a. tell the seller the highest price the buyer is willing to pay

b. tell the buyer the lowest offer the seller will accept

c. inform the buyer that the owner will consider any reasonable offer

d. suggest to the seller that the property is over-priced and he should take the offer

13. A salesperson should prepare all of the following for the purchaser who wants to make an offer on a property, EXCEPT:

a. an estimate of the buyer's closing costs

b. an estimate of the monthly principal, interest, taxes, and insurance payment

c. an offer to purchase agreement

d. a right of first refusal document

14. If personal property is included in the sale of real property, the following document is used:

a. purchase agreement

b. bill of sale

c. lease option

d. list contract

15. John and Janice Jones hire broker Bill Williams to locate a home for them in the exclusive Fairmont district. After searching for a home that fits the requirements of the Joneses, Williams locates a property listed with ABC Realty. An agreement to purchase is written and accepted by the sellers. Bill Williams's fee will be paid by:

a. whomever was stipulated in the contract

b. the sellers

c. ABC Realty

d. buyers

16. All of the following are essential to an agreement to purchase contract, EXCEPT:

a. purchase price

b. description of the property

c. buyer's and seller's signatures

d. mortgage assumption

17. The sale price of a property and the amount of the earnest deposit are all determined by:

a. state law

b. negotiation

c. the real estate board

d. the broker who has the property listed

18. When a salesperson represents both the buyer and the seller, the relationship is referred to as:

a. dual agency

b. subagency

c. buyer agency

d. broker's agency

19. Which of the following statements regarding a buyer's agent is NOT true?

a. the buyer's agent informs the seller's agent, before discussing any property, that she is representing the buyer

b. complete loyalty is given to the buyer

c. the buyer's agent only shows property she has listed, so no conflict arises

d. the commission may be paid by the buyer or seller

20. Coinsurance can best be described as:

a. an insurance policy that is held jointly by the mortgage company and the property owner

b. insurance that covers a loss partially

c. entitles the homeowner to collect the full amount without paying a premium that justifies the coverage

d. an insurance policy with an 80 percent coinsurance clause

21. A broker meets a prospect and before showing the property explains that she is an agent of the seller.

The agent's fiduciary obligation includes all the following, EXCEPT:

a. full disclosure of the property condition

b. presentation of a contract in a fair and timely manner

c. disclosure of any previous offers and the amount offered

d. showing various properties that fit the buyer's needs

Lending Institutions and Loans

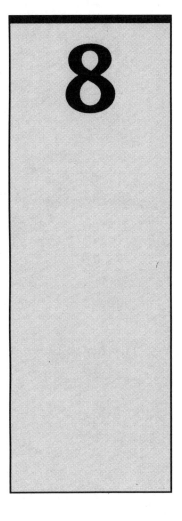

KEY WORDS

annual percentage rate (APR)

conventional loan

disintermediation

Equal Credit Opportunity Act (ECOA)

Federal Home Loan Mortgage Corporation (FHLMC)

Federal Housing Administration (FHA)

Federal National Mortgage Association (FNMA)

Federal Reserve Board

Government National Mortgage Association (GNMA)

land contract

mortgage-backed security (MBS)

mortgage banker

mortgage broker

novation

private mortgage insurance (PMI)

Real Estate Settlement Procedures Act (RESPA)

Regulation Z

Resolution Trust Corporation (RTC)

Savings Association Insurance Fund (SAIF)

secondary mortgage market

truth-in-lending law

underwriter

upfront mortgage insurance premium (UFMIP)

VA loans

OVERVIEW

We refer to the business enterprise whose purpose it is to make available various kinds of financing as the money market. Most of the funds used for financing real estate are savings from firms and individuals who deposit their money in return for interest earned on their savings. The lending institutions are called financial fiduciaries, and as such they are responsible to safeguard the funds entrusted to them by their depositors. These lending institutions and the loans they originate are covered in this chapter.

Until recently, bankers did not search for customers but waited for business to come to them. The borrower felt lucky to get a loan. Not so today. In today's competitive world of real estate finance it takes more than low rates and discount points to obtain business. When the real estate agent sells a property, the sales agent guides the borrower to a loan officer whose service and knowledge assist in providing a smooth closing for the customer.

In the 1970s most agents took their business to the savings and loan institutions where interest rates were relatively constant from month to month and discount points were almost nonexistent. Then in the mid to late 1970s, deposits left the savings and loans for the higher interest rates provided by the money market funds. The process whereby funds left the savings and loans to go to the higher paying money markets is called **disintermediation**. This left savings and loan institutions with insufficient reserves to make real estate loans, and the home borrower was forced to seek funds on Wall Street and compete with industry and government for the limited savings available for lending. Interest rates were now determined by the marketplace, and loans had to be sold on a **secondary mortgage market** to investors at a discount from face value. The situation led to the birth of a new multimillion dollar industry called mortgage banking. **Mortgage bankers** originate new loans and package them in million dollar pools. These pools form collateral for **mortgage-backed securities (MBS)**, which are sold to investors through an auction process. In this chapter you will learn where the money for home mortgages comes from, why we must now pay discount points, and the roles played by various financial institutions, along with Fannie Mae, Ginnie Mae, and Freddie Mac, to provide a source of mortgage money for home buyers. We will begin by taking a glance at how the supply of money is manipulated by the Federal Reserve Board.

THE FEDERAL RESERVE BOARD

Monetary policy control

We hear about the Feds manipulating the supply of money. How is this accomplished and how can the economy be regulated? The **Federal Reserve Board** controls the actual amount of money in circulation, determining the level of money available to our economy. There are 5 presidents of the Reserve Bank branches and 7 governors who serve on the board, and these 12 people make the crucial decisions on how much capital will be added or withdrawn from circulation. They have a twofold mission: to *regulate member banks* and to *set monetary policy*.

The board meets on the third Thursday of each month to analyze reports and make decisions that are reported to the New York Federal Reserve Bank, and that staff carries out the decisions rendered by these 12 people. The nation's monetary policy is based on money supply and prevailing interest rates and controls the direction of the economy, whether it grows or withdraws. In formulating policy, consideration is given to what the supply of money is, what spendable funds are available to the nation's consumers, the rate of inflation, and economic growth. Too much money causes inflation, which, as it eases off, results in recession. A balance must be adhered to and the right formula achieved for the situation at any given period. To accomplish this, the Federal Reserve Board looks at the future to determine where the economy is headed. Thus, the amount of money available at any one time for use in mortgage lending is dependent on the competition for these same funds and the money that is pumped into the system by the Federal Reserve Board.

SOURCES OF FINANCE

Savings and Loans: A Glance Back

The history of the savings and loan associations dates from January 1, 1831. In Frankford, Pennsylvania, a borough of 2,000 near Philadelphia, 6 men met to discuss forming a "building club." Modeled after a building society formed 50 years earlier in Birmington, England, the organization was named the Oxford Providence Building Association. Thirty-seven members made regular deposits into a common fund, and when each contributor had purchased a home, the Oxford Providence Club was dissolved. Five months after the association was formed, in May 1831, they had collected sufficient funds to grant their first loan. Comly Rich was the highest bidder, paying $10 for a $375 loan. The two-story, 450-square-foot frame home that he purchased with the loan still stands in Philadelphia.

In the years to follow many such organizations were patterned after the club. Groups of people purchased shares of stock from which they would later be able to borrow. It was necessary that each association collect enough money to have the funds available to make these loans. The borrower not only pledged his home, but also his shares as collateral. Today, the borrower at a savings and loan association does not have to be a depositor.

As housing needs increased, the expansion of savings and loans grew. By the time of the 1929 stock market crash, there were more than 12,000 savings and loan associations in the United States.

Following the Great Depression years, legislation was enacted to provide protection to depositors. The Federal Home Loan Act of 1932 required reserve funds from which the savings and loans could draw. The Homeowners Act of 1933 established a system for federal chartering of savings and loan associations. In 1934, the National Housing Act created the **Federal Housing Administration (FHA)**, which provides federal insurance on home mortgages. The Federal Savings and Loan Insurance Corporation (FSLIC) insured the savings of depositors in savings and loans for up to $100,000. Today, the FSLIC no longer exists. It has been replaced by the Savings Association Insurance Fund (SAIF). A savings and loan association must be state or federally chartered to operate.

Savings and Loans Today

The years following World War II up to the early 1970s were considered "the best of times" for the mortgage finance and the housing industry. We enjoyed a thriving economy that offered low interest rates that, coupled with inflation, created housing appreciation and income growth. Bankers and borrowers were stimulated by government policies that made housing a top priority, and business enjoyed one of the most productive periods in our history.

Savings and loans originated loans locally, kept them in their own portfolio, and serviced the loans. However, government regulations restricted rates to their depositors, and the S&Ls began to see money flow to higher yielding sources and *disintermediation* began to occur.

Disintermediation

Today the savings and loans are no longer the primary source of home financing. Their role has changed greatly in the past decade. During the early 1980s they were caught with long-term mortgages at 7 percent to 8 percent while existing market rates were running 12 percent to 16 percent. They needed to replace these loans with adjustable rate loans where the rate would move up or down with current market conditions. This type of loan places the burden of future interest rate increases squarely on the shoulders of the borrower. Consequently, savings and loans began to lend short-term mortgages, three to five years, or use adjustable rate mortgage (ARM) loans from their own portfolios.

In the mid 1980s we saw a trend wherein large savings and loans bought or formed their own mortgage banking operations that originated long-term, fixed-rate real estate loans and sold these loans on the secondary market to investors, such as insurance companies, pension and trust funds, and large corporations. Deregulation of the savings and loans in the 1970s changed their approach away from the primary market of home loans into diversified markets, resulting in less money for home financing. Savings and loans began to test areas out of their realm of expertise as they moved into riskier investments and placed more assets into commercial properties. The loans, coupled with poor regulatory supervision, led to losses among many S&Ls. Investments rose, but local markets began to crumble, and troubles began to mount. Failing thrifts offering higher depositor rates only put other thrifts at a disadvantage to attract capital. Blame was placed in part on poor appraisals, causing Congress to pass

*Resolution Trust
Corporation*

into law the requirement that all appraisers, when appraising real estate involved in a federally related transaction, must be licensed or registered. Today massive restructuring is occurring among savings and loan institutions. The **Resolution Trust Corporation (RTC)** was formed to liquidate the insolvent thrifts, which placed the FSLIC fund more than $14 billion in the red. With more than 500 failed savings and loans and the bailout cost estimated at $100 to 130 billion, the entire industry has been jeopardized. The FSLIC has been disbanded, and thrifts will become subject to more stringent banking regulations.

The Financial Institutions Reform, Recovery and Enforcement Act (FIRREA) of 1989 benefits customers in three primary ways:

Formation of SAIF

1. FSLIC insurance fund was replaced by the **Savings Association Insurance Fund (SAIF)**.
2. Disbandment of the Federal Home Bank Boards separated district banks from the role of regulator.
3. New regulations on investment and lending practices were designed to limit the risks that institutions take in the future.

This new insurance fund will be protected by some changes that will alter the day-to-day operations of the savings institutions, and beginning in 1991, higher capital reserves were required. Many savings and loans are unable to meet these new, higher reserve requirements, which will result in more failed S&Ls.

Insurance Companies

Other loan sources

Life insurance companies have funds available to invest in real estate and are heavy investors in mortgage-backed securities sold on the secondary mortgage market. Their large amounts of cash available from insurance premiums need to be invested to provide for future cash needs.

Insurance firms usually favor investment in larger apartment complexes and commercial loans greater than $1 million and are the biggest suppliers of funds for large mortgages on apartment complexes, commercial buildings, and shopping centers. Since they are not concerned with quick liquidity, they often enter into an equity position in the projects they finance. Referred to as participation financing, it affords them greater returns on the investment.

All insurance companies are state chartered, which means less regulation than savings and loans, and thus they have greater latitude in their investment approaches.

Commercial Banks

Commercial banks are either federally or state chartered. Originally they served the community in short-term (3- to 5-year), high-yield loans, such as automobile, mobile home, and household loans. Today, however, they also offer 15- and 30-year fixed rate loans and balloon loans.

These banks also make short-term construction and home improvement loans. They may also grant interim financing, called a bridge loan, to fill the gap if a purchaser buys a home prior to selling an existing one. Today commercial banks have begun to play a larger role in residential financing, especially FHA and VA loans. At the end of 1989, commercial banks' share of home loan originations surpassed S&Ls for the first time in 19 years, with a 38 percent share to the S&Ls' 35 percent, and with mortgage bankers accounting for 19 percent of all originations.

Trust Funds

Commercial banks and some title companies have trust departments that manage and supervise real estate holdings and properties of clients. The money held in trust funds is placed there for the benefit of a third party. Their fiduciary position includes acting as executor for estates, guardians for the estates of minors, and serving as trustees for individuals and corporations. They are known for their conservative approach since their responsibility is to safeguard the property entrusted to them. Little of this money is used for residential loans. It is usually placed in large commercial investments, or some of it may be used to purchase mortgage-backed securities.

Mutual Savings Banks

Primarily located in the northeastern section of the United States, mutual savings banks are all state chartered. They favor long-term investments since they are basically savings institutions owned by their depositors, and they prefer a low-risk position. They are also quite diversified in their investment approach; they buy blue chip stocks, bonds, and government securities. Mutual savings banks have no stockholders, so all earnings after operational costs are met are returned to depositors as interest earned. The majority of mutual banks holds membership in FDIC, with the balance state insured. However, some state-chartered mutual savings banks failed to protect depositors by not keeping sufficient funds in reserve. In such instances, the depositors lost their savings.

Credit Unions

Credit unions were founded by individual firms as savings programs for their employees, with regular payroll deductions taken from each participating employee's check. Many people feel this is a painless way to save, since most people don't miss money they never receive. Credit unions usually pay a higher rate of interest and offer lower interest rates to employees wishing to borrow money. Credit unions generally do not make many long-term real estate loans, but normally limit their funds to home improvement and personal property loans. Some credit unions are providing long-term, fixed-rate loans for their members and selling them to the Credit Union National Association (CUNA), much like mortgage bankers sell to the secondary market.

Pension Funds

The purpose of a pension fund is much like that of the social security program—it offers a forced savings program for its contributors. Pension funds are deducted from employees' salaries and held in trust until retirement, when they are paid out in monthly sums. This cash requirement dovetails nicely with the home buyer's need for money. Most pension funds are used for corporate and government stocks and bonds or mortgage-backed securities (MBS) that are generally purchased from the secondary market. Dividends are passed on to the subscribers to increase their retirement savings as inflation continues to climb.

MORTGAGE CORRESPONDENTS

Acting as the middleman, the loan correspondent is generally a mortgage broker or mortgage banker acting in the capacity of an agent for the lender, placing the loan for the borrower. With the expansion of the national and international markets, financing boundaries have widened, and the lenders require a network of knowledgeable correspondents to keep them informed on local economic markets in any given area.

Financial middlemen

Mortgage Brokers

The primary purpose of the **mortgage broker** is to locate lenders and borrowers and bring them together, much as the real estate broker brings together buyers and sellers of property. These financial middlemen do not lend their own money nor do they normally service (collect payments or handle foreclosures) the loan. For his effort, the mortgage broker earns a placement or finder's fee, usually a percentage of the loan. The mortgage broker ordinarily specializes in commercial loans, locating sources for loans as he finds borrowers for them. Care must be taken in placing the loans so that no high-risk loans affect the mortgage broker's credibility. Large investors, such as insurance companies, often prefer working through a mortgage broker rather than directly with the people seeking capital.

Mortgage Bankers

The services of mortgage bankers extends beyond just bringing the borrower and lender together. They originate mortgages and then sell the loans to investors through the secondary mortgage market or to private investors. They assume the risk of underwriting the loans and may have to buy the loan back if it does not meet the **Federal National Mortgage Association** (**FNMA** or Fannie Mae) standards. Funds are sometimes committed from the investors prior to the mortgage banker's original loan. Serving as an intermediary, mortgage bankers earn their income from origination fees and service fees for collecting monthly payments and handling foreclosures. The origination fee will generally be 1 percent of the loan amount, with the servicing fee generating an income of 1/2 percent to 1 percent of the monthly payment. Most mortgage bankers started in business in the 1930s after the Federal Housing Administration created FHA loans, which they originated and serviced, selling them to life insurance companies and other investors.

Mortgage bankers play a significant role in residential loan placement. Home loans are originated in what is referred to as the primary mortgage market. The borrower visits the mortgage banker and requests a loan on the property being purchased. The originator of the loan packages the loans and sells them on the secondary market to investors in million dollar blocks. The **Government National Mortgage Association** (**GNMA** or Ginnie Mae) is the primary source of these pools. Today the mortgage bankers originate nearly 30 percent of all mortgages, operating with little of their own funds.

GOVERNMENT REGULATIONS ON LOANS

The federal government has enacted legislation that requires credit arrangers to comply with certain laws as protection to the consumer. These federal lending laws include:

> Truth-in-Lending Act
> Real Estate Settlement Procedures Act (RESPA)
> Equal Credit Opportunity Act (ECOA)
> Fair Credit Reporting Act
> National Flood Insurance
> Community Reinvestment Act
> Americans with Disabilities Act (ADA)

The Truth-in-Lending Law

Truth-in-lending is a federal law enforced and administrated by the Federal Reserve. **Regulation Z**, as published by the Board of Governors of the Federal Reserve System, implements the act. As part of the A-1 Consumer Protection Act, truth-in-lending became effective July 19, 1969. However, the act was simplified and refined, and in October 1982 the Truth-in-Lending Simplification and Reform Act (TILSRA) became law.

The law requires that disclosure of the true **annual percentage rate (APR)** be made to the borrower within three days of the loan application. The APR shows the result of upfront finance charges made by the lender on the note rate. A disclosure statement form is used to disclose hidden finance charges to the borrower and allows the borrower to compare one lender's loan with a competitor. In the past, lenders may have advertised low rates and then charged the borrower large fees upfront on the day of closing, increasing the lender's yield on the loan. Now lenders must calculate the APR utilizing the net loan proceeds and disclose this to the borrower. The finance charges include all costs the consumer must pay either directly or indirectly over the life of the loan (such as discount points, private mortgage insurance, loan fees, and interest paid in advance). Designed to protect the consumer, Regulation Z requires the lender to reveal in writing where the borrower's money is going through a good faith estimate. This disclosure must be given at the time of the loan application and must include the following:

Disclosure of loan costs

1. the date the finance charge commences
2. the annual percentage rate
3. the number of monthly payments
4. the date payments are due
5. any pay-off penalties
6. charges made in case of late payment or default
7. sufficient description of the property
8. the total finance charges

Disclosure to borrower

The discount points and loan origination fees are added to the interest paid over the life of the loan to calculate the APR; the interest rate the lender quotes is known as the note rate. The note rate does not include the discount points or the loan origination fee.

This law applies to all extenders of credit on a regular basis, including savings and loan associations, commercial banks, mortgage brokers, and finance companies. It does *not* apply to arrangers of credit but only to lenders who actually extend credit. Assumptions of existing mortgages and contracts from creditors must also adhere to the law, if any terms are changed or the lender charges in excess of $50 for the assumption fee. While the real estate agent and mortgage broker bring the consumer and the lender together, they are not considered arrangers of credit since they do not finance the sale themselves.

Creditor

Exemptions to the Truth-in-Lending Act include:

1. business loans
2. commercial loans
3. loans to corporations and partnerships
4. installment loans with four or fewer installments
5. Loans on which no finance charges are made
6. Assumptions of a loan by a new borrower

Exempt from truth-in-lending

For some types of loans, such as refinancing of a residence or home improvement, the borrower may cancel the loan up until midnight of the third working day after signing the loan note. The buyer does not have this three-day "cooling off" period, however, with the loans that real estate salespeople help secure for their customers (such as a first mortgage or a deed of trust).

Three-day right of rescission

Advertising guidelines

Regulation Z of the act further determines how credit terms are advertised, a condition with which the real estate industry must comply. Advertising the annual percentage rate (APR) and the price of the property is permissible; however, if credit terms are further mentioned, all terms must be disclosed. No advertisement may say simply "7% mortgage" or "no down payment" unless all terms are disclosed.

In a mortgage assumption, the advertiser can state the rate of finance charge without any other disclosure, but the finance charge must be stated as an annual percentage rate; that is, "assume 10% mortgage" is wrong, but "assume 10% annual percentage rate mortgage" or "assumable loan" is right. However, you cannot advertise "assume 10% annual percentage rate mortgage" if the note rate is 10%. Remember, the note rate and the annual percentage rate are not the same thing.

If any credit terms are stated, the price, down payment, and the amount of the mortgage must be stated, together with the due date, the number of payments, and the annual percentage rate. An advertisement that mentions price alone is beyond suspicion.

Truth-in-Lending penalties

The penalty for not complying with the Truth-in-Lending Act when advertising is enforced by the Federal Trade Commission and includes:

1. Criminal liability of a fine of up to $4,000 and one year in jail or both.
2. Civil liability to the mortgagor, who must file a complaint within one year of the closing. The mortgagee's liability shall not exceed $1,000 and costs.
3. The arranger of credit may eliminate any fines by complying with the law within 15 days after notification.

RESPA

As of June 20, 1975, the **Real Estate Settlement Procedures Act (RESPA)** became effective. This act, administered by HUD, was intended to provide the purchaser and seller with regulated and standardized procedures in closing a federally related mortgage loan sale. Because of the many complaints from lenders and real estate brokers concerning the involved implementation of the act, it was modified in June 1976. In 1983 it was amended to address the emergence of "one-stop shopping," so financial institutions with service subsidiaries could offer their customers a variety of services. The controlled business amendment, while supported by the thrift industry, was opposed by traditional suppliers of services, such as title insurance companies. The position of Congress was that consumers would benefit from the bundling of services provided that safeguards were put in place.

RESPA applies only to *first mortgages* and includes:

1. savings and loans institutions that are insured by the FDIC
2. banks
3. FHA-insured loans
4. VA-guaranteed loans
5. HUD administered loans
6. any loan that the lender sells to Fannie Mae, Ginnie Mae, or Freddie Mac

HUD issued a new rule effective December 2, 1992, permitting a real estate broker to collect a fair fee for actual services in conjunction with a home sale transaction. A broker may use a computerized loan originator (CLO) system to assist a homebuyer in selecting a mortgage for a fee, provided the fee is disclosed in writing to the home buyer.

On a CLO system, a real estate broker can call up a menu of mortgage products and start the loan application and approval process. The broker may offer products of a single lender or multiple lenders.

If a controlled business arrangement exists in which the broker has an affiliate firm, such as a title company, escrow service, or mortgage brokerage, the broker may provide these services to the customer if the broker discloses the relationship in writing. The customer is free to obtain these services elsewhere. Fees are not exchanged between affiliated companies merely for the referral of business.

RESPA's main thrust is to eliminate any kickbacks that might occur through referrals by closing agents or attorneys for particular title companies. It also prevents the seller of the property from insisting that the purchaser buy title insurance from a specific title company.

Prevents kickbacks

The act further limits the amount of tax and insurance escrow funds that the lender can require the borrower to pay in advance. Only one-sixth of the amount due in a one-year period, commencing at the settlement date, may be collected. This amount will adequately cover the lender by the taxes and insurance due date, but will not leave more than necessary (one-sixth of the amount due in a one-year period) in the reserve account.

Limits escrow amount

When applying for a loan, the mortgagor can expect the following:

1. an information booklet from HUD explaining RESPA
2. the lender's use of the Uniform Settlement Statement as required by HUD (see Chapter 9)
3. the receipt of a good faith estimate of closing costs at loan application
4. the right to inspect the Uniform Settlement Statement one day prior to settlement

A good faith estimate of closing costs has been substituted for the repealed 12-day advance disclosure of settlement costs. The good faith estimate must be supplied by the lender within 3 days of the time of the loan application. When a good faith estimate cannot be provided, a range of charges must be supplied. HUD encourages but does not require estimates of loan-related fees. The booklet "Settlement Cost and You" is an information guide for borrowers that must also be given to the borrower applicant within 3 days.

Disclosure of closing costs

The settlement statement must be made available to the borrower at or prior to the settlement except when

1. the secretary of HUD exempts the above requirements in a particular locality, or
2. the borrower has waived the requirement, in which case the statement shall be mailed or delivered at the earliest practical date.

The Uniform Settlement Statement is virtually unchanged from the original RESPA Disclosure Statement. The new statement, however, has been revised to eliminate references to advance disclosure and truth-in-lending.

The Equal Credit Opportunity Act (ECOA)

In 1974 the **Equal Credit Opportunity Act (ECOA)** was passed to prohibit lenders from discrimination on the basis of sex or marital status. In 1977 it was amended to include a broader group of borrowers, including race, color, religion, and national origin, to ensure that lenders would not give favorable treatment to one group of people over another. Discrimination cannot occur because all or a portion of a borrower's income may stem from public assistance programs, alimony, separate maintenance, or child support. Exceptions to the law are individuals who are not citizens, since their

Lenders must not discriminate

status could affect a creditor's rights and remedies in the event of default. Also excluded are minors, since they do not possess contractual power.

Discounting a woman's income because she is of child-bearing age or has part-time employment is no longer permissible, nor can young adults and singles be refused a loan just because they may be considered likely to move more readily. The senior citizen is another category that cannot be ignored. Under the ECOA the focus is on job stability, net worth, credit rating, and sufficient income.

Fair Credit Reporting Act

Borrowers may see credit report

In April 1971 the Fair Credit Reporting Act was passed by the federal government entitling borrowers to see a summary of the report and examine information regarding their credit. If errors are found, such as may occur with common names, the borrower has a right to correct them. The act restricts access to the consumer's credit record to people who evaluate an applicant for credit, employment, or insurance and to those who secure consumer permission or court permission.

National Flood Insurance

Flood zone property must be insured

The National Flood Insurance Program was passed by Congress in 1968 and implemented in 1973. It requires flood insurance or a certificate stating the property is not in a flood zone on all government-insured mortgages or mortgages written by federally insured or regulated lending institutions. The objectives of the federal government and the insurance companies are to encourage cities to regulate and control development in flood zone areas and to provide flood insurance at reasonable rates. The policy is administered by HUD. Maps that recognize definite areas prone to flooding have been prepared by the Army Corp of Engineers.

Community Reinvestment Act

Redlining prohibited

To prevent lenders from refusing to make loans in older neighborhoods which may economically be higher risk areas, Congress passed the Community Reinvestment Act. The practice of *redlining* by lenders literally cut off funds in certain neighborhoods. One can equate it to encircling the area in red because of its income level, racial, cultural, or religious composition. Lenders must now comply with the act by taking care not to exclude homes in these areas. This does not imply that the lender has to loan on a property that does not meet city safety and building codes or a residence in an area that is primarily commercial in use.

Americans with Disabilities Act (ADA)

The Americans with Disabilities Act (ADA) was passed into law July 26, 1990. The four sections are:

1. Title I—Employment. Employers with 15 or more employees cannot discriminate against qualified individuals with disabilities.
2. Title II—Public Services. State and local government must adjust all government buildings and public transportation facilities to meet the accessibility needs of individuals with wheelchairs and others who are disabled.
3. Title III—Public Accommodations. All business establishments were given 18 months to comply with the act. By January 26, 1992, all private businesses were to have been made accessible to persons with disabilities.
4. Title IV—Public Communications. Telephone companies must provide telecommunications relay services for hearing-impaired and speech-impaired individuals 24 hours a day.

This civil rights legislation will have a significant impact on the sale and lease of buildings. Real estate salespersons and property owners must be versed on the requirements of Title III. Buyers and sellers will want assurances that the buildings they are going to purchase, sell, or lease are in full compliance with ADA standards for architectural accessibility.

LOANS

The Federal Housing Administration (FHA)

The Federal Housing Administration (FHA) has been in existence since 1934. Prior to that time, most borrowers in need of home financing were dependent upon banks to renew short-term (generally five-year) loans. During the Great Depression of the 1930s, many banks closed or could not renew loans, resulting in the debtor losing the property and any equity acquired.

The FHA was created during the depression to create construction jobs, stimulate the housing industry, and help Americans obtain good quality, affordable housing. FHA has been a boon to housing financing for the following reasons:

1. It establishes a set of standards concerning the construction and appraisal of property to qualify for FHA insurance.
2. It sets up new standards for qualifying buyers for mortgage insurance.
3. It initiates the long-term amortized mortgage loan, thereby providing lower monthly house payments so that more Americans could own their own homes.
4. The above innovations made it possible to sell mortgages through a national clearinghouse, later to be called the secondary mortgage market.

The FHA does not make loans, plan housing, or do any actual construction; it *insures* loans made by approved lenders. The FHA offers protection to the lender in the event of a foreclosure. If the borrower defaults on the loan, the lender may foreclose, and the FHA will repay the lender's loss, if any. If the homeowner misses two payments, FHA requires that the lender notify the local credit bureau and the local HUD office. The lender attempts to contact the borrower to establish an alternative to foreclosure. Prior to starting the foreclosure process, the lender must work with the borrower by providing a counseling agency, recasting the mortgage, or offering a long-term repayment plan. The borrower must provide a complete financial history, and the lender tries to determine the reason for default and assist the borrower with a solution. These steps reduce the losses paid out of the insurance fund from HUD to the lenders.

Because borrowers are required to show good employment patterns and reasonable credit control, the risk to the FHA or the lender has been minimal. To eliminate fraud and the misuse of FHA financing, guidelines have been tightened.

The mortgage insurance premium (MIP) payment program was changed in 1983 from a monthly premium to a one-time premium payable upfront, with additional changes in 1990. Most mortgages will be subject to an **upfront mortgage insurance premium (UFMIP)** and an annual premium. The UFMIP is a one-time fee that may be added to the mortgage and financed. The annual premium will be calculated on the unpaid principal balance. In the event the loan is paid off prior to the term, upon request, the unused portion of the UFMIP is refunded to the borrower based upon a formula given by HUD. As of December 27, 1992, the two formulas are as follows:

1. Finance the UFMIP and pay 3.8 percent of the loan amount for a 30-year loan or 2.0 percent for a 15-year loan.

2. Pay cash for the UFMIP amounting to 3.6 percent of the loan amount for a 30-year loan or 2.0 percent for a 15-year loan. If the complete MIP premium is paid in cash at closing, the reduced UFMIP fee, as stated above, may be paid by any party involved in the transaction.

Let's assume on the purchase of a $60,000 home the UFMIP is added to the loan:

Down payment:	3% of $25,000 =	$ 750.00	
(see discussion	5% of $35,000 =	1,750.00	
below of FHA		$2,500.00	required
down payment)			down payment

Loan Amount:	$60,000 − $2,500 = $57,500 loan
Add UFMIP:	$57,500 × 3.8% (UFMIP) = $ 2,185 UFMIP
	$57,500 + $2,185 = $59,685 loan

Adding the UFMIP has increased the loan by $2,185, but it provided the purchaser the opportunity to obtain housing with a minimum down payment. A problem that surfaces is that adding the UFMIP and closing costs to FHA loans can result in a loan greater than the value of the property.

FHA loans are based either on the acquisition cost (purchase price plus the FHA allowable closing costs) or on the FHA-appraised value, whichever is lower. To figure this on FHA loans the lender compares the purchase price with the appraised value, using the lower of the two amounts. Once this amount is derived, the lender figures the maximum allowable closing cost on the good faith estimate to arrive at the acquisition cost.

Discount points

The Federal Housing Administration requires the loan to be paid back in periodic payments, both principal and interest. The loans are generally issued for 15 or 30 years, with insurance and taxes included in the monthly payment. There is no prepayment penalty if the loan is repaid before maturity. Lenders may vary as to their requirements in making an FHA loan. Discount points are charged if the borrower wants a below current market interest rate. It is permissible to charge either the seller or the buyer for points if it is disclosed in the purchase agreement.

FHA down payment

FHA insures loans only for one- to four-family housing. The FHA section 203B program under Title II requires a minimum down payment with the maximum loan based on local market conditions, which vary across the nation. If the acquisition value is less than $50,000, the purchaser is only required to put 3 percent down. If the purchase price is $50,000 or more, 3 percent is paid up to $25,000, and the balance is at 5 percent down. If the home is less than one year old and not built under FHA specifications, the minimum down payment is 10 percent, unless the property carries a homeowner's warranty (HOW). FHA does not permit investor financing on a new loan, and effective December 15, 1989, the home must be purchased as the buyer's principal residence or, under certain conditions, a secondary residence. Borrowers must have down payment and prepaid expenses from their own funds, with the following exceptions:

1. The down payment may be a "gift" from a blood relative.
2. The money may be borrowed against any collateral to secure the cash needed for down payment and closing costs (understandably, the borrower must qualify for the added debt).
3. The seller may pay all of the closing costs, or the closing costs may be financed by acquisition as shown in our example.

Since some builders were adding excessive financing costs to the price of their new homes, FHA felt it necessary to limit the amount of dollars the seller could contribute to the buyer as an enticement to buy the home. The maximum seller contribution for an FHA loan is 5 percent of the sales price. If the contribution exceeds 5 percent, the FHA mortgage is reduced dollar for dollar of excess contribution.

Until November 1983, the government controlled the amount of interest the lender could charge on FHA loans. However, because of spiraling interest rates in the late 1970s and early 1980s, lenders were reluctant to loan out money at lower rates than they could receive on conventional loans. The alternative was to charge enormous discount points, which meant the seller was generally asked to pay them. This in effect meant sellers were taking less for their homes after deducting the cost of paying the points.

Controlled interest ceiling removed

Eliminating the controlled ceiling on the FHA interest rates allows the borrowers to "shop" rates for their loans. The rate will adjust or float with the market, and any party may pay the points. The rate will be determined by discount points paid; the formula is complex and has many variables. Rate and points may be locked in for a set period of time from the date of the loan application, or they may float and lock in at a time prior to the closing. The longer a lock, the more points a borrower will pay. For example: if the current rate is 10.5 percent with 2 points for a 60-day lock, then for every additional 30 days it could cost anywhere from .25 percent to .75 percent more (depending on the lender). So, using .50 percent for every 30 days, a 10.5 percent rate with 3 points would be good for a 120-day lock. When shopping for an FHA loan, not only should the rate and points be "shopped," but the length of the lock and the cost of extending it another 30 days should be considered.

The FHA buydown program offers the buyer a lower rate for the first two or three years, depending on the program, thus allowing the borrower to qualify for a higher loan amount. The buydown is a seller-subsidized loan with the funds placed in an escrow account by the seller.

Congress passed the HUD Reform legislation bill in November 1989, creating a new impact on FHA-insured mortgages. The new rules require the following:

1. Increased requirements on loan assumptions state that any subsequent purchaser must pass a credit check and qualify for the payment prior to title passing or the acceleration (due on sale) clause will be invoked. This substitution of liability to a new debtor is termed **novation**.
2. New loans issued after December 14, 1989, can only be assumed by a buyer who will occupy the property, thus eliminating the investor-purchaser.
3. No new loans will be issued to investors after the December 14, 1989, date.
4. The new guidelines recommend that borrowers use no more than 29 percent of their monthly gross income to make the mortgage payment and no more than 41 percent of their gross income for monthly payment of all debts.

FHA loan assumptions

FHA loan assumptions become extremely popular when interest rates are high. Not only is the interest lower, but the cost of originating a new loan is bypassed. Since the loans have generally been in force for a number of years and the owners equity has built up, a larger down payment will be necessary. However, since it is not a new loan the purchaser can borrow some of the down payment from the seller. Purchasers must be realistic in what amount they can allot for a monthly house payment. The guidelines set down by lenders are a wise plan for any buyer assuming an existing loan. Conversely, the larger down payment lessens the risk the seller has of foreclosure. With the new rulings from FHA, the loan assumptions will be cut considerably. While most FHA loans are under the 203B program, variations from the original FHA plan have developed to fill the needs of buyers.

Other FHA programs:

- The FHA 235 program subsidized lower and moderate income families by reducing their monthly payments through a government subsidy. However, at the current time these loans are no longer available.

Subsidized FHA plan
- The FHA 234 program covers loans for condominiums, a plan equivalent to the 203(b) program.
- The FHA 245 program requires a somewhat larger down payment than a 203B but offers a graduated payment plan which permits the borrower to begin payments at a substantially lower interest rate with a gradual increase the first four to five years of the loan. The 245 program is designed to assist buyers who initially need low monthly payments to qualify and whose income is expected to grow in the next four to five years. Since interest that occurred in the first year equals more than the payments, the outstanding principal balance increases, resulting in what is called *negative amortization*. That is, the debt increases over time instead of decreasing. At the end of five years the maximum mortgage is reached, and the debt will begin to decline just as a regularly amortized real estate loan.

FHA Adjustable Rate Mortgage (ARM)

FHA buydown program
In an unstable market, the FHA ARM program proves to be an excellent product. Down payment and qualifying guidelines do not vary from FHA standards; this buydown program allows the borrower to qualify at the first year rate. Some local HUD offices require the borrower to qualify at 1 percent above the first year rate. Two key words used in implementing this program are the *margin*, which adds 2 percent to the *index*, which is the weekly average of one-year Treasury bills (T-bills). The maximum the rate can increase is 1 percent per year, and the highest rate the ARM can increase is 5 percent above the first year rate. For example:

Year	Rate	Index
1st year	5%	N/A for 1st year
2nd year	6%	1 yr T/Bill 4%
3rd year	7%	1 yr T/Bill 5%
4th year	8%	1 yr T/Bill 6%
5th year	9%	1 yr T/Bill 7%
6th year	10%	1 yr T/Bill 8%

This example shows the worst-case scenario if T-bills were to go up every year after you obtained an FHA ARM loan.

FHA Title I

FHA home improvement loans
The FHA Title I Act authorized the FHA to insure lending institutions against losses on loans made to finance repairs and improvements to existing structures and to build new structures for nonresidential use. FHA liability is limited to 90 percent of the loss on individual loans and to 10 percent of all such loans made by the institutions. Borrowers must have a satisfactory income and credit record. They must own the property or have a lease expiring not less than six months beyond the maturity of the loan. The loan may not exceed $5,000 or have a maturity greater than 7 years and 32 days. The lender pays an insurance charge on each loan made. This revenue, plus recoveries on defaulted notes, is sufficient to make the program self-supporting and establish a substantial reserve for paying off losses.

VA Loans

The Department of Veterans Affairs (DVA) designed the **VA loans** for veterans who qualify under the law. A minimum of 90 or 181 days active service with an honorable discharge is required, depending on when the individual served. The eligibility entitlement covers World War II, the Korean Conflict, Vietnam, and the Persian Gulf War. This eligibility is valid until used and extends to widows and widowers of veterans who died on active duty if they have not remarried. In October 1992 the law was expanded to include members of the National Guard and military reserves who have served a minimum of six years.

Unlike FHA loans, there is no down payment with VA loans. VA loan terms can be for 15 or 30 years. These loans are guaranteed by the DVA, with maximum guarantees to eligible veterans as follows:

No down payment for VA loans

1. For loans of $45,000 or less, 50 percent of the loan is guaranteed.
2. For loans above $45,000, 40 percent of the loan is guaranteed up to $36,000, whichever is less, but not less than $22,500. For loans from $45,000 to $56,250, the minimum guarantee will result in a percentage of guarantee over 40.
3. For home purchases, construction, or condominium loans that are for an amount in excess of $144,000, 25 percent of the loan is guaranteed up to $46,000, whichever is less. These guarantees may not exceed the veteran's remaining entitlement.

If there is a default on a guaranteed loan, the government reimburses the lender for loss up to the amount of the VA guarantee (veteran's eligibility). The maximum loan depends upon the lending institution, with most lenders stopping at four times the veteran's entitlement with no down payment. In order to sell a VA loan on the secondary market, it cannot exceed a 75 percent loan-to-value ratio. The veteran must occupy the property as the principal residence, as the VA loan cannot be used solely for income property.

VA loans guaranteed

The veteran must secure a *certificate of eligibility* and sign a statement that the veteran intends to occupy the home. Loans can be made on one- to four-family housing units. When the loan is paid off, the veteran's eligibility will be fully restored. If a VA loan is assumed and if the assumption is with substitution of eligibility along with release of liability, the veteran will be given entitlement again. If the loan is paid off before maturity, there is no prepayment penalty.

Certificate of eligibility

As of October 1992, the government no longer fixes the interest rate on VA loans. Veterans and lenders may negotiate the interest rate. The seller no longer has to pay the veteran buyer's discount points.

The VA funding fee is figured on the amount of the down payment in four different levels.

Level one	no down payment	1.25% funding fee
Level two	5% down payment	.75% funding fee
Level three	10% down payment	50% funding fee
Level four	for disabled veteran	no funding fee

The funding fee may be paid in cash or financed; there is no preference for either.

With both FHA and VA loans, an escape clause is a mandatory part of the purchase agreement and is signed by both seller and buyer. If the lender does not appraise the property for the purchase price, the purchaser need not carry through with the purchase. If the purchaser agrees to buy the property, the difference between the purchase price and the appraisal will be renegotiated between the buyer and the seller or paid in cash.

Farmers Home Administration (FmHA)

The Farmers Home Administration (FmHA) was established in 1946 to make and insure loans to farmers for construction or repair of farm homes and farm buildings.

The FmHA is available for loans in towns and rural areas of up to 20,000 in population. In addition to the property location, borrowers must demonstrate limited income record and a need for housing. The loans are reviewed periodically, and payments are increased as the borrower's income rises. The loans are either: (1) made directly by FmHA or (2) made by a private lender with FmHA guaranteeing a certain percentage.

Private Mortgage Insurance (PMI)

PMI insurance covers conventional loans

A great boost to the housing industry in the early 1960s, the Mortgage Guarantee Insurance Corporation (MGIC) of Milwaukee, Wisconsin, introduced a mortgage that allowed borrowers to obtain homes with a minimal down payment. New houses not built under FHA and VA requirements could now be purchased with a minimum 10 percent down payment. Discount points were charged but could be paid by either the buyer or the seller. A 50 percent insurance premium was paid by the borrower for the first year and 25 percent from then on, on the mortgage amount. Other private mortgage insurance companies followed, and in 1971, they were approved by the Federal Home Loan Bank. **Private mortgage insurance (PMI)** accounts for a large percentage of loans, requiring only 5 percent to 15 percent as a down payment. The insurance expense will vary depending on the depth of exposure to the insuring company.

Similar to FHA, the PMI insures its lenders but only for the top 20 or 25 percent of the loan. After the loan is paid down to the insured amount, the insurance premium can usually be eliminated, at the discretion of the agency in the secondary market that purchased the loan from the local lender.

Conventional Loans

The lender of a **conventional loan** is not insured, nor is the loan guaranteed by the federal government. The lending institution sets its own requirements and policies. If a borrower requests a shorter-term loan with a larger down payment, the lender may decrease the interest rate, depending on the availability of funds. Conventional loans ordinarily require a minimum of 20 percent down except when private mortgage insurance is used. This type of loan will be discussed in greater detail in Chapter 9.

Private Loans

Private loans are often used when the credit of the borrower is not extremely good. Usually a private loan has a higher interest rate since there is a greater risk involved. A buyer may not have sufficient down payment or income to qualify for a loan so that a private lender is needed. When home mortgage interest rates are high, the position of lender has become attractive to individuals with the capital.

Land Contracts

Vendor retains title

Variously referred to as **land contracts**, land sales contracts, installment sales contracts, or contracts for deed, these financing arrangements are contracts to buy wherein the seller finances the purchaser. In this type of contract, the seller takes the role of lender. Historically, land contracts are used in the sale of vacant land, since lenders do not categorize bare land as property that is eligible for loans. Land contracts are also used if the property is not readily salable and would not qualify for a long-term loan, if the purchaser has insufficient funds for a minimum down payment or an unstable income, or if the seller does not want all the equity immediately but prefers to receive a regular monthly income from the land contract. In the tight-money period of the late 1970s and the early 1980s, land contracts were often the only means of obtaining financing.

In a land contract sale, the vendor (seller) retains legal title to the real property with the vendee (buyer) receiving the equitable title. While the vendee does not become the owner of record, he has the right to use, possess, and transfer the property and should record that right. Customarily, the purchaser pays the insurance and maintenance expenses. Upon fulfillment of the terms of the contract, the deed is delivered to the vendee. If the vendee fails to live up to the terms of the contract, the vendor may terminate the contract and recapture the property. Many purchasers are concerned about the risks involved in land contracts since title is retained by the seller. However, the seller would have to go through the normal foreclosure procedures of her particular state if the vendee defaulted. The greatest potential risk of a land contract would be claims brought against the vendor during the term of the contract that could prohibit the vendee from obtaining clear title.

Vendee receives equitable interest

Qualifying the Buyer

An **underwriter**, employed by a lending institution or mortgage banking company, reviews the borrower's loan application and makes a recommendation to the loan committee on the advisability of making the loan. The underwriter's opinion is largely based on the applicant's ability to repay the loan, credit history, and the property value. This is a vital part of the lending process. Some of the factors underwriters consider when qualifying the borrower include the following:

Underwriters' duties

1. credit report
2. job stability and ability to meet future debt retirement
3. cash equity invested
4. bonus (must be verified)
5. second job (these are usually short term so lenders are strict; they want a minimum 2-year work record)
6. child support payments (lender takes into account that it may not be received; the borrower must have one-year record of payment and must receive payments for five more years)
7. overtime pay (it must be consistent, substantiated, and guaranteed by employer; a two-year history is necessary)
8. bankruptcy (lenders consider if action was made to repay creditors, if two or three years have passed, and if applicant has a good credit history since the bankruptcy; they also consider if there was a valid reason for bankruptcy)
9. installment debts (usually a factor if for 10 or more months; credit cards carefully scrutinized)
10. total debt ratio (should not exceed 41 percent for VA loans and FHA loans and 36 percent for conventional loans)

Income qualifications

THE SECONDARY MORTGAGE MARKET

The secondary mortgage market refers to the sale of mortgages by the primary lender to investors (see Figure 8.1). The choice of resale affords lenders an opportunity to dispose of their inventory enabling them to obtain new funds and make new mortgages. The original lender continues to service the loan and receives a fee for this service.

Resale of mortgages

FNMA

The Federal National Mortgage Association (FNMA), dubbed Fannie Mae, was created by the government to stimulate the housing market. Originally chartered in 1938

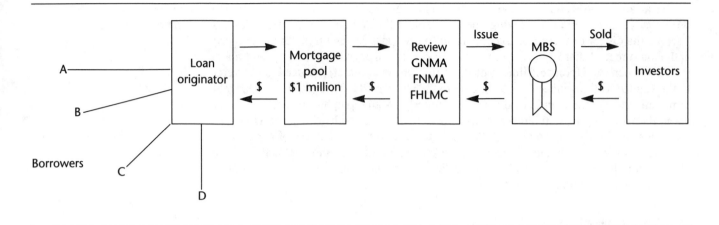

FIGURE 8.1 Secondary mortgage market.

as a government agency, it was primed with $10 million. FNMA purchased loans from commercial banks and savings and loans, providing the institutions with new funds to lend. Revised as a federal agency in 1954, FNMA was acquired from the Department of Housing and Urban Development by the private sector in 1968 and is now owned by stockholders, and the stock is traded on the New York Stock Exchange. It is called a quasi-government enterprise because the board of directors must get government approval before issuing bonds and making other financial decisions. Fulfilling its role as a "warehouse" for loans, FNMA buys, sells, and services loans. FNMA, along with Freddie Mac, are now the mortgage industry leaders in defining standards in underwriting loans and appraising property for one- to four-family dwellings.

GNMA

Government National Mortgage Association (GNMA), called Ginnie Mae, was established in 1968 and is operated by the Department of Housing and Urban Development. GNMA receives the funds to purchase loans from the sale of long-term bonds on Wall Street. These bonds are often purchased by insurance companies, pension and trust funds, and mutual funds or money market funds. GNMA's purpose is to provide housing and to stabilize mortgage money. GNMA provides reduced interest rates to lower-income home purchasers. Ginnie Mae is involved in the tandem plan, which is a program that allows FNMA to buy high-risk, low-yielding mortgages at full market price, and GNMA guarantees the payment, absorbing the difference between the market rate and the low yield expected. In recent years its largest focus has been on the purchase and sale of these mortgage-backed securities.

FHLMC

The **Federal Home Loan Mortgage Corporation (FHLMC)**, called Freddie Mac, was under the control of the Federal Home Loan Bank Board. It was created in 1970 to buy conventional loans from banks and S&Ls, much the same way FNMA initially bought FHA and VA loans from commercial banks and S&Ls. Originally owned by lending institutions, shares were sold to the public in 1988. Freddie Mac buys mortgages and pools them to sell in the marketplace, but does not guarantee them.

Mortgage-Backed Securities (MBS)

The secondary mortgage market affects everyone involved in real estate financing—builder, seller, borrower, lender, sales agent, broker, and investor—particularly in residential transactions.

Figure 8.2 explains where the money for home mortgages comes from and why we now have to pay discount points to obtain the funds for our mortgages.

The *loan originator* is the institution that takes the loan application and gets the loan approved and closed. It can be a bank, savings and loan, mortgage broker, or mortgage banker. After the loans are closed, they are placed in a mortgage pool with an aggregate amount of $1 million or more. All the loans in the mortgage pool must be homogeneous; that is, they must have a restrictive range of rates and the same term.

Loan originator

The mortgage pools are then reviewed for compliance with applicable regulations and are then approved by Fannie Mae, Ginnie Mae, or Freddie Mac. A *mortgage-backed security* (MBS) is then issued and auctioned to investors, such as insurance companies, pension and trust funds, or money market funds. The proceeds from the sale, after commissions and discount points are subtracted, are then sent to the originator (primary lender) to be lent out again for new mortgages. The average life of an MBS is 12 years; by then most of the loans have been paid off when the property was sold or refinanced.

Mortgage "pools"

The lower the interest rate of the MBS, relative to the current money market, the higher the discount. For example, if an MBS containing 32 mortgages with an average rate of 9 percent is being auctioned when the current market rate (as determined by long-term Treasury bills and bonds) is 10 percent, investors will only pay 94 cents on the dollar because they could buy T-bills with no risk for 10 percent. This discount of 6 cents on the dollar, or 6 points, is collected from the borrower or the seller at closing.

As many as three months may elapse between the time the borrower signs the note at closing and the time the MBS is sold on the secondary market. Mortgage bankers and brokers often play the market, betting that they can sell the mortgage three months later at a profit. This is a high-risk game, and millions of dollars are at stake.

SUMMARY

The backbone of the housing industry, savings and loan institutions, has historically provided the bulk of the funds for one- to four-family homes. Dating from the original building club of the early nineteenth century, the idea of saving money in savings and loan institutions spread tremendously. Today the borrower does not need to be a depositor in a savings and loan to obtain a loan. Along with savings and loans, mortgage bankers now provide a large percentage of home loans on their own or through various brokers.

Great changes in the savings and loan industry have occurred. In the late 1980s many insolvent savings and loans were closed down by the federal government, causing chaos in the housing industry. The great "bail out" began and the Resolution Trust Corporation (RTC) was formed to begin the liquidation and sale of the failed institutions. The bankrupt FSLIC was dissolved and replaced by the Savings Association Insurance Fund (SAIF). Chapter 9 will further explain the changes that have taken place in the mortgage market.

Mortgage brokers help join lenders and borrowers, but do not service the loans. Government regulations on lending are outlined by Regulation Z and the Real Estate Settlement Procedures Act. The government is also active in insuring FHA loans and

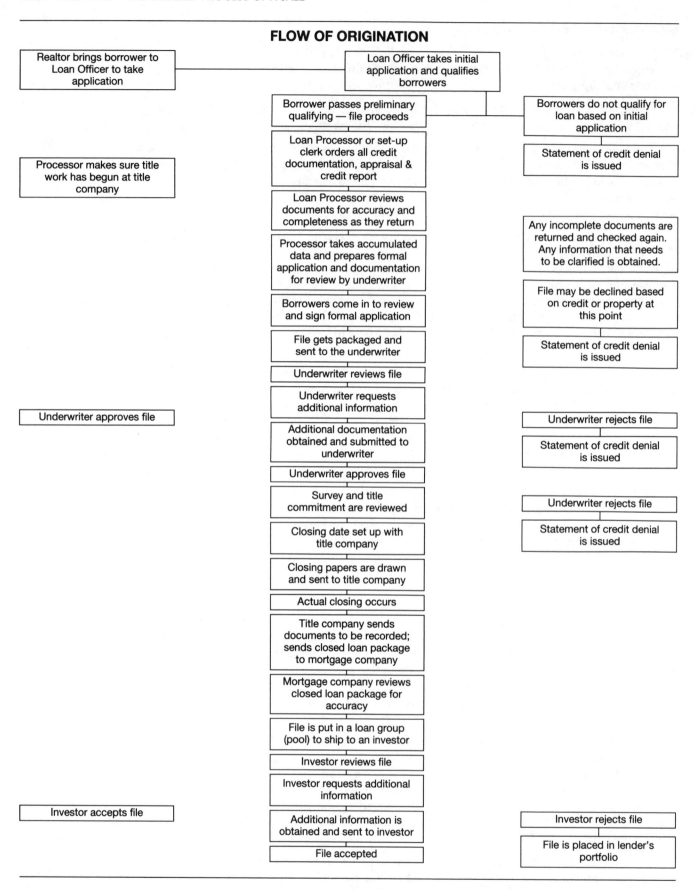

FIGURE 8.2 The cycle of a loan, from application to sale of the loan to the secondary market.

guaranteeing VA loans. Conventional loans, private loans, and land contracts may also be obtained to finance mortgages.

The secondary mortgage market involves the resale of mortgages. The FNMA, GNMA, and FHLMC all serve to provide a stable market for mortgages.

DISCUSSION QUESTIONS

1. Why is the Federal Reserve Board organized to control fiscal policy?
2. Explain how the FHA has changed its program since its inception in 1934. Why were these changes necessary?
3. Explain the purpose of mortgage-backed securities.
4. Why is there a need for the secondary mortgage market?
5. What causes disintermediation?
6. What effect, if any, have the failed savings and loans had on financing for housing?
7. Explain the reasons a purchaser would prefer to use FHA financing.
8. When would it be advisable to use a land contract as a means of financing?

REVIEW QUESTIONS

Answers to these questions are found in the Answer Key section at the back of the book.

1. Money for FHA financing is provided by:

   a. any governmental agency
   b. the FDIC
   c. any qualified lending institution
   d. the Federal Housing Administration

2. The Federal Housing Administration:

   a. makes loans
   b. builds houses
   c. purchases land
   d. insures loans

3. In order to make financing for homes available, the most common source of secondary mortgage money is:

   a. the seller taking a second mortgage
   b. the Federal National Mortgage Association
   c. insurance companies
   d. the Federal Housing Administration

4. Which of the following is NOT true regarding a federally chartered savings and loan?

   a. it must be a member of the Federal Home Loan Bank System
   b. it needs to be federally insured

   c. deposits are insured up to $100,000
   d. deposits of any amount are insured

5. In securing a residential loan:

   a. no down payment is required on conventional loans
   b. no down payment can be made on a VA loan unless the selling price of the home is greater than the appraised value
   c. a down payment is made when obtaining an FHA loan
   d. there always must be a 10% (or greater) down payment

6. Which of the following facts is/are true concerning VA loans?

   a. a VA loan on a fourplex cannot exceed 15 years
   b. a buyer must pay the difference between the amount the VA appraises the home and the purchase price
   c. a VA loan can be assumed by a nonveteran
   d. a VA loan can only be issued to a veteran of a foreign war

7. Which of the following is true regarding a property that has been financed with a VA loan?

   a. the loan may be assumed by a person who is not a veteran

b. the present owner can transfer the loan to a new home she is purchasing

c. the loan is not assumable

d. only another veteran that uses his eligibility can assume the loan

8. In securing a loan on a home:

a. escrow accounts are mandatory

b. through FHA, the buyer must occupy the home as a residence

c. through VA, the buyer must occupy the home as a residence

d. the VA loan has no guarantee limit

9. Which of the following is NOT exempt from Regulation Z of the Truth-in-Lending Act?

a. commercial or business loan

b. loans of four or fewer installments

c. loans to corporations or partnerships

d. loans of five or fewer installments

10. The maximum amount guaranteed by the government on any VA loan is:

a. the same as on an FHA loan

b. $36,500

c. 50 percent of the purchase price

d. $60,000

11. The Department of Veterans Affairs:

a. insures loans

b. guarantees loans

c. sells loans

d. originates loans

12. The private corporation that buys federally insured or guaranteed mortgages for resale is:

a. FNMA

b. PMI

c. MGIC

d. FDIC

13. When a purchaser of real estate assumes the seller's existing loan:

a. she buys out the lender's equity

b. she becomes responsible for the repayment of the debt along with the original borrower

c. the original borrower is always relieved of responsibility for repayment of the debt

d. the new owner is always solely responsible for the debt

14. Conventional loans are:

a. never insured

b. insured by FHA

c. not insured by the federal government

d. guaranteed

15. The substitution of a new contract for an existing agreement is known as:

a. novation

b. satisfaction

c. release

d. reversion

16. In an FHA loan, discount points are paid by:

a. the buyer

b. the seller

c. buyer and seller

d. buyer or seller

17. A young couple wants to buy a home. Their income is low, but should increase greatly in the next few years. They will apply for:

a. an FHA 203

b. a conventional insured loan

c. an FHA 245

d. an FNMA

18. The mortgage broker who brings the lender and borrower together receives a fee for her services, which is referred to as:

a. a finder's fee

b. a service fee

c. an insured fee

d. a participation fee

19. Which of the following government regulations entitles borrowers to review their credit report?

a. Truth-in-Lending

b. Fair Credit Reporting

c. Equal Credit Opportunity

d. Real Estate Settlement Procedures

20. The Mortgage Guarantee Insurance Corporation insures which of the following types of loans?

    a. FHA
    b. VA
    c. conventional
    d. land contract

21. The Community Reinvestment Act was passed to:

    a. prevent lenders from discriminating because of sex or age
    b. permit borrowers to view their credit report to be certain there were no errors
    c. assure all low-income borrowers that they can receive loans
    d. to prevent redlining

22. The primary lender may sell the mortgage to the secondary mortgage market. These transactions result in the issuance of certificates that are secured by a pool of mortgages. The certificates are referred to as:

    a. mortgage-backed securities
    b. second mortgages
    c. purchase money mortgages
    d. stock options

Financing

Key Words

adjustable rate mortgage (ARM)
amortization
balloon payment
blanket mortgage
deed of trust
discount points
equity
escrow agreement
estoppel certificate
foreclosure
general liens
hypothecation

interest
lien
lien theory
moratorium
mortgage
mortgagee
mortgagor
open-end mortgage
PITI
specific liens
title theory

Overview

One of the most important cogs in any real estate transaction is the financing. Since the purchase of a home is the largest investment the average person enters into, almost everyone needs to finance at least a portion of the purchase price. Without adequate financing the sale can be lost.

When interest rates for real estate mortgages escalated to all-time highs in the late 1970s and early 1980s, financiers developed many new creative financing techniques. The traditional financing practices gave way to innovative methods. Many of these practices remain with us today even though interest rates are lower.

This chapter explains interest rates, the various clauses found in notes and mortgages, and the different types of mortgages that are available to the borrower. The foreclosure procedure on a defaulted mortgage and the numerous specific and general liens complete this chapter.

INTEREST RATES

Interest is rent for the use of money. Interest rates depend upon many complex economic factors, including

1. the risk involved in making the loan.
2. the business outlook for the future.

Renting money

3. the market rate for alternate investments such as Treasury bonds: if there are fewer buyers for bonds, then bond prices fall, which results in a corresponding increase in rates. This is a simple application of the law of supply and demand.

4. the outlook for inflation in the future.

Since investors are in business to make a profit, they require a certain rate of return on their investments. Under the free market system in the United States, the market rates of interest are not set by the government, but by auction process.

MORTGAGE PAYMENT METHODS

Straight-Term Payments

Interest & principal repaid separately

Straight-term payments are arranged for the borrower to pay only the interest due with the sum borrowed repaid on the due date of the loan. Prevalent before the depression of the 1930s, they resulted in many people losing their homes because the banks were unable to negotiate a new loan when the principal became due. The borrower had no resources from which to repay the loan and foreclosures resulted. As mentioned in Chapter 8, the government intervened by creating the Federal Housing Administration, using amortized FHA loans. Today these straight-term loans are used by builders and land developers who need short-term financing.

Fully Amortized Mortgages

Interest & principal repaid in equal payments

The most common means of repaying a mortgage is by making equal payments that gradually reduce the balance of the loan within a stated period of time. The equal payment includes a portion for interest and a portion for principal, which reduces the unpaid balance. Basically, **amortization** is the liquidation of a financial obligation on the installment basis. For example, on a $90,000 loan at 9 percent interest for 30 years, the interest and principal payment would be $724.50 monthly. After the first payment, the balance due would be figured as follows:

$$\begin{array}{rl} \$90,000.00 & \textit{loan amount} \\ \times \quad\quad .09 & \textit{interest rate} \\ \hline \$ \ 8,100.00 & \textit{yearly interest} \end{array}$$

$8,100 ÷ 12 months = $675 monthly interest

$$\begin{array}{rl} \$ \quad 724.50 & \textit{principal and interest payment} \\ - \quad 675.00 & \textit{first month's interest} \\ \hline \$ \quad\ 49.50 & \textit{toward principal} \end{array}$$

$$\begin{array}{rl} \$90,000.00 & \\ - \quad\ \ 49.50 & \\ \hline \$89,950.50 & \textit{balance due after first payment} \end{array}$$

As this example shows, the debt is reduced by $49.50 the first month. Since the borrower pays each month on the unpaid balance due, a larger amount is attributed to the principal reduction each month. Some lending institutions require that monthly mortgage payments not only include the principal and interest (known as P and I) payment, but one-twelfth of the yearly taxes and insurance also. This amount is kept in an

Impounding funds

escrow or reserve account from which the lender pays the taxes and insurance as they become due. The lender is then assured protection on the investment; for example, if the dwelling burns down, it is covered by insurance. Similarly, the taxes are paid, so there will be no tax foreclosure sale.

The following equation demonstrates the calculation of a **PITI** (principal, interest, taxes, and insurance) payment. To the $724.50 payment on a $90,000 loan at 9 percent interest, add one-twelfth of the $2,200 yearly tax and one-twelfth of the $360 yearly insurance premium.

$\quad$ $ $\quad$ 724.50 $\quad$ *P&I*
$\qquad$ 183.33 $\quad$ *taxes*
$\qquad$ $\underline{\quad 30.00}$ $\quad$ *insurance*
$\quad$ $ $\quad$ 937.83 $\quad$ *total PITI monthly payment*

A departure from the traditional 30-year mortgage is the 15- or 20-year fixed-rate loan. One advantage is that it is often available at a lower interest rate and with reduced discount points. The following examples illustrate the difference in interest paid on 15-, 20-, and 30-year mortgages. Check the amortization chart to determine the P and I payment (see Figure 9.1).

A. $50,000 loan for 30 years at 10% interest
$\quad$ $439.00 P&I $\times$ 360 payments = $158,040
$\quad$ $158,040 − $50,000 loan = $108,040 interest paid

15-year vs.
30-year mortgage

Equal Monthly Payments to Amortize a Loan of $1000

Years	6.00%	7.00%	8.00%	8.50%	9.00%	9.50%	10.00%	10.50%	11.00%	11.50%	12.00%
1	86.07	86.53	86.99	87.22	87.46	87.69	87.92	88.15	88.39	88.62	88.85
2	44.33	44.78	45.23	45.46	45.69	45.92	46.15	46.38	46.61	46.85	47.08
3	30.43	30.88	31.34	31.57	31.80	32.04	32.27	32.51	32.74	32.98	33.22
4	23.49	23.95	24.42	24.65	24.89	25.13	25.37	25.61	25.85	26.09	26.34
5	19.34	19.81	20.28	20.52	20.76	21.01	21.25	21.50	21.75	22.00	22.25
6	16.58	17.05	17.54	17.78	18.03	18.28	18.53	18.78	19.04	19.30	19.56
7	14.71	15.10	15.59	15.84	16.09	16.35	16.61	16.87	17.13	17.39	17.66
8	13.15	13.64	14.14	14.40	14.66	14.92	15.18	15.45	15.71	15.98	16.26
9	12.01	12.51	13.02	13.28	13.55	13.81	14.08	14.36	14.63	14.91	15.19
10	11.11	11.62	12.14	12.40	12.67	12.94	13.22	13.50	13.78	14.06	14.35
11	10.37	10.89	11.42	11.69	11.97	12.24	12.52	12.81	13.10	13.39	13.68
12	9.76	10.29	10.83	11.11	11.39	11.67	11.96	12.25	12.54	12.84	13.14
13	9.25	9.79	10.34	10.62	10.90	11.19	11.48	11.78	12.08	12.38	12.69
14	8.82	9.36	9.92	10.20	10.49	10.79	11.09	11.39	11.70	12.01	12.32
15	8.44	8.99	9.56	9.85	10.15	10.45	10.75	11.06	11.37	11.69	12.01
16	8.12	8.68	9.25	9.55	9.85	10.15	10.46	10.78	11.10	11.42	11.74
17	7.84	8.40	8.99	9.29	9.59	9.90	10.22	10.54	10.86	11.19	11.52
18	7.59	8.16	8.75	9.06	9.37	9.68	10.00	10.33	10.66	10.99	11.32
19	7.37	7.95	8.55	8.86	9.17	9.49	9.82	10.15	10.48	10.82	11.16
20	7.17	7.76	8.37	8.68	9.00	9.33	9.66	9.99	10.33	10.67	11.02
21	6.99	7.59	8.21	8.53	8.85	9.18	9.51	9.85	10.19	10.54	10.89
22	6.84	7.44	8.07	8.39	8.72	9.05	9.39	9.73	10.08	10.43	10.78
23	6.69	7.30	7.94	8.27	8.60	8.93	9.28	9.62	9.98	10.33	10.69
24	6.56	7.18	7.83	8.16	8.49	8.83	9.18	9.53	9.89	10.25	10.61
25	6.45	7.07	7.72	8.06	8.40	8.74	9.09	9.45	9.81	10.17	10.54
26	6.34	6.97	7.63	7.97	8.31	8.66	9.01	9.37	9.74	10.10	10.47
27	6.24	6.88	7.55	7.89	8.24	8.59	8.95	9.31	9.67	10.05	10.42
28	6.16	6.80	7.47	7.82	8.17	8.52	8.88	9.25	9.62	9.99	10.37
29	6.08	6.73	7.40	7.75	8.11	8.47	8.83	9.20	9.57	9.95	10.33
30	6.00	6.66	7.34	7.69	8.05	8.41	8.78	9.15	9.52	9.91	10.29

FIGURE 9.1 Amortization chart.

B. $50,000 loan for 20 years at 10% interest
$483.00 × 240 payments = $115,920
$115,920 − $50,000 loan = $65,920 interest paid

C. $50,000 loan for 15 years at 10% interest
$537.50 × 180 payments = $96,750
$96,750 − $50,000 loan = $46,750 interest paid

Partially Amortized Mortgage

The partially amortized mortgage requires periodic payments on the principal, but at the due date, a balance remains because the principal has only been partially reduced. If a loan does not amortize out at the due date, the total unpaid sum is much larger than the regular monthly payment. In some situations the mortgagor may only make interest payments, with the full amount of the principal due at an agreed upon time. This results in a **balloon payment**.

Balloon payment

Balloons are used when the lender prefers not to lend money for a long period of time. The mortgage is generally a 3- to 5-year fixed loan with an amortization schedule of 15 to 30 years. The mortgage holder is under no obligation to refinance the loan, so the borrower must find other means of financing when the balloon payment is due.

Budget Mortgage

A *budget mortgage* requires the borrower to not only repay the principal and interest in set monthly payments, but also one-twelfth of the annual taxes and insurance. This frees the borrower from the expense of paying taxes and insurance in a lump sum when they become due, thus the term *budget* is often applied to this mortgage. Budget mortgages are synonymous with direct-reduction mortgages, as used in FHA, VA, and some conventional loans.

Equity

Difference between value and debt

The **equity** an owner has in property represents the difference between the value of the property and what is owed. A $60,000 property with a $50,000 mortgage represents a $10,000 equity for the owner. As the principal is paid off through the monthly amortized payments, the equity increases. In the early years of the mortgage, the equity build-up is gradual. Since the payments are on the unpaid balance, this equity increases as the loan is paid off. If there is more than one loan, equity is the difference between the total owed and the market value.

Usury

Illegal interest

Interest charged or accepted by a money lender in excess of the amount allowed by law is considered usury and is illegal. Usury laws are not federal laws, but are set by state statutes. With the unprecedented rise of interest rates during the early 1980s, many states placed a **moratorium** on their usury laws, since many were originally lower than the national market for mortgage money. During the first three months of 1980, Congress placed a suspension order on all state usury laws. Designed to protect the borrower from paying excessive interest rates, the usury laws may indeed be a symbol of the past. Some states change the legally allowed rate as interest rates fluctuate.

Discount Points

Discount points are charged by money lenders to increase the yield on the money lent to the borrower. Originally, discount amounts were based on the quality of the property, market conditions, and the ability of the purchaser to borrow and repay. Today the amount is determined by market conditions.

Percentage charges made on new loans

If yields on mortgage loans are lower than yields on other investments, funds will be drawn away from the home mortgage market, and money for home mortgages will become scarce and more expensive. The fixed-rate mortgage lender has to determine the cost of doing business and allow for a reasonable profit to arrive at the yield needed to make the sale of a mortgage at a given discount economically sound.

One discount point is equal to 1 percent of the loan amount. Thus, if a lender charges two discount points on a $30,000 loan, the lender will be receiving 2 percent of $30,000, or $600. This will be paid to the lender at the time the loan closes. While most loans are paid off before the 30-year maturity, a general rule is that each discount point lowers the note rate by one-eighth of 1 percent. So the two discount points in the example would lower the interest rate by .25 percent. As the interest rate increases, the discount points are lower until you reach the market or "par" rate at which no points are charged.

Do not confuse discount points with the *origination fee*. The origination fee is paid by the borrower to the lender for the originating and processing of the new loan and is generally an additional 1 percent of the loan. Both the discount points and loan origination fee are considered prepaid interest and can be deducted on your income tax form.

Origination fee

Loan-to-Value Ratio (LTV)

The lender makes a loan on the property for a proportionate value of the real estate. If the property appraises for $40,000 and the purchaser is putting 20 percent down, the loan-to-value ratio will be 80 percent of the $40,000, or $32,000. Needless to say, the greater the loan-to-value ratio, the greater the risk involved for the lending institution, since the down payment represents the borrower's equity. Mortgages are made as high as 95 percent LTV; however, the borrower must have excellent credit to qualify. The property must appraise at the purchase price. If not, the lender will only loan on 80 percent of the appraised value, and the buyer will need to pay the balance at closing except if a PMI loan is used. However, if the property appraises higher than the purchase price, the lender will loan on the basis of the purchase price. The lender loans on whichever is lower, purchase price or appraised value.

Percentage loaned by lender

The Promissory Note

In real estate financing the borrower signs a promissory note in which the promise is made to pay the specified debt at a stated rate and at a time specified in the note. The note is backed by a mortgage that pledges the property as security for the loan.

Promise to repay debt

The note and mortgage may be incorporated into a single document, but technically they are two legal instruments. The note must state the terms of payment, the due date, and interest rate and sometimes will include a prepayment penalty. Since lenders often sell their loans to the secondary mortgage market, a standardized form is used in all states.

The promissory note shown in Figure 9.2 has no prepayment penalty. If the mortgagor pays the note off before its due date, no charge is made for prepaying the amount borrowed. This may be important to the borrower since the average person

NOTE

__May 15, 1994__ Any City Any State
City State
1040 Clear Street
Property Address

1. BORROWER'S PROMISE TO PAY

In return for a loan that I have received, I promise to pay U.S. $ 67, 200.00 (this amount is called "principal"), plus interest, to the order of the Lender. The Lender is Ready Savings and Loan
I understand that the Lender may transfer this Note. The Lender or anyone who takes this Note by transfer and who is entitled to receive payments under this Note is called the "Note Holder."

2. INTEREST

Interest will be charged on unpaid principal until the full amount of principal has been paid. I will pay interest at a yearly rate of 10 %
The interest rate required by this Section 2 is the rate I will pay both before and after any default described in Section 6(B) of the Note.

3. PAYMENTS

(A) TIME AND PLACE OF PAYMENTS
I will pay principal and interest by making payments every month.
I will make my monthly payments on the 1st day of each month beginning on July 1, 1994 . I will make these payments every month until I have paid all of the principal and interest and any other charges described below that I may owe under this Note. My monthly payments will be applied to interest before principal. If, on July 1, 2024 , I still owe amounts under this Note, I will pay those amounts in full on that date, which is called the "maturity date."
I will make my monthly payments at Ready Savings and Loan, 8250 Alert Dr., Any City, USA
or at a different place if required by the Note Holder.
(B) AMOUNT OF MONTHLY PAYMENTS
My monthly payment will be in the amount of U.S. $ $590.02 .

4. BORROWER'S RIGHT TO PREPAY

I have the right to make payments of principal at any time before they are due. A payment of principal only is known as a "prepayment." When I make a prepayment, I will tell the Note Holder in writing that I am doing so.
I may make a full prepayment or partial prepayments without paying any prepayment charge. The Note Holder will use all of my prepayments to reduce the amount of principal that I owe under this Note. If I make a partial prepayment, there will be no changes in the due date or in the amount of my monthly payment unless the Note Holder agrees in writing to those changes.

5. LOAN CHARGES

If a law, which applies to this loan and which sets maximum loan charges, is finally interpreted so that the interest or other loan charges collected or to be collected in connection with this loan exceed the permitted limits, then: (i) any such loan charge will be reduced by the amount necessary to reduce the charge to the permitted limit; and (ii) any sums already collected from me which exceeded permitted limits will be refunded to me. The Note Holder may choose to make this refund by reducing the principal I owe under this Note or by making a direct payment to me. If a refund reduces principal, the reduction will be treated as a partial prepayment.

6. BORROWER'S FAILURE TO PAY AS REQUIRED

(A) LATE CHARGE FOR OVERDUE PAYMENTS
If the Note Holder has not received the full amount of any monthly payment by the end of 10 calendar days after the date it is due, I will pay a late charge to the Note Holder. The amount of the charge will be .4 % of my overdue payment of principal and interest. I will pay this late charge promptly but only once on each late payment.
(B) DEFAULT
If I do not pay the full amount of each monthly payment on the date it is due, I will be in default.
(C) NOTICE OF DEFAULT
If I am in default, the Note Holder may send me a written notice telling me that if I do not pay the overdue amount by a certain date, the Note Holder may require me to pay immediately the full amount of principal which has not been paid and all the interest that I owe on that amount. That date must be at least 30 days after the date on which the notice is delivered or mailed to me.
(D) NO WAIVER BY NOTE HOLDER
Even if, at a time when I am in default, the Note Holder does not require me to pay immediately in full as described above, the Note Holder will still have the right to do so if I am in default at a later time.
(E) PAYMENT OF NOTE HOLDER'S COSTS AND EXPENSES
If the Note Holder has required me to pay immediately in full as described above, the Note Holder will have the right to be paid back by me for all of its costs and expenses in enforcing this Note to the extent not prohibited by applicable law. Those expenses include, for example, reasonable attorney's fees.

7. GIVING OF NOTICES

Unless applicable law requires a different method, any notice that must be given to me under this Note will be given by delivering it or by mailing it by first class mail to me at the Property address above or at a different address if I give the Note Holder a notice of my different address.
Any notice that must be given to the Note Holder under this Note will be given by mailing it by first class mail to the Note Holder at the address stated in Section 3(A) above or at a different address if I am given a notice of that different address.

MULTISTATE FIXED RATE NOTE-Single Family-FNMA/FHLMC UNIFORM INSTRUMENT Form 3200 12/83

F1046.CTI (10/90) 91-00534 Page 1 of 2

FIGURE 9.2 Promissory note. *(continued)*

8. OBLIGATIONS OF PERSONS UNDER THIS NOTE

If more than one person signs this Note, each person is fully and personally obligated to keep all of the promises made in this Note, including the promise to pay the full amount owed. Any person who is a guarantor, surety or endorser of this Note is also obligated to do these things. Any person who takes over these obligations, including the obligations of a guarantor, surety or endorser of this Note, is also obligated to keep all of the promises made in this Note. The Note Holder may enforce its rights under this Note against each person individually or against all of us together. This means that any one of us may be required to pay all of the amounts owed under this Note.

9. WAIVERS

I and any other person who has obligations under this Note waive the rights of presentment and notice of dishonor. "Presentment" means the right to require the Note Holder to demand payment of amounts due. "Notice of dishonor" means the right to require the Note Holder to give notice to other persons that amounts due have not been paid.

10. UNIFORM SECURED NOTE

This Note is a uniform instrument with limited variations in some jurisdictions. In addition to the protections given to the Note Holder under this Note, a Mortgage, Deed of Trust or Security Deed (the "Security Instrument"), dated the same date as this Note, protects the Note Holder from possible losses which might result if I do not keep the promises which I make in this Note. That Security Instrument describes how and under what conditions I may be required to make immediate payment in full of all amounts I owe under this Note. Some of these conditions are described as follows:

Transfer of the Property or a Beneficial Interest in Borrower.

If all or any part of the Property or any interest in it is sold or transferred (or if a beneficial interest in Borrower is sold or transferred and Borrower is not a natural person) without Lender's prior written consent, Lender may, at its option, require immediate payment in full of all sums secured by this Security Instrument. However, this option shall not be exercised by Lender if exercise is prohibited by federal law as of the date of this Security Instrument.

If Lender exercises this option, Lender shall give Borrower notice of acceleration. The notice shall provide a period of not less than 30 days from the date the notice is delivered or mailed within which Borrower must pay all sums secured by this Security Instrument. If Borrower fails to pay these sums prior to the expiration of the period, Lender may invoke any remedies permitted by this Security Instrument without further notice or demand on Borrower.

WITNESS THE HAND(S) AND SEAL(S) OF THE UNDERSIGNED.

_____(Seal)
Borrower

_____(Seal)
Borrower

_____(Seal)
Borrower

_____(Seal)
Borrower

FIGURE 9.2   (Continued).

changes residence every seven years due to employment transfers, changes in family size, or other personal reasons. The following descriptions match the corresponding numbers on Figure 9.2.

1. Shows the amount borrowed, the name of the lender, and permits the lender to transfer the note. *Elements of a note*
2. Indicates the amount of interest to be charged to the borrower.
3. Provides for the time, place, and amount to be paid.
4. States that the borrower has the option to prepay all or a portion of the note without penalty.
5. Explains that if a law should be established that causes the interest rate to exceed the amount that is lawful, the lending institution will reduce the principal to the amount necessary to meet the new requirement and refund to the borrower any excess collected.

6. Addresses the borrower's failure to repay the note as promised. A late penalty will be charged, and the lender has the right to call the note due and payable in full. It further explains that any costs and expenses incurred by the lender will be borne by the borrower.

7. Any notices given to the borrower will be sent by first class mail to the address stated or to a different address if the lender is so notified of such address.

8. Provides for all the signers (also known as makers) of the note to be jointly responsible for repayment.

9. The borrower waives any rights requiring the note holder to demand payment of the amounts due or to inform other persons that the note is past due.

10. States that the note is secured by a mortgage, deed of trust, or security instrument. The last paragraph gives the lender the right to call the note due and payable if the property is sold or transferred without permission of the note holder.

THE MORTGAGE

Pledging property as security

A **mortgage** is an instrument that pledges the property as collateral for a debt. To pledge property without giving up possession is referred to as hypothecating the property or **hypothecation**. There are two parties to the mortgage—the **mortgagee** and the **mortgagor**. The mortgagee (the creditor) is the person or lender to whom the mortgage has been given as security. The interest can be assigned to another and occurs when the mortgage is sold to the secondary mortgage market as covered in Chapter 8.

The mortgagor is the owner (debtor) of the property put up as security. The mortgagor is also referred to as the obligor and possesses all the rights of ownership but must live up to the terms of the mortgage that has been given to the mortgagee (obligee). The note described above is backed by the mortgage that pledges the property as security for the loan. This pledge gives the lender security while permitting the mortgagor use of the property. If the borrower does not make the payments as agreed, the creditor has the right to seize and sell the property through foreclosure to satisfy the debt. Thus, the mortgagor is not paying on a mortgage but on a note (a promise to pay.) A mortgage note is a negotiable instrument and, as such, can be bought or sold.

The mortgage contains certain covenants that the mortgagor makes to the mortgagee, as shown in Figure 9.3:

Section 1 sets forth the borrowers' names, the amount of the loan, the lender's name, and the street address and legal description of the property.

In *Section 2*, the mortgagors affirm that they have title to the property.

Section 3 explains that the mortgage is an open-end mortgage and that Ready Savings and Loan will loan, at its option, additional money not to exceed 110 percent of the original note. (A section on open-end mortgages appears later in this chapter.)

Defeasance clause

Section 4 is the *defeasance clause*, which states that the mortgage is defeated when the debt is paid in full; that is, when the mortgagors have abided by the terms of the mortgage and the debt has been paid, the rights that the mortgagee held to take the property if the terms were not met have been defeated. However, if the mortgagors do not repay the debt as scheduled in the mortgage, they lose the property to the lender, and their opportunity to defeat the clause is lost. The section further states that the mortgagors must (a) make payments as they are due, or the lender can call the mortgage due and payable. The mortgagors also covenant that (b) they will keep insurance on the property for not less than the loan amount, with the lender co-named as beneficiary. Finally, they agree that (c) the taxes must be kept current, and (d) if the property is sold, the note is due and payable.

MORTGAGE

1
KNOW ALL MEN BY THESE PRESENTS: That <u>Kurt K. Kindly and Susan A.</u>
<u>Kindly, husband and wife</u>_____(hereinafter called the
Mortgagors) in consideration of the sum of _____
_____<u>Sixty-seven thousand two hundred and no/100 ——— Dollars ($ 67,200.00)</u>
loaned to Mortgagors, do hereby grant, bargain, sell and convey unto READY
SAVINGS AND LOAN ASSOCIATION of Any City, USA (hereinafter called
"Ready"), its successors and assigns, the following described real estate; situated
in the County of _____ State of _____ , to-wit:

Lot Eight (8) Block One (1) Confusion Hill Subdivision

2
Said Mortgagors hereby covenant with said Ready, its successors and
assigns, that Mortgagors are lawfully seized of said premises, that they are free
from encumbrances, and that they will forever warrant and defend the title to said
premises against the lawful claims of all persons whomsoever.

3
Provided, nevertheless, these presents are upon the following conditions:
That whereas this mortgage shall secure any additional advances, with interest, which may, at the option of Ready, be made by Ready to the undersigned
Mortgagors or their successors in title for any purpose, at any time before the
release and cancellation of this mortgage, but PROVIDED, HOWEVER, at no time
shall the aggregate principal amount secured by this mortgage, being the amount
due at any time on said original note and any additional advances made, exceed
an amount equal to 110 percent of the amount of the original note, but in no event
shall said note exceed the maximum amount permitted by law.

4
If the said Mortgagors shall pay or cause to be paid the said sums of money
when due, as set forth in said note, then this mortgage shall be null and void;
otherwise, to be and remain in full force and effect;
(a)   If default should be made: in any of the payments due on said note, and
any other note for additional advances made, as therein agreed to be made for
three months, or
(b)   In keeping the improvements on said premises insured against loss by
reason of fire, lightning, and other hazards included in extended coverage insurance in an amount not less than the unpaid balance of said mortgage loan, in a
company or companies acceptable to Ready Savings & Loan, the original of such
policy or policies to be held by Ready Savings & Loan, and with a mortgage clause
attached to said policy or policies, in favor of Ready; or
(c)   In the payment of taxes and assessments levied upon said premises, or
on this mortgage, before they are delinquent; or
(d)   If there is any change in the ownership of the real estate mortgaged
herein, by sale, either outright or by land contract, or by assignment of any interest
thereon or otherwise;

5
then, in any of the above set-forth events, the whole indebtedness hereby
secured shall, at the option of Ready Savings & Loan, immediately become due
and payable without further notice. The amount due under said note and any other
note for additional advances made shall, from the date of the exercise of said
option, bear interest at the maximum legal rate per annum, and this mortgage may
then be foreclosed to satisfy the amount due on said note, and any other note for
additional advances, together with all sums paid by Ready Savings & Loan for
insurance, taxes, assessments and abstract extension charges, with interest
thereon from the date of payment at the maximum legal rate.

6
PROVIDED, further, that in the event that default occurs, Ready shall be entitled to the immediate possession of the premises above described, together with
all rents, proceeds and issues arising out of the premises, and may in its discretion
use the rents so far as it deems necessary to the purpose of making repairs upon
the premises and for payment of insurance premiums, taxes and assessments

FIGURE 9.3
A mortgage instrument.

(continued)

6 upon such premises, and for necessary expenses incurred in renting said premises and collecting rent therefrom, and to apply same on said note and any notes evidencing future advances hereunder until the indebtedness secured is fully paid; and for such purposes, the undersigned does hereby sell, assign, set over and transfer unto Ready all of said rents, proceeds and incomes including any land contract payments due mortgage owners or any other incomes of any type whatsoever from said property to be applied on the notes above-described, but said Ready shall in no case be liable for the failure to procure tenants, to collect rents, or to prosecute actions to recover possession of said premises.

7 The Mortgagors hereby agree that if Ready either voluntarily or involuntarily becomes or is made a party to any suit or proceeding relating to the hereinbefore described real estate, or to this mortgage or said note or notes, other than a foreclosure instituted by Ready, Mortgagors will reimburse Ready for all reasonable costs incurred in said suit or proceeding. The Mortgagors further agree that if the hereinbefore described real estate or any part thereof be condemned under the power of eminent domain, or is otherwise acquired for a public use, the damages awarded, the proceeds for the taking, and for the consideration for such acquisition to the extent of the full amount of the remaining unpaid indebtedness secured by this mortgage, be, and they hereby are, assigned to Ready and shall be paid forthwith to Ready to be applied on account of the last maturing installments of such indebtedness.

Dated this _____15th_____ day of _____May_____ , 19 _94_ .

8 IN THE PRESENCE OF:

_____
Name

_____

_____

FIGURE 9.3
(Continued).

Alienation clause

Section 5 reconfirms that the mortgage will be foreclosed upon if any of the items under Section 4 are violated. Known as the *alienation clause*, it allows the lender to call the balance due and payable upon the sale of the property. It is commonly referred to as the *due-on-sale clause*. This protects the lender in the event that interest rates have risen since the loan was originally placed. If the purchaser desires to assume the existing mortgage, the lender can raise the interest rate. Some states passed into law mandatory compulsion on the part of the lender to permit conventional loan assumptions. However, in July 1982 the U.S. Supreme Court ruled that federally chartered savings and loan associations can enforce the due-on-sale clause, thus superseding the state law. The news media related the ensuing pandemonium that took place in the states where sales were being consummated on the basis of the state's law.

Acceleration clause

Section 6 relates that if the owner does default in payment, the lender can immediately take possession of the premises. This clause, called the *acceleration clause*, is recited in deeds of trust, mortgages, and land contracts. It permits the lender or creditor to declare the entire sum due and payable upon certain default by the debtor. The legality of the call clause, as it is commonly known, has been upheld for loans issued by federally chartered savings and loans.

Assignment of rent clause

This section also provides the lender protection in the event that the mortgagor rents the property and fails to make the mortgage payment. Referred to as an *assignment of rents clause*, this provision states that the mortgagee can notify the tenants that the mortgage is in default and future rents shall be paid to the mortgagee. The lender in this case is called the *mortgagee in possession*.

Section 7 helps protect the lender's rights by stating that if the mortgagor is involved in a lawsuit and it results in expenses to the lender, the mortgagor will pay all costs. This section further states that the mortgagee will be first in line for payment if the property should be taken by the government. (The right of the government to take property by condemnation is called the right of eminent domain.)

Section 8 includes the date and the witness and mortgagor signatures.

Deed of Trust

A **deed of trust** is a conditional deed to secure money for the payment of a debt involving three parties to the instrument. The borrower transfers the property to a *trustee*, who holds it for the benefit of the lender until the debt is repaid in full. Remember, the purpose of a trust deed is to secure the loan. Widely used in some parts of the country, a trust deed is considerably easier to foreclose on than a mortgage. The lender does not hold title, only the *right* to request the trustee to hold a foreclosure sale in the event of a default in payment. If the trustee is not an authorized public trustee, the law states the foreclosure must proceed through the courts in the same manner as a routine mortgage foreclosure (see Figure 9.4). There are three parties to a deed of trust:

1. the trustor: the owner or borrower
2. the trustee: a public trustee; the disinterested third party
3. the beneficiary: the lender

OTHER MORTGAGE CLAUSES AND CONDITIONS

The Subordination Clause

The subordination clause states that the rights of the mortgage holder shall be secondary to subsequent encumbrances. This agreement provides that the mortgage lien will be second in priority to any specific existing or future liens. Since the risk involved to the lender is greater, interest rates on such mortgages are usually higher. For example, a purchaser of an $80,000 parcel of land puts down $50,000 and requests the seller to take a first mortgage of $30,000 with a subordination clause. The buyer needs a $250,000 mortgage to erect an office building. The lender of the $250,000 insists on being first in priority, even though this mortgage is technically a second mortgage. Thus, the subordination clause in the first mortgage clears the path for the buyer to obtain the $250,000 mortgage. The building loan becomes first in line and the lien on the land second.

Interest of holder is secondary

The Prepayment Penalty Clause

The prepayment penalty clause permits the mortgagee to charge a penalty to the borrower if the loan is paid off prior to its maturity. The prepayment penalty protects the mortgagee in the event interest rates decrease; borrowers will not refinance at a lower rate if they must pay a penalty to do so. It also is a form of reimbursement to the lenders for loss of time for interest that would have been earned while they find and approve new borrowers. While FHA and VA loans never carry prepayment penalties, other mortgages may. In times of plentiful money for mortgage loans, the competition dictates that prepayment penalties not be used.

F1029.LM (12/90)

[Space Above This Line For Recording Data]

DEED OF TRUST

THIS DEED OF TRUST ("Security Instrument") is made on _____, _____.
The trustor is _____
_____("Borrower").
The trustee is _____ ("Trustee").
The beneficiary is _____, which
is organized and existing under the laws of _____, and whose address is
_____ ("Lender").
Borrower owes Lender the principal sum of _____
_____ Dollars (U.S.$_____). This debt is evidenced by Borrower's note
dated the same date as this Security Instrument ("Note"), which provides for monthly payments, with the full debt, if not paid earlier, due
and payable on _____.
This Security Instrument secures to Lender: (a) repayment of the debt evidenced by the Note, with interest, and all renewals, extensions
and modifications; (b) the payment of all other sums, with interest, advanced under paragraph 7 to protect the security of this Security
Instrument; and (c) the performance of Borrower's covenants and agreements. For this purpose, Borrower irrevocably grants and conveys
to Trustee, in trust, with power of sale, the following described property located in _____ County, Nebraska:

which has the address of _____ , _____ ,
Nebraska _____ ("Property Address");
     Zip Code

    TOGETHER WITH all improvements now or hereafter erected on the property, and all easements, rights, appurtenances, rents,
royalties, mineral, oil, and gas rights and profits, water rights, and stock and all fixtures now or hereafter a part of the property. All
replacements and additions shall be covered by this Security Instrument. All of the foregoing is referred to in this Security Instrument as
the "Property."

    BORROWER COVENANTS that Borrower is lawfully seised of the estate hereby conveyed and has the right to grant and convey the
Property and that the Property is unencumbered, except for encumbrances of record. Borrower warrants and will defend generally the title
to the Property against all claims and demands, subject to any encumbrances of record.

    THIS SECURITY INSTRUMENT combines uniform covenants for national use and non-uniform covenants with limited variations by
jurisdiction to constitute a uniform security instrument covering real property.

    UNIFORM COVENANTS. Borrower and Lender covenant and agree as follows:

    1. PAYMENT OF PRINCIPAL AND INTEREST; PREPAYMENT AND LATE CHARGES. Borrower shall promptly pay when due the
principal of and interest on the debt evidenced by the Note and any prepayment and late charges due under the Note.

    2. FUNDS FOR TAXES AND INSURANCE. Subject to applicable law or to a written waiver by Lender, Borrower shall pay to Lender
on the day monthly payments are due under the Note, until the Note is paid in full, a sum ("Funds") equal to one-twelfth of: (a) yearly
taxes and assessments which may attain priority over this Security Instrument; (b) yearly leasehold payments or ground rents on the
Property, if any; (c) yearly hazard insurance premiums; and (d) yearly mortgage insurance premiums, if any. The items are called "escrow
items." Lender may estimate the Funds due on the basis of current data and reasonable estimates of future escrow items.

Form 3028 12/83 NEBRASKA Single Family FNMA/FHLMC UNIFORM INSTRUMENT

F1029.LM (12/90)
                                       Page 1 of 4

FIGURE 9.4
Deed of trust.

(continued)

The Funds shall be held in an institution the deposits or accounts of which are insured or guaranteed by a federal or state agency (including Lender if Lender is such an institution). Lender shall apply the Funds to pay the escrow items. Lender may not charge for holding and applying the Funds, analyzing the account or verifying the escrow items, unless Lender pays Borrower interest on the Funds and applicable law permits Lender to make such a charge. A charge assessed by Lender in connection with Borrower's entering into this Security Instrument to pay the cost of an independent tax reporting service shall not be a charge for purposes of the preceding sentence. Borrower and Lender may agree in writing that interest shall be paid on the Funds. Unless an agreement is made or applicable law requires interest to be paid, Lender shall not be required to pay Borrower any interest or earnings on the Funds. Lender shall give to Borrower, without charge, an annual accounting of the Funds showing credits and debits to the Funds and the purpose for which each debit to the Funds was made. The Funds are pledged as additional security for the sums secured by this Security Instrument.

If the amount of the Funds held by Lender, together with the future monthly payments of Funds payable prior to the due dates of the escrow items, shall exceed the amount required to pay the escrow items when due, the excess shall be, at Borrower's option, either promptly repaid to Borrower or credited to Borrower on monthly payments of Funds. If the amount of the Funds held by Lender is not sufficient to pay the escrow items when due, Borrower shall pay to Lender any amount necessary to make up the deficiency in one or more payments as required by Lender.

Upon payment in full of all sums secured by this Security Instrument, Lender shall promptly refund to Borrower any Funds held by Lender. If under paragraph 19 the Property is sold or acquired by Lender, Lender shall apply, no later than immediately prior to the sale of the Property or its acquisition by Lender, any Funds held by Lender at the time of application as a credit against the sums secured by this Security Instrument.

3. APPLICATION OF PAYMENTS. Unless applicable law provides otherwise, all payments received by Lender under paragraphs 1 and 2 shall be applied: first, to late charges due under the Note; second, to prepayment charges due under the Note; third, to amounts payable under paragraph 2; fourth, to interest due; and last, to principal due.

4. CHARGES; LIENS. Borrower shall pay all taxes, assessments, charges, fines and impositions attributable to the Property which may attain priority over this Security Instrument, and leasehold payments or ground rents, if any. Borrower shall pay these obligations in the manner provided in paragraph 2, or if not paid in that manner, Borrower shall pay them on time directly to the person owed payment. Borrower shall promptly furnish to the Lender all notices of amounts to be paid under this paragraph. If Borrower makes these payments directly, Borrower shall promptly furnish to Lender receipts evidencing the payments.

Borrower shall promptly discharge any lien which has priority over this Security Instrument unless Borrower: (a) agrees in writing to the payment of the obligation secured by the lien in a manner acceptable to Lender; (b) contests in good faith the lien by, or defends against enforcement of the lien in, legal proceedings which in the Lender's opinion operate to prevent the enforcement of the lien or forfeiture of any part of the Property; or (c) secures from the holder of the lien an agreement satisfactory to Lender subordinating the lien to this Security Instrument. If Lender determines that any part of the Property is subject to a lien which may attain priority over this Security Instrument, Lender may give Borrower a notice identifying the lien. Borrower shall satisfy the lien or take one or more of the actions set forth above within 10 days of the giving of notice.

5. HAZARD INSURANCE. Borrower shall keep the improvements now existing or hereafter erected on the Property insured against loss by fire, hazards included within the term "extended coverage" and any other hazards for which Lender requires insurance. This insurance shall be maintained in the amounts and for the periods that Lender requires. The insurance carrier providing the insurance shall be chosen by Borrower subject to Lender's approval which shall not be unreasonably withheld.

All insurance policies and renewals shall be acceptable to the Lender and shall include a standard mortgage clause. Lender shall have the right to hold the policies and renewals. If Lender requires, Borrower shall promptly give to Lender all receipts of paid premiums and renewal notices. In the event of loss, Borrower shall give prompt notice to the insurance carrier and Lender. Lender may make proof of loss if not made promptly by Borrower.

Unless Lender and Borrower otherwise agree in writing, insurance proceeds shall be applied to restoration or repair of the Property damaged, if the restoration or repair is economically feasible and Lender's security is not lessened. If the restoration or repair is not economically feasible or Lender's security would be lessened, the insurance proceeds shall be applied to the sums secured by this Security Instrument, whether or not then due, with any excess paid to Borrower. If Borrower abandons the Property, or does not answer within 30 days a notice from Lender that the insurance carrier has offered to settle a claim, then Lender may collect the insurance proceeds. Lender may use the proceeds to repair or restore the Property or to pay sums secured by this Security Instrument, whether or not then due. The 30-day period will begin when the notice is given.

Unless Lender and Borrower otherwise agree in writing, any application of proceeds to principal shall not extend or postpone the due date of the monthly payments referred to in paragraph 1 and 2 or change the amount of the payments. If under paragraph 19 the Property is acquired by Lender, Borrower's right to any insurance policies and proceeds resulting from damage to the Property prior to the acquisition shall pass to Lender to the extent of the sums secured by this Security Instrument immediately prior to the acquisition.

6. PRESERVATION AND MAINTENANCE OF PROPERTY; LEASEHOLDS. Borrower shall not destroy, damage or substantially change the Property, allow the Property to deteriorate or commit waste. If this Security Instrument is on a leasehold, Borrower shall comply with the provisions of the lease, and if Borrower acquires fee title to the Property, the leasehold and fee title shall not merge unless the Lender agrees to the merger in writing.

7. PROTECTION OF LENDER'S RIGHTS IND THE PROPERTY; MORTGAGE INSURANCE. If Borrower fails to perform the covenants and agreements contained in this Security Instrument, or there is a legal proceeding that may significantly affect the Lender's right in the Property (such as a proceeding in bankruptcy, probate, for condemnation or to enforce laws or regulations), then Lender may do and pay for whatever is necessary to protect the value of the Property and Lender's rights in the Property. Lender's actions may include paying any sums secured by a lien which has priority over this Security Instrument, appearing in court, paying reasonable attorneys'fees and entering on the Property to make repairs. Although Lender may take action under paragraph 7, Lender does not have to do so.

Any amounts disbursed by Lender under paragraph 7 shall become additional debt of Borrower secured by this Security Instrument. Unless Borrower and Lender agree to other terms of payment, these amounts shall bear interest from date of disbursement at the Note rate and shall be payable, upon notice from Lender to Borrower requesting payment.

If Lender required mortgage insurance as a condition of making the loan secured by the Security Instrument, Borrower shall pay the premiums required to maintain the insurance in effect until such time as the requirement for the insurance terminates in accordance with Borrower's and Lender's written agreement or applicable law.

8. INSPECTION. Lender or its agent may make reasonable entries upon and inspections of the Property. Lender shall give Borrower notice at the time of or prior to an inspection specifying reasonable cause for the inspection.

9. CONDEMNATION. The proceeds of any award or claim for damages, direct or consequential, in connection with any condemnation or other taking of any part of the Property, or for conveyance in lieu of condemnation, are hereby assigned and shall be paid to Lender.

In the event of a total taking of the Property, the proceeds shall be applied to the sums secured by this Security Instrument, whether or not then due, with any excess paid to Borrower. In the event of a partial taking of the Property, unless Borrower and Lender otherwise agree in writing, the sums secured by this Security Instrument shall be reduced by the amount of the proceeds multiplied by the following fraction: (a) the total amount of sums secured immediately before the taking, divided by (b) the fair market value of the Property immediately before the taking. Any balance shall be paid to Borrower.

If the Property is abandoned by Borrower, or if, after notice by Lender to Borrower that the condemnor offers to make an award or

FIGURE 9.4
(Continued).

(continued)

settle a claim for damages, Borrower fails to respond to Lender within 30 days after the date the notice is given, Lender is authorized to collect and apply the proceeds, at its option, either to restoration or repair of the Property or to the sums secured by this Security Instrument, whether or not then due.

Unless Lender and Borrower otherwise agree in writing, any application of proceeds to principal shall not extend or postpone the due date of the monthly payments referred to in paragraph 1 and 2 or change the amount of such payments.

10. BORROWER NOT RELEASED; FOREBEARANCE BY LENDER NOT A WAIVER. Extension of the time for payment or modification of amortization of the sums secured by this Security Instrument granted by Lender to any successor in interest of Borrower shall not operate to release the liability of the original Borrower or Borrower's successors in interest. Lender shall not be required to commence proceedings against any successor in interest or refuse to extend time for payment or otherwise modify amortization of the sums secured by this Security Instrument by reason of any demand made by the original Borrower or Borrower's successors in interest. Any forbearance by Lender in exercising any right or remedy shall not be a waiver of or preclude the exercise of any right or remedy.

11. SUCCESSORS AND ASSIGNS BOUND; JOINT AND SEVERAL LIABILITY; CO-SIGNERS. The covenants and agreements of this Security Instrument shall bind and benefit the successors and assigns of Lender and Borrower, subject to the provisions of paragraph 17. Borrower's covenants and agreements shall be joint and several. Any Borrower who co-signs this Security Instrument but does not execute the Note: (a) is co-signing this Security Instrument only to mortgage, grant, and convey that Borrower's interest in the Property under the terms of this Security Instrument; (b) is not personally obligated to pay the sums secured by this Security Instrument; and (c) agrees that Lender and any other Borrower may agree to extend, modify, forbear or make any accommodations with regard to terms of this Security Instrument or the Note without that Borrower's consent.

12. LOAN CHARGES. If the loan secured by this Security Instrument is subject to a law which sets maximum loan charges, and that law is finally interpreted so that the interest or other loan charges collected or to be collected in connection with the loan exceed the permitted limits, then: (a) any such loan charges shall be reduced by the amount necessary to reduce the charge to the permitted limit; and (b) any sums already collected from Borrower which exceeded permitted limits will be refunded to Borrower. Lender may choose to make this refund by reducing the principal owed under the Note or by making a direct payment to Borrower. If a refund reduces principal, the reduction will be treated as a partial prepayment without any prepayment charge under the Note.

13. LEGISLATION AFFECTING LENDER'S RIGHTS. If enactment or expiration of applicable law has the effect of rendering any provision of the Note or this Security Instrument unenforceable according to its terms, Lender, at its option, may require immediate payment in full of all sums secured by this Security Instrument and may invoke any remedies permitted by paragraph 19. If Lender exercises this option, Lender shall take the steps specified in the second paragraph of paragraph 17.

14. NOTICES. Any notice to Borrower provided for in this Security Instrument shall be given by delivering it or by mailing it by first class mail unless applicable law requires use of another method. The notice shall be directed to the Property Address or any other address Borrower designates by notice to Lender. Any notice to Lender shall be given by first class mail to Lender's address stated herein or any other address Lender designates by notice to Borrower. Any notice provided for in this Security Instrument shall be deemed to have been given to Borrower or Lender when given as provided in this paragraph.

15. GOVERNING LAW; SEVERABILITY. This Security Instrument shall be governed by federal law and the law of the jurisdiction in which the Property is located. In the event that any provision or clause of this Security Instrument or the Note conflicts with applicable law, such conflict shall not affect other provisions of this Security Instrument or the Note which can be given effect without the conflicting provision. To this end the provisions of this Security Instrument and the Note are declared to be severable.

16. BORROWER'S COPY. Borrower shall be given one conformed copy of the Note and of this Security Instrument.

17. TRANSFER OF THE PROPERTY OR A BENEFICIAL INTEREST IN BORROWER. If all or any part of the Property or any interest in it is sold or transferred (or if a beneficial interest in Borrower is sold or transferred and Borrower is not a natural person) without Lender's prior written consent, Lender may, at its option, require immediate payment in full of all sums secured by this Security Instrument. However, this option shall not be exercised by Lender if exercise is prohibited by federal law as of the date of this Security Instrument.

If Lender exercises this option, Lender shall give Borrower notice of acceleration. The notice shall provide a period of not less than 30 days from the date the notice is delivered or mailed within which the Borrower must pay all sums secured by this Security Instrument. If Borrower fails to pay these sums prior to the expiration of this period, Lender may invoke any remedies permitted by this Security Instrument without further notice or demand on Borrower.

18. BORROWER'S RIGHT TO REINSTATE. If Borrower meets certain conditions, Borrower shall have the right to have enforcement of this Security Instrument discontinued at any time prior to the earlier of: (a) 5 days (or such other period as applicable law may specify for reinstatement) before sale of the Property pursuant to any power of sale contained in this Security Instrument; or (b) entry of a judgment enforcing this Security Instrument. Those conditions are that Borrower: (a) pays Lender all sums which then would be due under this Security Instrument and the Note had no acceleration occurred; (b) cures any default of any other covenant or agreements; (c) pays all expenses incurred in enforcing this Security Instrument, including, but not limited to, reasonable attorneys' fees; and (d) takes such action as Lender may reasonably require to assure that the lien of this Security Instrument, Lender's rights in the Property and Borrower's obligation to pay sums secured by this Security Instrument shall continue unchanged. Upon reinstatement by Borrower, this Security Instrument and the obligations secured hereby shall remain fully effective as if no acceleration had occurred. However, this right to reinstate shall not apply in the case of acceleration under paragraph 13 or 17.

NON-UNIFORM COVENANTS. Borrower and Lender further covenant and agree as follows:

19. ACCELERATION; REMEDIES. Lender shall give notice to Borrower prior to acceleration following Borrower's breach of any covenant or agreement in this Security Instrument (but not prior to acceleration under paragraph 13 or 17 unless applicable law provides otherwise). The notice shall specify: (a) the default; (b) the action required to cure the default; (c) a date, not less than 30 days from the date the notice is given to Borrower, by which the default must be cured; and (d) that failure to cure the default on or before the date specified in the notice may result in acceleration of the sums secured by this Security Instrument and sale of the Property. The notice shall further inform Borrower of the right to reinstate after acceleration and the right to bring a court action to assert the non-existance of a default or any other defense of Borrower to acceleration and sale. If the default is not cured on or before the date specified in the notice, Lender at its option may require immediate payment in full of all sums secured by this Security Instrument without further demand and may invoke the power of sale and any other remedies permitted by applicable law. Lender shall be entitled to collect all expenses incurred in pursuing the remedies provided in this paragraph 19, including, but not limited to, reasonable attorneys' fees and costs of title evidence.

If the power of sale is invoked, Trustee shall record a notice of default in each county in which any part of the Property is located and shall mail copies of such notice in the manner prescribed by applicable law to Borrower and to the other persons prescribed by applicable law. After the time required by applicable law, Trustee shall give public notice of sale to the persons and in the manner prescribed by applicable law. Trustee, without demand on Borrower, shall sell the Property at public auction to the highest bidder at the time and place and under the terms designated in the notice of sale in one or more parcels and in any order Trustee determines. Trustee may postpone sale of all or any parcel of the Property by public announcement at the time and place of any previously scheduled sale. Lender or its designee may purchase the Property at any sale.

—— ——

F1029.LM (12/90)   Page 3 of 4

FIGURE 9.4
(Continued).

(continued)

Upon receipt of payment of the price bid, Trustee shall deliver to the purchaser Trustee's deed conveying the Property. The recitals in the Trustee's deed shall be prima facie evidence of the truth of the statements made therein. Trustee shall apply the proceeds of the sale in the following order: (a) to all expenses of the sale, including, but not limited to, Trustee's fees as permitted by applicable law and reasonable attorneys' fees; (b) to all sums secured by this Security Instrument; and (c) any excess to the person or persons legally entitled to it.

20. LENDER IN POSSESSION. Upon acceleration under paragraph 19 or abandonment of the Property, Lender (in person, by agent or by judicially appointed receiver) shall be entitled to enter upon, take possession of and manage the Property and to collect the rents of the Property including those past due. Any rents collected by Lender or the receiver shall be applied first to payment of the costs of management of the Property and collection of rents, including, but not limited to, receiver's fees, premiums on receiver's bonds and reasonable attorneys' fees, and then to the sums secured by this Security Instrument.

21. RECONVEYANCE. Upon payment of all sums secured by this Security Instrument, Lender shall request Trustee to reconvey the Property and shall surrender this Security Instrument and all notes evidencing debt secured by this Security Instrument to Trustee. Trustee shall reconvey the Property without warranty and without charge to the person or persons legally entitled to it. Such person or persons shall pay any recordation costs.

22. SUBSTITUTE TRUSTEE. Lender, at its option, may from time to time remove Trustee and appoint a successor trustee to any Trustee appointed hereunder by an instrument recorded in the county in which this Security Instrument is recorded. Without conveyance of the Property, successor trustee shall succeed to all the title, power and duties conferred upon Trustee herein and by applicable law.

23. REQUEST FOR NOTICES. Borrower requests that copies of the notices of default and sale be sent to Borrower's address which is the Property Address. Borrower further requests that copies of the notices of default and sale be sent to each person who is a party hereto at the address of such person set forth herein.

24. RIDERS TO THIS SECURITY INSTRUMENT. If one or more riders are executed by Borrower and recorded together with this Security Instrument, the covenants and agreements of each such rider shall be incorporated into and shall amend and supplement the covenants and agreements of this Security Instrument as if the rider(s) were a part of this Security Instrument.

[Check applicable box(es)]

☐ Adjustable Rate Rider ☐ Condominium Rider ☐ 2-4 Family Rider

☐ Graduated Payment Rider ☐ Planned Unit Development Rider

☐ Other(s) Specify

BY SIGNING BELOW, Borrower accepts and agrees to the terms and covenants contained in this Security Instrument and in any rider(s) executed by Borrower and recorded with it.

_____ SEAL   _____ SEAL
Borrower   Borrower

_____ SEAL   _____ SEAL
Borrower   Borrower

_____ [Space Below This Line For Acknowledgment] _____

STATE OF

COUNTY OF   } ss:

I,_____, a Notary Public in and for said county and state, do hereby certify that

_____

_____, personally appeared

before me and is (are) known to me to be the person(s) who, being informed of the contents of the foregoing instrument, have executed same, and acknowledged said instrument to be _____ free and voluntary act and deed and that _____
                  (his, her, their)   (he, she, they)
executed said instrument for the purposes and uses therein set forth.

Witness my hand and official seal this _____ day of _____, _____.

My Commission Expires:

_____ SEAL
Notary Public

This instrument was prepared by:

FIGURE 9.4
(Continued).

The Assumption Clause

*Buyer assumes
existing mortgage*

If a loan is assumed by new owners, the assumption clause in the deed says that the buyers are obligating themselves to pay off the loan. This transfers the responsibility onto the buyers. In case of default, the lender will expect the new owners to fulfill their promise. If they fail to do so, the original owners are still primarily liable since their names are on the promissory note. However, if the sellers obtain a release of liability from the lender, the sellers' obligation ends when the title is transferred. If the clause in the deed states that the buyers are purchasing the property "subject to the existing loan," the buyers acknowledge the existing loan, promise to pay, but are only secondarily liable. Assumption clauses are usually found only in VA and FHA loans.

TYPES OF MORTGAGES

Open-End Mortgages

*Right to borrow
additional money*

An **open-end mortgage** allows the mortgagor to extend the amount of the loan. The loan company has the option of advancing additional money to the borrower at a later date. The borrower may not have taken the full amount that could have been requested at the time the mortgage was initiated, or the loan may have been paid down enough for the mortgagor to borrow more. However, the terms of the mortgage can be changed by the lender if the borrower requests more money. For example, 10 years ago a borrower obtained a $30,000 open-end mortgage on a new home. Inflation has since added $10,000 to the original value of the home; furthermore, the mortgage is now reduced to $26,000. The lending institution agrees to loan an additional $4,000 to the borrower for remodeling. The loan is back to $30,000, the interest rate may remain the same, and the time period of the loan extended back to the original term.

Package Mortgages

The package mortgage is often used in the financing of new homes, since it expressly includes built-in appliances and any such equipment that may be offered for sale with a new home. This may include carpets, drapes, and furniture. The loan includes both real and personal property, so the purchaser is able to finance the equipment over a longer period of time and at a more favorable interest rate than if they were separately financed. This type of loan can also be used to buy a farm and tractor.

Blanket Mortgages

*Coverage of several
properties*

A single mortgage that covers more than one piece of property is referred to as a **blanket mortgage**. Developers of subdivisions often use this type of mortgage and then obtain partial releases as they sell off individual lots. A partial release clause is included in the mortgage so that specific lots can be released as they are purchased. The lender requires a specified amount to be paid on the mortgage before allowing the release of the lots.

A real estate agent may be approached by an individual who desires to purchase a new home but currently owns another home. If the borrower's equity is sufficient, a blanket mortgage might be placed on the two properties. When either home is sold later, it would be released from the loan.

Open Mortgages

An open mortgage is an overdue mortgage that has not yet been foreclosed on. The mortgagee can request payment when this type of mortgage has reached its maturity and is due. The name is derived from the fact that the mortgage is open for payment.

Purchase Money Mortgages

In a purchase money mortgage the seller takes back a note as all or part of the purchase price in a transaction. In some cases the buyer may not have or be able to obtain or borrow sufficient funds to purchase the property. By means of a purchase money mortgage, the transaction is consummated. The seller agreeing to hold a note may have made the difference in making the sale. Purchase money mortgages may be first or second liens. If there is an existing first lien, the purchase money mortgage the seller holds would take second lien priority. It can be a wise investment for sellers if they do not need all their cash immediately. The interest may be greater than the interest the money would earn in a bank.

Seller holds mortgage

Second Mortgages (Junior Mortgages)

A second mortgage pledges the owner's equity in the real estate with the property as collateral. It is second in priority to the first mortgage in case of default. Since it represents a greater risk to the lender, a higher rate of interest is required. Sometimes a seller of real estate will carry back a second mortgage to help finance the new owner. If a buyer has limited cash to invest in a home, the buyer may assume the balance of the existing mortgage, make a down payment, and obtain a second mortgage for the money needed to make up the remainder of the purchase price. The actual interest rate is in reality a combination of the old lower rate and the new second mortgage rate. The combined rate is generally lower than the current market rate on the total amount borrowed. Generally the combined loan-to-value ratio of both first and second mortgages should be less than 80 percent.

Second in priority

Term Mortgages

Not commonly used, term mortgages are for specified periods of time and demand full payment at the end of those periods. As stated under the mortgage payment methods earlier in this chapter, they are not amortized and are issued for only short periods of time, usually three to five years. Builders will use term mortgages since there are no monthly payments and their money is not tied up. The borrower's credit must be extremely good to obtain this type of loan.

Wraparound Mortgages

The wraparound mortgage is two or more mortgages consolidated into one payment. This mortgage may allow the buyers to purchase with a small down payment and the added benefit of a low-interest-rate first mortgage. The sellers receive all of their cash at the time of closing. The lender wraps new money around an existing assumable loan. If in the future the borrowers have the cash available, they could pay off the new money and resort to the original, low-interest mortgage. If the mortgage contains a due-on-sale clause, it cannot be wrapped.

Two mortgages, only one payment

Wrap mortgages are used when interest rates are high, allowing the buyer to take advantage of the lower rate existing mortgage without having to come up with a large down payment as in the case of a loan assumption. The following example will clarify the use of the wrap mortgage.

Assume a sale price of	$80,000	
FHA first mortgage of	50,000	8½%
Seller's equity	$30,000	

The buyers do not have $30,000 to invest; their savings are only $16,000. The sellers refuse to carry back a second mortgage because they need all their equity to purchase another home. The dilemma is solved by the lender who makes wrap loans. The buyer will obtain an 80 percent loan of $64,000:

$50,000	*at 8½% rate (existing first mortgage)*
14,000	*at 11% rate (current rate)*
$64,000	*wrap mortgage*

The $64,000 will be paid back over the same period as remains on the first mortgage. Assume the existing first mortgage is 5 years old, then the amortization of the wrap mortgage will be 25 years.

The buyers are pleased because they receive a less-than-market-rate loan that has only 25 years remaining instead of 30 years for a new loan; if in the future they have $14,000, they can pay off the new money and resort to the underlying first mortgage of $50,000 at 8.5 percent.

In today's market, a wraparound mortgage would only be used when the lender warehouses the loan and does not sell it to the secondary market.

ALTERNATE MORTGAGE PLANS

Most of the alternate financing available is an outgrowth of the tight money market and high interest rates of the 1980s. With the rapid rise of interest, the housing market went into a slump. Innovative and creative financing techniques were developed by lenders and real estate agents to keep homes affordable. This smorgasbord of mortgages meets a variety of needs.

Adjustable Rate Mortgages (ARMs)

Variable rates In the late 1970s the variable rate mortgage became the first vehicle that allowed for interest rates to be moved up or down on home mortgages. This allowed the yield to the lender to be kept close to the market interest rates being paid to depositors. This loan was followed by the renegotiable rate mortgage in 1980, which permitted adjustments every one, three, and five years to correlate with market conditions. The Federal Home Loan Bank Board (FHLBB) sanctioned the **adjustable rate mortgage (ARM)** in 1981, and in 1988 the board set guidelines that must be conformed to in all federal transactions.

Like the variable rate mortgage, the adjustable rate offers protection to the mortgagee because it allows the mortgagee to vary the interest rate in the future. The interest rate may be adjusted up or down depending on the current cost of funds (called an *Index* index), usually one-year U.S. Treasury securities (referred to as T-bills). Thus, with an adjustable rate mortgage, the yield to the lender may be kept close to market interest *Margin* rates. The lender adds a profit margin to the index, which varies from 2 percent to 3 percent. This margin compensates the lender for any risk involved in making the loan and allows for a reasonable profit. If the rate is increased, the monthly payments do not necessarily increase; however, negative amortization is possible. Another way to avoid increased payments is to extend the life of the loan up to a maximum of one-third of the original term. The time will not be extended, however, to a point that would reduce the payments.

Adjustment period The adjustment period is the time during which the interest rate can be changed. Usually this is one year although three or five years also are used. The longer time span is an advantage to the borrower if market rates are increasing, and conversely if rates are declining, the borrower would prefer the shorter time span.

Cap Rate The amount that the interest rate may change is limited by rate caps. Federal law mandates that the lenders reveal the interest cap rate. The periodic cap rate is the amount that the rate may increase at any given time. The aggregate cap rate is the upper limit to which the rate can be raised.

Reverse Annuity Mortgages (RAMs)

In the reverse annuity mortgage (RAM), retired homeowners can convert the equity they have acquired in their homes into cash. The lender pays a net amount over a specified period of time or until a stated event such as death or the sale of the property. This means that the loan increases—an exact *reverse* of the normal procedure of reducing the debt. If the owners sell the home, their equity will naturally be less. Spendable income may be more important than accumulated wealth to the retirees, and the RAM can provide an income stream or a lump-sum payment.

Owner collects payment from lender

With the elderly population growing, the Department of Housing and Urban Development made 2,500 reverse mortgages available to homeowners 62 years and older through their local area lenders. In effect through September 30, 1991, this small amount restricted area lenders to just 50 insured mortgages apiece, too low a level to justify staffing and administrative expenses for many of these lending institutions, and thus they dropped their allotment. To have the program become feasible, expansion of the volume from the 2,500 initial allotment to 25,000 was passed by Congress in 1990.

FHA will insure loans that take any of the three basic payment formulas, plus some add-on features: (1) A "tenure" loan that guarantees the homeowner will receive an agreed-upon amount for as long as the owner occupies the home as the principal residence. (2) Term loans with a definite repayment plan, such as 10 years. (3) "Line of credit" loans, which allow borrowers to take money in increments and frequency as they so choose with a fixed cap on the maximum amount. Additionally, FHA allows lump sum withdrawals on any of the plans. FHA will also insure fixed-rate, adjustable rate reverse mortgages, and the borrower can receive lower rates on loans in exchange for the lender receiving a percentage of future appreciation on the home, thus sharing in the equity. An example issued by FHA was a 75-old person who owns a debt-free home valued at $100,000 can qualify for $810 a month payment on a 5-year, fixed-term reverse mortgage at 10 percent with no appreciating sharing. If the same person extended the term to 10 years, the monthly payments would be $510. Since some of the elderly population are house rich and cash poor, expect to hear more about reverse mortgages for this expanding group of people.

FNMA Rewrites

The FNMA (Fannie Mae) rewrite is used to obtain a new loan, generally at a lower-than-market interest rate if the property has an existing mortgage carried by the Federal National Mortgage Association.

Shared Appreciation Mortgages (SAMs)

With the shared appreciation mortgage (SAM), the borrower agrees to share future benefits with the lender in exchange for a fixed, below-market interest rate. The future appreciation percentage is known as contingent interest, since the money due the lender is dependent upon the property's appreciation in value. The prearranged percentage can reach a maximum of 40 percent of the net appreciated value of the mortgaged property, payable when any one of the following occurs:

Lender shares profit

1. The house is sold.
2. The loan is paid off.
3. Ten years have passed.

If the property is not sold within the 10-year period, most SAMs would require that the buyer pay the lending institution a percentage of the appreciation due. The

SAM program is useful in high-growth areas where home values are likely to escalate in the future. The lender can qualify more buyers because of the lower payments and at the same time receive a potentially higher rate of return than on a fixed-rate mortgage. The lender guarantees the borrower that refinancing is available.

Temporary Buydown

Mortgage bought down for first few years

The temporary buydown is a mortgage differential allowance program that permits the seller of the property to place a percentage of the sale proceeds at closing with the lender in an escrow account. This money is used to reduce the effective interest costs and monthly payments for the first two or three years of the loan. The buyer makes the offer-to-purchase contingent on the seller establishing a mortgage differential account for the purchaser, in the purchaser's name, at the time of closing. The account will have sufficient funds to effectively reduce the purchaser's monthly payment to reflect a lower interest rate for the first few years of the purchaser's loan. The buyer will still be signing the note and mortgage at the current interest rate. In essence, the seller is prepaying interest for the buyer. The differential will be established in a savings account in the purchaser's name with the lender who makes the loan.

3-2-1 Buydowns

The 3-2-1 buydown program offers the buyer 3 percent off the first year's rate, 2 percent off the second year's rate, and 1 percent off the third year's rate. These buydowns may be used with almost any type of mortgage whether it is VA, FHA, or conventional loans. Borrowers will qualify at the first-year rate if they put down 10 percent or carry a 90 percent loan-to-value (LTV) mortgage. The borrower will need to qualify at the end rate on all conventional buydowns if the LTV is greater than 90 percent. The buydown program can also be used in six-month or one-year increments. Buydowns are an appealing incentive but are meeting with disapproval from the secondary market buyers because of the high foreclosure rate.

Blend Mortgages

New money blended with old loan

The blend mortgage is like a wrap mortgage except that if the new money is paid back, the borrower cannot revert to the original first mortgage. It is a "blend" between the existing mortgage rate on the property and current market rates. The purchaser assumes the existing mortgage at a renegotiated rate. For example:

Sale price	$90,000
20% down payment	18,000
New mortgage	$72,000

The existing mortgage is $36,000 at 10 percent. Q-T Savings and Loan will increase the 10 percent by .5 percent to 10.5 percent. The purchaser needs another $36,000, which will be loaned at the prevailing rate of 18 percent. The two rates will then be blended for a total rate of $72,000 at 14.5 percent. Blends are used only when current interest rates are very high.

Growing Equity Mortgage (GEM)

Monthly payments increase

In today's market the growing equity mortgage (GEM) is similar to a graduated payment mortgage without negative amortization and considered second in popularity to the fixed-rate mortgage. GEM's monthly payment for the first year is identical to the traditional fixed-rate mortgage. However, monthly payments increase each year with this increase applying to the principal. This provides for a shorter payment period of 10 to 15 years as opposed to the traditional 25- to 30-year loan. The buyer must be able to afford these increased payments and have a desire to build equity faster. The advantage of this loan is that the borrower saves interest over a 30-year loan and pays back with inflated dollars.

Reduction of the principal is accomplished with the use of curtailments. Curtailments are usually predetermined annual percentage increases in the monthly payments that are applied directly to the principal balance of the loan, generally a 7 percent per year increase in payment. Since these curtailments are applied directly to the loan balance, the mortgage will be paid off at almost twice the rate of a fully amortized 25-year mortgage.

Many growing equity mortgages also provide a temporary buydown option. The buydown amount is placed in a pledged account and used to reduce monthly payments in the early years of the loan.

Construction Loans

Construction loans are used as interim financing. Money is advanced in installments as progress on construction is made. Payouts are usually limited to 80 percent of the loan until final inspection is made. The borrower must own the lot before construction begins. This type of mortgage is advantageous to the borrower because interest is paid only on the amount advanced. The lender disburses principal only upon inspection and when the security has been improved. As a high-risk loan, a construction loan generally does not extend beyond three years, and interest rates are higher than conventional real estate loans.

Construction loan

INSTRUMENTS RELATIVE TO FINANCING

An **estoppel certificate** is an instrument executed by the mortgagor stating the validity of the full mortgage debt. In other words, it declares the exact balance of the debt to the new owner of the mortgage. It is sometimes called a *certificate of no defense* or a *declaration of no set off*. When a mortgage is assigned by the mortgagee to the new owner of the mortgage, the mortgagee must issue an assignment. The person to whom the mortgage is assigned (the assignee) acquires title and interest in the mortgage and note.

Declaring full balance of note

A *satisfaction piece* or a mortgage release is an instrument for recording and acknowledging full payment of an indebtedness that is secured by a mortgage. It means "satisfied in full." It is recorded to show the debt has been paid.

A *pledge* is money kept on deposit with the lending agency. It is held as security for a debt until the extra amount loaned to the purchaser is paid off. The pledge is an interest-bearing account but is technically a "frozen" asset that cannot be removed until the amount specified on the loan is paid. For an example of a pledge, consider a young couple wishing to purchase a home. They have the required down payment but are short in qualifying for the loan. A second party could put up the necessary amount in a pledge account with the lender. A pledge may also be used to avoid monthly payments to the lender for taxes and homeowner insurance. The owner will pay these from personal funds, or the lender will seize the account.

Pledge held as security

An **escrow agreement** is used by the parties to a contract to carry out the terms of the agreement. The parties involved appoint a third party to act as *escrow agent*. This agent should be a disinterested party who will not benefit in any way.

For example, you have just purchased a new home but at the time of closing the carpet has not been installed. The lending institution will hold a sufficient sum back from the builder until the carpet is in place, at which time the escrow fund will be released to the builder. Another example is the loan that requires monthly payments that include not only the principal and interest payment, but one-twelfth of the annual taxes and insurance. This tax and insurance payment accumulates in an escrow account so that the lender can pay the taxes and insurance premium when they are due.

FORECLOSURE ON A MORTGAGE

Nonpayment of debt

If the mortgagor fails to abide by any of the terms of the mortgage, the lending institution may bring **foreclosure** action. Usually foreclosures are the result of delinquent payments. Lenders may attempt to work out another option for payments by the debtor since they prefer not to foreclose. If the debtor sees that he cannot fulfill the commitment to meet the financial obligation, he will attempt to sell the property. Failure of the owner to obtain a sale will result in the need for the lender to foreclose. At this point the lender may pursue two courses of action: foreclosure by judicial or nonjudicial proceedings.

Judicial Foreclosure

Right of redemption

A judicial foreclosure is a court action to cut out the right of redemption the debtor has in the property. In some states after a decree of foreclosure has been entered, the mortgagor may, under certain conditions, obtain a court order postponing the foreclosure sale. The courts give the mortgagor a statutory period within which to redeem the property. Failure of the mortgagor to do so would result in losing the property. This right is known as the *right of redemption* or *equitable redemption*. If the mortgagor has considerable equity in the property, the courts may order the property sold; however, the debtor may pay the delinquent debt up until the property goes up for sale. Usually constructive notice is given by filing notice that the property is in litigation. Any prospective purchaser can conduct a title search and will learn there is a notice of *lis pendens*, a lawsuit is pending.

Junior lien holder rights

Generally, a petition is filed with the court against the debtor and anyone holding a junior lien position, stating the property involved and the amount due. A junior lien holder that is included as a defendant may take the property by redeeming the senior lien holder, and the foreclosure would be stopped. The junior lien holder would want to be certain the property value was sufficient to warrant buying out the first lien holder.

The other course of action for the second lien holder would be to permit the foreclosure and file a *surplus money action*. If the proceeds from the sale are sufficient, both the first lien holder and the junior lien holder will receive payment.

Sale by auction

The sheriff auctions foreclosed property either at the site of the property or at the court house in an attempt to obtain market price. The lender and any prospective buyers will attend the auction. If no bids are made above the indebtedness, the mortgagee will always bid for the property at the balance due on the mortgage, less penalties and legal fees. If a bid is made by a third party for a higher amount than the mortgagee's bid, the mortgagor will receive the amount above the existing costs. A foreclosure sale does not dismiss property tax liens that may be against the property. This is one reason lenders like to escrow for taxes if they are carrying a mortgage with a large loan to value ratio.

Once the foreclosure by judicial sale takes place, the court confirms the price to ascertain that it was fair. If the price was extremely low, the court has the power to set the sale aside.

The successful bidder will receive a sheriff's deed, which will convey whatever title the debtor held, exclusive of the debt. This deed carries no warranties, but title insurance may be purchased by the buyer.

Nonjudicial Foreclosure

In a nonjudicial foreclosure the state permits a foreclosure by *power of sale* providing the mortgage carries this clause. If the debt instrument is a deed of trust, the trustee is normally provided with the power of sale. In that situation once the lender/beneficiary gives proper statutory notice by recording a notice of default, the right to sell the property at public auction exists. This allows for a quick recovery of the property for the lender/beneficiary. Any interest the debtor has is terminated, the property is sold, and the lender is reimbursed from the proceeds of the sale.

In lieu of foreclosure, the debtor may deed the property over to the mortgagee. If the lender/beneficiary accepts the deed, it would bring with it any junior liens that may be attached, which is not the case when the property is sold at auction.

Deed in lieu of foreclosure

The foreclosure procedure on a mortgage was originally designed to allow the farmer sufficient time to harvest crops before losing the right to redeem. These same lengthy foreclosure procedures are a disadvantage to the lender on a residential property. The delayed time period of foreclosure, set by state statute of usually six months to two years, permits the debtor to stay on the property. The mortgage may provide for the appointment of a receiver who is court appointed and would be responsible to collect rents and see that the property is maintained during this period. However, the reader should keep in mind states which use the deed of trust can foreclose quicker.

REAL ESTATE MORTGAGE THEORIES

Title Theory

The **title theory** evolved from the days when the rights of the mortgagee were primary. If the borrower defaulted on the loan, the mortgagee could dispossess the borrower without notice, and all the equity the borrower built up was forfeited. Today the states that adopted the title theory of real estate finance have modified the law with the defeasance clause in the mortgage pledging the property to the mortgagee, and upon payment in full the property reverts to the mortgagor. It further gives the debtor the right of redemption and a reasonable time after default to redeem the property. Title theory states use the mortgage as the security instrument.

The Lien Theory

The **lien theory**, used by most of the states, acknowledges that borrowers retain their legal rights in the property, with the beneficiary having equitable rights. This means that borrowers keep possession and title in their property, while the lender must follow the state's legal foreclosure procedures. Lien theory states use the deed of trust as the security instrument.

Intermediate Theory

Some states have a modified plan of either the title or the lien theory, referred to as an *intermediate theory,* whereby the lender does not have to wait until foreclosure to obtain possession of the property. Title is not turned over, however, until the statutory redemption period has ended.

Deficiency judgment

If mortgagees do not receive the full amount due upon the foreclosure sale, they have the right to enter a *deficiency judgment* against the mortgagor. For example, if the owner has a mortgage balance due of $12,000 and the property brings only $10,000, the mortgagee may request the courts to file a deficiency judgment for the $2,000 balance due.

LIENS

Placing liens on property

Ownership of real property can be lessened by the interest of another party, and while we have covered the mortgage, there are other liens that can also affect the rights of ownership.

A **lien** represents the legal monetary claim held against property that provides the lien holder security for a debt or obligation. Liens are generally enforced by court order when legal action has been commenced by the creditor, and the courts authorize sale of the property to fully or partially satisfy the debt.

Liens are established as either voluntary or involuntary. A *voluntary* lien is created by the property owner, such as a mortgage. It has been contracted by the agreement of the parties. An *involuntary* lien is created by statute, such as a tax lien, and is referred to as a statutory lien. The debtor is known as the *lienee* and the person who holds the mortgage and receives payments is the *lienor*.

Liens may be *specific* (*in rem*) and attach to a particular property, or the lien may be general (*in personam*) and attach to *all* the property of the debtor.

Specific Liens

Specific liens affect only the property they are placed against. These liens can be used to force a sale and include:

Liens that can force a sale

1. The *mortgage* which pledged the property as collateral for the loan.
2. *Property taxes* result in a lien against the property if they are not paid. The majority of states place property tax liens before all other liens, even preexisting liens. If the taxes remain delinquent for the time specified by state law, the property may be sold at a tax sale or by tax foreclosure. Notice is published and an auction held with the successful bidder receiving a tax certificate. The debtor must pay the taxes and interest accrued or permanently lose the property. After the redemption period expires, the person holding the tax certificate will be issued a tax deed or treasurers deed.

Improvement to property

3. *Special assessments* are liens placed against real property to pay for an improvement to the property, such as sidewalks, pavement, street lights, and public utilities. If the assessment is not paid, the governing body within whose jurisdiction the property is located will place a lien on the property. For example, a street is paved, and one property has an 85-foot frontage and the other property a frontage of 95 feet. The properties will be assessed in relation to the front feet and not the value of the respective properties. If, however, a sewer line is being extended into the neighborhood, each of the properties will be equally assessed since they will benefit equally.
4. *Mechanic's liens* are placed upon property without consent of the owner. In most states a supplier of labor and materials may levy a lien against a property for nonpayment of services and material. This includes general contractors, subcontractors, laborers, and materialmen. The lien offers security to those who supply labor or furnish material in the improvement of real property. It is created by state statute and must be filed within a specified time after the work has been

completed. It can only be against that one property upon which the work was performed or to which material was delivered. The mechanic must prove that an express or implied contract existed, and in some states lawsuit action must be taken by the claimant against the homeowner within a specified time or the lien is discharged.

5. *An attachment* may be placed against personal property by a court order and is referred to as a *writ of attachment*. This prevents the property owner from leaving the state with the merchandise. Once the order is issued by the court, the sheriff of the county will seize the property in satisfaction of the debt.

Writ of attachment

General Liens

General liens are broader in scope and are capable of affecting all the property of the lienee, real and personal. General liens include the following:

1. *Federal liens* give the government the authority to place a lien on all of a debtor's personal and real property for failure to pay income taxes. The statutory period for federal tax liens is 10 years. The law permits the government to issue a tax warrant, record it in the federal tax docket in the county records, and attach a federal tax lien. Sale of the property will be made if the debt is not satisfied.

Affect all debtor's property

2. *Judgment liens* are legally determined by the courts as to the rights of the parties involved in the dispute. The party that wins is awarded a judgment stating the amount of the claim. When the judgment (decree) is recorded, it automatically becomes a general lien upon all the real and personal property of the debtor within that particular jurisdiction. The creditor would need to file the lien in other counties to cover the lien in those counties.

   If the lienee does not comply with the judgment order, the general lien holder can file action to force a public sale of the real estate to satisfy the judgment. However, specific liens have priority, so mortgages, taxes, and mechanic's liens will be paid first. If the lienee decides to sell the real estate, all the liens will need to be paid in order to give clear title. A judgment lien is a lien *in personam*, since it is against all the debtor's property.

Lien in personam

3. The *federal estate tax* is a tax imposed upon the estate of the deceased, and it must be paid, or liens can be filed against the property. A federal estate tax is levied against the decedent's estate upon transfer of the property to the devisee. The estate must file an estate tax return nine months after the date of the decedent's death. If unpaid, federal law provides for a general lien to be placed upon the property.

Estate of deceased is taxed

   A person, referred to as the donor, may "gift" a recipient, known as the donee, and the gift tax is the obligation of the donor. No income tax is paid on the gift since it is not considered income.

4. *State inheritance tax* provides for any inherited property to be taxed at the state level. Clear title cannot be issued until payment of the tax is made. A lien will be placed against the property until the tax is paid in full. This is a state government imposed tax upon the heirs, not the estate. If property is held in joint tenancy, the survivor inherits the deceased spouse's half-interest and, in theory, becomes obligated for payment of the inheritance tax, if any.

Tax liens must be paid

5. *Decedents' debts* become general liens against all the deceased assets and must be paid, or a lien will be placed against the real property. In settling the estate, all debts must then be paid out of the proceeds from the sale.

6. *Child support* liens usually just consist of paperwork to clear. The person obligated to pay the support has a lien attached to any parcel of real estate bought. If the child support has been paid, the ex-spouse will sign a voluntary release without having to go to court. If the support has not been received, the party goes to

court to see that the lien is not released, thus preventing the defaulted party from selling the real estate.

7. *Corporation franchise tax* is paid by corporations in accordance with state statute. The tax is based upon capital stock that has been issued or income derived from the business. If unpaid, the tax becomes a lien upon the property owned by the corporation.

A *vendor's* (seller's) *lien* arises from the sale of property financed by a land contract when the vendee (buyer) defaults on payment. The law permits the vendor to place a lien on the unpaid balance. The vendee will forfeit the property along with all the payments made up to the time of default. Many states have a redemption period which allows the vendee to pay any overdue payments in full plus interest due within a specified time limit.

A *vendee's lien* results if the vendor fails to deliver a deed after the vendee has fulfilled his obligation. As stated in the land contract, the vendee can place a lien on the property for all the payments made to the vendor and can also include the cost of any improvements made to the property.

Municipal liens can be placed against property by municipalities that supply water to property owners who fail to pay their water bill or other utility services.

Surety bail bond liens are the result of a bail bond being used to secure the release of a person arrested for a crime. Until the trial is held, the bail bond is surety that the person will not leave the area. The bail bond can be paid in cash or by pledging real property as surety. A bail bond lien will be filed against the property. Upon the person's release, the lien is discharged by the court.

Moratorium   A moratorium is the legal right to delay meeting a money obligation. The lending institution must agree to permit the mortgagors a legal right to delay payment.

Lis pendens means suit pending; it is public notice that a lawsuit is filed against a specific property that may affect the right to ownership of land.

SUMMARY

The many terms and types of mortgages and mortgage clauses relevant to the financing of real estate are covered in this chapter. New creative financing programs surfaced due to the rising cost of home financing and the shortage of funds to lend. Since our population dictates that the market for housing will not diminish, the need for making housing affordable for this generation and generations to follow is imperative.

Among the many creative financing techniques developed in the search for funds is the adjustable rate mortgage. This mortgage allows the lender the option of raising or lowering the interest rate after one, three, or five years. The adjustable rate is extremely popular today.

There have been many changes in the mortgage market. The savings and loan industry had been the mainstay of the one- to four-family home mortgage, and its continuance could only be assured by using renegotiable mortgages. However, with the lowering of interest rates in the early 1990s, less need for innovative mortgage plans exists. Today, the mortgage banker provides most of the fixed-rate mortgages. It is not unusual for borrowers to select 15- and 20-year term mortgages instead of the traditional 30-year in an effort to save interest.

Since competition among lenders of money is high, new marketing ideas and techniques will continue to be presented in an effort to meet the consumer's financing needs.

Liens are legal claims against the property of the debtor and are either voluntary or involuntary. The mortgagor voluntarily pledges the property as security for the debt, whereas an involuntary lien is created by statute as a tax lien. Liens are either specific and attach to a particular property only, or they are general and attach to all the property of a debtor.

DISCUSSION QUESTIONS

1. A borrower is applying for a loan, and while she prefers to extend the payments for 30 years, her plans include repaying the loan sooner. What type of loan should she consider?
2. Explain the difference between an amortized loan and a straight payment loan.
3. Why is a mortgage necessary if the note is the promise to repay?
4. Why would a borrower choose an adjustable rate mortgage in preference to a fixed rate conventional mortgage?
5. Explain the steps in a mortgage foreclosure for your state.
6. Why would a lender prefer a deed of trust to a note and mortgage?
7. A property carries a mortgage of $30,000; taxes of $1,760 are delinquent for two years; and a second mortgage of $7,500 was filed four years ago. Place the debts in the order of their priority.
8. Explain the difference between the title theory and the lien theory. Which does your state use?
9. Explain what a buydown mortgage is.
10. Why do mortgage lenders require property taxes and insurance to be paid in advance along with the monthly principal and interest payments? Is this requested on all types of loans?

REVIEW QUESTIONS

Answers to these questions are found in the Answer Key section at the back of the book.

1. When monthly payments made on a loan are amortized over a period of years:

   a. the debt is liquidated all at once
   b. the payments include both principal and interest
   c. there must be a balloon payment
   d. principal is paid first

2. Discount points are charged by lending institutions:

   a. to make the loan more favorable to the lender
   b. to help the mortgagor with his down payment
   c. because the law requires they be collected
   d. to meet FDIC requirements

3. Under the terms of the mortgage, the mortgagor:

   a. has all the rights of ownership
   b. can automatically assign the mortgage to another
   c. signs a note that pledges the property as security
   d. is the primary lender

4. If the mortgagor defaults on the note:

   a. the mortgagor is given a six-month grace period
   b. the mortgage becomes due and payable
   c. upon a foreclosure sale, all the equity paid belongs to the debtor
   d. an immediate foreclosure sale ensues

5. An open-end mortgage is favorable to the mortgagor because:

   a. the loan cannot be paid off ahead of time
   b. more than one piece of property can be under a single mortgage
   c. the mortgagor may have the option of extending the amount of the loan
   d. the mortgage does not carry a prepayment clause

6. An assignment of rents allows the mortgagee to take possession:

   a. when the mortgage is assigned to another
   b. when the mortgagor defaults in meeting his payments on rental property
   c. if the mortgagor takes a second loan on the property
   d. upon a writ of execution

7. A second mortgage taken on real property:

   a. has precedence over the first mortgage
   b. is usually subordinate to any previously issued mortgage on the property
   c. has priority if it was executed earlier than the first mortgage
   d. is equal to a performance bond

8. The advantage of a deed of trust for a mortgagee is that:

   a. the title is held in trust and the foreclosure procedure is quicker
   b. no second mortgage can be made on the property
   c. there is no advantage
   d. it allows all creditors to file claims

9. Who signs the note that goes along with the mortgage?

   a. mortgagor
   b. mortgagee
   c. mortgagor and mortgagee
   d. mortgagee and assignee

10. Which lien is attached to a specific property?

   a. judgment lien
   b. general lien
   c. federal income tax lien
   d. property tax lien

11. Abigail Jones purchases a home for $90,000. She puts 20 percent down with the balance due over 20 years at 7 percent. Her monthly principal and interest payments are $558.72. What is the amount of interest paid the first month?

   a. $504.00
   b. $420.00
   c. $138.72
   d. $58.72

12. Relating to the above question, what is the approximate amount of interest Abigail Jones will have paid on the loan at its maturity?

   a. $134,092.80
   b. $62,092.80
   c. $72,000.00
   d. $56,984.30

13. The repayment of principal and interest within a specified time is characteristic of a(n):

   a. delinquent loan
   b. amortized loan
   c. accelerated loan
   d. equalized loan

14. The clause in a mortgage that allows the mortgagee to declare the entire sum due upon default by the mortgagor is:

   a. the escalator clause
   b. the acceleration clause
   c. the forfeiture clause
   d. the termination clause

15. The type of mortgage that encompasses more than one property is:

   a. a package mortgage
   b. a wraparound mortgage
   c. a blanket mortgage
   d. a net mortgage

16. This mortgage, though not commonly used, is for a specific period of time and demands full payment at the end of that period:

   a. junior mortgage
   b. direct reduction mortgage
   c. term mortgage
   d. construction loan

17. An act performed by a creditor to receive payment on a real estate loan is called:

   a. redemption
   b. escrow
   c. foreclosure
   d. assignment

18. To charge interest in excess of the amount allowable by law is:

   a. truth-in-lending

b. discount points

c. rent

d. usury

19. Which mortgage allows the mortgagor to extend the amount of the loan?

    a. an open mortgage

    b. a blanket mortgage

    c. an open-end mortgage

    d. a wraparound mortgage

20. A note, as opposed to a mortgage, is a:

    a. lien

    b. personal obligation

    c. second mortgage

    d. judgment

21. On a $45,000 loan at 8 percent interest for 30 years, the interest and principal payment is $330.30. After the first payment, the loan balance would be:

    a. $44,750.00

    b. $44,969.70

    c. $43,785.00

    d. $44,650.00

22. Which permits the seller to subsidize the buyer's interest so that the first few years require lower payments from the buyer?

    a. open-end mortgage

    b. temporary buydown

    c. blanket mortgage

    d. balloon payment

23. Which clause in a mortgage allows the mortgagee to collect rents directly from a tenant when the mortgage is in default?

    a. mortgagee in possession

    b. foreclosure clause

    c. possession by law

    d. acceleration clause

24. Jane Street sold her property for $120,000. The buyer put $25,000 down, and Jane took a note back for $95,000, agreeing to transfer title when the note is paid. Jane holds a(n):

    a. land contract

    b. second mortgage

    c. interim loan

    d. purchase money mortgage

25. What do mortgages and deeds of trust have in common?

    a. number of parties

    b. redemption clause

    c. foreclosure initiation

    d. nothing

Closing Statements

10

OVERVIEW

We have covered the listing, marketing, and financing of real property. The final step in the sale is the closing of the transaction. At this point, title is transferred to the purchaser.

The procedure for closing the sale will vary from state to state. When a sale is handled by a real estate company, the buyer and seller rarely meet. The real estate agent writes the offer with the buyer and presents it to the seller for acceptance (Chapter 7). Once the seller signs the contract, the agent puts into motion the procedures for closing the sale. The sale may be closed through escrow and, in some states, by the real estate company. In other states, such as Illinois, the court has ruled that brokers and salespeople are only authorized to fill in blanks and/or make deletions as required on the preprinted contracts. The licensee may thus prepare the contract for signature but not compose. It is considered unauthorized practice of law to suggest additions and/or give advice or interpretation. The sales agent is also prevented from preparing any subsequent documents, such as mortgages, deeds, a bill of sale, or notes. The law stipulates that attorneys cannot counsel sellers or buyers in which they are acting as a broker or salesperson. In those states the closing is processed by an escrow company.

This chapter explains both closing procedures by escrow, and the settlement prepared by the real estate company. The example of Kurt and Susan Kindly buying a home from Harvey and Della Wender will continue to be followed in this section. We will use the settlement procedures as handled by a real estate company.

ESCROW CLOSING

In some states, the process of title closing is concluded by an escrow agent and is referred to as an **escrow closing**. The escrow agent is a disinterested third party who handles the closing procedure for the buyer and seller. The escrow agent's obligation commences when the buyer's earnest deposit is received and placed in the trust account of the escrow agent. The deed and all papers relating to the sale are delivered to the escrow agent. Escrow closings are most often handled by attorneys, title insurance companies, or the escrow departments of lending institutions. As a third disinterested party, these paid professionals are accountable by law to perform their duties in a timely and accurate manner. In most states the escrow agent represents both parties to the contract, there being no question of a conflict of interest, since the closing is a procedural matter and the decisions of "who pays what" has been spelled out in the purchase agreement. The escrow agent follows the exact instructions outlined in the purchase contract between the buyer and the seller, carrying out all the duties necessary to exact a uniform closing which is finalized when the escrow agent collects the balance of the funds due from the buyer, passes the deed to the buyer (or the buyer's lender), and disburses the funds to the seller. Following this chain of actions results in a paper trail of documentation that leads to the smooth closing.

SETTLEMENT

The **settlement or closing** procedure is carried out by the real estate firm that listed the property. The real estate broker prepares closing statements which are presented to the purchaser and seller when the sale is finalized. The **closing statement** itemizes debits (costs) and credits (assets) incurred in the purchase and sale of the property. The loan papers are prepared by the lending institution, and both the lender and the real estate agent close with the buyer, usually at the lender's office or the conference room of the real estate firm.

Since we have followed the sale of the property at 1040 Clear Street, we will now follow the closing procedure from the time the purchase agreement was accepted by the seller to the culmination of the sale.

If the purchaser needs a loan (the cash buyer is indeed rare), the real estate agent that sold the property sets an appointment with the lending institution and the buyer, thus facilitating the start of the loan processing. A copy of the purchase agreement is given to the lender in addition to any information regarding the property. The lender will complete a loan application on the borrower, inquiring as to income, employment record, assets, and liabilities (see Figure 10.1).

Fees are collected from the borrower to cover the cost of the credit report and property appraisal. In compliance with RESPA, if the loan is federally related, the lender must furnish the borrower with a HUD information booklet and an estimate of the closing costs on the HUD good faith estimate (see Figure 10.2). The HUD booklet is a buyer's guide to settlement costs, explaining home buyer's rights and obligations and standard closing procedures (see Chapter 8).

Lender's responsibility

The lending institution follows a series of preliminary steps prior to setting the closing date. The lender:

1. Immediately orders a **credit report.** The credit report reveals the borrower's past record in paying debts. If the borrower has been slow or delinquent in payments, the lender takes this into consideration while evaluating the risk involved in issuing a loan.

2. Orders an appraisal. The lender's appraiser inspects the property to ensure that the purchase price is not more than the property's market value.

3. Obtains verification of employment from the borrower's employer. A borrower's employment record should indicate that the borrower has been regularly employed and, preferably, possesses a marketable job skill. If the borrower's work is seasonal, difficulty may arise in meeting a monthly payment obligation. Lenders

Form Approved
OMB No.2900-0144

☐ VA APPLICATION FOR HOME LOAN GUARANTY	☐ USDA-FmHA APPLICATION FOR FmHA GUARANTEED LOAN	☐ HUD/FHA APPLICATION FOR COMMITMENT FOR INSURANCE UNDER THE NATIONAL HOUSING ACT	1. AGENCY CASE NUMBER	2A.LENDER'S CASE NUMBER	2B. SECTION OF THE ACT (HUD only)

3A. NAME AND PRESENT ADDRESS OF BORROWER (Incl. ZIP Code)
Kurt K. and Susan A. Kindly
11250 Cherry Blossom Lane
Any City, USA

3B. BORROWER'S SOCIAL SECURITY NO.
515-51-5151

5A. BORROWER: If you do not wish to complete items 5B or 5C, please initial in the space to the right.

INITIALS

5B. RACE/NATIONAL ORIGIN
1 ☒ WHITE, NOT HISPANIC   4 ☐ ASIAN OR PACIFIC ISLANDER
2 ☐ BLACK, NOT HISPANIC   5 ☐ HISPANIC
3 ☐ AMER. INDIAN OR ALASKAN NATIVE

5C. SEX
1 ☒ MALE
2 ☐ FEMALE

4A. NAME AND ADDRESS OF LENDER (Include Zip Code)
Ready Savings & Loan
8052 Alert Drive
Any City, USA

6A. COBORROWER: If you do not wish to complete items 6B or 6C, please initial in space to the right.

INITIALS

6B. RACE/NATIONAL ORIGIN
1 ☒ WHITE, NOT HISPANIC   4 ☐ ASIAN OR PACIFIC ISLANDER
2 ☐ BLACK, NOT HISPANIC   5 ☐ HISPANIC
3 ☐ AMER. INDIAN OR ALASKAN NATIVE

6C. SEX
1 ☐ MALE
2 ☒ FEMALE

4B. ORIGINATOR'S I.D.(HUD) OR LENDER I.D. CODE (VA)

4C. SPONSOR'S I.D.(HUD Only)

7. PROPERTY ADDRESS INCLUDING NAME OF SUBDIVISION, LOT AND BLOCK NO., AND ZIP CODE
1040 Clear Street, Any City, USA
Lot 8, Block 1, Confusion Hill Subdiv.

8A. LOAN AMOUNT $ 67,200

8B. INT.RATE 10% %

8C. PROPOSED MATURITY 30 YRS. MOS.

8D. DISCOUNT AMT. (Only if borrower permitted to pay) $

VA ONLY: Veteran and lender hereby apply to the Secretary of Veterans Affairs for Guaranty of the loan described here under Chapter 37 ,Title 38, United States Code to the full extent permitted by the veteran's entitlement and severally agree that the Regulations promulgated pursuant to Chapter 37, and in effect on the date of the loan shall govern the rights, duties, and liabilities of the parties.
HUD/FHA ONLY: Mortgagee's application for mortgagor approval and commitment for mortgage insurance under the National Housing Act.

SECTION 1 - PURPOSE, AMOUNT, TERMS OF AND SECURITY FOR PROPOSED LOAN.

9A. PURPOSE OF LOAN - TO:
1 ☒ PURCHASE EXISTING HOME PREVIOUSLY OCCUPIED
2 ☐ FINANCING IMPROVEMENTS TO EXISTING PROPERTY
3 ☐ REFINANCE
4 ☐ PURCHASE NEW CONDO. UNIT
5 ☐ PURCHASE EXISTING CONDO. UNIT
6 ☐ PURCHASE EXISTING HOME NOT PREVIOUSLY OCCUPIED
7 ☐ CONSTRUCT HOME-PROCEEDS TO BE PAID OUT DURING CONSTRUCTION
8 ☐ PURCHASE PERMANENTLY SITED MANUFACTURED HOME
9 ☐ PURCHASE PERMANENTLY SITED MANUFACTURED HOME AND LOT
10 ☐ REFINANCE PERMANENTLY SITED MANUFACTURED HOME TO BUY LOT
11 ☐ REFINANCE PERMANENTLY SITED MANUFACTURED HOME/LOT LOAN
12 ☐ HUD ONLY-FINANCE COOP- PURCHASE

9B. TYPE OF AMORTIZATION
1 ☒ REG. FIXED PAYMENT   6 ☐ ARM
2 ☐ GPM LOAN BAL. NEVER TO EXCEED REASONABLE VALUE
3 ☐ OTHER GPM   7 ☐ OTHER (Specify)
4 ☐ GEM (GROWING EQUITY MORT.)
5 ☐ TEMPORARY BUY DOWN

9C. HUD ONLY - BORROWER WILL BE
1 ☒ OCCUPANT
2 ☐ LANDLORD
3 ☐ BUILDER
4 ☐ OPERATIVE BUILDER
5 ☐ ESCROW COMMITMENT
6 ☐ FIRST TIME HOME BUYER

10. VA ONLY - TITLE WILL BE VESTED IN
☐ VETERAN
☐ VETERAN AND SPOUSE
☐ OTHER (Specify)

11. LIEN: ☒ First Mortgage ☐ Other (Specify)

12. ESTATE WILL BE: ☐ Fee Simple ☐ Leasehold (Show expiration date)

13. IS THERE A MANDATORY HOMEOWNERS ASSOC.? ☐ YES ☒ NO (If "yes", complete item 14F.)

14.ESTIMATED TAXES,INSURANCE AND ASSESSMENTS

A. ANNUAL TAXES	$ 1550.00
B. AMOUNT OF HAZARD INSURANCE ON SECURITY	
C. ANNUAL HAZARD INSURANCE PREMIUM	390.00
D. ANNUAL SPECIAL ASSESSMENT PAYMENT	
E. UNPAID SPECIAL ASSESSMENT BALANCE	
F. ANNUAL MAINTENANCE ASSESSMENT	

15.ESTIMATED MONTHLY PAYMENT

A. PRINCIPAL AND INTEREST	$
B. TAXES AND INSURANCE DEPOSITS	
C. OTHER	
TOTAL	$

SECTION II - PERSONAL AND FINANCIAL STATUS OF APPLICANT

16. PLEASE CHECK APPROPRIATE BOX(ES). IF ONE OR MORE ARE CHECKED, ITEMS 18B,21,22 AND 23 MUST INCLUDE INFORMATION CONCERNING BORROWER'S SPOUSE (or former spouse if Box D is checked). IF NO BOXES ARE CHECKED, NO INFORMATION CONCERNING THE SPOUSE NEED BE FURNISHED IN ITEMS 18B, 21, 22, and 23.

A. ☒ THE SPOUSE WILL BE JOINTLY OBLIGATED WITH THE BORROWER ON THE LOAN.
B. ☐ THE BORROWER IS MARRIED AND THE PROPERTY TO SECURE THE LOAN IS LOCATED IN A COMMUNITY PROPERTY STATE.
C. ☐ THE BORROWER IS RELYING ON THE SPOUSE'S INCOME AS A BASIS FOR REPAYMENT OF THE LOAN.
D. ☐ THE BORROWER IS RELYING ON ALIMONY,CHILD SUPPORT, OR SEPARATE MAINTENANCE PAYMENTS FROM A SPOUSE OR FORMER SPOUSE AS A BASIS FOR REPAYMENT OF THE LOAN

17A. MARITAL STATUS OF BORROWER
1 ☒ MARRIED
2 ☐ SEPARATED
3 ☐ UNMARRIED

17B. MARITAL STATUS OF CO-BORROWER OTHER THAN SPOUSE
1 ☒ MARRIED
2 ☐ SEPARATED
3 ☐ UNMARRIED $

17C. MONTHLY CHILD SUPPORT OBLIGATION $

17D. MONTHLY ALIMONY OBLIGATION $

18A. AGE OF BORROWER 38

18B. AGE OF SPOUSE OR CO-BORROWER 37

18C. AGE(S) OF DEPENDENT(S) 12, 9

19. CURRENT MONTHLY HOUSING EXPENSE $ 420.00

20. UTILITIES INCLUDED? ☐ YES ☒ NO

21. LIABILITIES (Itemize all debts)

NAME OF CREDITOR	MO. PAYMENT	BALANCE
Nifty Credit Union	$ 57.00	$ 1500.00
Foster Furniture Co.	45.00	180.00
Visa Card	45.00	300.00

22. ASSETS

A. CASH (Including deposit on purchase)	$ 2,578.00	
B. SAVINGS BONDS - OTHER SECURITIES	10,000.00	
C. REAL ESTATE OWNED	51,500.00	
D. AUTO	11,900.00	
E. FURNITURE AND HOUSEHOLD GOODS	10,000.00	
F. OTHER (Use separate sheet, if necessary)	JOB-RELATED EXPENSE (Specify)	
G. TOTAL $ 85,978.00	TOTAL $ 147.00	$ 1980.00

23. INCOME AND OCCUPATIONAL STATUS

ITEM	BORROWER	SPOUSE OR COBORROWER
A. OCCUPATION	Engineer	Artist
B. NAME OF EMPLOYER	Village Engineer	Facto Art Co.
C. NUMBER OF YEARS EMPLOYED	8	6
D. GROSS PAY	MONTHLY $ 2750.00 HOURLY $	MONTHLY $ 600.00 HOURLY $
E. OTHER INCOME (Disclosure of child support,alimony and separate maintenance income is optional)	MONTHLY $	MONTHLY $

NOTE - If land acquired by separate transaction, complete items 25A and 25B

25A. DATE ACQUIRED April 8, 1994

25B. UNPAID BALANCE $ 82,000

24. ESTIMATED TOTAL COST

ITEM	AMOUNT
A. PURCHASE EXISTING HOME OR CONSTRUCTION	$ 84,000.00
B. ALTERATIONS, IMPROVEMENTS, REPAIRS	
C. LAND (If acquired separately)	
D. REFINANCE (Attach list of debts to be paid)	
E. PREPAID ITEMS	
F. ESTIMATED CLOSING COSTS	
G. HUD MIP OR VA FUNDING FEE PAID IN CASH	
H. DISCOUNT (Only if borrower permitted to pay)	
I. TOTAL COSTS (Add Items 24A through 24H)	84,000.00
J. LESS CASH FROM BORROWER	2,000.00
K. LESS OTHER CREDITS	
L. LOAN AMOUNT EXCLUSIVE OF MIP OR FUNDING FEE FINANCED	67,200.00
M. MIP/FUNDING FEE FINANCED	
N. LOAN AMOUNT INCLUDING MIP/FUNDING FEE	$ 67,200.00

VA Form 26-1802a, FEB 1988
HUD Form HUD-92900.1

SUPERSEDES VA Form 26-1802A and HUD FORM 92900.1, JUN 1985, WHICH WILL NOT BE USED.

Lender _____
Borrower _____

VA/HUD COPY 1

F1074.CTI (02/91)   91-00534

FIGURE 10.1
Loan application for borrower.

GOOD FAITH ESTIMATE

NAME(S):
PROPERTY ADDRESS:

DATE:
DEPOSIT RECEIVED $ __April 19, 1994__

FHA_____ VA_____ CONV _X_ ARM_____ RATE _10.000_ YEARS _30_

This list gives an estimate of most of the charges that you will have to pay at settlement of your loan. The figures shown, as ESTIMATES, are subject to change. The figures shown are computed based upon a sales price of $ _84,000_ and proposed mortgage amount as stated on your loan application of $ _67,200_.

The numbers listed in the left hand column of the estimated settlement charges correspond to the line numbers on the HUD-1 Form which will be used in conjunction with the settlement of your loan. For further explanation of these charges, consult your booklet on Settlement Costs.

ESTIMATED SETTLEMENT CHARGES:

801	Loan Origination Fee _1.000_%	$ _672.00_	903	Hazard Insurance Premium First Yr.		$ _390.00_
802	Loan Discount _____%	$ _____	1001	Hazard Insurance _2_	Months	$ _65.00_
803	Appraisal Fee	$ _215.00_	1002	Mortgage Insurance _____	Months	$ _____
804	Credit Report	$ _45.00_	1003-4	City/County Taxes _5_	Months	$ _645.83_
809	Underwriting Fee	$ _75.00_	1005	Homeowners Assoc.		$ _____
810	Tax Service Fee	$ _____	1108	Title Insur/Abstract & Atty Opinion		$ _159.63_
901	**Interest _15_ days	$ _280.00_	1101	Closing Fee		$ _150.00_
902	Mortgage Insurance Premium First Yr.	$ _____	1201	Record Deed & mortgage		$ _11.00_
			1301	Survey		$ _50.00_
			1302	Pest Inspection		$ _____

MONTHLY PAYMENTS (ESTIMATED):

$ _590.02_ Principal & Interest

$ _____ Mort. Insur. Premium

$ _129.17_ Taxes

$ _32.50_ Insurance

$ _____ Homeowners Assoc.

$ _751.69_ **TOTAL PAYMENT (EST.)**

REQUIREMENTS (ESTIMATED):

$ _16,800.00_ Downpayment

$ _1,377.63_ Closing Costs #801,803,804,809 1101,1201,1301.

$ _1,100.83_ Prepaid Expenses 901,903,1001

$ _280.00_ _15_ days Int. Adj 1003,1004

$ _19,558.46_ **TOTAL REQUIRED (EST.)**

**NOTE: This interest calculation represents the greatest amount of interest that you could be required to pay at settlement. The actual amount will be determined by which day of the month your settlement is conducted. To determine the amount you will have to pay, multiply the number of days remaining in the month in which you settle times $ _____, which is the daily interest charge of your loan.

THIS FORM DOES NOT COVER ALL ITEMS YOU MAY BE REQUIRED TO PAY IN CASH AT TIME OF SETTLEMENT. YOU MAY BE REQUIRED TO PAY OTHER ADDITIONAL AMOUNTS AND YOU MAY WISH TO INQUIRE AS TO THE AMOUNTS OF SUCH OTHER ITEMS.

(2) TRUTH-IN-LENDING DISCLOSURES

ANNUAL PERCENTAGE RATE The cost of your credit as a yearly rate. 10 %	FINANCE CHARGE The dollar amount the credit will cost you. $ 145,207.20	AMOUNT FINANCED The (proposed) amount of credit provided to you or on your behalf. $ 67,200.00	TOTAL OF PAYMENTS The amount you will have paid when you have made all scheduled payments. $ 212,407.20

Your PAYMENT SCHEDULE will be:

Number of Payments	Amount of Payments	When Payments Are Due
360	596.02	Monthly beginning May 15, 1994

☐ VARIABLE RATE: The annual percentage rate may increase during the term of this transaction if the index changes. The "INDEX" is the weekly average yield on U.S. Securities adjusted to a constant maturity of _____ years. Any increase will take form of higher payment amount. If the rate increases by 1% in one year, the payment will increase to _____. The rate may not increase more often than once a year and may not increase more than _____% each year. The rate will not go above _____%.

☐ DEMAND: ☐ This loan will have a demand feature. ☐ This loan will be payable on demand and all disclosures are based on an assumed maturity of one year.

SECURITY: You will be giving a security interest in: ☐ (brief description of the property)

☒ The goods or property being purchased. 1040 Clear Street, Any City, USA

☐ Collateral securing other loans with us may also secure this loan.

☐ Your deposit accounts and other rights you may have to the payment of money from us. FILING FEES: $ _____

LATE CHARGE: If a payment is late you will be charged _4.000_% of the payment, which is $ _23.60_.

PREPAYMENT: If you pay off this loan early, you ☐ may ☒ will not have to pay a penalty.

☐ may ☒ will not be entitled to a refund of part of the finance charge.

ASSUMPTION: Someone buying your house ☐ may, subject to conditions, be allowed to ☒ cannot assume the remainder of the mortgage on the original terms.

All numerical disclosures are estimates (except_____).

You can see contract documents for any additional information about nonpayment, default, any required repayment before scheduled date, and prepayment refunds and penalties.

PROPERTY INSURANCE: You may obtain property insurance from anyone you want that is acceptable to us. If you get the insurance from or through us, you will pay $_____ for _____ of coverage assuming the property has insurable value of $_____.

CREDIT LIFE AND CREDIT DISABILITY INSURANCE are not required to obtain credit and will not be provided unless you sign (a separate form) and agree to pay additional cost. Assuming we lend you the amount financed on the terms stated above:

The cost of Credit Life is $_____ for a term of _____.

The cost of Credit Disability is $_____ for a term of _____.

The cost of Joint Credit Life is $_____ for a term of _____.

BY SIGNING BELOW, I ACKNOWLEDGE RECEIPT OF A COPY OF THIS DISCLOSURE ON DATE OF DELIVERY INDICATED ABOVE.

X_____ X_____ X_____
91-00534

FIGURE 10.2
Good faith estimate.

usually like to see no more than a quarter of the borrower's monthly gross income used for housing. This may vary depending on the type of financing the borrowers are requesting and their total debt ratio. The number and ages of dependents the borrower must support is also taken into consideration, and if the borrower's spouse is employed, it is credited to their ability to repay the loan.

Since the federal Equal Credit Opportunity Act (ECOA) has been in force, the lender cannot discriminate as to race, marital status, sex, or age. Today a single woman or an older person can purchase a home provided she meets the requirements of sufficient income, good credit rating, and employment stability (see ECOA in Chapter 8.)

4. Obtains verification of bank deposits.
5. Obtains a survey. Surveys are often required if the lender plans to sell the mortgage (see Figure 10.3).
6. Prepares settlement statement for borrower.

If the credit report reveals no adverse information—that is, if the borrower's employment is verified as stated in the loan application; if the bank verifies the deposits as stated by the applicant; and if the appraisal is at the purchase price—the lender informs the broker they are ready to proceed with the closing.

The real estate firm that had the property listed then proceeds to carry out the duties for which it is responsible:

1. If there is an existing loan on the property, it must be paid off unless it is being assumed by the purchaser. The holder of the mortgage issues a pay-off letter (reduction certificate) stating the exact mortgage balance.   *Real estate firm's responsibility*
2. Obtains the sellers' signatures on the deed.
3. Obtains a general lien waiver in which the sellers attest that there are no unpaid debts against the property.
4. Orders inspections which may include: (a) a wood infestation report certifying that there is no damage, (b) a structural inspection of the building if it is required in the area, and (c) any appliance and general inspections if requested in the purchase contract.
5. Orders the abstract to be extended or sees that title insurance is obtained. Either the abstract to the property will be brought up to date or title insurance will be issued. In some states this will depend on state law, and no choice will exist.
6. Completes closing statements for the buyer and seller.

As mentioned in item 5, a title search is made on the property either through examination of the abstract or title insurance purchased.

ABSTRACTS

The division of land from the time of the original land grant to the present time is explained in an **abstract** of the property. An abstract is a condensed history of the title. It reveals the "chain of title," listing all the previous owners of the land, along with any instruments affecting the title. The term *instrument* refers to a deed, mortgage, or any legal paper that has been acknowledged (sworn to under oath) and recorded in the office of the Registrar of Deeds.

If an abstract is used, a title search is performed by a bonded abstractor or attorney and extended (brought up to date). The abstractor lists any additional instruments recorded against the property since the current owner took title. The abstract does not guarantee good title; it merely lists the instruments of public record. However, the abstractor is liable if an item of record is overlooked in the search. Once the abstract is

Project No. ___13130___   Location ___1040 Clear St.___

Field Notes:
Found all iron pipe as shown, using SE corner, Lot 1 Old Home estates and NE corner Lot 6 Confusion Hill Subdivision. Established A12' offset line. Checked remaining distance around survey.

LAND SURVEYOR'S CERTIFICATE

I hereby certify that this plat, map, survey or report was made by me under my direct personal supervision and that I am a duly Registered Land Surveyor under the laws of the State of _____.

Legal Description:
Lot 8, Block 1 in Confusion Hill Subdivision, An Addition to Any City, Kent County, _____, as Surveyed, platted and recorded.

Plat to scale showing tract surveyed with all pertinent points.

Signature of Land Surveyor

Date Received: April 16, 1994
Official Address: Yards, Measure & Associates, Inc.
                        11421 Goldenrod Lane, Any City, USA

Bldg. Permit No.:

FIGURE 10.3
Certificate of survey.

brought up-to-date, it is sent to the lender's attorney, who gives an opinion as to the condition of the title, stating who the current owners are, whether their property taxes are paid, and if there are any liens against the property. This certifies the condition of the title and, in some states, is referred to as a *certificate of title*. The buyers also have their attorney check the abstract to certify the title. The attorney for the buyers examines the complete abstract beginning with the original land grant and issues an opinion on the title (see Figure 10.4). *Searching the title*

Certificate of title

TITLE INSURANCE

Title companies guarantee good title by having the title searched, as in the abstract method, and by issuing **title insurance**. After the title searcher sets forth the information on the property, the title insurance company's attorney renders an opinion, and the title report is written and acts as the support for a commitment (binder) to be issued. The title insurance policy states the date the **title search** was made, the owner's name, and the property address. It further states any outstanding liens, mortgages, or easements of record against the property (see Figure 10.5). As with the title opinion drawn up by the attorney who examined the abstract, the title insurance policy states any possible obstacles to clear title, such as: *Insuring the title*

1. unpaid taxes or assessments not of public record
2. unrecorded liens and mortgages
3. repair work completed but not paid for
4. questions on exact locations of boundary lines (proclaiming that a survey should be obtained if there are any such questions)
5. any interest or claims not of public record that the purchaser could determine by inspecting the property and inquiring of the person in possession
6. any zoning restrictions which should be checked

The insurer (title company) inspects the title and validates it to the title holder; the title policy is a contract of indemnity against loss or damage arising out of matters that have occurred in the past rather than what may happen in the future. There are many possible causes of title defects that are not disclosed by examination. If the claim, lien, or defect has never been recorded, it will not appear on record. Title insurance protects against such undisclosed and hidden risks, which could include forged deeds, illegal acts of trustees, guardians, or attorneys, or false claims of ownership. Human errors in copying and recording or the loss or destruction of records could also occur.

Title insurance policies are divided into four main classes. The two types most commonly issued are the owner's policy and the mortgagee's policy.

1. An *owner's policy* is issued to the property owner to ensure good title, guaranteeing the owner of the real property against any title loss or damages suffered as a result of liens or defects in title that were not revealed when the examination of the title was made. *Owner's policy*

   Title insurance rates are not paid annually as with other types of insurance; the coverage runs indefinitely. That is, the insured will be protected against claims based upon the insured warranty of title to successors in interest. However, if the property is sold, the new owners would want to obtain a policy to cover their interest, since the owner's policy is not transferable. The owner's policy is issued for the full purchase price of the property.

2. The *mortgagee's* (lender's) *policy* is issued to the holders of the mortgage because of their interest in the property created by the mortgage. The mortgagee's only concern is to provide security for the loan, so the policy is for the loan amount only. The mortgagee's policy protects the investor for the term of the mortgage. If *Mortgagee's policy*

Righteous, Righteous & Caveat
Attorneys At Law
321 Legal Drive
Any City, USA

May 12, 1994

Kurt K. & Susan A. Kindly
11250 Cherry Blossom Lane
Any City, USA

Dear Mr. & Mrs. Kindly:

We have carefully examined Abstract of Title to the property described as:

Lot 8, Block 1, Confusion Hill Subdivision,
Any City, Kent County, USA

consisting of plat and 103 entries last certified to October 10, 1978, at 8:00 a.m. by Title Services, Inc.

We find the fee simple title to said real estate as of that date to be vested in Harvey J. Wender and Della J. Wender, husband and wife as joint tenants, subject only to the following:

1. A mortgage to Ready Savings and Loan Association dated October 13, 1984 in Book 1670 at Page 314 in the original sum of $47,500.

2. The restrictions shown in the deed at entry 163 regulating the size of any dwelling which may be erected in the addition giving the utility companies the right to install and maintain their lines along the rear lot lines.

3. The first half taxes are paid, in the sum of $775.00. There are no special assessments.

You are required to take notice of the rights of any persons in possession of the premises. Also, whether or not any labor has been performed or materials delivered on the premises within the last four months which might result in a lien. Also as to whether any special improvements have been planned or commenced which might later result in special taxes against the property.

Yours truly,

I. M. Righteous

IMR:rm

FIGURE 10.4
An attorney's abstract
opinion.

the mortgagee assigns the loan to someone who does not see the property, the title insurance eliminates any risk problems. The policy is reassigned by the lender upon sale of the loan.

Also available are the following:

3. A *leasehold policy* insures and protects the interests of a lessee under the terms and conditions of the lease as it would pertain to the property.

SCHEDULE A
Date of Policy

Policy Number	May 15, 1994	Amount	Premium
O-121756-ram	at 2:30 P.M.	$67,200	$319.20

1. Name of Insured

   Ready Savings and Loan

2. The estate or interest in the land described in this Schedule and which is encumbered by the insured Mortgage or Deed of Trust is:

   Fee Simple Title

3. The estate or interest referred to herein is at Date of Policy vested in:

   Kurt K. Kindly and Susan A. Kindly, husband and wife

4. The Mortgage or Deed of Trust herein referred to as the insured Mortgage or Deed of Trust, and the assignments thereof, if any, are described as follows:

   Mortgage from Kurt K. Kindly and Susan A. Kindly, husband and wife to Ready Savings and Loan to secure $67,200, dated May 15, 1994 and recorded May 16, 1994 in Book 2210 at Page 295, Mortgage Records.

5. The land referred to in this policy is described as follows:

   Lot 8, Block 1 in Confusion Hill Subdivision, an Addition to Any City, USA, as Surveyed, platted and recorded.

SCHEDULE B - PART I

This policy does not insure against loss or damage by reason of the following:

1. Rights or claims of parties in possession not shown by the public records.

2. Easements, or claims of easements, not shown by the public records.

3. Discrepancies, conflicts in boundary lines, shortage in area, encroachments, and any facts which a correct survey and inspection of the premises would disclose and which are not shown by the public records.

4. Any lien, or right to a lien, for services, labor, or material heretofore, or hereafter furnished, imposed by law and not shown by the public records.

5. General taxes paid for first 1/2 year. Special taxes or assessments now assessed or levied, but payable in future installments: None certified to the office of the County Treasurer at date hereof.

6. Protective Covenants dated March 27, 1987, filed April 3, 1984 in Book 379 at Page 709 of the Miscellaneous Records of Kent County, USA, shall run with the land for a period of twenty-five years. A five foot (5) easement across and along the rear and side boundary lines of each of said lot is hereby reserved for the construction, maintenance, operation and repair of electric and communication lines and for the erection of poles thereon, with privilege of access thereto.

SCHEDULE B - PART II

In addition to the matters set forth in Part I of this Schedule, the title to the estate or interest in the land described or referred to in Schedule A is subject to the following matters, if any be shown, but the Company insures that such matters are subordinate to the lien or charge of the insured mortgage upon said estate or interest: None.

Issued at ___Any City, USA___   Countersigned by *G. B. Goodwin*
                                              Authorized Signatory

FIGURE 10.5
A title insurance policy.

4. An *easement policy* is used to insure easement interests of the insured over or across a particular parcel of real estate.

The American Land Title Association (ALTA) is a group of approximately 2,000 land title companies who have banded together to promote professional standards and ethics among their members. While some members are both abstractors and title insurance agents, other members only offer one service.

THE TORRENS SYSTEM

Registering the title

Robert Torrens was the originator of the **Torrens System** of title registration. Adopted in Australia in 1857, this system requires that application for title be made by the landowner. A petition requesting initial registration of the title is filed by the owner in the county where the land is located. A notice is published in the newspaper that a hearing of a suit to quiet title will be held before a court of law. All known parties having an interest in the real estate are sent copies of the publication. Once the hearing takes place, the court mandates that the owner has good and merchantable title. The Torrens Certificate of Title System requires *all* deeds to be registered to authenticate legal title. The certificate of title reveals the owner of record and any encumbrances against the title. Similar to the method used in car registration, this system negates the need for a title search when the property is sold. Follow-up evidence of title is comparably inexpensive as no costly examination need be made once the title is recorded. Although approximately 10 states recognize its use, lack of public acceptance has limited more active use of this system.

OTHER PREREQUISITES TO CLOSING

Termite Inspection

In many states a termite and wood infestation inspection requirement is a standard part of the purchase agreement. Our purchase agreement (see Chapter 7, Figure 7.1 at Section G) states, "purchaser, except for a VA loan, agrees to pay the cost of a termite inspection of the house and attached structures, and Seller agrees to pay for any treatment or repair work found necessary. If repairs are found to be needed for issuance of termite warranty, upon completion of repairs, Purchaser agrees to accept said treated real estate."

Structural Inspection

In some areas of the country, structural inspections are required to be performed by qualified inspectors, with the stipulation being made a part of the offer to purchase. Questions of whether the structure is built on solid ground or the soil properly compacted are of concern to sales agents and buyers of homes situated on slopes, hillsides, and newly excavated areas where the soil has been moved considerably. This was the problem faced by the Eastons in the landmark case where the California courts awarded damages to them because of structural problems that arose when the land began to buckle and slide. A standardized disclosure form is now used in California with a checklist of inspections for potential problem areas (see Chapter 7, Figure 7.3).

Appliance Inspection

Across the country there are insurance plans that buyers and sellers may purchase warranting against mechanical defects. The policy may cover electrical, plumbing, heating, air conditioning, and major appliances. This provides protection to the buyer in the event that a costly defect occurs after the sale. Some of the insurers require that an inspection be made prior to issuing the policy.

Homeowner's Insurance

For anyone purchasing a home and obtaining a mortgage, lending institutions require the mortgagor to carry homeowner's insurance. This protects the lender's interest in the property should loss or damage to the premises occur. The borrower must give proof of fire and extended coverage by presenting an insurance binder to the mortgagee at the time the loan is closed. Some lenders will not accept a binder but insist upon a paid policy at closing. The lender will be named on the policy along with the homeowner, and if damage occurs, the checks will be made out jointly to the lender and borrower.

There is a variety of coverage available to the homeowner, ranging from Homeowner 1 (HO-1) to Homeowner 5 (HO-5). The HO-5 policy is the more comprehensive plan covering all possible types of perils, excluding only such catastrophes as earthquakes, floods, war, settling, and cracking (see the discussion in Chapter 7 on insurance and warranties).

Lien Waivers

To ensure the buyers that there are no unpaid liens against the property, the real estate firm may request that the sellers sign an affidavit attesting to the fact that there are no unpaid bills that could result in a lien against the property. This affidavit is called a **lien waiver**.

CLOSING EXPENSES

There are costs involved in the sale for both the buyer and the seller. The parties to the agreement can negotiate who will pay these expenses, and the purchase agreement will clarify who is to be charged. Items that may be expenses of the closing are:

1. *Transfer tax*. Most states have a tax, either referred to as a transfer fee or tax stamps, that is due upon the sale and transfer of the property. As discussed in Chapter 2, this tax is usually paid by the seller, although customs may vary.
2. *Loan fees*. Charges generally made by the lending institution include:
   a. An *origination fee* (also called a service or placement fee) for issuing the loan. This fee is paid by the buyer.
   b. An *assumption fee* if the buyer is assuming an existing loan. This is a buyer expense.
   c. *Discount points*, which are paid at the time the loan is made, are based on a percentage of the loan. They can be paid by either buyer or seller, whatever was agreed upon in the purchase contract. Discount points are considered prepaid interest and are tax deductible if paid by the buyer.
   d. *Prepayment penalty* on existing loan. Some loans carry a prepayment clause that requires the seller to pay a penalty for repaying the loan before its maturity date.
   e. *Mortgage insurance premiums* are charged on some loans. An FHA loan will have an upfront mortgage insurance premium (UFMIP). This will be paid by the buyer at the time of closing or added to the loan. A conventional insured loan levies a fee of 1 percent to be prepaid at the time the loan is closed. It is paid by the borrower.

3. *Recording fees*. Charges are made to record the documents involved in the trans-action, the seller paying for release of the existing mortgage and the buyer paying the cost of recording the deed and usually the new mortgage or deed of trust.

4. *Attorney fees*. If an attorney's services are used by the seller or buyer, they may be charged on the settlement statement.

5. *Broker's commission*. Paid by seller and negotiated between the listing broker and the principal (seller) at the time the sellers employed and listed with a broker to represent their interests. If the buyers employ an agent/broker, they must pay their broker (selling agent) or negotiate a share of the listing broker's commission (see Chapter 6).

6. *Appraisal fee*. The appraisal fee is paid by the person for whom the appraisal was ordered. Usually the lending institution requires an appraisal, and the borrower pays the fee along with the credit report at the time the loan application is taken.

7. *Survey fees*. Usually paid by the buyer unless stated otherwise in the purchase agreement.

8. *Title expense*. If an abstract is being brought up to date, a title search is made, and an attorney's opinion is given. Local customs will vary as to who is charged. If title insurance is being issued, the common practice in many states is to split the cost between the buyer and the seller. In other states, the buyer pays the entire cost.

9. *Escrow account*. Taxes and insurance are collected by the lender on some loans and placed in a reserve (impound) account so that the funds wil be available to pay the insurance premium and property taxes when they are due. Added to the monthly principal and interest payment is one month's insurance and taxes. At the time of closing, the lender will collect enough to establish sufficient funds in the account to pay the taxes and insurance when they are due. For example, if the loan is closed February 15 and taxes for the first half of the year are not due until June 15, the lender will collect for the months of January, February, and March so that six months' taxes will be in the account by June 15. Since interest is paid in arrears, the buyers will not be making a payment until April.

All of the mentioned fees may not appear in the closing statement but are common costs involved in a sale.

Proration

First, let's review the total transaction to date. In Chapter 6, the property owned by Harvey J. Wender and Della Wender at 1040 Clear Street was listed by the A-1 Real Estate Company. A purchase agreement was written for $84,000 (Chapter 7), and the property was purchased by Kurt K. Kindly and Susan A. Kindly on April 8, 1994.

The Kindlys gave A-1 Real Estate Company a $2,000 earnest deposit and signed for an 80 percent loan at 10 percent interest for 30 years. The taxes for the first one-half of the year have been paid by the Wenders. The Kindlys will take possession upon closing, and all calculations regarding who owes what will be figured as of that date, based on a 30-day month. The division of expenses and credits between the buyer and seller is called **proration**.

The purchase contract in Chapter 7 indicates that certain items will be prorated at the time of settlement. Expenses such as taxes, rent, interest, and escrow deposits will be divided according to who received the benefits. If the taxes are paid in advance, as in our transaction, the sellers will receive the portion back that they did not use, and the buyers will be charged. Had the taxes been unpaid, the sellers would pay for the time the property was in their possession.

Proration requires the division of expenses between the buyer and the seller in proportion to the time each has owned or will own the property. Keep in mind that the "user" pays. In some states, the buyer is responsible for costs on the day of closing, and in other states the seller has the obligation up to and including the day of closing.

Prorations usually are computed on a 30-day month, using a 360-day year. However, some areas of the country require a 365-day year, with calculations based on the actual number of days in the month being prorated. All prorated items paid in arrears will appear as debits (charges) to the seller and credits to the buyer.

Items that are **prepaid** (paid in advance) include:

1. *Insurance* policy. When the buyer assumes the seller's policy, the unused portion will be credited to the seller. Most parts of the country require the buyer to purchase a new policy; thus policies are seldom assumed.
2. *Rent*. Rent is always paid in advance, so the seller will credit the buyer commencing the day after closing.
3. *Security deposits*. These deposits were required from the tenant to cover any damage made by the tenant and should be credited to the buyer.
4. *Mortgage interest*. Almost always paid in arrears, thus when a payment is made, the interest paid is for the past month.

Items that are paid in arrears have accrued, have accumulated, and are payable at a later date. Use has been had before payment is made. These items may include:

1. *Utilities*. They will be credited to the buyer since the buyer is the person who will receive the bill.
2. *Mortgage interest*. If the seller's mortgage is being assumed, the purchaser will be paying for the month the seller had possession (interest is paid in arrears); so a credit to the purchaser should be made.

An item that may be prepaid or paid in arrears is *property taxes*. The payment of taxes may vary within a state. If paid in advance, the sellers will receive credit, as they will not be using what they have prepaid for. If paid in arrears, the buyers will be paying the taxes at a later date. Since the seller had the use of the property, the taxes will be prorated and a credit given to the buyers.

EXAMPLES:

1. Property taxes of $2,160 have been paid for the current year. Closing and possession is September 1. Compute the amounts debited and credited to buyer and seller.

   $2,160 ÷ 12 months = $180 a month
   4 months × $180 = $720
   A credit to the seller and a debit to the buyer.

2. Taxes of $1,860 are payable twice annually, April 15 and September 15. Closing and possession are July 15. Compute the amount debited and credited to buyer and seller.

   July 1 to July 15 are used by seller but not paid for
   $1,860 ÷ 12 months = $155 month, ½ of $155 = $77.50
   The seller is debited and the buyer is credited.

Proration is discussed again and examples are given in the math chapter, Chapter 19.

THE PURCHASER'S SETTLEMENT STATEMENT

Figure 10.6 shows a purchaser's settlement statement as prepared by the real estate company.

1. On the **debit** side, the first item shown is the purchase price. Since the buyers owe this amount, it appears as a cost to them.
2. The Kindlys deposited $2,000 as earnest money at the time they entered into the purchase contract. Since it was paid in advance and held in the broker's trust account, it now appears as a **credit** on the settlement statement.
3. The buyers requested an 80 percent loan on the cost of the property. Since the purchase price is $84,000 and the buyers are making a 20 percent down payment, the loan is in the amount of $67,200. *All* mortgages are always a credit to the purchaser.
4. Title insurance will be purchased at a cost of $319.26. In some states this cost will be equally divided between the buyer and seller, representing a $159.63 debit to the buyer. (Keep in mind that some areas of the country may charge the entire fee to either the seller or the buyer.)
5. Bleecher Insurance Company will issue a homeowner's policy for $390.00 per year, effective upon the closing date. The year's premium is payable at the time of issuance, since insurance is always payable in advance and is shown as a debit.
6. The property taxes are paid for the *first half* of the current year, so the buyer will be charged for the amount prepaid by the seller. As per our listing contract in Chapter 6, the total annual taxes are $1,550. This breaks down to $129.17 per month. Since closing and possession are set for May 15, the buyers are charged for one and one-half months of taxes which is shown as a debit.
7. The columns must balance. By adding the credits and subtracting the total from the debit column, we find the buyer will need $15,543.38 in the form of a certified check at the time of closing.

FIGURE 10.6
A purchaser's settlement or closing statement. In compliance with license law, the purchaser receives a copy of the settlement statement at the time of closing. A copy is also given to the lending institution as required by the Real Estate Settlement Procedures Act, and the broker keeps a copy in the office files.

A-1 REAL ESTATE
1104 Homestead Avenue
Any City, USA

PURCHASER'S CLOSING STATEMENT

NAME Kurt K. and Susan A. Kindly   DATE 5/15/94
ADDRESS   1040 Clear Street, Any City, USA

		Debit	Credit
Purchase Price	1	$84,000.00	$
Earnest Deposit			2,000.00 2
First Mortgage-Ready S&L			67,200.00 3
Title Insurance (½ cost)		159.63 4	
Bleecher Ins. Co. (1 yr. Prem.)		390.00 5	
Prorated Taxes ($1,550@ 1½ mo. 5/15/94 to 7/1/94)		193.75 6	
Balance due from Purchaser			15,543.38 7
Totals		$84,743.38	$84,743.38

THE LENDER'S SETTLEMENT STATEMENT

The lending institution will also have a settlement statement for the borrower. In compliance with RESPA, lending institutions use a standard form as shown in Figure 10.7. The costs will vary from region to region and may also vary among lenders in a given location. Since the A-1 Real Estate Company is closing the transaction, the only collection made by the loan company will be under J, number 103: $2,368.46. These costs are the lender's charges in connection with placing the loan.

The statement reveals the following:

1. borrowers' names
2. sellers' names
3. lending institution
4. property address
5. name of the settlement agent
6. place of settlement
7. date the sale is being closed
8. sale price (J is the borrower's summary and K is the seller's)

Proceeding through the borrower's transaction (Section L):

9. This section shows the loan **origination fee** charged by the lender—the $672 charge (line 801) represents 1 percent of the $67,200 loan the borrowers are receiving. The lender's appraisal fee is $215 (line 803), the credit report is $45 (line 804), and the lender's underwriting fee is $75 (line 809).

10. The lender will charge interest on the loan from the settlement date to the next month. The closing date is May 15, so interest is charged from that date to June 1. Many lenders do not request a full PITI payment until the following month (in this case, July 1) so the interest will always be one month in arrears. When the borrowers make their July 1 payment, they would then be paying the June interest. The loan of $67,200 times 10 percent interest equals $6,720 interest per year. This amount, divided by 12 months, equals $560; 15 days (one-half month) equals $280 (line 901).

11. **Reserves** will be needed if the lender is going to establish a reserve account and collect monthly taxes and insurance along with the principal and interest payments. Some lenders prefer to escrow these items to ensure their payment. The yearly insurance premium is $390. The lender will need that amount when the policy is due next May. Since the payments will not begin until July 1, the lender will be short two months, so $65 will be charged the purchaser at the time of the closing so that the full $390 will be in the account when the premium is due, which was paid and shown on the real estate firm's statement (line 1001).

12. The same procedure will be applied to the taxes. The date when taxes are due and payable will determine the amount needed for the reserve account. Assuming the second-half taxes are due and payable August 1, the lender will require five months escrow. Since the yearly taxes are $1,550, there must be $645.83 in the reserve account. In the event the taxes or insurance are subsequently increased, the monthly payments will be raised accordingly. If the taxes were due and payable only once annually, another six months' escrow of taxes would have been added (line 1004).

13. Ready Savings & Loan charges $150 for document preparation (line 1105).

14. The title charge will differ among lenders (and in various areas of the country), so all of the items in this section are pertinent to this particular settlement. If the settlement was handled by an attorney, title company, or escrow agency, these expenses would be noted here. Since the lenders are placing a new loan on the

U.S.DEPARTMENT OF HOUSING AND URBAN DEVELOPMENT   OMB No.2502-0266

A. SETTLEMENT STATEMENT

B. TYPE OF LOAN

1. ☐FHA 2. ☐FMHA 3. ☒ CONV.UNINS. 4. ☐VA 5. ☐CONV.INS.	**6. File Number** 1007-70 **7. Loan Number** 007 **8. Mortgage Insurance Case Number**

C. NOTE: This form is furnished to give you statement of actual settlement costs. Amounts paid to and by the settlement agent are shown. Items marked "(p.o.c.)" were paid outside the closing; they are shown here for informational purposes and are not included in the totals.

D. NAME AND ADDRESS OF BORROWER	E. NAME AND ADDRESS OF SELLER	F. NAME AND ADDRESS OF LENDER
Kurt K. Kindly and Susan A. Kindly **1**	Harvey J. Wender and Della Wender **2**	Ready Savings & Loan **3**

G. PROPERTY LOCATION	H. SETTLEMENT AGENT
1040 Clear Street Any City, USA **4**	Ready Savings & Loan **5** **7**
	PLACE OF SETTLEMENT 8052 Alert Drive **6** **I. SETTLEMENT DATE** May 15, 1994 DISBURSEMENT DATE

J. SUMMARY OF BORROWER'S TRANSACTION		K. SUMMARY OF SELLER'S TRANSACTION	
100. GROSS AMOUNT DUE FROM BORROWER		**400. GROSS AMOUNT DUE TO SELLER**	
101. Contract sales price **8**	84,000.00	401. Contract sales price **8**	84,000.00
102. Personal Property		402. Personal Property.	
103. Settlement charges to borrower (line 1400) **18**	2,368.46	403.	
104.		404.	
105.		405.	
ADJUSTMENTS FOR ITEMS PAID BY SELLER IN ADVANCE		*ADJUSTMENTS FOR ITEMS PAID BY SELLER IN ADVANCE*	
106. City/Town taxes to		406. City/Town taxes to	
107. County taxes to		407. County taxes to	
108. Assessments to		408. Assessments to	
109. Real Estate Taxes **19**	193.75	409. Real Estate Taxes 5/18-7/1	193.75
110.		410.	
111.		411.	
112.		412.	
120. GROSS AMOUNT DUE FROM BORROWER **20**	86,562.21	**420. GROSS AMOUNT DUE TO SELLER** **28**	84,193.75
200. AMOUNTS PAID BY OR IN BEHALF OF BORROWER		**500. REDUCTIONS IN AMOUNT DUE TO SELLER**	
201. Deposit or earnest money	2,000.00	501. Excess Deposit (see instructions)	
202. Principal amount of new loan(s)	67,200.00	502. Settlement charges to seller (line 1400) **29**	6,171.13
203. Existing loan(s) taken subject to		503. Existing loan(s) taken subject to	
204. Application deposit		504. Payoff of first mortgage loan **30**	45,320.10
205. Second lien mortgage		505. Payoff of second mortgage loan	
206.		506.	
207.		507.	
208.		508.	
209.		509.	
ADJUSTMENTS FOR ITEMS UNPAID BY SELLER		*ADJUSTMENTS FOR ITEMS UNPAID BY SELLER*	
210. City/Town taxes to		510. City/Town taxes to	
211. County taxes to		511. County taxes to	
212. Assessments to		512. Assessments to	
213.		513.	
214.		514.	
215.		515.	
216.		516.	
217.		517.	
218.		518.	
219.		519.	
220. TOTAL PAID BY/FOR BORROWER **21**	69,200.00	**520. TOTAL REDUCTION AMOUNT DUE SELLER** **31**	51,491.23
300. CASH AT SETTLEMENT FROM OR TO BORROWER		**600. CASH AT SETTLEMENT TO OR FROM SELLER**	
301. Gross amount due from borrower (line 120)	86,646.21	601. Gross amount due to seller (line 420)	84,193.75
302. Less amounts paid by/for borrower (line 220) **22**	(69,200.00)	602. Less reduction amount due seller (line 520) **32**	( )
303. CASH ☒ FROM ☐ TO BORROWER	17,446.21	603. CASH ☒ TO ☐ FROM SELLER	32,702.52

I have carefully reviewed the HUD-1 Settlement Statement and to the best of my knowledge and belief, it is a true and accurate statement of all receipts and disbursements made on my account or by me in this transaction. I further certify that I have received a copy of the HUD-1 Settlement Statement.

Kurt K. Kindly
Susan A. Kindly
Borrowers

Harvey J. Wender
Della G. Wender
Sellers

To the best of my knowledge, the HUD-1 Settlement Statement which I have prepared is a true and accurate account of the funds which were received and have been or will be disbursed by the undersigned as part of this transaction.

Settlement Agent   Date

WARNING: It is a crime to knowingly make false statements to the United States on this or any other similar form. Penalties upon conviction can include a fine and imprisonment. For details see: Title 18 U. S. Code Section 1001 and Section 1010.

Previous Edition is Obsolete
F2366.CTI (03/91)   91-00534   HUD-1 (07-87) RESPA, HB 4305.2

FIGURE 10.7
The lender's settlement statement.

(continued)

U.S. DEPARTMENT OF HOUSING AND URBAN DEVELOPMENT
SETTLEMENT STATEMENT
Page 2

L. SETTLEMENT CHARGES	PAID FROM BORROWER'S FUNDS AT SETTLEMENT	PAID FROM SELLER'S FUNDS AT SETTLEMENT
700. TOTAL SALES/BROKER'S COMMISSION(based on price)		
Division of commission (line 700) as follows: $ @ %=		
701. $ to A-1 Real Estate		
702. $ to		
703. Commission paid at Settlement	23	5,880.00
704.		
800. ITEMS PAYABLE IN CONNECTION WITH LOAN		
801. Loan Origination Fee 1.000 %	672.00	
802. Loan Discount %		
803. Appraisal Fee to Tower Appraisers	215.00	
804. Credit Report to Landow Credit Bureau	45.00	
805. Lender's Inspection Fee		
806. VA Funding Fee to 9		
807. Assumption Fee		
808.		
809. Lenders Underwriting Fee	75.00	
810.		
811.		
900. ITEMS REQUIRED BY LENDER TO BE PAID IN ADVANCE		
901. Interest from 5-15 to 6-1 @ $ 24.25x15 /day 10	280.00	
902. Mortgage Insurance Premuim for mos. to		
903. Hazard Insurance Premium for yrs. to (paid through Real		
904. yrs. to Estate Firm)		
905.		
1000. RESERVES DEPOSITED WITH LENDER FOR		
1001. Hazard Insurance 2 mos. @ $ 32.50 /mo. 11	65.00	
1002. Mortgage Insurance mos.@ $ /mo.		
1003. City Property Taxes mos. @ $ /mo.		
1004. County Property Taxes 5 mos. @ $127.17 /mo. 12	645.83	
1005. Annual Assessments mos. @ $ /mo.		
1006. mos. @ $ /mo.		
1007. mos. @ $ /mo.		
1008. mos. @ $ /mo.		
1100. TITLE CHARGES		
1101. Settlement or Closing Fee to		
1102. Abstract or Title Search to		
1103. Title Examination to		
1104. Title Insurance Binder to		
1105. Document Preparation to Ready Savings & Loan 13	150.00	
1106. Notary Fees to		
1107. Attorney's Fees to		
(includes above Items No.:)		
1108. Title Insurance to Security Title Co. 14	159.63	159.63 24
(includes above Items No.:)		
1109. Lender's Coverage $ 67,200.00		
1110. Owner's Coverage $ 84,000.00		
1111.		
1112.		
1113.		
1200. GOVERNMENT RECORDING AND TRANSFER CHARGES		
1201. Recording Fees: Deed $ 5.50 ; Mortgage $ 5.50 ; Release $ 5.50 15	11.00	5.50 25
1202. City/County tax/stamps: Deed $; Mortgage $		
1203. State tax/stamps: Deed $ 126.00 ; Mortgage $		126.00 26
1204.		
1205.		
1300. ADDITIONAL SETTLEMENT CHARGES		
1301. Survey to Grand Vista Surveyors 16	50.00	
1302. Pest Inspection to		
1303.		
1304.		
1305. 17		
1400. TOTAL SETTLEMENT CHARGES (enter on line 103, Section J and line 502, Section K)	2,368.46	6,171.13 27

The Undersigned Acknowledges Receipt of This Settlement Statement and Agrees to the Correctness Thereof.

Buyer _____   Seller _____

Buyer _____   Seller _____

Date _____

HUD-1B Settlement Statement
F2367.CTl (11/90)   91-00534

FIGURE 10.7
(Continued).

property, they are also servicing the customer by handling the closing transaction. One-half of the title costs ($159.63) are charged to the borrower (line 1108).

15. The recording fees include $5.50 for recording the buyer's deed and another $5.50 for recording the buyer's mortgage (line 1201).

16. The survey fee of $50 is entered on line 1301.

17–18. The gross amount due from the borrower is entered on line 1400 and carried back to number 18 (line 103) under Section J on page 1 of the settlement statement.

19. The buyer's tax cost is credited to the seller on line 409. In this instance, the seller prepaid taxes, thus the buyer will reimburse the seller for the unused portion, as shown on line 109.

20. The amount due from the borrower is entered on line 120, and the credits of the earnest deposit and the loan that will be issued are on line 201 and 202.

21. The total credits (lines 201 and 202) in the amount of $69,200 to the borrower is entered on line 220.

22. The difference between line 301 (costs) and line 302 (credits) is recorded, and the total amount due from the borrower of $17,446.21 is shown on line 303.

Upon closing with the buyer, the deed will be passed to the lender, who will record the deed and the mortgage (see Chapter 9, Figure 9.3). Now let's proceed through the seller's closing costs on page 2 of the settlement statement in the right hand column under section L.

23. If two brokerage firms had been involved in the sale, one firm listing the property and another firm selling it, the division of commission might be shown. In this instance, A-1 Real Estate handled both the listing and the sale, so the sum of $5,880 is shown on line 703.

24. The sellers are charged half of the title insurance on line 1108.

25. The sellers are charged $5.50 for release of their mortgage on line 1201.

26. The state transfer tax is generally paid by the sellers and will vary from state to state. In this example, it is payable on the full sales price at $1.50 per $1,000 ($1.50 times $84,000 equals $126) (line 1203).

27. The total charged to seller, $6,171.13, is shown on line 1400.

28. Returning to page 1, under the K column, the selling price of $84,000 is shown at number 8 (line 401) of the seller's summary. This figure, added to the $193.75 tax credit, is brought down to number 28 (line 420).

29. The settlement charges of $6,171.13 due from the seller are brought forward from number 27 (line 1400 to line 502).

30. The amount of $45,320.10 due on the first mortgage, which will be paid off, is listed on line 504.

31. The costs in numbers 29 and 30 are totaled on line 520.

32. The balance due to the seller is entered on line 603. The $32,702.52 represents the difference between the debits at number 31 and the sale price of $84,000 and the tax credit of $193.75 totaling $84,193.75 at line 601. This sum must balance with the real estate firm's statement (see Figure 10.8).

THE SELLER'S SETTLEMENT STATEMENT

Now let's proceed to the analysis of the seller's statement as prepared by A-1 Real Estate (Figure 10.8). When the real estate broker delivers the proceeds from the sale to the seller, he also presents the closing statement, showing all disbursements. These include the following:

A-1 REAL ESTATE
1104 Homestead Avenue
Any City, USA

SELLER'S CLOSING STATEMENT

NAME Harvey J. and Della Wender _____ DATE 5/15/94 _____

ADDRESS 1040 Clear Street, Any City, USA _____

	Debit	Credit
Selling Price	$	$84,000.00 [1]
Title Insurance	159.63 [5]	
State Transfer Tax		
$1.50 per 1,000	126.00 [4]	
Mortgage Release	5.50 [3]	
Balance of First Mortgage		
Ready S & L	45,320.10 [2]	
Prorated Taxes ($1,550 @ 1½ mo.		
5/15/94 to 7/1/94)		193.75 [6]
Professional Services Fee (7%)	5,880.00 [7]	
Balance due to Seller, Proceeds	32,702.52 [8]	
Totals	$84,193.75	$84,193.75

FIGURE 10.8
The seller's closing statement.

1. The selling price (a *credit* to the owner).
2. The mortgage balance of $45,320.10, which appears as a *debit* since it is owed by the seller.
3. The charge (debit) of the release of the mortgage. This is filed at the county courthouse to prove the note has been paid in full and the mortgage is no longer a lien on the property.
4. The state transfer tax, as previously explained, is based on the rate of $1.50 per $1,000 of the sale price. This rate will vary from state to state, and is generally paid for by the grantor.
5. The cost of one-half of the title insurance is $159.63.
6. The prorated taxes are a credit, since the first half are paid and the buyers will reimburse the owner for the unused portion. Keep in mind that the person who has the use of the property will be expected to pay the taxes.
7. The brokerage fee of 7 percent is based on the gross sales price of $84,000, so we debit the seller $5,880.
8. The amount of $32,702.52 is the sum due the seller as proceeds from the sale. This figure was arrived at by totaling the credit side, which shows the $84,000 sale price and the tax proration of $193.75, and subtracting the debit column from the credits.

At the time the new loan (for the buyers) closes with the lending institution, the broker gives the lender a copy of the seller's closing statement.

SUMMARY

This chapter furnishes invaluable information on the closing of the transaction. The steps taken prior to the actual closing are reviewed, with the lending institution's responsibility defined. Numerous documents used in the preparation of the closing are

A-1 REAL ESTATE COMPANY
TRUST ACCOUNT BALANCE SHEET

Wender, H.

Kindly, K.

1040 Clear Street, Any City, USA

Date	Name	Ck#		Credit	Balance
1/20/XX	Kurt A. Kindly and Susan A. Kindly		$	$ 2,000.00	$ 2,000.00
5/15/XX	Balance due from K. Kindly			15,543.38	17,543.38
5/15/XX	Proceeds from Ready Savings and Loan			21,874.40*	39,417.78
5/15/XX	Best Title Company	441	319.26		39,098.52
5/15/XX	Bleecher Insurance Co.	442	390.00		38,708.52
5/15/XX	Register of Deeds	443	126.00		38,582.52
5/15/XX	H. Wender and D. Wender Proceeds from Sale	444	32,702.52		5,880.00
5/15/XX	A-1 Real Estate Co.	445	5,880.00		–0–

The balance sheet from A-1 Real Estate Company Trust Account is completed as shown. This ledger sheet shows the receipts and disbursements for this sale.

*The proceeds from Ready Savings and Loan to A-1 Real Estate represent the difference between the existing loan of $45,320.10 and the new loan of $67,200, minus the $5.50 deduction to record the release of the old mortgage.

The last check written will be to the real estate company for their brokerage fee due. It will be placed in the firm's business account and from there will be paid to the salesperson(s) involved in the listing and sale of the property.

FIGURE 10.9
A trust account
balance sheet.

included, and the closing statement the lender completes for the buyer as required by federal law is evaluated step by step.

The real estate firm's obligation in preparing the settlement statement is reviewed, with a detailed accounting for both buyer and seller. Real estate firms need to maintain accurate records, so a ledger sheet revealing the disbursements from the trust account is also included in this chapter.

DISCUSSION QUESTIONS

1. Explain the difference between an escrow closing and a settlement closing.
2. Why is it necessary to have both a lender's closing statement and a statement from the closing department of the real estate firm or the escrow company?
3. Explain the three methods used in determining the condition of the title.
4. Explain prorating of the costs and why it is performed.
5. Who purchases title insurance and determines when it is essential?
6. Some of the steps involved in preparing for a closing appear below. Determine which are handled by the lender and which by the real estate firm or escrow company. When applicable, indicate whether a cost to the buyer or the seller.

Responsibility of   **Paid by**

a. credit report
b. appraisal
c. verification of employment
d. bank deposit verified
e. property survey
f. order loan payoff
g. get deed signed
h. termite inspection ordered
i. extend abstract/title insurance
    buyer's title insurance
    lender's title insurance
j. lien waiver signed
k. prepare closing statements
l. homeowner insurance policy
m. broker's commission
n. attorney fee
o. loan assumption fee
p. discount points
q. origination fee
r. recording fees

REVIEW QUESTIONS

Answers to these questions are found in the Answer Key section at the back of the book.

1. At the time of the closing, any prepaid taxes would be considered a:

    a. credit to the buyer
    b. credit to the seller
    c. debit to the seller
    d. debit to both buyer and seller

2. The mortgage release is charged to:

    a. the seller
    b. the buyer
    c. the loan company
    d. the seller's agent

3. The HUD Settlement Statement is best defined as:

    a. a means of establishing the prorations of a closing
    b. a means of regulating the real estate closing
    c. a summary of charges to be paid by the borrower and the seller at the closing of a sale
    d. a means of prohibiting the finder's fee

4. Before the closing, the lender does all of the following, EXCEPT:

    a. obtains verification of the borrower's employment
    b. orders an appraisal on the property
    c. obtains the buyers' signatures on the deed
    d. orders a credit report on the borrower

5. The cost of recording the deed is charged to:

    a. the seller
    b. the buyer
    c. the real estate firm
    d. the lending institution

6. The most accurate definition of a closing statement would be:

    a. the reconciliation of credits and debits to the buyer and seller
    b. the proration of credits due the brokerage firm
    c. the establishment of the brokerage fee due from

the purchaser

d. the establishment of all expenses due to the lender from the purchaser

7. Which of the following charges is usually the responsibility of the buyer?

a. the insurance premium
b. the transfer tax
c. release of existing mortgage
d. unpaid taxes

8. The brokerage fee is charged to:

a. the buyer
b. the seller
c. the lender
d. whoever is stipulated by agreement of all parties

9. A reserve held by the lender to pay for taxes and insurance when due is called the:

a. closing statement
b. proration
c. earnest deposit
d. escrow or impound account

10. At closing, the settlement statements do NOT show:

a. how much the buyer pays at closing
b. how much the seller is to receive as proceeds from the sale
c. interest rate of loan
d. commission proceeds

11. In the settlement statement for the sale of a house, all of the following are credited to the buyer, EXCEPT:

a. the purchase price
b. the down payment
c. the earnest deposit
d. the purchase money mortgage

12. A copy of the buyer and seller closing cost statement should go to:

a. buyer and seller, respectively
b. the recorder's office where the deed is being held
c. seller only
d. buyer only

13. A closing takes place and the seller is delinquent $572 on his taxes. This would show on the statement as a:

a. debit to the seller
b. credit to the seller and debit to the buyer
c. credit to the buyer
d. credit to the seller

14. Mr. Smith's property tax is $948 per year and is paid in advance semiannually January 1 and July 1. He sold the property to Ms. Huff, and closing took place August 1. The settlement would show:

a. Mr. Smith will have to pay $553
b. Mr. Smith will be credited $79
c. Ms. Huff will be credited $79
d. Mr. Smith will be credited $395

15. Beverly Buyer purchases a house for $35,000. She deposits 10 percent on the contract and acquires a 75 percent loan. The lender charges her a 1 percent origination fee. How much money will Ms. Buyer need at closing?

a. $5,512.50
b. $5,250.00
c. $5,750.00
d. $9,012.50

16. When an existing mortgage is assumed by the buyer, it appears as a:

a. credit to the seller
b. credit to the buyer and the seller
c. credit to the buyer, debit to the seller
d. debit to the buyer

Answer questions 17–20 from the following information.

On May 10, 1992, Jane Sellum, a broker for A-1 Realty, listed Harry Brown's house for $82,950 for a period of 90 days. The commission is to be 7 percent of the gross sales price with 30 percent for the listing agent. Taxes of $1,320 per year are paid, and the $302 insurance for one year was paid March 20. Agent Isaac Blake with ABC Realty sold the property July 6 for $81,000, with an August 20 possession date.

17. What commission does the listing agent earn?

a. $1,741.95
b. $1,701.00

c. $5,806.50

d. $4,105.50

18. The prorated tax amount is:

a. $843.40

b. $953.40

c. $476.67

d. $513.33

19. The taxes would appear on the closing statement as a:

a. debit to the buyer

b. debit to the seller

c. credit to the buyer

d. taxes do not appear on closing statements

20. If the buyer assumes the existing insurance policy, the prorated amount will be a:

a. credit of $125.81 to seller

b. credit of $176.19 to seller

c. debit of $125.81 to seller

d. credit of $125.81 to seller

CLOSING PROBLEM

Complete the buyers' and sellers' closing statements from the following information.

On July 15 Jane and Jerry Jones listed their home at 8484 Lincoln Drive for $93,500 with A-1 Real Estate Company and agreed to pay a 7 percent commission on the sale price. June and James Jury's offer of 3 percent less than the listed price was accepted by the Joneses. Taxes of $1,320 are due in the current year and are paid in full. The title insurance policy of $430 will be paid by the buyers. Homeowner's insurance will cost the buyers $350. The mortgage release will be $7.00. Recording the deed will cost $6.00. The buyers will acquire a $72,600 loan, and the sellers have agreed to pay 1/2 of the 2 percent points charged by the lender. Closing and possession will be August 10. All prorations are based on a 30-day month. The Jones's mortgage balance is $58,548.

Buyer			Seller		
	Debit	Credit		Debit	Credit
Balance due			Proceeds due to seller		
Total			Total		

Other Aspects of Real Estate Ownership

PART THREE

This section deals with other aspects of ownership. Chapter 11 covers diverse forms of residences, including the condominium, townhouse, cooperative, and the concept of time-sharing.

Chapter 12 explains leases and the interest the lease holder has in the real estate of another. The various types of leases that the lessee may hold and the rights of both the landlord and the tenant are included in this chapter.

Chapter 13 discusses the business of managing real estate for other people. All aspects of real estate management—residential, office space, commercial, and farms—are defined.

Chapter 14 considers investing in real estate. The chapter begins with the homeowner's investment and concludes with the reasons for investing in income-producing properties. The tax aspects of real estate investment are covered.

Chapter 15 discusses the appraisal of real estate and the expertise required to place a value on the property. The three approaches to value—sales comparison, cost, and income—and how they are employed in the appraisal process are explained.

Chapter 16 completes this section, introducing the reader to the controls and regulations various units of government exercise over the use of land. Zoning laws are explained, and the development of a subdivision is covered.

Condominiums and Cooperatives

11

Key Words

air lot
bylaws
common elements
condominium
cooperative
declaration
homeowners' association

Horizontal Property Act
master deed
proprietary lease
time-sharing
townhouse
unit conversions
vacation license

Overview

New life-styles have emerged, and along with them have come new variations of homeownership. While shelter used to be limited to either homeownership or apartment rental, many new options have appeared in the housing market. The single-family home with its picket fence and rose hedge has been the traditional American dream, but it is being replaced across the country by a new mode of living. There is a growing trend toward **condominium** ownership. The word *condominium* is derived from the Latin words meaning "for exercising domain with others." Condominium ownership is the individual ownership of a single-family unit in a multifamily structure or group of buildings, together with joint ownership of common areas. A form of ownership, it is a way of life, not just a type of building or living complex. A condominium can be a townhouse, a duplex, a fourplex, a high-rise structure, an office, or a commercial building. This form of group ownership provides the owners with individual and absolute title to their own living space, just as in a single-family home. Along with receiving a deed to the property, the owner has an undivided interest in the common areas of the property.

Large metropolitan cities have seen the concepts of condominium and townhouse ownership spreading. In fact, so many apartment houses were converted to condominiums that some cities placed temporary moratoriums on future conversions. In other sections of the country, the trend toward condominiums reduced rental units to a point where adequate rental housing was in jeopardy.

The history of condominiums has not been smooth. Condominium pioneers came under attack by government agencies and consumer interest groups, especially in resort and retirement areas. Unscrupulous developers took advantage of inefficient or vague laws, leaving a trail of dissatisfied buyers. Most of the misunderstanding arose over assessment fees that were far below what was necessary for proper maintenance of common areas and unit exteriors. Thus, shortly after the purchase, heavy increases in the dues were levied. Some unfortunate buyers found they had to pay extra for a garage or parking space that they had erroneously believed was part of owning a unit. Some developers also retained too much control, even to the point of retaining ownership over recreation areas and holding a long-term lease binding the association. Most of these early problems have been eliminated through enactment of stiffer laws now governing the development of condominiums.

This chapter begins by explaining the formation of a condominium regime. The townhouse, the cooperative, time-share, and vacation license will also be covered.

CREATION OF A CONDOMINIUM REGIME

Single ownership within a master deed

Condominium ownership was created by a special real estate law that allows individual ownership within a larger estate. The owner of the development files a **master deed** in the land records of the county where the property is located, along with a declaration of the condominium regime. *Regime* refers to the governing system of a condominium complex. The plot and plans of the area to be developed are defined in the declaration and set forth the sponsor's intention to create the condominium. A general description of the common areas and the restrictive covenants under which the regime will operate are also included. A property that was previously a single traditional estate is thus divided into a number of units within a common area. Basically, the declaration does the following:

1. Converts the property to single deed estates.
2. Gives a description of the units and the common areas.
3. Establishes the undivided interest percentages of common areas.
4. Through the bylaws, authority and power is placed with the board of directors of the **homeowners' association**.

Recognized in all 50 states, the **Horizontal Property Act** provides for ownership of a specific unit of space that differs from traditional ownership of property with rights to the surface, subsurface, and air space above the property. The individual unit is not complete without an undivided interest in the whole area.

Single condominium units can be grouped together with the owner possessing surface, subsurface, and air rights in fee simple title plus ownership as tenants in common of the common areas and recreation facilities with the other owners in the regime (see Figure 11.1).

As we learned in Chapter 3 covering land descriptions, property boundaries are established by surveying a particular parcel of land. By relying on previously established reference points, the boundaries are staked out and recorded. As Figure 11.2 indicates, the boundaries are defined, and the individual has ownership of that area into the earth's surface and up into the sky above the owner's ground lot.

Air lot in a high-rise condominium

The condominium owner may also own space in the sky and beneath the earth's surface if the unit is a duplex or a townhouse. In a high-rise type of condominium, in lieu of having title to a piece of land on the earth's surface, ownership is created that allows the individual a cubic unit of space. This space is called an apartment **air lot** (see Figure 11.3). According to this horizontal property division, the individual owners of these cubes of space also have ownership in the common areas.

There is no legal difference between a high-rise condominium building and **townhouse** units. The townhouse is a form of condominium construction. It is an individual unit joined to another unit by a common wall. The land beneath the unit is sometimes

FIGURE 11.1
Condominium ownership.

FIGURE 11.2
Single family residence.

deeded to the townhouse owner and not included as part of the common area. The townhouse resembles the single-family home since the units do not have neighbors above or below. However, land costs are saved, since the units can be attached or clustered together.

Bylaws

The condominium **declaration** states the covenants, restrictions, and conditions of the condominium regime. The **bylaws** provide for a homeowners' association to administer the affairs of the common elements and facilities and state any special rules that control the project. This gives the individual a greater voice in these matters and also

Creation of bylaws

air lot

FIGURE 11.3
High-rise condominium.

allows the association board to levy charges against individual owners for the mainte-nance of the common areas. If monthly assessments are not paid by an individual, the bylaws provide for the legal enforcement of placing a lien against the delinquent owner's unit.

The developer controls the condominium from its inception through the initial stages or until the developer no longer owns the majority of the units. Later, when most of the units have been sold, control passes to resident members of the board of directors. The following articles are included in the bylaws:

1 the responsibilities of the officers and directors
2. the owner's obligations
3. a statement of the assessment to be levied and how the fees will be collected to maintain the common areas and to legally enforce payment of overdue monthly assessments
4. the establishment of an operating budget
5. any rules governing the use of recreation areas
6. provisions to maintain liability, fire, and hazard insurance on structures (this does not include unit interiors)

The Association

Owners' association The homeowners' association, or the condominium council, is the governing board whose responsibilities are spelled out in the bylaws. As in corporations, the board of directors and officers are elected by members and are responsible for the control of what happens in the governing of the condominium regime. Every unit owner auto-matically belongs to the homeowners' association, and membership carries with it the right to voice opinions and vote at both regular and annual meetings which are held in accordance with the bylaws. A large development may hold meetings on a regular basis, whereas a smaller regime may only hold quarterly or annual meetings. Members may vote to raise or lower monthly assessments; hire or terminate a management firm; approve, disapprove, or change the annual budget; and release or withhold payment to a contractor. The governing body is based on majority rule and will provide for:

1. an operating budget, including general operation reserve for replacement of com-mon elements
2. collection of monthly charges and assessments
3. notice to lenders of any unpaid assessments

4. professional management, if needed

5. right of entry and rules of conduct with respect to the common areas

6. rules for use of recreational areas

7. refuse collection, water, sewer, and outside lighting

What the Condominium Owner Receives

The owner receives an *undivided interest in common* in a portion of a parcel of real estate, together with *fee simple title* to an individual interest in his unit.

1. Each unit has an individual deed in fee simple title.

2. Each unit is separately assessed for taxes.

3. Each unit can be individually mortgaged.

4. Each unit is eligible for title insurance just as a separate piece of property is eligible.

5. Each unit has an interest in common areas and facilities that are part of the entire building and land.

Interest held by owner

Purchasers obtain a mortgage on terms agreeable to their particular needs and are not liable for default of other owners in the condominium unit. One owner may have paid cash while another may have an FHA loan or a conventional mortgage. If the loan is defaulted upon, only that unit goes into foreclosure.

Taxes and Assessments

Just as in a single-family home, all taxes and special assessments on a condominium are levied against the individual units and not against the whole condominium regime. Owners receive an individual tax assessment and are liable solely for their taxes. A lender may require that a tax escrow be included in the monthly mortgage payment, thus ensuring the other owners that taxes on all the units are paid. The maintenance and repairs of the common elements require funds, so each unit is assessed association dues according to the ratio of that unit to the total condominium units. If an owner has 1,000 square feet, that unit will be assessed for less than an owner with 1,500 square feet. Some states require that a definite formula be followed regarding this ratio which may be by value, by living area, by market price, or in equal shares.

Maintenance fees

Limited and Common Elements

Condominium living offers ownership both exclusively and in common. The unit is individually owned, whether an air space in a high-rise or an attached unit in a cluster arrangement.

Depending on the condominium style, the **common elements** (common areas) owned by the group may include the land and the exterior surfaces of the buildings, such as foundations, roofs, and stairways. Exterior areas will incorporate driveways, walks, parking areas, and gardens while the interior common areas will consist of corridors, lobbies, stairs, club rooms, entrances and exits, storage areas, and elevators. Recreational areas may encompass swimming pools, putting greens, tennis courts, saunas, and exercise rooms. A *limited common element* refers to a common area limited to an individual unit owner, such as a balcony or parking stall. Sharing the monthly cost of maintenance and repair of the common areas with the other residents tends to reduce expenses, since the costs are divided by the group. Many of these special amenities would prove to be cost prohibitive for the single-family homeowner.

Shared areas

The Best of Both Worlds

Carefree ownership

Who buys condominiums? A government survey made in 1975 predicted that one in every two households will be living in some form of condominium by the year 2000. That may seem unrealistic if you live in a rural area or small town, but not when you consider the highly populated urban cities such as New York, San Francisco, Boston, or Chicago. A desire for easy commuting to employment centers and scarcity of land in large metropolitan areas has resulted in the need for more living in less space.

The condominium life-style also carries particular appeal to people who do not want the hassle of property maintenance, including singles, divorcees, empty nesters, career-oriented couples, and retirees. Due to high land costs and growing construction costs, more living space can generally be obtained in a condominium for the same number of dollars invested. Thus, in some areas of the country it is less expensive to purchase a condominium than a single-family dwelling. Others purchase the condominium as a second home or vacation retreat. Resort areas abound with high-rise units.

We want more for less, and the condominium can fulfill this want in terms of facilities, amenities, and creature comforts. Many condominium residents feel they have the best of both worlds: the advantages of homeownership and the benefits of apartment living. The owner has the security of living in a compound and the tax benefits of homeownership. Another attraction of condominium living is freedom from lawn care, snow removal, and exterior maintenance. This carefree life-style, which eliminates these outside maintenance chores for the owners and offers the availability of recreational facilities, draws many people to the condominium way of life. Investing in a condominium is also more appealing than collecting rent receipts as the owner has an opportunity to build up equity. Renting provides no deductions for income tax purposes, while the condominium owner may deduct the interest on the mortgage payments and property taxes.

The benefits of owning a condominium include:

Ownership benefits

1. Amenities not often available to single-family homeowners, such as pools and tennis courts, though these amenities will vary according to cost and location.
2. Freedom from exterior maintenance.
3. A feeling of security which may include sophisticated security systems.
4. Peace of mind for the owner who is often away.
5. Enjoyment of the homeowners' association meetings; a camaraderie not unlike old-fashioned town hall meetings.
6. Social involvement is available for those who want to participate. Some large units have organized activities for all ages and occasions.
7. Pride of ownership.
8. More living space is often obtained for the investment since maximum use of the land is made due to rising land costs.
9. Minimized upkeep—limited to the unit's interior.
10. Choice of desirable location.

The disadvantages associated with condominium living may include:

Disadvantages of condominium life-style

1. Lack of privacy because of the close proximity to other units.
2. Limited private outdoor space.
3. Restrictions and rules that must be adhered to.
4. Majority rule; decisions are made jointly by the owners, so one is not in complete control of surroundings.
5. Parking areas may be limited.

COMMERCIAL CONDOMINIUMS

The rapid growth of available office space that was stimulated by tax advantages offered by the government encouraged an oversupply of commercial buildings. This phenomenon was particularly noticeable when an industry moved from the area and those services that needed office space were no longer there. Some farsighted property owners began to offer individual space for sale. Aimed primarily at small businesses who may not have the need or resources to build their own building, purchasing space gives them tax benefits and the pride of ownership plus an opportunity to build equity.

One of the disadvantages of business condominiums is the inflexibility of the space. If the business needs to expand, adjoining space would probably be nonexistent. A means of avoiding this would be to purchase more space than needed and lease the extra space temporarily.

CONVERSIONS

Converting, which changes the use of real estate, began to surface widely in the late 1970s. Across the nation, 25 percent of all condominium **units** produced in 1977 were **conversions**. They became prevalent in communities that imposed rent controls, limiting the amount owners could charge tenants. With taxes and other costs rising due to inflation, owners began to view converting as the answer. For owners of apartment rentals that lent themselves easily to conversion, large profits could be made. Some concerned communities began to place moratoriums on conversions since they were reducing the amount of rentals available.

From apartment to condominium

Some convertees only did superficial "face lifting" that consisted of a few cosmetic changes, such as fresh paint, wallpaper, and new carpeting. The buyer must realize there may be deferred maintenance, inadequate insulation, and soundproofing and that the plumbing, electrical, heating, and air conditioning should be checked. Another form of conversion is occurring in urban areas that are being revitalized. Old warehouses, offices, and school buildings are being converted to residential condominiums. The sturdy brick construction of many of these buildings lends itself to aesthetically pleasing living units close to employment centers. These buildings will require more architectural and construction changes than conversion of apartment buildings already divided into living areas.

Disclosure on the resale of a unit is required in some states. A copy of the basic condominium documents and a current statement of the financial solvency of the homeowners' association and whether there are adequate reserves for any anticipated capital expenditures should be reviewed by the purchaser.

COOPERATIVES

In **cooperative** ownership of an apartment unit, the purchaser buys shares of stock in a nonprofit corporation, partnership, or trust that holds title to the real estate with the shareholders owning stock. The purchaser of a cooperative apartment is thus a shareholder in a corporation whose principal asset is the building. Owning stock in the corporation allows the purchaser to occupy a specific unit in the building, referred to as a **proprietary lease**. The owner does not have fee simple title as the shares owned are considered personal property and as such the stock purchase must be financed by means other than a mortgage.

Owning shares of stock in real estate

The shareholder is responsible for a pro rata share of the corporation expenses, which include real estate taxes, maintenance, mortgage payment, and other miscellaneous costs. The owners can deduct their proportion of taxes and interest charges on the mortgage for income tax purposes only if 80 percent of the cooperative's income is derived from tenant owner rentals.

As a corporation, a cooperative is a single entity and thus if mortgaged will have a single mortgage covering the buildings. If a stockholder defaults in his or her share of assessments, the other owners are liable or risk losing their investments.

Due to this inherent hazard, a few states have passed laws to permit stock to be used as collateral and pledged to the lender, just as in purchasing a condominium. This places the burden of payment directly where it belongs, upon the debtor. Mortgaging each unit individually enables the owner to sell the property easier. When there is a single mortgage, the seller of a unit had to either carry the financing for the purchaser or the single mortgage had to be renegotiated. These states further permit assessment of taxes on units individually, thus circumventing passing the liability on to all the shareholders.

When offering a cooperative unit for sale, the owner is offering stock and occupancy rights. A purchaser may be turned down by the vote of the cooperative board who participate in the operation of the cooperative. The shareholders may be quite selective in their decision of who they accept as purchasers.

TIME-SHARING

Have you heard of "buying time"? That sounds like a ridiculous statement until you realize that we are discussing the use of a piece of real estate, known as **time-sharing**.

Joint ownership

The evolution of real estate ownership and its use began with primitive people who lived on the *first* dimension of real estate, on the land as they found it: the *length and width*. Through the ages people moved into a more permanent structure and entered the *second* dimension, house; and now ownership could be measured in *length, width, and height*. We discovered a *third* dimension, owning a part or unit of a building, the condominium. Now ownership meant possessing *length, width, and height* and a specific unit of a building. The *fourth* dimension is buying *time* within the unit of the building.

If it can be divided, it can be sold as a time-share. Time-shares have been sold in jet airplanes, cruise ships, campsites, hotels, single-family homes, and just about any type of property that caters to people who like to travel and take vacations.

While there are many legal structures for a time-share plan, they basically can be grouped into two broad areas: (1) buying an ownership interest for an amount of time or (2) buying the right to use a living space without actually owning an interest in the real property.

Buying "right to use"

A purchaser buys an *interval ownership* and is deeded an undivided interest in a particular unit and holds title as tenants in common with other buyers of the unit. They can use, rent, give away, or will the amount of time they have purchased in the unit. Time-shares are usually sold in one- or two-week increments.

Mainly used in resort areas where full-time ownership is not practical or necessary, time-sharing allows each owner a time slot for a fixed or floating period to use the accommodations. Owners are charged an annual assessment for the costs of maintenance, upkeep of the recreational facilities, furniture replacement, and maid service.

An example of a fee title time-share follows:

Judy and Kyle Browning purchase an annual week of time in a condominium in Hawaii for the second week in January. They pay $10,000 for their share of the unit and an annual maintenance fee of $200. They receive a deed for one-fifty second (1/52) undivided interest in the unit. The Brownings are guaranteed the exclusive use of the unit on the second week of January every year for as long as they retain their interest. They receive the same tax benefits and equity as from any other type of real estate ownership. They may sell their share for whatever the market will provide.

Let us consider the scenario of this time-share sale:

Fifty (50) units are in the building. Each unit sells for $10,000, thus each unit represents a sale of $500,000 *if* they were sold to *one* owner. Selling 50 weeks (2 weeks are usually reserved for refurbishing the units) at $10,000 × 50 units results in a sale price of $25,000,000. Now 2,500 people own the 50 units. The $200 annual maintenance fee paid by the 2,500 owners totals $500,000 which amply takes care of redecorating, maintenance, and staff salaries plus a management fee for the promoter-owner of the complex who is now managing the development. While a tidy profit was made by the original owner, the purchasers have prepaid lodging for one week a year for as long as they retain their ownership.

VACATION LICENSES

A **vacation license** is a form of time-sharing that offers the purchaser the *right to use* for a stated period over a given duration of time with the project developer retaining ownership. In some instances the unit will revert to the developer at the end of the specified time.

Buying future vacations

In vacation areas that were overbuilt with condominiums, interval ownership has provided developers with a means of selling units.

One of the selling points to buyers is that they are purchasing vacation lodging for the future at today's prices. Luxury units in such exotic places as Mexico, Hawaii, the Virgin Islands, the Bahamas, and Spain offer vacations that many people could not aspire to take on an annual basis, but by prepaying "rent," these vacations are within their grasp.

EXCHANGE PROGRAMS

One of the most evident objections to time-sharing is the idea of vacationing at the same time and same place year after year. Exchange programs are alleviating this concern: the owner swaps time with another owner at a different resort. Resorts across the country are forming exchange groups between their owners, so the owner of a time-sharing plan in California could swap for equal time in Florida. As the concept of time-sharing spreads, exchange companies are being formed across the world to meet the needs of their members. For membership dues an individual owner may join an exchange group and make application to use a unit in another resort.

Swapping use

Leisure time is on the increase. If the average person does not want or cannot afford a second home, a time-share program may be the answer. Potential buyers are warned that if they are thinking of buying a time-share they should make sure it is for the right reason. It should be to guarantee a vacation site every year and perhaps save money on what is charged for comparable motel or hotel accommodations. Too many people bought time-shares as an investment, and today the market is flooded with owners who want to sell, but there are few buyers.

Summary

Although the traditional dream of middle-class Americans has been to own a single-family home, other types of housing have surfaced to accommodate the need for shelter, especially in areas where land is scarce, as in high-employment centers.

The condominium offers individual ownership of living space in a multi-unit building or group of buildings along with an interest in the common areas and facilities. This form of ownership is appealing to people who desire to own real estate without the burden of maintenance.

The bylaws require that a homeowners' association is formed and officers elected to govern the association.

Apartment houses have been converted into condominium units. Many times the conversion units have just had "cosmetic" face lifts, perhaps by replacing paint and carpeting. Depending on the age of the structure, the purchaser may be buying a unit that will soon need a new furnace, an air conditioner, and appliance replacements. It behooves the purchaser of a conversion unit to carefully examine these component parts.

Because so many condominium units are available in vacation areas such as ski resorts and beach resorts, the developers in these areas have sold units on a time-share basis. Still others have sold vacation licenses where the purchaser buys only the right to use the unit for future vacations. These licenses are sold on the premise that housing costs will continue to escalate and that the purchaser can save money by buying future vacations at today's prices.

When purchasing a cooperative, the buyers receive shares of stock for which they obtain the right to possession of a unit. Since the building is taxed as a single, whole unit and necessary assessments are divided proportionally among the owners, the solvency of the investment depends to a great degree upon the other shareholders. Some exclusive buildings are sold as cooperatives so that the owners can select their buyers carefully. In essence, these owners can "tactfully" discriminate on who they wish to have as neighbors.

Retirement and vacation condominiums especially continue in popularity, and often the developer plays a second role in operating a management firm to oversee the rental of a vacation site project.

The varied choices on the types of housing available today literally offer something for everyone. Some authorities feel that traditional single-family homeownership will before long be a remnant of the past.

Discussion Questions

1. Explain the basic difference between a condominium and a cooperative.
2. Why would a purchaser decide to buy a time-share?
3. How do a time-share and a vacation license differ?
4. Explain the difference between separate, limited, and common elements.
5. Ownership of an air lot in real estate and ownership of a single-family lot differ in what respect?
6. Why is a homeowners' association necessary in a condominium regime?

REVIEW QUESTIONS

Answers to these questions are found in the Answer Key section at the back of the book.

1. In a condominium development, decisions regarding repairs or improvements to the common areas are made by:

   a. individual tenants

   b. the homeowners' association

   c. a board of governors

   d. the real estate commission

2. What type of ownership does a condominium owner hold?

   a. fee simple

   b. estate in trust

   c. estate in rescission

   d. group ownership

3. Under the condominium type of ownership:

   a. individual units are mortgaged separately

   b. a blanket mortgage covers the regime

   c. only common areas are mortgaged

   d. none of the above

4. Individual fee ownership of a single unit in a multi-family structure is characteristic of:

   a. a cooperative

   b. a condominium

   c. a vacation license

   d. all of the above

5. Which of the following statements is true regarding condominium ownership?

   a. failure of an owner to pay taxes on his condominium creates a lien on his unit only

   b. the entire condominium regime is responsible for any tax default

   c. a tennis court in a condominium project is individually owned

   d. the condominium owner owns stock or shares in the project

6. The amenities of condominium ownership would NOT include:

   a. no exterior maintenance

   b. reduced maintenance and repair expenses in group ownership

   c. income tax deductions on interest payment

   d. shares in the project

7. The difference between a condominium and a townhouse is:

   a. only condominium owners may have fee simple title

   b. condominiums are high-rise structures

   c. townhouses have no common areas

   d. the form of construction

8. The time-sharing plan of ownership is best explained as:

   a. a condominium owner shares his individual unit

   b. several purchasers own a property and share in its use

   c. an easy payment plan is used in purchasing a condominium

   d. none of the above

9. The "cube of space" owned in a high-rise condominium is called:

   a. a space lot

   b. an air lot

   c. a tax lot

   d. an apartment lot

10. The owner of a condominium shares in all of the following, EXCEPT:

    a. a unit deed

    b. a master deed

    c. a proprietary lease

    d. the bylaws of the owners' association

11. In a cooperative apartment complex, each unit owner usually is individually responsible for:

    a. the building insurance

    b. paying her own taxes

    c. exterior maintenance of apartment

    d. interior maintenance of apartment

12. A time-sharing estate is an example of:

    a. severalty ownership

    b. a leasehold estate

c. a nonfreehold estate in a condominium

d. the right to exclusive use for a specified time each year

13. Which of the following statements about a unit in a condominium building is NOT correct?

    a. it is eligible for title insurance as a separate piece of property

    b. it can be individually mortgaged

    c. there are no common areas

    d. an owner can take income tax deduction on interest paid

14. In which of the following must the owners or occupants in a building be stockholders of the corporation that owns the building?

    a. a cooperative apartment house

b. a condominium building

c. a townhouse

d. time-share ownership

15. The horizontal property regime refers to:

    a. setbacks from the perimeter of a property

    b. condominium ownership

    c. homestead laws

    d. cooperatives

16. Which fee would a condominium owner least likely be expected to pay?

    a. a recreation fee

    b. a condo maintenance fee

    c. a stock transfer fee

    d. a hazard insurance fee

Leases

12

OVERVIEW

All individuals need the use of real estate as shelter or for business purposes, but many do not need or desire absolute ownership. For the segment of our population that is nomadic in nature, the desire and need for permanent ownership is not of primary concern. In fact, because many households are headed today by younger and older people, the population age distribution favors apartments. Many students living away from home, young adults working in cities, retired people, and newly married couples not certain of permanency in a locality prefer to rent until they establish definite residency. It must also be remembered that the continued trend of climbing construction costs and interest rates price many people out of homeownership.

Commercial rentals are used by small businesses without the cash flow required to purchase land and erect buildings, and real estate investors meet these needs by leasing office and retail space.

The types of leases and the rights and conditions imposed by a lease for both residential and commercial uses are discussed in this chapter.

THE LEASE

A **lease** is a *contract* and a *conveyance* between a **lessee** (tenant) and a **lessor** (landlord) of real property. A legal and binding agreement, it specifically documents the obligation of the lessor and the lessee. An example of a lease is shown in Figure 12.1. A lease contract between the two parties is considered a conveyance that gives the right of possession to the tenant for which rent is paid to the landlord. This conveyance is referred to as a **demise**, or the conveyance of an estate under lease.

Conveying use of real property

THIS AGREEMENT Witnesseth: That I or we, _____

_____

have this day rented to _____

_____

in the present condition thereof, the premises known as; _____

_____

_____

for the period of _____
from the _____ day of _____, 19____, on the following terms and conditions, to-wit: for the use and rent thereof the said lessee, hereby promises to pay the lessor, or to his, her or their order _____
_____ Dollars
per _____ for the whole time above stated, and to pay the same _____
_____ on the _____ of each _____; that lessee will not sub-let or allow any other tenant to come in with or under him, her or them without the written consent of said lessor; that lessee will repair all injuries or damages done the premises during his, her or their occupancy, or pay for the same; that all of his, her or their property, whether subject to legal exemption, or not, shall be bound and subject to the payment of rents and damages thereof; that lessee will comply with all city ordinances, will take good care of the buildings and premises, and keep them free from filth, from danger or fire, and will keep the side-walks free from ice and snow and the house and premises shall be kept clean. If in default of the payment of rent for a period of _____ days after the same is due, lessee will at the request of said lessor quit and render to lessor the peaceable possession thereof; but, for this cause, the obligation to pay shall not cease; and finally at the end of lessees term, lessee will surrender to the said lessor, his, her or their heirs and assigns, the peaceable possession of said demised premises with all keys, bolts, latches and repairs, if any, in as good condition as the same was received, the usual wear and tear.

The said lessor reserves the privilege of entering and showing above property to prospective renters during the last thirty-day period of this lease or for any other reasonable purpose at any time. _____

_____

_____

_____

_____

IN WITNESS WHEREOF the parties hereto have subscribed to two copies hereof, one to be retained by each party.

Dated this _____ day of _____, 19____.

_____   _____
Lessor   Lessee

_____   _____
Lessor   Lessee

FIGURE 12.1
House lease.

Many leases use the phrase "to grant, demise, and let." These are the conveying terms that give the lessee the right of possession.

Upon expiration of the lease, the lessor again gains possession of the property. The lessor has a **reversionary interest** in the property while it is under lease, with the property reverting to the lessor when the lease terminates, and thus the lessor's interest includes the leased fee and the reversionary right to the property.

LEASEHOLD INTERESTS

As mentioned in Chapter 4, a lease is a nonfreehold estate in that it is set for a definite period of time with the rights granted by a lease constituting a leasehold interest. Leasehold estates can be classified into four main types:

1. **Tenancy for years.** This estate is for a definite or fixed period of time as agreed *Interests under lease terms* to between the lessee and the lessor. The main characteristic of this lease is that it must have a stated expiration date. The term of a lease for years may actually be less than a year, perhaps only for a week or a month. Upon the termination of a lease for years, the tenant must vacate and surrender possession of the property. This estate is not terminated upon the death of the lessor or lessee.
2. **Periodic tenancy.** This type of estate is for a specified period to period, such as a month-to-month or year-to-year agreement. There is no set termination date, as the lease is automatically renewed at the end of each period. If one of the parties wishes to cancel the lease, notice to quit must be given to the other party. A tenancy from month-to-month usually requires a 30-day notice prior to the due date of the next month's rent to cancel the lease.
3. **Tenancy at will.** This nonfreehold estate at will provides for either the lessee or the lessor to terminate the agreement whenever they so desire. Most states require the party to give proper notice to terminate the lease. If one of the parties dies, the tenancy at will is automatically terminated.
4. **Tenancy at sufferance.** A tenant who remains in possession of the premises after the lease has expired has a tenancy at sufferance. The tenant stays in possession without the right or consent of the landlord and is referred to as a holdover tenant. A possessory interest in the land is held by the tenant only because the tenant stayed past the expiration date, so technically an estate in land no longer exists. The lessor may evict the lessee or may decide to accept rent from the tenant according to the terms of the previous lease. If the landlord does not evict the tenant, a periodic estate will usually be created.

LEASE CONTENTS

The following terms and conditions should be stipulated in the lease:

1. *Names* of the lessee and the lessor. *Provisions in a lease*
2. A *description* of the leased property.
3. *Duration of the lease.* The commencement and termination dates of the lease should be set forth. If the lease is renewed, a new agreement should be written.
4. The *amount of rent* to be paid should be stipulated, along with the time and the place payment is to be made.
5. *Possession, maintenance, and improvements.* Any conditions imposed upon the lessee and any exceptions to the lessee's rights should be enumerated.
6. *Liability of the parties.* The person held responsible for injuries resulting from conditions of the premises should be included.

7. *Transfer by the lessee*. It is to the lessee's benefit to have a clause of transfer in the lease.

8. *Special covenants, conditions, and provisions*. Any special rights and privileges of the parties should be included in the lease.

TERMINATION OF A LEASE

A lease may be terminated under the following conditions:

1. *Expiration of the lease*. When the term of the lease expires, the tenancy understandably ends. Usually a written notice must be given by the party desiring to terminate the lease, especially under the terms of a tenancy at will or a periodic tenancy. A tenancy for years expires at the termination time stated in the lease so no notice need be given. In a tenancy at sufferance, the tenant has overstayed the lease term so it may be terminated at any time.

2. *Agreement between the parties*. By mutual agreement the landlord and tenant can sever the lease, the lessee surrendering the lease and the lessor accepting the terms. This is referred to as **surrender and acceptance**.

3. *Breach of condition*. If either the lessee or lessor breaks the terms of the lease, a breach has been committed, and the injured party may cancel the lease.

4. *Condemnation*. If a property is condemned under the right of eminent domain, the lessee must vacate the premises. In some instances compensation is given to the tenant based on the value of the remainder of the lease. The present value is the difference between the *contract rent* (lease) and the *economic rent* (market value) at the time of the condemnation.

5. *Notice*. If the lessee does not give notice to quit to the lessor as required in the lease, the lessor can hold the tenant to another full term. For instance, if the lease calls for a 60-day notice if the tenant is not renewing the lease, the landlord must be notified before that 60-day time limit. Such notices to quit are usually incorporated into estates for years, periodic estates, and estates at will.

Landlord's right to cancel lease

6. *Eviction of the lessee*. The lessee may be evicted through actual eviction or constructive eviction.

   a. *Actual eviction*. The tenant is dismissed from the premises and the lessor can regain possession of the leased premises because of a contract breach. The tenant may have stayed over after the expiration of the lease (as a holdover tenant) or failed to live up to the terms of the lease (for example, failure to pay rent). A tenant's failure to move is referred to as unlawful detainer. Possession must be surrendered, or the lessor will take legal action to evict the lessee and have an office of the court forcibly remove the tenant from the premises. The term *distraint* refers to the owner's right, pursuant to a court order, to seize the lessee's personal property if the lessee is in arrears (is behind) in the rent payment.

Tenant's right to cancel lease

   b. **Constructive eviction**. A lessee may break the terms of the lease if the owner violates the covenants or terms of the lease and interferes with the quiet enjoyment of the lessee. If the owner fails to maintain the property according to the terms of the lease, the tenant may terminate the lease under constructive eviction. In many states after receiving notice that repairs are needed, the landlord has 14 days to make repairs or the tenant can make them and deduct the cost from the rent payments. A tenant's withholding rent because of the landlord's failure to maintain the property in a livable condition is referred to as *rent abatement*. The landlord may not evict a tenant, restrict utilities, or withhold other services in retaliation against the tenant for exercising her rights.

LEASE PROVISIONS

Leases for one year or less do not need to be in writing. However, according to the statute of frauds in most states, if the lease is for more than one year, it must be in writing. In lieu of a written lease, the fact that the lessee takes possession is sufficient to affirm his acceptance of the lease and delivery by the lessor. A written lease provides protection for both parties and makes it easier to resolve any disputes that may arise.

Lease clauses

Rent is customarily payable in advance, in money, chattel, labor, or provisions. The lessee has the right to enjoy the use of the property as specified in the lease, without interruption or invasion by the lessor or another.

An **option clause** allows the lessee the right to renew the lease upon the expiration date. The lessee may be uncertain at the time of entering into the lease agreement if he will want to remain past the initial term of the lease. For example, a real estate broker decides to open a second office and rents the branch office location with an option that will allow the broker the choice of continuing or discontinuing business at the new location.

Option clause

A commercial lease will generally provide that if the building were destroyed by fire, flood, tornado, or winds and becomes unusable, the tenant is relieved from rent payment. Some businesses will carry insurance covering interruption of business due to damages outside of the business owner's control. Most commercial leases require the tenant to carry liability insurance in case of injury to a third party.

The lease should state the use to which the tenant intends to use the property, giving the landlord the option of terminating the lease if the tenant violates the covenant. This does not imply that an infraction would be committed if the tenant leased office space for an insurance business and later decides to add a real estate firm. A problem would be created, however, if it were a shopping center and say a dress shop decides to open a section for shoes, and a shoe store with a similar line is leasing space and has a clause in the lease stating no competitive shoe outlet would be leased space.

A *tax participation clause* is an agreement in a lease whereby the lessee agrees to pay all or a stated portion of any increase in real estate taxes on the leased property. If a lessor's taxes increase $1,000 over the year and she has five tenants leasing equal square footage, each tenant's rent would rise $200 for the year. A tax participation clause is often used on office or commercial rentals, thus offering the lessor protection against rising costs of ownership.

The landlord is under no obligation to make improvements or alterations to the property unless it is specifically stated in the lease. If the lessee decorates and makes changes, it must be done with the agreement of the lessor, and any improvements become the property of the lessor upon termination of the lease. The exception is *trade fixtures* installed by the lessee for use in conducting business, such as display cases and shelves. These trade fixtures must be removed by the tenant by the expiration date of the lease.

Trade fixture

When an unexpired portion of the lease is reconveyed to and accepted by the lessor, it is termed surrender and acceptance. If the lessee abandons the demised property without the owner's acceptance, he remains liable for the lease. The landlord should endeavor to find a new tenant, but any costs of advertising or commission paid to an agent would be charged to the lessee who abandoned the lease.

Surrender and acceptance

Assignment and Subletting

When one **assigns** a lease, the lessee is giving the remainder of the lease over entirely. The lessees may assign their interest unless the terms of the lease expressly state

Assigning lease to another

otherwise. The assignee (new lessee) obtains all the rights and interests that the assignor possessed. If the assignee does not live up to the terms of the lease, the assignor will be held responsible until released by the owner. When a property is sold and there are existing leases on the premises, the leases are assigned to the new owners and are binding on them.

When a lessee **sublets** the property, the lessee retains a portion of the lease, or a portion of the premises. The lessee may sublet a room or the entire property for a limited time and then retake possession at a later date.

Obligations of the Parties

Tenant responsibilities and rights

The Uniform Residential Landlord and Tenant Act in force in many states lists the obligations of the parties to a lease. If the lease does not clearly indicate who is responsible for the conditions of the premises, this act clarifies the responsibility.

Basically, the tenant is required to keep the property clean and in good condition with the exception of the expected normal wear and tear through use. The tenant is held responsible for destroying or damaging the premises, and garbage and other wastes must be disposed of in a clean and safe manner. The tenant must not disturb other tenants or nearby neighbors and is expected to conform to the law concerning occupation of the property.

The landlord, in turn, must comply with the minimum housing codes. He must keep the premises in good repair and in a safe livable condition or as otherwise provided in the lease. By agreement between the landlord and tenant, the tenant may prefer to perform certain repairs in lieu of part of the rental payment. The landlord must also see that all electrical, plumbing, and other facilities are in good repair and basically provide a habitable dwelling. It is understood the tenant will have *quiet enjoyment*, that is, the use of the property without interruption or invasion by the lessor or another.

Leases often contain a notice of intent to move clause requiring a 30- or 60-day notice. The notice may need to be in writing, or verbal notice may be acceptable.

Security Deposits

A **security deposit** is often required when the lessee takes possession of the property. This deposit is refundable upon expiration of the lease, providing the property has not been materially damaged.

In most states the landlord cannot request more than one month's rent as a security deposit. This deposit must be returned, with deductions for any repairs itemized, within a reasonable time after the tenant vacates and requests the refund. Some states provide that interest must be paid on the deposit.

Rent Control

Rent control is the action of a local governing board to place a ceiling on the rent charged by a landlord. This places a great burden on the landlord if maintenance costs, insurance, and taxes increase to any extent. In some communities where rent control is in effect, building owners are neglecting to maintain their property. Other landlords are converting apartments into condominium units. Rent control is generally mandated when apartments are scarce and rents have been greatly increased.

TYPES OF LEASES

Leases generally fall into the following categories:

The **net lease** requires the tenant to assume all or a portion of the property expenses normally paid by the owner, leaving the rent net to the lessor. Many long-term commercial and industrial leases are triple net leases. This type of lease places the responsibility of all the expenses upon the tenant, including taxes, repairs, maintenance, insurance, and generally even exterior maintenance. The triple net lease has a special appeal to the institutional lessor, such as a college or insurance company, since such a lessor would desire to avoid repairs and management concerns.

Lessee shares building expenses

The **percentage lease** is based on a flat fee plus a percentage of the gross income received by the tenant doing business on the premises. Several factors must be considered in a percentage lease. The base rent may be low, but a percentage of the business income must be paid to the lessor. If the business income exceeds the lessee's expectations, the rent is subsequently increased. The percentage should be at a rate that permits the lessee to obtain a reasonable profit and provides the lessee with an incentive to gain additional volume. A percentage lease can be advantageous to both parties, allowing a lower base rent for the lessee who may be just starting in business and, as the sales volume increases, the lessor receives a percentage.

In the *straight, gross, or flat lease*, the lessee makes periodic payments of rent over a fixed period of time with the lessee's responsibility limited to the rental payment. This lease may have a renewal option and may provide for an escalator clause to accommodate increased costs. An example of a flat lease would be an apartment lease.

The **ground lease** is used when a parcel of unimproved land is leased, usually for a long period of time. If the owner does not wish to sell the land and has no plans to build on it, a ground lease may be the answer. The tenant agrees to erect a building, so it is desirable for him to have a long-term lease. It usually is a net lease and should remain fixed for a specified period of time. Renegotiation of rent is normally based on current market value of the land. It allows the lessee to build the building without the cost of purchasing the land, and it gives the lessor a fixed, long-term return on the land.

Leasing bare land

An example of a place where ground leases might be used is on homesites in a recreational area. A provision in the lease generally stipulates the disposition of the improvements at the termination of the lease. The reversionary interest may revert to either the lessee or the lessor.

The *oil and gas lease* gives the lessee the right to explore on the land of the lessor. A flat rent is usually paid, and if oil or gas is discovered, the landowner receives royalties.

The *sandwich lease* develops when there is a sublease. The lessor is on the top layer, the lessee is in the middle, and the sublessee is on the bottom layer.

The *reappraisal lease* protects the owner by requiring periodic reappraisals of the value of the leased property. A long-term lease usually is reevaluated every five years. If the property has increased in value, the rent is increased by the percentage called for in the original lease. If the value has decreased, the rent will likewise decrease.

The **sale-leaseback** of real estate provides for the property to be sold on the condition that it is leased back to the seller. The buyer becomes the lessor, and the seller is the lessee. The seller's money is released and available for inventory or reinvesting, and the seller retains possession, leasing back from the buyer. In addition, the rental payments are deductible from the seller's income tax. The sale-leaseback arrangement is desirable for the buyer also, since the investor has a guaranteed tenant and may

Seller rents back from buyer

deduct depreciation on the structure from taxable income, lessening tax liability. The new owner will also be building up equity in the investment.

The *graduated lease* is also referred to as a stepped-up lease, as it provides for a series of graded increases in the rent at stated intervals. This type of lease is advantageous to the lessee because it can start at a lower rental and increase as the business matures.

An *index lease* calls for periodic increases or decreases in rent. This change is locked into some national index, such as the cost-of-living index.

An *air lease* gives the right to occupy the space of another over a designated property. A restaurant built over a freeway and elevated walkways that connect buildings across streets are examples of property under air leases.

Summary

Since not all people own real estate, a segment of the population leases housing or business space from investors. The majority of state statutes requires that a lease must be in writing if it is for more than a year. The tenant has a nonfreehold estate in the property of the landlord and under the terms of the lease acquires the right to the use of the property for the time period stipulated in the lease.

The four major leasehold interests include the estate for years, which is for a specified time period; the periodic lease, which is for an indefinite period with no stated termination date; the tenancy at will, which allows for either the lessee or the lessor to decide the length of the lease; and the tenancy at sufferance, which occurs when the tenant has stayed past the lease term and becomes a holdover tenant. The lease should define the time period, the amount of rent, the liability, possession, and responsibilities of each party.

If the lessee violates the terms of the lease, the lessor may institute proceedings for actual eviction of the tenant. If the lessor does not maintain the property in a livable manner, the lessee can abandon the property under the terms of constructive eviction.

For commercial tenants who lease space for a business, leases vary. Many owners request the tenant pay a portion of the expenses under a net lease arrangement. These expenses may include repairs, tax escalations, insurance, and maintenance. Percentage leases are often imposed upon retail merchants, requiring them to pay a flat fee plus a percentage of their profits based on the volume of business they transact.

There are specific leases to cover houses, apartments, farms, office buildings, retail stores, and commercial and industrial tracts. Each type of lease is specially designed to cover the rights and privileges of lessor and lessee of the property.

Discussion Questions

1. Explain the advantages of the sale-leaseback to the seller-lessee and to the buyer-lessor.
2. Under what conditions can a lessee remove improvements made when the lease terminates?
3. If you were leasing an apartment but planned to buy a home in the near future, which type of lease would you prefer?
4. Explain the difference between an estate for years and a periodic estate.
5. What rights does the lessee have under the terms of a tenancy at sufferance?
6. Explain the difference between a sublease and the assignment of a lease.

REVIEW QUESTIONS

Answers to these questions are found in the Answer Key section at the back of the book.

1. When the lessee assigns the lease to another:

   a. the lessee gives up the remainder of the lease
   b. a portion of the lease is retained
   c. the existing lease is terminated
   d. a portion of the space is leased for a specific time

2. When a property is sold:

   a. leases automatically expire
   b. leases are assigned to the new owner
   c. a lessee can break the terms of her lease
   d. the lessee can assign the lease to another without agreement of the purchaser

3. Demise refers to:

   a. the death of a grantor
   b. a gift by will
   c. interest by decree
   d. an estate of lease

4. One of the features of a ground lease is:

   a. it is always a net lease
   b. it is a long-term lease
   c. the term is short
   d. it is a tenancy at will

5. Which lease calls for periodic changes in the amount of the lease fee?

   a. a graduated lease
   b. a percentage lease
   c. a gross lease
   d. a net lease

6. A percentage lease refers to:

   a. a straight lease
   b. a lease with a sliding scale whereby the rent gradually increases
   c. a minimum base rent plus a percentage of the volume of sales
   d. a flat fee that diminishes over a period of years

7. Who is the final tenant on a sale-leaseback?

   a. the buyer
   b. the seller
   c. the optionor
   d. the optionee

8. A lease that requires the tenant to pay all or a stated portion of the expenses is a:

   a. gross lease
   b. flat lease
   c. percentage lease
   d. net lease

9. When the premises reach a physical condition in which the tenant is unable to occupy them for the purpose intended, the situation is legally recognized as:

   a. actual eviction
   b. constructive eviction
   c. surrender and acceptance
   d. income conversion

10. All of the following are necessary in a lease, EXCEPT:

    a. the names of the parties
    b. a description of the property
    c. a renewal option
    d. the rent and terms of the lease

11. Under the terms of the estate for years, if either the lessor or lessee dies the lease is:

    a. canceled
    b. renegotiated
    c. unchanged
    d. liable for breach of contract

12. In a net lease arrangement, a lessee may be liable for:

    a. utilities
    b. depreciation
    c. mortgage payments
    d. special assessments

13. Cancellation of a lease by mutual consent of the lessor and lessee is referred to as:

    a. assignment of the lease
    b. renegotiation of the lease

c. surrender and acceptance

d. novation

14. The tenant has the least interest in a(n):

    a. estate at will

    b. periodic tenancy

    c. estate for years

    d. tenancy at sufferance

15. The reversionary interest is owned by:

    a. the mortgagor

    b. the life tenant

    c. the grantee

    d. the lessor

16. A lease may best be described as:

    a. an option and a contract

    b. consideration

    c. a contract and a conveyance

    d. an assignable contract

17. A lessee may terminate a lease by:

    a. assignment

    b. moving prior to termination date and not paying the remaining balance due

c. constructive eviction

d. subletting

18. A person renting an apartment would most likely have what type of lease?

    a. gross

    b. net

    c. percentage

    d. graduated

19. The lease that would be least affected by death is:

    a. tenancy at sufferance

    b. tenancy for life

    c. estate for years

    d. periodic estate

20. A landlord-tenant relationship would be which of the following?

    a. at will

    b. severalty

    c. tenancy by entireties

    d. a freehold estate

Property Management

KEY WORDS

Certified Property Manager (CPM)
industrial parks
management budget
management contract
neighborhood shopping centers
office parks

property management
regional centers
resident manager
residential property management
strip centers

OVERVIEW

In many states a real estate license is required to manage the real estate of another. It is a natural progression for the real estate firms that specialize in the sale of investment properties to operate a management department to supervise their clients' investments. A property manager is employed to take over the management responsibility for the owner, and by applying knowledge and expertise, the manager tries to produce the greatest net return possible for the investor. The manager has a fiduciary relationship with the principal and is responsible to protect the clients' investments. This chapter will cover the diversified properties that require management and the duties and obligations of the property manager.

THE NEED FOR MANAGEMENT

Property management has escalated due to the many investors that have busy schedules allowing little spare time for the problems of management. These owners prefer to turn the responsibility of their investments over to capable management specialists who, because of their expertise, are able to create greater profits. Investment syndicates, composed of a number of individuals who band together to purchase investment properties, also need management firms to administer their investments. Absentee owners are becoming more prevalent and need the reliable services of management companies to care for their investments.

Managing property as career

The owner-investor is hiring a manager to oversee a large capital investment and should select a management firm that has the ability to bring a profitable return to the investor. There are several professional trade organizations that train managers, offering designations and accreditation to members who complete a variety of courses in property management. The Institute of Real Estate Management (IREM), an affiliate of the National Association of REALTORS®, offers a **Certified Property Manager (CPM)** and an accredited property manager (APM) designation to qualified persons.

They award the accredited management organization (AMO) to qualified management firms. The Building Owners and Managers Association (BOMA) offers management courses that lead to the Real Property Administrator (RPA) designation.

Far from being merely rent collectors, today's managers possess technical knowledge in such areas as marketing, accounting, finance, and social psychology. They must be detail-oriented since they will be involved with large dollar volumes, and they must be people-oriented so that they maintain a high rate of occupancy. By reviewing the manager's credentials and past performance as you would if hiring a manager to administer any other business, you can help to ensure competency that will generate high profits coupled with attention to property maintenance.

Specialization of property management

A property manager may specialize in just one type of property and, since there are vast differences between properties, an expert in apartment management may not necessarily be as knowledgeable in managing farm properties, shopping centers, or office buildings.

Property managers also act as consultants to owners who want advice about upgrading their investment in an effort to produce a greater yield. Updating and modernizing may make a difference in profits, or converting the building to condominium units may be recommended. The building's location, economic conditions, and competition are all factors that will be analyzed in making the decision. Property management may involve the following specializations.

The Residential Property

Duties of the residential manager

Residential property management includes the management of single-family homes, duplexes, apartment buildings, and condominium complexes. The apartment building, generally owned by one or more investors, represents the greatest opportunity for the residential manager.

Among the apartment complex manager's concerns are securing and retaining tenants, collecting rents, advertising, providing cleaning and maintenance services, and keeping financial records and accounts. Investigating the prospective tenant's credit record and present employment should be standard procedure, and obtaining references from past landlords gives additional assurance of the tenant's stability. Exercising care in screening applicants results in fewer vacancies and less collection loss.

Proper maintenance and quick attention to tenant complaints means contented occupants who tend to remain longer. When vacancies do occur, a careful analysis of why is important. The most effective ways to advertise and promote are also important. This requires a well-planned budget that includes a percentage allotted to advertising.

The federal fair housing laws must be adhered to in renting residential space. An amendment to the Fair Housing Act became effective March 12, 1989, and prohibits discrimination based on handicap or families with children. See Chapter 17 for the complete fair housing law.

Condominium management has surfaced in the past few decades because of the increase in this residential type of ownership. Condominiums can be divided into the complexes used by permanent residents and the recreational units purchased by investors or families as vacation retreats. They require management just as do apartment buildings, except the owner-occupied units dispense with the need for interior maintenance. The need for maid services and periodic interior refurbishing exists in the leasing of furnished units. The assessments must be collected by management of both owner-occupied and rental units.

The **resident manager** is an "on site" manager who administers the day-to-day affairs of a residential building. Living on the premises, the manager is available to consult with the tenants on any problems or concerns that arise. A pleasant, congenial *Lives on premises* resident manager is extremely helpful to the management firm in retaining good tenant relations. Resident managers collect the rent, show and lease vacancies, and see that maintenance is executed by the staff hired to perform those tasks. Any rules and regulations regarding recreational facilities, parking and storage areas, and trash removal should be presented to the tenants at the inception of the lease so that no misunderstandings develop. Resident managers are usually compensated with a living unit plus a salary that will vary depending on the size of the complex and the duties they are required to render.

Office Space

Managing leased office space is another specialty requiring careful analysis of the prospective tenants in a given building. If all the tenants create excessive traffic, the available parking area may prove insufficient. While accounting firms, attorneys, and *Managing office space* small businesses may not need an abundance of parking space, a physician or dental clinic could mean considerable traffic. The needs of the tenants must be carefully considered if the property manager expects to do justice by the owner and the tenant.

Large office buildings, especially high-rise structures, require supervision of the considerable staff needed for the operation and maintenance of the building. Trained specialists such as electricians, engineers, and purchasing agents must be supervised by trained management. The personnel needed for the accounting system alone is considerable. Cleaning, security, and maintenance usually require around-the-clock attendance to the property.

A trend toward business or **office parks** has become prevalent in some areas of the country. Usually built as one-story office buildings, this office community offers a variety of options for both the small business and the very large user. While rental cost of residential space is monthly based on the unit size, with one bedroom less than a two bedroom, commercial space is generally priced for annual use per square foot. Thus, if a 1,500 square foot space rents for $10 a square foot, that equals $15,000 annual rent, or $1,250 per month.

Retail Properties

Shopping centers can be divided into three categories: neighborhood shops, strip centers, and regional centers. **Strip centers** generally consist of a single building with 4 to 12 bays that are conveniently located with easy access to and from main arteries. The larger **neighborhood shopping centers** may be made up of several buildings grouped together with 15 or more retail bays. **Regional centers** house several nationally recognized stores such as Sears, Ward's, and Penney's, known as anchor stores, with a broad mix of other shops. Many times these stores are all under one roof and offer covered parking, theaters, cafes, and seating facilities for the weary shopper in a central mall. Some regional centers have skating rinks to occupy youngsters while their parents shop. Any such amenities in the center enhance it in the eye of the shopper.

Periodic redecorating and refurbishing need to take place to keep competitive with new shopping malls developed in the community. Competition among retailers is keen, and with the ever growing small specialty stores that are franchised, it is easier today for the entrepreneur to set up a shop and start into business with training pro- *Managing retail stores* vided by the franchisor. The commercial manager needs to understand the type of tenant best suited to the particular center. A prospective tenant may desire a clause in the lease that disallows competition from a similar store. To place several beauty salons, dress shops, or bookstores in a small neighborhood center may result in insufficient volume for any of the businesses. Many shopping bays have heating and air conditioning ducts above suspended ceilings that could conduct odors across to adjoining spaces. A restaurant specializing in fish or fried foods next door to a dress shop could create unpleasant odors in the clothing store. The rent on retail space in shopping malls is generally a flat fee plus a percentage based on the volume of business transacted, so it is important to the owner that the merchant is successful in the business venture.

Industrial Property

Managing industrial parks

The need for industrial centers to have easy access to major traffic arteries, interstate highways, and rail transportation has led to tracts strictly developed for industrial use. The tracts are more strategically located away from the central core of the city. Referred to as **industrial parks**, they are built in suburban areas that will accommodate industrial needs. A listing of a warehouse will recite such items as trackage available, ceiling heights, utilities, and docks. Light industry manufacturers, bottling companies, paint distributors, and businesses in need of warehousing space are examples of merchants who locate in industrial tracts. Managers of this space will generally be the same real estate firms that sell the property. Industrial use properties that are built for a special purpose usually carry long-term leases contracted on a net basis and thus require less managing.

Farmland

A farm management company provides complete services for the farm landowner. Concerned with assuring the owner maximum returns from the land, a farm management specialist analyzes the farm to evaluate its production potential.

Managing agricultural property

One of the first steps is to take an inventory of the farm's soil and physical resources. The management service will also evaluate the farm's conservation practices, with the proper use of waterways and/or terrace construction, and maintenance. The farm may be adaptable to irrigation and might therefore produce a greater return for the tenant and the owner. If the soil is wet, it may be necessary to complete a tilling program to carry water away from the wet areas and thus provide more land for farming or to make the area less prone to flooding and therefore produce a higher-yielding crop. The farm manager takes preventive measures to eliminate as much soil erosion as possible.

Rotating crops prevents the exhaustion of the land's natural minerals. Crop planning also includes cost-efficient fertilizer in co-op quantities. Savings can be passed on to the owners.

The professional farm manager is responsible for the selection of the best tenant possible with lease terms on a share crop, cash rent, guaranteed bushel, or net lease basis.

By keeping abreast of the many marketing techniques available, the manager is able to offer suggestions on handling the sale of the crop to maximize profits. This may include deferred payment, price-later contracts, cash sales, or hedging.

Finally, the farm manager maintains accurate records on the farm's production to improve the returns of the farm. Complete accounting is provided for the landowner with completely audited financial statements listing expenses paid and income received from the farm. The farm management firm reviews proper insurance programs and makes recommendations to the landowner. The firm reviews and pays the real estate taxes and incorporates the data into the financial statements. The managers prepare annual summaries for the landowners for use in their income tax preparation.

With the increase of farmland being sold to corporations, the need for knowledgeable farm managers has become greater.

MANAGEMENT CONTRACTS

As you can see, the operations involved in such diversified real estate requires specialized training in the role of manager to properly serve the owner. Likewise, the **management contract** will differ, depending on the real estate under management.

The contract between the principal and the manager should clearly define the responsibilities, obligations, and duties of the manager and the owner (see Figure 13.1). The contract should include the following basic items:

Contents of a management contract

1. names of the parties to the contract
2. description of the property
3. the duration of the contract
4. terms of the contract
5. the management fees
6. the authority vested in the agent (owners will vary in the responsibility they relinquish to the manager)
7. a budget for operating expenses
8. a provision for monthly accounting by the manager to the owner
9. a statement as to purpose and goals

THE MANAGEMENT PLAN

Before the contract is signed, a physical inspection of the exterior and interior of the property should be made. Deferred maintenance may need immediate attention, and minor problem areas should be prioritized. The manager must know the owner's objectives and make the owner aware of current market conditions, what the competition is, and what rents can be expected. The owner should be informed of this information on an ongoing basis. Since the owner's potential income is in direct proportion to vacancies and operating expenses, a careful plan should be formed to meet these objectives.

Organizing a management plan

A typical plan used by an office building management firm would include:

1. Assigning an experienced licensed property manager to the project.
2. Supervision of all services performed whether by in-house or by outside contractors. Bids would be solicited and awarded for contractor services such as cleaning and security. Supervision of contractors once bids are awarded.
3. Will serve as a general contractor or to supervise general contractors for leasehold and capital improvements.
4. Handle all tenant relations including lease renewals.
5. Collect rents, pay bills, and provide operating statements itemizing income and expenses on a timely basis.
6. Prepare an annual budget of the financial operation.
7. Provide maintenance personnel, as necessary, to perform repairs and maintenance of the property.
8. Maintain 24-hour accessibility of assigned property manager to immediately handle emergencies which may arise at the property regardless of time or duration.
9. Set up all mechanical systems not under warranty on either service contracts or in-house maintenance programs.

MANAGEMENT AGREEMENT

_____ (hereinafter called Owner), and _____ (hereinafter called Agent), agree as follows:

A. The Owner hereby employs the Agent exclusively to rent and manage the property known as _____ upon the terms hereinafter set forth, for a period of _____ years beginning on the _____ day of _____, 19___, and ending on the _____ day of _____, 19___, and thereafter for yearly periods from time to time, unless on or before _____ the expiration of any such renewal period, either party hereto shall notify the other in writing that it decides to terminate this Agreement, in which case this Agreement shall be thereby terminated on said last mentioned date.

B. The Agent Agrees:

1. To accept the management of the above mentioned property and agrees to furnish services for the rental operation and management of the Premises.

2. To render a monthly statement of receipts, disbursements and charges to the Owner and to remit each month the net proceeds (provided Agent is not required to make any mortgage, escrow or tax payment on the first day of the following month). Agent will remit the net proceeds or the balance thereof after making allowance for such payments to the Owner. In case the disbursements and charges shall be in excess of the receipts, the Owner agrees to pay such excess promptly, nothing herein contained shall obligate the Agent to advance its own funds on behalf of the Owner.

3. The Agent agrees to have all employees who handle any money to be bonded.

C. The Owner Agrees: To give the Agent the following authority and powers (all or any which may be exercised in the name of the Owner) and agrees to assume all expenses in connection therewith:

1. To advertise the property, to display signs, and to rent said property. Agent will investigate prospective tenants and to sign leases, renew and or cancel existing leases and prepare and execute the new lease. To terminate tenancies and to sign and serve such notices as are deemed needful by the Agent; to institute and prosecute actions to remove tenants and to recover possession of the property; to sue for and recover rent: and, when expedient, to settle, compromise and release such actions or suits, or reinstate such tenancies.

2. To collect rents due or to become due and issue receipts to deposit all funds collected hereunder in the Agent's custodial account.

3. To refund tenants' security deposits at the expiration of leases.

4. To hire, discharge and pay all caretakers and other employees; to make all ordinary repairs and replacements necessary to preserve the property in its present condition and for the operating efficiency thereof and all alterations and decorating required to comply with lease requirements and to enter into agreements for all necessary repairs and maintenance; to purchase supplies and pay all bills.

a. To indemnify, defend and save the Agent harmless from all suits in connection with the Premises and from liability for damage to property and injuries to or death of any employee or other person whomsoever, and to carry at his (its) own expense public liability, and workmen's compensation insurance naming the Owner and the Agent and adequate to protect their interests.

5. To pay any expenses incurred by the Agent, including, without limitation, attorney's fees for counsel employed to represent the Agent or the Owner.

6. Owner agrees to pay to said agent _____ per month or _____ percent (_____%) of the monthly gross receipts from the operation of the Premises during the period this Agreement remains in full force and effect, whichever is the greater amount.

7. This Agreement may be cancelled by Owner before the termination date specified in Paragraph 1 on not less than _____ days prior written notice to the Agent, provided that such notice is accompanied by payment to the Agent of a cancellation fee in an amount equal to _____% of the management fee that would accrue over the remainder of the stated term of the Agreement. For this purpose the monthly management fee for the remainder of the stated term shall be presumed to be the same as that of the last month prior to service of the notice of cancellation.

IN WITNESS WHEREOF, the parties hereto have affixed or caused to be affixed their respective signatures this _____ day of _____, 19___.

_____   _____
Witness   Owner

_____   _____
Witness   Agent

FIGURE 13.1
Example of a
management contract.

FUNCTIONS OF THE MANAGER

The manager's function is considered threefold:

1. secure and retain tenants, thus generating income
2. preserve the property's value by conscientious care and maintenance
3. provide financial accounting and records for the investor

RENTING THE SPACE

The primary goal of the manager is to market the client's space to yield the greatest net return. Whether the space is living accommodations, office space, or commercial space, the prospective tenant will be seeking the most advantageous location for the tenant's needs at the best price available. The manager's task is to achieve and maintain a high occupancy rate with a low turnover rate.

Marketing the space

The manager may need to adjust the rental rate if the supply of rentals is greater than the demand. However, care must be taken not to favor any one tenant by reducing rent on a particular unit.

In leasing commercial areas it is wise to reserve space for a growing tenant to expand into by filling in with a tenant needing less space. Allowing the larger tenant an area for expansion may prevent the business from moving at a later date. It is not unusual to give a large anchor tenant concessions to induce other businesses to the complex.

EMPLOYEES

Property managers will select personnel with care, since the managers are accountable to the employer for their actions. By carefully interviewing applicants to evaluate their abilities, desires, and ambitions and following up with a good training program and adequate supervision, the manager can build a staff of conscientious employees. As word of the manager's expertise spreads, her business will expand.

Selecting the staff

MAINTENANCE

To preserve the property's physical condition the manager sees that the property is kept clean and attractive. Prompt attention to tenant repairs will result in contented and cooperative tenants. The manager conducts routine inspections and supervises the maintenance of the complex. Manicured lawns, trimmed hedges, clean walls and floors in the corridors, and keeping all facilities in working conditions are the manager's responsibility to ensure the preservation of the client's investment.

SECURITY

Adequate safety precautions are necessary to ensure the safety of the tenant and lessen the possibility of crime. Sufficient lighting in parking areas and hallways should be standard care. Some apartment buildings and office complexes have television monitors at entries, and in other situations, security guards are employed. Security arrangements to handle emergencies should be provided but will vary greatly depending on whether it is an apartment, office, or industrial building.

THE BUDGET

Operating statement

The manager has prepared a financial plan that includes an annual budget for financial operation of the property. Operating statements itemizing income and expenses will be presented to the owner on a timely basis. The budget will outline the expected return and expenses calculated from past years' performances, but expected trends relative to economic conditions must be considered. The budget will provide the investor with a criterion from which to measure the property manager's performance. Managers are often paid incentives for keeping the property at maximum capacity.

The detailed accounting of expenditures and disbursements to the owners indicates whether the manager is controlling expenses and producing the greatest net return possible for the owners without neglecting maintenance needs. He supervises the maintenance employees to ascertain that the work is skillfully accomplished with materials acquired at a reasonable rate. By insisting upon proper vouchers and receipts, the manager maintains efficient control of costs.

A typical **management budget** for an apartment complex should contain the following items:

I. Expenses
   A. Operating expenses and maintenance service
      1. supplies
      2. painting and decorating
      3. salaries
      4. services
      5. repairs
   B. Utility expenses
      1. heating fuel
      2. electricity
      3. gas
      4. water
   C. Fixed charges
      1. real estate taxes
      2. insurance

The property manager should create a monthly written income and expense report for the owner (see Figure 13.2).

SUMMARY

The need for responsible management to supervise and administer property investments is discussed in this chapter. Many investors pool their funds in joint ventures with others and employ management firms to supervise their investments. While some investors may purchase farmland, others buy shopping centers, office buildings, or residential complexes. Since investments vary so greatly, specialization in management is required. A great deal of expertise is mandatory since the property manager must try to protect the owner's investment and obtain the largest net return the property is capable of producing.

Property management firms are increasing in numbers as more and more people are investing in real estate. Some real estate firms have separate management departments to handle the properties they have sold to investors. The management fee varies in different areas of the country and also is dependent on the type of property managed

INCOME & EXPENSE REPORT

Property Address: 12534 Money Lane   June 1994

Income:

18 units @ $375	$ 6,750	
8 units @ $350	$ 2,800	
6 units @ $325	$ 1,950	
Total	$11,500	

Less Vacancy

1 unit @ $375	$ 375	
Manager's unit	350	

Total rent $10,775

Other income:

Garages - 20 @ $15 $ 300	300	
TOTAL INCOME	$11,075	

Expenses:

Salaries:

Resident manager	500	
Property manager	1,000	1,500

Fixed expenses

Insurance	305	
Taxes	380	685

Variable expenses

Maintenance	402	
Utilities	500	902

Capital expenditures

1 refrigerator	420	
Paint	30	450
TOTAL EXPENSES		$3,537
NET INCOME			$7,538.00
DEBT SERVICE		$4,400
CASH FLOW			$3,138.00

FIGURE 13.2
A typical monthly income and expense report on an apartment complex.

and the quantity of units. For example, 24 single-family homes will create more work than a 24-unit apartment building.

While investing in real estate provides a hedge against inflation, the time involved in renting and maintaining the property can be a troublesome chore for the investor. Owners often prefer to pay a fee to have a professional handle the management details.

The obligations and duties of the property manager are defined in the contract between the parties. The manager is the liaison between the owners and the tenants, handling the tenants' complaints and guarding the owners' interests. The manager sees to the physical care of the building and hires maintenance personnel and resident managers (when a residential complex is involved).

At the end of each month a detailed accounting of expenditures and disbursements must be given to the owners. A typical manager's budget for an apartment complex is included in the chapter.

DISCUSSION QUESTIONS

1. Explain why specialization in property management is important.
2. Once a commercial building is leased, why is continuous management necessary, since the leases are often long term?
3. List some of the responsibilities and obligations of the apartment manager. How do the duties of the resident manager differ from those of the property management firm?
4. What items should be incorporated into a management contract?
5. Who plans the operating budget and why is one necessary?
6. Discuss which recurring expenses are monthly costs and which are annual costs.
7. You have decided to specialize in property management. What type of property would you prefer to handle? Give reasons for your answer.
8. Why can an investor derive more net income from hiring a management firm?

REVIEW QUESTIONS

Answers to these questions are found in the Answer Key section at the back of the book.

1. A property management contract would NOT contain:

   a. the responsibilities assigned to the manager
   b. terms of the contract
   c. the property owner's obligations
   d. renters' names

2. The manager's responsibilities include:

   a. selecting tenants on the basis of the space they require
   b. selecting and retaining tenants
   c. keeping an accurate account of his own salary
   d. advertising only when the building becomes 15 percent vacant

3. Upon signing a management contract with an owner, a broker becomes a:

   a. trustee
   b. receiver
   c. management director
   d. fiduciary

4. All of the following would be included in a typical manager's operating budget, EXCEPT:

   a. the investor's profit
   b. decorating and painting
   c. the manager's salary
   d. cleaning supplies

5. Management is NOT needed by which of the following?

   a. an absentee owner
   b. an investment syndicate
   c. busy investors
   d. resident

6. Which of the following considerations is important in selecting tenants?

   a. the compatibility of tenants
   b. the ethnic background of tenants, since this would be proof of stability
   c. the number of employees in the tenant's business and the number of customers they will serve
   d. obtaining percentage leases from tenants of office space

7. A resident manager will usually perform which of the following duties?

   a. efficient marketing of the space
   b. showing units and obtaining leases
   c. paying complex's taxes
   d. paying complex's mortgage

8. A property manager's responsibilities include all of the following, EXCEPT:

   a. paying utilities
   b. investing profits
   c. renting units

d. collecting security deposits

9. When calculating operating income, a property manager would include which of the following?

   a. income taxes
   b. allowance for vacancies and collections
   c. mortgage payments
   d. allowance for depreciation

10. All of the following statements concerning property management are true, EXCEPT:

    a. a manager of commercial property would not necessarily understand farm management
    b. residential management includes the managing of condominiums
    c. managers care for the absentee owner's property
    d. the largest role of the manager is in the management of commercial property

Investment and Tax Aspects of Ownership

OVERVIEW

Since food, clothing, and shelter are essential to our very existence, most Americans decide it is more prudent to permanently own that shelter than to rent. Ownership of real estate creates the greatest portion of the estate the average person acquires. Inflation contributes to the appreciation of real estate, and most homeowners soon become cognizant of the equity building up in their homes. The sector of the country where the property is located and the local demands for housing determine appreciation of real estate. The high interest rates of the early 1980s slowed that appreciation to a standstill in many parts of the country. As interest rates began to drop in the latter part of 1982, real estate transfers again began to increase. In early 1986 interest rates dropped to 10 percent and 10.5 percent and began to stabilize, causing an increase in refinancing that kept financing institutions busy as homeowners sought the lower rates. Home sales were brisk with the backlog of consumers who felt they could now afford to purchase a home. In early 1987 interest rates had dropped to 8 percent and 8.5 percent, something not seen for many years, making homeownership even more within the realm of possibility for the average American.

The decade of the 1990s began with interest rates at 9.5 percent to 10.5 percent, and a slowing of the economy began. By 1993 the recessionary conditions brought interest rates down to 6 percent and 6.5 percent. As we approach the mid-90s we see a rise in these rates as the economy stabilizes.

This chapter is divided into two distinct areas:

1. investing in a residence
2. investing in income-producing real estate

It will explain the advantages of homeownership as an investment, illustrating the true principal and interest payments when the tax deductions are considered.

The income benefits that the investor in real estate receives will also be covered with a step-by-step analysis of an investment.

HOMEOWNERSHIP AS AN INVESTMENT

Homeownership provides more than shelter; it is one of the most substantial investments that can be made. Owning a home not only enhances pride and self-worth, but also provides a hedge against inflation.

Mortgage interest & tax deductible expenses

The Tax Reform Act of 1986 (TRA 86) brought some sweeping changes to the nation's tax laws, some of which affect the real estate investment market, but the benefits of homeownership remain intact. Itemized deductions are retained on real estate taxes, and mortgage interest continues to be deductible for first and second homes.

The owner of a primary residence and a second vacation home can still deduct interest paid on the mortgages and the real estate taxes. To qualify as a vacation home, the property must be occupied more than 14 days annually or 10 percent of its useful rental period. If it is used fewer than 14 days or less than 10 percent of its useful period, it is considered investment property and is eligible for depreciation in addition to deducting property taxes and mortgage insurance. An added incentive to purchase real estate is that interest is deductible from taxable income.

Home equity loans

Taxpayers can borrow on their homes (such loans are referred to as home equity loans) up to the original purchase price, plus any added improvements, and the interest on such a loan will be deductible. The Tax Reform Act of 1986 stipulates that loans backed by the appreciated value of a home, but used for purposes other than home improvements (consumer loans), are not deductible unless the proceeds are used for tuition or other educational costs, or for medical expenses. Generally, it is not permissible to deduct interest paid on loans above the market value of the property.

CALCULATING THE BENEFITS OF HOMEOWNERSHIP

Tax benefits of investing in real estate are reflected by an individual's gross income. For example, assume a married couple, filing jointly, will pay 31 percent income tax on their earnings. Owning a home allows the following deductions if the couple is paying on a $70,000 mortgage at 10 percent interest:

$70,000	*mortgage*
× .10	*interest rate*
$ 7,000	*annual interest*
× .31	*tax bracket*
$ 2,170	*tax savings allowable*

Now assume the mortgage is for 15 years. Principal and interest payments would be 10.75 for $1,000 (see amortization chart in Chapter 9), or $752.50 per month. With the tax deduction for interest that is paid, the monthly payment is effectively lowered by $180.83 to $571.67 ($2,170 interest ÷ 12 months = $180.83 per month).

In addition, the homeowner may also deduct a portion of the property taxes paid. If the taxes are $1,800 per year, 31 percent of $1,800 = $558 tax savings. Dividing $558 by 12 months reduces the monthly payment another $46.50, leaving an actual monthly house cost of $525.17. Add to these tax advantages the fact that equity is building and that the investment is very likely appreciating in value, and we see why people purchase rather than rent.

Appreciation and Homeownership

As construction costs and land prices rise, real estate continues to appreciate in value in many parts of the country. As discussed in Chapter 1, the supply of funds and market conditions in a given area will affect this value. More people are becoming aware that owning shelter not only brings pride of ownership but also a degree of appreciation in their investment. The demand for housing continues to grow as young adults are realizing the value of owning real estate. With people living longer, housing requirements are being constructed to meet the particular needs of each generation.

Depreciation of a Residence

A homeowner cannot depreciate property considered a residence unless a portion of that residence is used as an office; in such a case, depreciation is allowable along with deductions of business expenses. In effect, the law refrains from considering the building a residence if a portion is used for business. For example, if one room in a six-room house is used as an office, then one-sixth of the expenses of that residence may be deductible. With the advent of computers, fax machines, and other communication technology, combined with the entrepreneurial spirit of many self-employed persons, the home office is becoming more prevalent.

Home business deductions

Sale of a Residence

All sales or exchanges must be reported on IRS form 2119 for the tax year in which the transaction takes place. A tax is imposed upon any gain realized from selling a residence. This tax is postponed, however, if:

1. the taxpayer purchases a new principal residence within a 24-month period preceding or following the sale
2. the cost of the replacement is equal to or more than the house that was sold

Under the above two conditions, the owner is excused from paying tax on any gains realized at the time of the sale. The **gain** is carried over to the new residence and is not taxed until there is a sale without replacement. If the cost of the replacement home is less than the old, any gain realized is taxable immediately to the extent of the difference.

DEFERRING CAPITAL GAINS TAX

When a capital gains tax is deferred, the cost of any improvements to the first home is added to the original purchase price. To minimize taxes, the homeowner should keep accurate records of all improvements. Regular maintenance costs are not deductible. Only capital improvements are deductible, for example, installing an air conditioner, building fences, landscaping, and adding decks or patios.

Costs incurred in the sale are deductible from the amount realized. These selling expenses are the actual costs involved in the sale, such as the broker's commission, legal fees, state transfer fees, and title insurance or abstract fees.

The **basis** is **adjusted**; that is, the gain on the old residence is subtracted from the costs of the new residence. For example:

1985 purchase price	$65,000
1987 added family room	8,500
Adjusted basis	$73,500
1993 sale price	88,000
Less selling expenses	6,330
	$81,670
Less adjusted basis	73,500
Gains from sale	8,170
New purchase	95,000
Less gain from sale	8,170
Adjusted basis	$86,830

The Age-55-and-Older Exclusion

The $100,000 exclusion for homeowners 55 or older was introduced by the Revenue Act of 1978. The amount has since been increased to $125,000 and generally applies to residences sold or exchanged after July 20, 1981. To qualify for this exclusion, the taxpayer must file an election and meet these conditions:

1. The taxpayer must have reached the age of 55 before the date of the sale or exchange, and, if married, only one spouse needs to be 55, but both must join in making the election and *neither* will be eligible for the exclusion a second time.
2. The taxpayer must have owned and used the property as a principal residence for at least *three* of the *five years just before the sale*.

Assume a retired couple sell their home and purchase a smaller, less expensive residence. Using the over-55 exclusion rule:

Adjusted sale price	$185,000
Less: tax basis	45,000
Taxable gain	
(before exclusion)	$140,000
Less: over-55 exclusion	125,000
Taxable gain	
(unless deferred)	$15,000

To defer the tax on the $15,000 gain, the retirees must purchase a home for no less than $60,000, which represents the difference between the sale price and the one-time exclusion of $125,000. Rollover rules allow the taxpayer to defer taxes when buying and selling a home.

Selling at a Loss

If a homeowner is forced to sell at a loss, the tax laws regretfully do not provide any assistance benefits. The loss is not tax deductible. The rationale used is that the home was not purchased as a "for profit" investment. Gains from the sale of personal assets are taxable income, but losses are not deductible.

REAL ESTATE AS AN INCOME-PRODUCING INVESTMENT

The investment in real estate serves many functions. With the realization that real estate is a great hedge against inflation, the number of people investing in income-producing property has grown. Leading economists have found by tracking real estate values through the years that prices keep pace with inflation.

Investing in real estate

Purchasing Real Estate vs. Fixed Income Investment

The main reasons for investing in real estate are:

1. appreciation
2. cash flow
3. equity buildup
4. tax shelter

The primary purpose of the investor is to generate income (cash flow) and to achieve long-term growth of capital without substantial risk. Our most precious resource is time, and income gained other than through one's labor can be realized by limiting present spending in favor of future benefits. A person seeking a fixed return can invest in Treasury bills, certificates of deposit (CDs), municipal bonds, or savings accounts. These forms of savings are secure and produce a fixed income that is easily converted to cash. However, inflation erodes the future purchasing power of these investment dollars. In the case of real estate, appreciation has been a big factor in attracting investors, and for many of these investors, the compelling motive is not only income but the favorable tax advantages connected with investment property.

Advantages of real estate investment

Financial planners will recommend a balanced portfolio, altering the investments to accommodate the individual's age and present and projected incomes. Investments may include buying silver, gold, coins, paintings, stamps, automobiles, and other desirable collector items. An element of risk is involved in speculative investments and liquidating them may prove difficult with the true value unobtainable when the investor wants to cash out. Young people may look at speculative stock while retirees will prefer investments in annuities and CDs to augment their social security payments. A well-rounded portfolio of investments may include several approaches to saving. Unfortunately, when people reach the recognized retirement age of 65, less than 10 percent have saved sufficiently to meet their retirement years with total independence. This is a startling revelation, but it is never too late to begin an investment program. For people involved in real estate, the obvious answer is to purchase what they sell.

Most people accumulate the largest portion of their estate through the equity that builds in homeownership. Thus, it only seems logical that investing in income-producing real estate would further enhance their savings.

The Time Value of Money

Regardless of what is used as a vehicle to increase one's wealth, the old adage "the higher the risk, the greater the return" holds true. A premium is paid for certainty and security. If we can receive 8 percent on a CD that requires no risk or management concerns, why would we invest in real estate and only receive 8 percent return? The bright side of risk is the potential of gain, and the dark side is the potential of loss. When money is lent in the anticipation of receiving the principal (money lent) back plus a return on the principal, referred to as interest, we are risking the return.

Cash Flow

Calculating net return

Ideally, an investment property will yield a positive **cash flow**. The cash flow represents the net proceeds after all expenses are met and may be measured before or after taxes are considered. If an investor has a property that generates an annual income of $44,000 and expenses total $35,000, a net return (cash flow) of $9,000 has been earned.

Income from office building		$44,000
Expenses	17,000	
Debt service (mortgage payment)	18,000	
Cash flow		$ 9,000

Negative cash flow

If the tax deductible expenses involved in a property are greater than the income, there will be, for tax purposes, a **negative cash flow**. To some investors this negative cash flow is desirable because their main concern is to have a **tax shelter**. A tax shelter is best defined as a book loss; it is simply a phrase used to describe some of the advantages of real estate investments. Since investment property can be depreciated as an expense when figuring income tax, it provides a tax shelter for its owner. For example:

Income		$44,000		
Expenses	22,000			
Interest deduction	16,000			
Depreciation deduction	8,000			
	$46,000	$44,000	=	($2,000 loss)

The owner has a book loss of $2,000. Prior to the passage of the TRA 86, owning improved real estate proved to be one of the few, as well as one of the best, methods for sheltering income. The optimum situation results when the property shows a book loss but still has a positive cash flow.

With TRA 86, much of the special tax treatment that was accorded to taxpayers' investment activities was phased out. Generally, the bill considers these investments (including rental properties) **passive income**, that is, not containing the taxpayers' active involvement. Previously a taxpayer's income or loss from all sources were combined and the net amount taxed (with the exception of capital gains or losses) at the graduated rates. Today there are three classifications for income:

Income classification

1. *Active income*: earned by salaries or a business in which the taxpayer materially participates.
2. *Portfolio income*: interest, annuities, dividends, royalties, and profit from the sale of portfolio assets.
3. *Passive activity income*: invested funds.

Losses from passive investments may no longer be used to offset ordinary income. The taxpayer may only deduct these losses from passive investments against income from passive investment; they may not be applied against active or portfolio income. The IRS has described passive investments as all rental income, interests in limited partnerships, and all other business involvements in which the taxpayer is not involved in the operation on a regular and substantial basis. Exempt are working oil and gas properties.

Losses up to $25,000 from real estate rental activities in which the taxpayer actively participates may be used to offset salaries and active business income. This $25,000 amount, however, is phased down to a 50 percent ratio for those taxpayers with income between $100,000 and $150,000. Any losses on real estate investments in excess of these amounts will be treated as passive investment losses; and the $25,000 amount is eliminated entirely.

Rate of Return

The value of an asset is determined by the stream of income it produces over the expected life of the investment. The return on the individual's cash investment can vary greatly, depending on the ratio of cash invested to the purchase price, and also on the cost of financing.

To evaluate the feasibility of an investment, the investors decide what percentage of return they want on their investment and examine the return on the actual investment. If they know they can receive a certain percentage return on CDs or Treasury bonds, they will expect more from a real estate investment because of the risks involved. However, income tax must be paid on the interest earned from savings. With a real estate investment, the earnings can be sheltered since the improvements can be depreciated.

Determining investment return

In the income approach technique for evaluating property investments, the property's net annual income is divided by the desired rate of return. If an investor requires a 12 percent annual return and the property has a $15,000 net annual income, he should pay no more than $125,000.

$$\frac{\$15,000 \text{ (net annual income}}{12\% \text{ (investor's desired}} = \$125,000 \text{ (value of property if investor}$$
$$\text{rate of return} \qquad \text{is willing to accept a 12\% rate of return)}$$

The rate of investor's desired rate of return relates net operating income to the investment.

In using this capitalization method of evaluating an income-producing property, the future income is converted to present value. When the risk is greater, the capitalization rate is higher, thus the value of the income stream is lessened as the capitalization rate increases. Since a property will depreciate and lessen in value as its economic life is depleted, this must be taken into consideration when analyzing the possibility of recapturing the investment. If the remaining life of the property is 25 years, and it is depreciated on a straight-line basis, the property will depreciate at 4 percent a year. As the property depreciates, the income will likewise decline. Since the investor desires a 12 percent return on her investment, the 4 percent (recapture rate) must be added to supply the full return on the investment. Thus, in looking for a 16 percent return, the value of the property in the previous example is now reduced to $93,750.

$$\frac{\$15,000}{16\%} \quad \frac{(income)}{(rate\ of\ return)} = \$93,750\ (property\ value\ to\ investor)$$

Depreciation

Depreciation, as we will discuss it here, is an accounting concept used in federal tax law. It makes available to an investor in real estate a deduction from income derived from a property. For accounting and tax purposes, depreciation is based on estimates of a property's future decrease in value. Even as the investor depreciates his property, it continues to increase in value due to rising construction costs and land values. The realization of this depreciation allowance is further enhanced if the investor has used little of his resources to purchase the property. (For example, if a $60,000 property was acquired with $12,000 in cash and the balance from a loan, the investor was still able to depreciate on the *full* value of the structure.) After the value of its **useful life** (economic life) is over, the **salvage value** remains.

The past ten years have brought dramatic changes in the depreciation methods allowed by the Internal Revenue Service. Prior to 1981, an investor chose one of four methods to depreciate any property or asset eligible for the depreciation allowance. In 1981 Congress passed the Tax Recovery Act, referred to as the Accelerated Cost Recovery System (ACRS). This act replaced the concept of "depreciating" the property with "recovering the cost," enabling the investor to use short-term write-off periods for tax purposes.

Straight-line depreciation

Further changes were introduced as a result of TRA 86. This act stated that residential rental property placed in service after January 1, 1987, must be depreciated on a straight-line basis over 27½ years, and that nonresidential real estate must be depreciated on a straight-line basis over 31½ years. TRA 1993 amended this to increase the depreciable lives of nonresidential properties placed in service on or after May 13, 1993. Straight-line depreciation is depreciation of the asset figured in equal installments over a predetermined period of time. Automobiles and light trucks may be depreciated over five years and manufacturing equipment over a seven-year period. Additionally, any losses resulting from depreciation cannot be used to shelter other "earned" income.

Depreciation only on improvements

Depreciation can be taken only on the improvements on land and not on the land itself, since land does not diminish in value—literally, it does not wear out. Tax assessors separate the land and improvements when they appraise the property for tax purposes. Assuming that the market value and the cost of the property were the same as the assessed value, the following is an example of the annual depreciation cost of a single-family residential rental:

Address:	7007 Mulberry Drive
Legal:	Lot 3, Block 7, Fall Rapids Subdivision
Land value:	$ 32,000
Improvements:	$ 88,000
Assessed value	$120,000

Since the example that we have used here is a residential property rental, the amount that can be depreciated must be done over 27½ years. Continuing with our example,

Improvements: $ 88,000 ÷ 27.5 (years)

$ 3,200 = Annual amount available for depreciation

Leverage

Using other people's money

The investor may borrow money to finance the greater share of an investment. By using other people's money the investor's buying power is increased. This use of borrowed funds is called **leverage**. The investor will want to put the least possible amount down and obtain the lowest available interest rate over the longest period of time. This allows the investor to accumulate the maximum amount of real estate with the minimum amount of personal funds.

However, for the investor expecting a cash flow, the expenses and mortgage costs may well exceed the returns if too much leverage is used. While tax shelters, appreciation, and cash flow are all great motivators for purchasing, the investment must not be leveraged to the point that a cash flow is impossible. The choice the investor selects must have reasonable likelihood of satisfying the objective of increasing the purchaser's net worth. Not only does the present value need to be considered, but its future income stream should be analyzed. Mentioned earlier in this text were the forces that influence value. If the investor buys with the intention of selling or if conditions develop that necessitate a sale, economic conditions may not be conducive to a quick sale. The *lack of liquidity* is one of the biggest risk factors involved in owning real estate.

Let us take a property and analyze the difference on the rate of return when cash is paid versus leveraging with a mortgage.

1. Cash investment:
   $125,000 investment with a $15,000 net income
   $15,000 ÷ $125,000 = 12 percent return

2. Investment financed:
   $125,000 investment
   $93,750 mortgage (75%) = $31,250 equity invested
   subtract one year's interest at 10% ($9,375.00) from $15,000
   net income = $5,625 net income.
   $5,625 (net income) ÷ $31,250 (initial investment) = 18% return annually.

Remember, the above figures on investment/financing are predicated on the rate of return on the investment. To many investors this is more meaningful since it considers only the amount of cash they have invested. The investment will be growing in equity and hopefully appreciating in value.

There are various types of real estate investments from which to choose. The investor may purchase single-family homes, duplexes, fourplexes, apartments, condominiums, office buildings, strip shopping centers, farms, acreage, or bare development land. There is literally something for everyone. If the investor needs immediate income, vacant land would be a poor choice. Holding power is needed since property taxes, interest, and insurance are constant costs. The speculator gambles on the premise that the land will increase in value, a risk that all investors are not ready to assume.

Investment opportunities

Consider a typical American couple who own their own home. They have been able to accumulate $6,000 in savings, $5,000 of which they decide to use to purchase a rental house. After searching every weekend for the perfect unit, they make concessions and finally decide on an older two-story house that has been converted into two apartments and is located in a modest neighborhood. Inspections reveal newer wiring and two modern furnaces. No measurable deferred maintenance is observed. They purchase the property for $45,000 with a $40,000 loan at 10 percent interest for 20 years with monthly payments of $386.40. Insurance coverage costs $140.00 a year and annual taxes are $450. The units rent for $280 and $320 each.

Income

$280 @ 12 mos.	=	$3,360.00
$320 @ 12 mos.	=	3,840.00
Gross income	=	$7,200.00

Expenses

Insurance policy	$140.00	
Supplies & materials	180.00	
Taxes	450.00	
Maintenance	320.00	
Mortgage payments	4,636.80	
	$5,726.80	$7,200.00 (income)
Net Income		$1,473.20

This is not taking into consideration income tax deductions for interest and real estate taxes.

All physical labor such as yard care and minor repairs are done by the owners, and technically they should place a value on their time. Had the investors taken their $5,000 and invested it in a CD at 7 percent, the annual yield would have been $350, before taxes.

They realize that their profit can be wiped out if a unit remains vacant for a period of time. They have discussed with one tenant carpet replacement for his unit, with the tenant agreeing to a raise in rent from $280 to $305 a month. To recover the cost of the carpet will take 2½ years, but they are assured of a happy tenant who will not vacate the unit. The couple is pleased with their investment, and when their savings build up, they plan to search for another property.

The principle of increasing and decreasing returns must be acknowledged. Continued improvement of a property will eventually reach a leveling-off point beyond which rents cannot be raised. To place microwaves, fireplaces, and jacuzzis in the units would not be a justifiable expense and would result in overimprovement.

The couple's upkeep and care of the property have enhanced its value, and they can use the equity in that investment to leverage buying another. They could either draw some of the equity out or use it as collateral for a blanket mortgage that could cover both properties.

Now the pyramiding begins. If they were to continue the process, a portfolio of investments could be secured. The careful investor will not overleverage or the pyramid will come tumbling down. It should be built with the stability of an Egyptian pyramid and withstand all foreseeable obstacles.

The Investment Scenario

The investor now has additional taxable income; that is, the investor has spendable income plus the capital gains or equity income in the property. The investor can depreciate the real estate holdings, and the interest on the loan is deductible. The taxable income is the investment net, less interest and depreciation. The spendable income is the investment net, less principal, interest, and tax costs. The equity income is the investment net, less the income and interest, but adding the appreciation of the investment.

Rehabilitation Tax Credit

Congress passed an investment tax credit for investors who rehabilitate buildings that qualify as historical buildings or older buildings that can be placed back in service. The investor is saving a building and bringing it back onto the tax rolls. The allowable credit is 20 percent for certified historical buildings and 10 percent for other buildings built before 1936. A tax credit receives full value as a deduction on income tax, which is more favorable than the property tax. For example, if a taxpayer is in the 28 percent tax bracket, only that percentage of the property taxes is deductible; 28 percent of $1,500 (assumed taxes) = $420. The Rehabilitation Tax Credit would allow the full $1,500.

Refinancing Versus Selling

Freeing equity by refinancing

Equity builds up in an investment property through increased value of the property and principal reduction on the amortized loan. The owner can then refinance the property with a new loan and use the tax-free money to purchase another property. Since this is borrowed money, it is not taxable. By refinancing, taxes on gains are avoided since taxes are payable only on the sale of the property. The owner is now able to purchase additional properties with the money obtained through refinancing and thus can pyramid her holdings. By carefully choosing properties that increase in value, the owner can refinance each after holding the property for a reasonable period of time, depending on current market conditions, and use the money to purchase other properties. If the investor so chooses, she can avoid taxes forever by leaving the properties to heirs.

Tax-Deferred Exchanges and Installment Sales

To defer capital gains, an investor can make a **tax free exchange** of the property for another like property. This simply means that real estate must be exchanged for real estate. A duplex could be exchanged for a sixplex, or an apartment could be traded for an office building. The quality of the property is not questioned. "Like kind" refers to the nature, class, or character of the real property. If it is not an equal exchange and additional money or goods are included, the extra money is called *boot* and, if it represents a gain, is taxed at the time of transfer. The depreciated book value of the old property will be carried to the new, and the adjustments for the additional compensation (boot) will be added to the property.

Exchanging property defers capital gains

Had the investor of the duplex at 7007 Mulberry Drive exchanged his property for another, taxes could have been deferred as follows:

Duplex sale price	$120,000	New fourplex	$180,000
Adjusted basis	$ 41,000	Boot needed	$ 60,000

The new **basis** for the fourplex is $101,000. This is the basis of the duplex, $41,000, carried over to the new purchase, plus the boot of $60,000.

When payment on the gross sale price of a property is received for a period of two or more years, the transaction qualifies as an **installment sale**. The seller is permitted to defer paying the capital gain tax on a prorated basis with receipt of the installments. A portion of the installment is treated as interest, a portion as capital gain, and a portion is nontaxable.

Capital Gains

The Tax Reform Act of 1986 repealed the long-term capital gains deduction for gains realized. Capital gains income will be taxed as ordinary income, with a top bracket of 28 percent. Most affected by this ruling will be the recapture of depreciation since profit from a sale is now treated as ordinary income. If the gains tax were lowered, the investment market would be stimulated, resulting in economic growth and increased revenues.

GROUP BUSINESS VENTURE

Many times business enterprises are formed by a group of individuals who have a common purpose in mind. Partnerships, corporations, syndications, and trusts hold real estate for business purposes. Investors join others in a **joint venture** or **limited partnership**, since they can acquire larger properties by pooling their funds.

Pooling funds

Partnerships are formed by two or more people who join forces to carry out an idea together for profit-making reasons. The partnership may be operated in the name of the owners or in a trade name selected by the partners.

Two types of legally recognized partnerships exist: the *general partnership* and the *limited partnership*.

In the general partnership the individuals involved manage and operate the business. The partners take total responsibility for both profits and losses. Some of the disadvantages are as follows:

1. Each partner is personally liable for any debts incurred, and his personal assets may be attached.
2. One partner can obligate the others.
3. Death will terminate the partnership.

4. Consent of all partners for decisions.
5. Lack of liquidity, since it may be difficult to sell a partnership interest.

The advantages include the following:

1. The partnership is not taxed (as a corporation is).
2. Partners can share their money and expertise to build a business.
3. Partners are treated for tax purposes as active investors.

Joint investing in a limited partnership

A limited partnership involves a general partner and two or more limited partners. Although the limited partners are the investors, they do not take an active role in management but are passive investors, and a general manager is paid to handle the investment. The limited partners are held responsible for losses only to the amount of their investment; the general manager usually conceives and organizes the partnership. The agreement is so drawn that the death or withdrawal of one of the partners does not affect the partnership.

The investors' liability is limited, and they have no management obligations. The general manager, however, must be capable and have a good track record and is the responsible party. Furthermore, limited partnership shares are difficult to sell or transfer since all partners usually must agree to the transfer. There are many combinations of limited partnerships. A typical joint venture is illustrated in Figure 14.1.

The joint purchasers of the property outlined in Figure 14.1 have an additional gross income added to the total cost:

$3,000,000   *cost to acquire property*
1,000,000   *gross income*
$4,000,000   *sale price to limited partners*

The development and management expenses are deducted from the gross income:

$1,000,000   *gross income*
475,000   *expenses*
$ 525,000   *net income*

The limited partners will receive the full amount of their invested funds plus a percentage—say 10 percent. The balance of the profits will be evenly divided between the limited partners and the general manager.

Owning stock in a corporation

Corporations are legal entities formed by two or more parties and are considered by law as individual "persons." The stockholders of a corporation may obtain money without becoming personally liable. Unlike a partner, a stockholder has only her own investment at stake. The corporation may hold title to property and enter into contracts

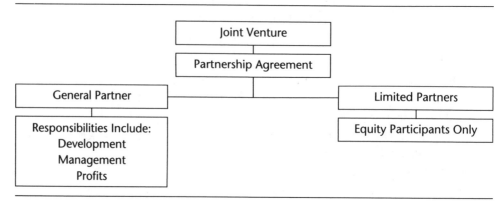

FIGURE 14.1
A typical joint venture in real estate.

under its articles of declaration. There is a cost to incorporate, and corporations are subject to double taxation: the corporation pays taxes on its earnings, and when the stockholders receive dividends, they are personally taxed on the income.

The *Subchapter S* corporation permits investors to avoid double taxation resulting from earnings of the shareholders and of the corporation. Income is not taxed at the corporate levels, but Subchapter S corporations are limited to 25 shareholders. The type of income allowed is limited, and there are firm limitations on losses.

Avoiding double taxation

Syndication is a term used to denote multiple participation in a real estate investment. A syndication group is composed of a general partner and two or more limited partners. Although the limited partners are the investors, they do not take an active role in management. The general partner is paid to manage the investment.

Syndicating

A syndication must comply with federal and state regulations. If the syndication is formed with the intent of making money on the investment, it is considered a security and must be registered with the **Securities and Exchange Commission (SEC)**.

Real Estate Investment Trusts (REITs) make available the investment in real estate to individuals by selling shares in large investment properties. By pooling the funds of many investors, the trust can purchase large properties, and the shares are easily transferable. The trustee (manager) manages the properties for the investors, and the income received is passed to the beneficiaries (investors). One of the advantages of REITs is that the revenue is not treated as corporate income, that is, it is not taxed twice.

Selling shares in real property

REAL ESTATE OFFERINGS AS SECURITIES

If real estate is purchased for investment, it will be considered a security and subject to jurisdiction under the Securities Act when it meets the four elements of an "investment contract" as defined by the federal Securities Act of 1933. The four elements are:

1. It must be an investment of money.
2. It must be in a common enterprise.
3. It must be undertaken with the prospect of making a profit.
4. It must be one in which profit will be derived solely or substantially from the management efforts of others (whose efforts affect the success or failure of the enterprise).

A typical example of a security would be a limited partnership in which shares are sold.

The purpose of the Securities Act was to provide full and fair disclosure of securities sold in interstate commerce and through the mails and to prevent frauds in the sale of securities.

Provides disclosure

Anyone selling a security must register it with the SEC before offering the security for sale. A disclosure statement giving basic preliminary information of the enterprise must be delivered prior to or with any solicitation of an offer for the sale of the securities. This statement is referred to as a **prospectus**. A detailed accounting must be included, revealing the number of investors the partnership is seeking, all pertinent data pertaining to the property offered, and the distribution of profits and losses.

There are exceptions, as when the offering is *intrastate*—that is, offered solely in the state where the issuer resides and does business. However, the offering will need to be registered in that particular state, unless it would be exempt as a private offering. A private offering is of a limited scope and is directed to a selected type of sophisticated investor who does not need the protection offered by the SEC disclosure.

Exceptions to SEC filing

A securities license is required of anyone who offers securities for sale. The securities laws that regulate the registration and sale of securities were passed to prevent people from buying or selling a "piece of the blue sky," thus the reason for referring to the laws as blue sky laws.

SUMMARY

The many aspects of real estate as an investment have been covered in this chapter. The advantages include the following:

1. The continual rise of property values has been a great hedge against inflation.
2. The attractive high rate of return on the investment.
3. The leverage available. Since the investor borrows money to finance the purchase, his buying power is substantially increased.
4. The investor's equity buildup, since a portion of the payments apply to reducing the principal.

The major disadvantages of a real estate investment are as follows:

1. The nonliquidity. While stocks and bonds can be sold quickly through a stockbroker, it usually takes a period of time to find a buyer for real estate.
2. The risk. An investor must be a knowledgeable buyer and understand the risks involved, which include
   a. the importance of property location
   b. the ratio of rental returns to payments
3. The investment requires a large sum of money.
4. Fixity, its immobility.
5. Maintenance is required.
6. The management of the property (if the investors do not have the time, a professional management service will need to be hired).

Many investors are not overly concerned if the property does not create an immediate return on the capital invested since they use their real estate investments in part as tax shelters. However, the Tax Reform Act of 1986 affects the passive investor who is involved only for purposes of sheltering income.

Depreciation schedules used in investment properties are discussed in this chapter along with a brief analysis of the need for reinvesting to avoid capital gains when the property is sold. The importance of tax-free exchanges to defer the resulting gains in the investment is also covered.

For the serious investor who wants to accumulate wealth through real estate ownership and have a steady flow of income, the new tax reform law will not deter investing. Proponents of the Tax Reform Act of 1986 felt such changes were necessary because of a glut of properties built with no concern for real use or occupation. Called "see-through" buildings because of the lack of tenants, they are an example of the abuse of the law by people merely seeking tax shelters.

DISCUSSION QUESTIONS

1. What elements should any investment possess?
2. In what instances can the capital gains tax be deferred?
3. Explain the philosophy of leverage.

4. Explain which of the following are depreciable for income tax purposes and give reasons for your answers: (a) personal residence, (b) office building, (c) land.

5. Why would an investor refinance a property rather than sell it?

6. According to the Tax Reform Act of 1986, when is rental income considered passive income?

REVIEW QUESTIONS

Answers to these questions are found in the Answer Key section at the back of the book.

1. When expenses are greater than the income produced, it is called:

   a. taxable income
   b. cash flow
   c. renters
   d. lenders

2. Depreciation of real property is available to:

   a. homeowners
   b. investors
   c. both of the above
   d. neither of the above

3. The function of a real estate investment is NOT to give the investor:

   a. equity gains
   b. appreciation
   c. income
   d. a second home

4. All of the following are true, EXCEPT:

   a. the primary purpose of an investment is to generate income
   b. portfolio income includes interest and royalties
   c. losses from passive income can be used to offset ordinary income
   d. the value of an asset can be determined by the stream of income it produces

5. Capital gains occur when:

   a. a homeowner sells his home and reinvests in a like property
   b. an investor sells property at a loss
   c. an investor sells depreciated property and does not reinvest
   d. the rollover rule is used

6. A disclosure statement that describes an investment opportunity is called a(n):

   a. contract
   b. shelter
   c. option to purchase
   d. prospectus

7. Leverage is best defined as:

   a. borrow the least amount of money for the shortest period of time
   b. put the least amount down, obtain the lowest interest for the longest period of time
   c. a tax-free exchange
   d. postponing capital gains

8. An owner is exempt from paying taxes on gains realized from a sale:

   a. if another home is purchased within a 48-month period
   b. if the new purchase is at least equal in value to the property sold
   c. if the new purchase is at least 1¼ more than the property sold
   d. a homeowner is never exempt from paying taxes on gains

9. The following factor(s) have influenced people to invest in real estate:

   a. the inflation of real estate values
   b. the need for shelter
   c. both of the above
   d. neither of the above

10. Investments that can be depreciated include:

    a. a home, when a room is used solely as an office
    b. a private residence
    c. savings deposited in a federally insured bank
    d. personal property

11. A homeowner has recorded the following expenditures: $2,300 mortgage interest, $1,250 property tax, $1,800 depreciation, $700 addition of a garage, and $1,500 sale of an easement. What would the allowable income tax deduction be?

    a. $3,550
    b. $5,350
    c. $6,050
    d. $7,550

12. After the economic life of an apartment complex has been exhausted, the owner has left:

    a. an unearned value
    b. pure profit
    c. salvage value
    d. adjusted basis

13. A retired person on a pension buys a 24-unit apartment complex. What would the buyer most likely be looking for?

    a. depreciation
    b. gross income
    c. rent income
    d. net spendable money

14. Professor Smith purchases a home for $60,000. She installs a $12,000 tennis court and a $3,000 air conditioner. Five years later she sells the home for $96,000. Her taxable income is:

    a. $78,000
    b. $36,000
    c. $21,000

    d. $18,000

15. Upon the sale of an investment property, any profits in excess of straight-line depreciation are considered:

    a. ordinary income
    b. earned income
    c. 30 percent tax sheltered
    d. entirely tax sheltered

16. A Real Estate Investment Trust (REIT) can best be described as:

    a. a management group that oversees investments
    b. a group of investors who pool their funds to purchase real estate
    c. a fund used to purchase vacation homes
    d. a syndication group monitored by the SEC

17. An investment is considered a security when all of the following components are present, EXCEPT:

    a. it is an investment of money
    b. it is a common enterprise
    c. the investor hopes to make a profit
    d. all the investors share in managerial duties

18. The Tax Reform Act of 1986 brought forth some sweeping new changes to the tax laws. It had the greatest impact on:

    a. homeowners
    b. investment property
    c. vacation homes
    d. motor homes

The Appraisal Process

15

KEY WORDS

ad valorem tax
appraisal
cost approach
depreciation
economic obsolescence
Financial Institutions Reform,
    Recovery and Enforcement Act
    (FIRREA)
functional obsolescence
gross income multiplier (GIM)
gross rent multiplier (GRM)

highest and best use
income approach
market price
market value
obsolescence
physical depreciation
quantity survey method
sales comparison approach
tax assessment
unit-in-place cost approach method

OVERVIEW

Appraising is far from an exact science, but a degree of relative uniformity may be achieved by applying proven appraisal techniques along with the use of factual information. Many professional appraisers concentrate all their time on the profession and are recognized for their knowledge, skill, and experience in the field. They interpret the facts in an unbiased manner from pertinent available information. An independent fee appraiser may be called upon to support his opinions in a court of law, so diligent care is taken with each parcel appraised. Although real estate brokers and salespersons need not qualify as professional appraisers, they should be familiar with the three approaches to determining value by means of the appraisal process and should be capable of arriving at the market value of the property they intend to list and market.

This chapter will explore the many purposes for which the fee appraiser may be requested to determine valuation of a property, the steps in an appraisal, and how valuation is arrived at and shown in the written, documented appraisal report furnished to the client. Title XI of the Financial Institutions Reform, Recovery and Enforcement Act of 1989 (FIRREA) and the new regulations placed upon appraisers are addressed in this chapter.

APPRAISALS

An **appraisal** is simply an estimate of value. It is an opinion as to the worth of a particular piece of property. An appraiser must measure the value of each parcel of real estate appraised and furnish a supportable opinion.

A definite sequence of steps is followed in the appraisal process.

1. Defining the problem: identifying the parcel of real estate by the legal description and street address and stating the purpose of the appraisal
2. Collecting the data
   a. economic
   b. neighborhood
   c. property
3. Analyzing and applying the three approaches
   a. sales comparison
   b. cost
   c. income
4. Correlating the data and analyzing the results
5. Writing the appraisal report

THE PURPOSE OF AN APPRAISAL

Defining Value

Since value means different things to different people, the purpose of the appraisal is the first question asked by the appraiser. To the owner of the property, value would be considered as market value, investment value, and value in use. The insurance agent will think in terms of insured value, while the lender is concerned with loan value. The appraiser's report will clearly state the nature of the assignment. Value is defined as the present worth of future benefits that accompany the ownership of real property, and for value to exist there must be benefits. Valuation may be sought to determine any of the following:

Market value vs. market price

1. *Market value*. The most *probable* selling price at which a willing seller will sell and a willing buyer will buy, with neither being under abnormal pressure, is commonly referred to as **market value**. It is the highest price a property is expected to bring if exposed for sale on the open market, allowing a reasonable amount of time to find a purchaser who is fully aware of the uses to which the property may be put. Keep in mind that value is created by the desire of people for a commodity or a service. **Market price** is the actual sale price of the property set through bargaining and negotiation. Market price may differ from market value if the seller needs to sell quickly.
2. *Loan value*. Prior to committing to a loan, a lending institution has an appraiser give a report on the property's value since it is the collateral for the loan.
3. *Insurance value*. The lender requires the borrower to insure the property to protect the lender's interest. The insurance policy will need to cover the amount of the loan, with the lender named as co-beneficiary.

   The property owner will also want to insure the investment, regardless of whether a loan is involved. In case of damage or destruction, the owner is assured of sufficient coverage to replace the structure.
4. *Estate tax value*. The value of a deceased person's real property will need to be determined for inheritance tax purposes.
5. *Lease interest*. If a commercial property carries a long-term lease, it may contain a reappraisal clause since the leasehold value may change over a period of time. Some properties, such as vacation homes or commercial buildings, are built on leased land, and the land value may vary over the length of the lease.
6. *Tax assessment*. Real property is assessed for taxation purposes according to its value, referred to as an **ad valorem tax**. The county assessor's office appraises the

property for taxation purposes, and the assessed value is provided by the law of the municipality. The city council or governing board then sets the mill levy according to the amount of money needed to meet the budget and expenses of the local government. This budget is submitted by the county auditor and approved by the council.

Determining value for taxation

To determine the amount of taxes on a property, the assessed value is multiplied by the mill levy. (A mill equals one-tenth of a cent.) Property may be taxed at its full assessed value or at a percentage of the appraised value as shown in the following example:

$70,000	*appraised value*
.30	*percentage taxed*
$21,000	*assessed value*
.070	*mill levy*
$1,470	*annual taxes*

Taxes are sometimes expressed in dollars, as $2.00 per $100 of appraised value. Thus, the $70,000 appraised value times $2.00 would equal $1,400 annual taxes.

7. *Eminent domain.* As discussed in Chapter 2, under the right of eminent domain the police power of a governmental body may take the property of an individual for public use. The property is condemned, and appraisers determine its fair market value.

Property condemned for public use

When a fraction of an individual's property is condemned and taken (as under the right of eminent domain), the appraiser determines what the value of the property was before that portion was taken and what the remainder is now worth. This before-and-after method awards *just compensation* to the condemnee (property owner) for the loss of that portion of land.

8. *Financial statement.* If a person needs to borrow capital, the lender may require a current appraisal of the borrower's real estate holdings to establish the net worth of the individual.

9. *Third-party companies.* An appraisal will serve as a basis for corporations or third-party companies that buy out (purchase) the homes of transferred employees.

10. *Liquidation.* In a forced sale or auction, a liquidation value will be necessary.

11. *Divorce cases.* An appraisal is necessary to settle disputes over distribution of assets.

At this point the difference between a competitive market analysis (CMA) as discussed in Chapter 6 and a *fee appraisal* should be clarified. The CMA is different in both purpose and form. The broker and salesperson need to arrive at the probable market value each time they list a property. This is approached by comparing the selling price of similar properties that have recently sold in the same neighborhood or a corresponding area and by checking the listed price of expired listings. Through continuous evaluation of recent sales and expired listings, the broker and salesperson keep abreast of values and the changing market conditions that affect them. However, they are not expected to give written and certified reports such as the fee appraiser prepares. The real estate salesperson's only concern is pricing the property at a realistic selling price in today's market.

Comparable market analysis vs. fee appraisal

Collecting the Data

The appraiser maintains a data bank of information as a ready resource. General data on the region, the city, and the neighborhood will be collected and maintained in the data bank.

Regional effects on value

Regional and city information will include knowledge of the economic conditions of the area. For example, an influx of new industry creates additional employment which will bring new families, children, bank accounts, and retail sales into the area. The community with diversified employment provides a healthy economic outlook. The environmental or physical conditions that affect property values include parks, highways, airports, public transportation, available utilities, and shopping centers in the region. The political conditions in regional and local governments are also considered. Understanding social factors includes evaluating the population trends of the area as the prevalent age groups determine the demand for various types of housing, such as single-family homes, condominiums, apartments, or retirement complexes.

The neighborhood data covers information on the area within certain street boundaries in which the dwellings are of comparable price range and age. The average income and age of residents, convenience to shopping, public transportation, churches, and schools are other factors considered.

After assembling the regional, city, and neighborhood data, the appraiser begins analyzing the property itself. The site is evaluated, and the lot size determined. The square footage and street frontage are measured. Any special assessments against the property are recorded in the report. (A special assessment is a charge against real estate to pay for the cost of a public improvement to the property. This assessment is made by a unit of government. Special tax assessments are levied against the property for the cost of street paving, curbing, sidewalks, and sewers.)

PRIMARY FORCES AFFECTING VALUE

The appraiser must consider the forces that continually affect value as property values are influenced at national, regional, and the local community level. The four major forces that have the greatest influence on residential real estate values are as follows:

1. governmental (political)
2. economic (financial)
3. physical
4. sociological

These four forces can modify value, can create value, or can destroy value. The influence of federal control over policies that affect inflation has an impact on the cost of housing. Interest rates are directly responsive to government action that determines how many people will be buying real estate.

Location determines value

While housing values are affected at the regional level by political stability, economic conditions, and employment statistics, the most important levels of influence are conditions at the local level. The physical location of a property in a community affects its value. Certain neighborhoods in a given area will be in greater demand and command higher sale prices. The topography may also be a factor, affecting construction costs.

Sociological factors reflect the attitude of the people in the community. Property taxes and services rendered to the residents are local forces that affect property values. How the residents feel toward the local government and their opinion of the community as a good place to live also have an impact on value. Cultural amenities such as theaters, arts, parks, and recreational facilities are all amenities that enhance the lives of the area residents.

In the final analysis, value is created when there is

1. *Desire*: The commodity must be wanted.
2. *Utility*: This considers the degree to which it can be used.

3. *Scarcity*: Supply is limited.

4. *Effective purchasing power*: Money is available to buy it.

Other Factors Affecting Value

Three approaches are used in the appraisal of real property: the cost approach, the sales comparison approach, and the income approach. Before the appraiser begins to analyze each of these approaches to value, certain basic principles that affect the value must be applied. These principles are discussed below.

Highest and Best Use

When we speak of the **highest and best use** of property, we are referring to the most profitable use to which it can be put. Briefly, the highest and best use can be defined as the use that, at the time of the appraisal, is most likely to produce the greatest net return on the land and/or building over a given period of time. *Net return* is the key phrase in this definition. It means whatever is left from gross yield after all costs are met. Sometimes net return takes a form that may not bring the greatest monetary return, for example, land for a children's zoo, a city park, or a forest preserve that will give enjoyment to thousands every year.

Net return affects value

Principle of Substitution

If the property can be substituted for another, its value is set to an extent by the cost of acquiring a like property. The knowledgeable purchaser today will "shop" and compare properties before making a selection. This is the principle of substitution, used in the sales comparison approach to appraising.

Utility Value

The utility value of a property, how it can be used, is also important in determining value. A lovely wooded lot may appear to be a perfect location for a homesite, but investigation uncovers that it has a ravine running through it, leaving no feasible spot for a building. Zoning laws and restrictive covenants can also affect the use of a property. A location that may seem ideal for a commercial building but which is zoned only for office buildings will be limited to the use designated by the zoning ordinance. Protective covenants in an area may prohibit the building of a two-story house since it would obscure the views of surrounding homeowners. When appraisers place a value on a particular property, they must carefully weigh its utility value.

Use dictates value

Functional utility refers to the usability of a building. A contractor may build one house with a highly desirable, very livable floor plan and choose a plan for another house with a poorly arranged interior. The latter may lack good window placement, have a traffic pattern that necessitates walking through the middle of one room to reach another, or lack storage area. As new innovations and more amenities are incorporated into new construction, older houses that do not have these appointments are considered less functional.

Functional utility

Principle of Contribution

The principle of contribution is the principle the appraiser applies to the *return on improvements* to the property. To improve a property may not necessarily mean that the total cost of the improvement can be added to the value of the property. While a recreation room will expand the living space of the home and make it more desirable to a buyer, the owner may not recapture the entire cost of the remodeling. Enclosing

Improvements may add value

porches and updating kitchens and baths may add appeal to the property but may not return the seller's total costs.

Principle of Change

Age changes value

Principles of change acknowledge that the life cycle of a building dictates change, for as a neighborhood ages, new land uses may be introduced. Multifamily units may begin to emerge in once affluent neighborhoods as covenants expire and new uses develop through zoning changes. As new styles and plans are built in the suburbs, people on a higher economic scale move beyond the city's urban area. A great thrust in many cities has been to revitalize the older sectors in an effort to slow suburban sprawl and prevent the decay of the inner city areas.

Changes in a neighborhood may transpire slowly, but the appraiser is trained to detect the implied as well as the evident indications that result in changing conditions. As the area ages, change may occur in not only zoning regulations but also the income level and average age of the residents. As buyers' needs and desires change, the forces of change also affect certain neighborhoods and cities.

New styles in home designs with the use of large expanses of well-designed windows, automated kitchens, and palatial baths appeal to still other buyers. *Amenities* are the extras that come with ownership. A desirable view, a wooded lot, or the privacy or location of a particular property can all be considered amenities. The amenities desired may vary with different buyers. The proximity to transportation, a shopping center, or schools may be prime considerations for one purchaser, while special energy-conserving features may be most important to another.

Scarcity

The supply will dictate the value; if property is not in demand, the value will decrease.

Principle of Supply and Demand

The law of supply and demand holds true in real estate as in any other commodity. Consumers must have a need and a desire, and the result will be value in the product. If 20 houses are built in a new subdivision, but demand is not present, the contractor will have an excess of 20 houses unless the price is lowered to encourage buyers. Conversely, if there is a demand for housing and few are available, prices will rise. The investor must determine the prospects for future growth or decline.

Transferability

Good title that can be transferred with comparable ease is important to value. While this is a legal concept and not an economic factor, value will not exist if the property cannot be transferred. Regardless of the demand, title must be capable of being transferred or its worth is nonexistent.

Principle of Anticipation

Future value

Value is created by anticipating the use or income that will be derived from the property in the future. The homeowner sees value in the property based on the amenities it offers, its ability to meet the buyer's needs, and consequently its present worth, while the investor will view it from the potential net income to be received from the investment.

Principle of Regression and Progression

If a property has been overimproved, the value of the overimprovement is decreased and the principle of *regression* applies. To add a $40,000 family room on a house in an area where surrounding homes are being appraised for $50,000 would not result in adding $40,000 to the market value of the overimproved property.

Overimprovements

If a particular property was underimproved and in an area of more expensive homes, the principle of *progression* applies, which would increase the value of the subject property.

Principle of Conformity

When a neighborhood is homogeneous, that is, the homes have a relative degree of uniformity, values tend to be higher. If the construction is architecturally compatible and an overall appearance of conformity is adhered to, values will be stabilized in the area. This is one of the reasons for covenants and restrictions in the platting of subdivisions; the property owners are assured that their investment will be secure from that standpoint.

Plottage Value

The combining of two or more parcels is called *assemblage*. The increase in the value of the new parcel is referred to as *plottage*. For example, if zoning laws permit a 6-unit building on a lot that has 15,000 square feet, the acquisition of the adjacent lot of equal size would permit the owner to build a 12-unit building. If a value of $15,000 is placed on each unit, the value has increased from a total of $90,000 ($15,000 × 6 units) to $180,000 ($15,000 × 12 units).

Assemblage

APPROACHES TO APPRAISAL

When using the three approaches to value, the appraiser makes the decision as to which approach best typifies the subject property. Little credence is given to the income approach when appraising single-family residences, since few are purchased for rental purposes. For these appraisals, greater reliance is placed on the cost and comparison approaches. Conversely, these approaches to value would not be given as much weight in appraising an income-producing property. When appraising a single-purpose building, such as a church, the cost approach would be most applicable since comparable properties would be difficult to locate and the church is not considered income producing.

Sales Comparison Approach

The **sales comparison approach** is often referred to as the market analysis approach to value because the subject property (the property being appraised) is compared with properties recently sold in the same general area or in neighborhods of similar value.

Determining value by comparison

The appraiser will seek comparable properties that have recently sold. Properties currently on the market for sale are not considered since no agreed upon contract between buyer and seller exists. A minimum of three comparables provides the appraiser with the necessary data to form an opinion as to the value of the subject property. The more similar the properties, the easier it is to conclude value. Allowances and adjustments are made for any differences in the properties. The sales comparison approach to value is the most commonly used method in appraising residential property as it depends on what similar properties are actually selling for.

When locating comparables, the appraiser will first look for recently sold properties in the immediate location of the subject property. If no recent sales are available in the neighborhood, an area similar in value should be searched. It is important that the comparables have sold recently; this is especially true if the market is volatile. Depending on local conditions, adjustments for time lapsed are made either upward or down.

It is necessary to locate the same style of house; for instance, two-story houses are not compared with ranch-style houses.

Adjustments

In the preparation of a market value analysis the use of adjustments is of prime importance. Some of the adjustments appraisers look for include:

1. *Time.* Since market conditions change, the comparables used are kept within a short time span, usually six months to one year.
2. *Age.*

Adjusting for differences

3. *Location.* Understanding the differences in neighborhoods that affect lot value (location does not affect building value).
4. *Lot size.*
5. *Quality of construction.* This should not be confused with the condition; if the quality is higher or lower than normal for the area, a reasonable adjustment should be made.
6. *Porches, decks, and patios.*
7. *General condition.* The cost of updating a house to bring it to the standard of other houses in the area is considered. This can include the need for exterior paint, new roofing or siding, and landscaping. Interior refurbishing would include painting, new carpeting, and wallpaper.
8. *Living area.* The appraiser uses the outside measurements in determining the square footage.
9. *Bedrooms.*
10. *Baths.* Consideration is given to tiled baths, full, ¾ or ½ baths.
11. *Basements.* Full, half, and walkout basements and whether they are finished and the quality of the finished work.
12. *Garages.* Detached, singles, double, or triple garages.
13. *Air conditioning and heating systems.*
14. *Fireplaces.*
15. *Extras.* Built-in appliances, garage door openers, any special amenities the house may have.

Figure 15.1 indicates the process used in comparing residential properties. Let us analyze each step. Our subject property is at 1040 Clear Street, which is the model used throughout this book.

A. This line lists the property addresses. All three comparables are in the same subdivision as the subject property.

B. This line states the sale price of the comparable properties.

C. Line C allows for the change in value that occurs since the date of sale. The appraiser must track carefully any economic changes that have occurred since the sale date of the properties. If property is selling for less, it will be necessary to adjust the comparables down. In the example, the area is in demand, and properties do not have a long market time even though prices have leveled off and inflation has slowed. In view of this information, comparable #1 needs no adjustment since it sold just one

	SUBJECT	COMPARABLES					
A. Address	1040 Clear Street	1155 Clear Street		2201 Main Street		3215 Lincoln Street	
B. Sale Price			$86,000		$84,000		$85,500
C. Time Adjustment		1 mo.	0	6 mos. add 2%	+ 1,680	3 mos. add 1%	+ 850
D. No. of rooms	6	6	0	6	0	6	0
E. No. of Bedrooms, baths	3-2	3-2	0	3-2	0	3-2	0
F. Square Footage	1350	1300 50 less	+ 2,500	1400 50 more	− 2,500	1350	0
G. Style, Const.	Ranch, frame	Ranch, fr.	0	Ranch, fr.	0	Ranch, fr.	0
H. Garage	2 car attd.	2 car attd.	0	1 car attd.	+ 1,500	2 car attd.	0
I. Age, Condition	7 yrs., good	2 yrs. excellent	− 2,500	7 yrs. excellent	− 1,000	10 yrs. good	+ 1,800
J. Lot, size extras	85 × 120	85 × 120	0	85 × 110	0	90 × 110	0
K. Special Features	wood deck, fenced	wood, deck, fenced	0	patio, view	0	new carpet, fenced	0
L. Method of Sale		loan assumption	− 1,000	conv.	0	VA	− 2,000
M. Net Adjustments			− 1,000		+ 320		+ 650
N. Adjusted Market Price			$85,000		$84,320		$86,150
O. Indicated Value	$85,000						

FIGURE 15.1   Comparing residential properties.

month ago. Comparable #2 sold six months ago, and its value has increased 2 percent, and comparable #3 sold three months ago and has a 1 percent increase.

Remember, *adjustments must be made to the comparable properties and not the subject*. This is sometimes difficult for the person first approaching the appraisal process to understand. Think of it in these terms: since the value of the subject property is unknown, we cannot make adjustments to it.

D. and E. No adjustments are necessary here since there are no variations.

F. Property #1 is 50 square feet smaller, so considering that the cost per square foot is $50.00 × 50 square feet, + $2,500 is given to the property. Comparable #2 has 50 square feet more, so we give it a − $2,500.

G. Style and construction of the properties are all the same.

H. Comparable #2 has a one-car garage, so we added $1,500. This takes into consideration that it would be worth an additional $1,500 if it had an extra garage.

I. Allowance needs to be made for the differences in the age and condition of properties. Comparable #1 is only two years old and in excellent condition. Since it is five years newer than the subject and in excellent condition, a minus $2,500 is given. Comparable #2 is the same age as the subject property; however, its condition is excellent, so a minus $1,000 is credited to it. Comparable #3 is ten years old so it has developed three years of additional depreciation, and $1,800 is added to it.

J. The lot sizes vary so slightly that no allowances are made.

K. Special features can have a great affect on the sale price of a property. Wood decks and fenced yards are very fashionable in this area. While comparable #2 has neither, it does have a spectacular view that the appraiser felt "equaled out" not having the former. Properties that are treed, that offer privacy, or that are unusually well landscaped have amenities that also enhance value. Houses with professionally decorated interiors, that sparkle with cleanliness, or that have extra features such as built-in appliances, skylights, and jacuzzis have enhanced market value.

L. The financing involved in the sale can influence the price paid for the property. If a seller carries financing or an existing loan is assumed, the purchaser may pay more for favorable loan terms. The appropriate adjustments were made on comparables #1 and #3.

M. The net adjustments are totaled.

N. The adjusted market price reflects the adjustments.

O. When looking at the three comparables, no correlation is necessary since the three properties are all very similar to the subject property. We give equal value to each of the properties, and the indicated market value is $85,000. After the correlation of the properties, the appraiser states the conclusion, and the final step for the appraiser is to certify the report.

Cost Approach

The **cost approach** to appraising is sometimes referred to as the *replacement cost method* or the *summation approach*. In this approach, an estimate is made of the cost to replace the improvements at today's prices, less depreciation, and adding the value of the land as if it were vacant and used to its highest potential as governed by covenants and zoning laws. Keep in mind that to replace a dwelling is to construct a building similar in design and quality. To actually reproduce a structure would probably not be feasible, as it would mean recreating the structure exactly as it is.

Analyzing value by cost to replace structure

In implementing the cost approach, the appraiser first estimates replacement costs by using the square-foot method. Cost data from recent construction of a similar structure will be divided by the square footage of the building, thus establishing the cost per square foot. The base cost estimate of the actual property is found by multiplying the square footage times the cost per foot.

Remember that in the cost approach the formula is: replacement cost less depreciation plus land value equals the appraisal value. Figure 15.2 indicates how the appraised value of the example property located at 1040 Clear Street was determined. The appraiser did not feel the seven-year-old residence suffered from functional or economic obsolescence. The annual physical depreciation of .5 percent was multiplied times the seven years, and the resulting 3.5 percent was then multiplied times the replacement cost (including the concrete). Most lenders now require appraisers to use the form approved by the secondary mortgage market (Freddie Mac and Fannie Mae), to facilitate the sale of the mortgage to this market (see Figure 15.3).

In a new building, a contractor may use the **unit-in-place cost approach method**. In this approach, the cost of all the component parts, including the kitchen cabinets ($8,700), the built-in appliances ($2,300), the fireplace ($2,200), and so on, are computed.

If contractors want a precise cost breakdown, they can use the **quantity survey method**. This is the most detailed approach to appraising. For example, 42 kitchen cabinet hinges may cost $1.30 each or 19 drawer pulls $.93 each. The cost of the labor is then added, and contractors can come very close to figuring the exact cost of constructing the house. They can then decide the percentage of profit they desire for time and labor and add this to the cost of the building.

The cost approach should be used on special purpose properties such as schools, police stations, or new construction. The cost of reproducing a duplicate does not lend

1040 Clear Street

Replacement cost estimate:
  Buildings:
    Residence ____1350____ sq. ft. at __$50.00__   __$67,500.00__
    Garage __2-car attd. 400__ sq. st. at __12.00__   __4,800.00__
    Other __(concrete) 700__ sq. ft. at __1.20__   __840.00__

Total replacement cost   __$73,140.00__
Less depreciation:
    Physical __(1/2%)__   __$2,530.50__
    Functional __(0)__   __-0-__
    Economic __(0)__   __-0-__

Total depreciation   __$ 2,530.50__
Present value of building   __$70,609.50__
Net value of land improvements (walks, fences, landscaping, etc.)   __2,400.00__
Land value (approximately $100 per front foot in this area)   __11,900.00__
Total value   __$84,909.50__
                                    Rounded: __$85,000.00__

FIGURE 15.2
The cost approach to appraisal, computed by square footage less depreciation plus land improvements and land.

itself to what a typical buyer would pay for the property. The most important thing to remember about the cost approach is that cost does not equal value.

Depreciation

In using the cost approach method, the appraiser must determine if there is any **depreciation**. Depreciation of the property is subtracted from the replacement cost of the structure. Depreciation of real estate is defined as loss of value from any cause. It includes physical depreciation, functional obsolescence, and economic obsolescence.

Physical depreciation includes the normal wear and tear of a structure through use and the actions of natural elements. This form of depreciation may be either curable or incurable. Curable depreciation may include the need for painting and decorating. Incurable depreciation occurs on items that are still serviceable but that will need replacement before the economic life of the structure is depleted, such as an obsolete furnace. Economic life refers to the period over which a building can be profitably utilized.

Loss in value through wear and tear

Functional obsolescence refers to the changes in design or construction that outdate a building. Curable obsolescence could include the need for modernizing a bathroom while incurable **obsolescence** is the result of a poor floor plan or a serious lack of closets. A five-bedroom home with only one bathroom suffers from functional obsolescence. (Undoubtedly, it also suffers from a very crowded bathroom!)

Loss caused by outdated design

Economic obsolescence is the most difficult for the property owner to control since it relates to conditions external to the property, such as the desirability of the neighborhood or changes in nearby land use. The value of a property might be diminished if the surrounding structures were not compatible. Overimprovement of a home may also result in economic obsolescence, since a $90,000 home surrounded by $50,000 homes would be less likely to attract $90,000 purchasers.

Neighborhood conditions affect value

Income Approach

The **income approach** is also referred to as the *capitalization approach* to value and is based on the *net income* produced in relation to the value of the property.

Property Description & Analysis   **UNIFORM RESIDENTIAL APPRAISAL REPORT**   File No.

SUBJECT

Property Address		Census Tract	LENDER DISCRETIONARY USE
City	County	State Zip Code	Sale Price $
Legal Description			Date
Owner/Occupant		Map Reference	Mortgage Amount $
Sale Price $	Date of Sale	PROPERTY RIGHTS APPRAISED	Mortgage Type
Loan charges/concessions to be paid by seller $		☐ Fee Simple	Discount Points and Other Concessions
R.E. Taxes $	Tax Year HOA $/Mo.	☐ Leasehold	Paid by Seller $
Lender/Client		☐ Condominium (HUD/VA)	
		☐ De Minimis PUD	Source

NEIGHBORHOOD

LOCATION	☐ Urban	☐ Suburban	☐ Rural	NEIGHBORHOOD ANALYSIS	Good	Avg.	Fair	Poor
BUILT UP	☐ Over 75%	☐ 25-75%	☐ Under 25%	Employment Stability	☐	☐	☐	☐
GROWTH RATE	☐ Rapid	☐ Stable	☐ Slow	Convenience to Employment	☐	☐	☐	☐
PROPERTY VALUES	☐ Increasing	☐ Stable	☐ Declining	Convenience to Shopping	☐	☐	☐	☐
DEMAND/SUPPLY	☐ Shortage	☐ In Balance	☐ Over Supply	Convenience to Schools	☐	☐	☐	☐
MARKETING TIME	☐ Under 3 Mos.	☐ 3-6 Mos.	☐ Over 6 Mos.	Adequacy of Public Transportation	☐	☐	☐	☐

PRESENT LAND USE	%	LAND USE CHANGE	PREDOMINANT	SINGLE FAMILY HOUSING		Recreation Facilities	☐	☐	☐	☐
				PRICE $ (000)	AGE (yrs)	Adequacy of Utilities	☐	☐	☐	☐
Single Family		Not Likely	OCCUPANCY ☐			Property Compatibility	☐	☐	☐	☐
2-4 Family		Likely	Owner ☐			Protection from Detrimental Cond.	☐	☐	☐	☐
Multi-family		In process	Tenant ☐	Low		Police & Fire Protection	☐	☐	☐	☐
Commercial		To:	Vacant (0-5%) ☐	High		General Appearance of Properties	☐	☐	☐	☐
Industrial			Vacant (over 5%) ☐	Predominant		Appeal to Market	☐	☐	☐	☐
Vacant				—						

Note: Race or the racial composition of the neighborhood are not considered reliable appraisal factors.
COMMENTS: _____

SITE

Dimensions		Topography	
Site Area	Corner Lot	Size	
Zoning Classification	Zoning Compliance	Shape	
HIGHEST & BEST USE: Present Use	Other Use	Drainage	

UTILITIES	Public	Other	SITE IMPROVEMENTS	Type	Public	Private	View	
Electricity	☐		Street		☐	☐	Landscaping	
Gas	☐		Curb/Gutter		☐	☐	Driveway	
Water	☐		Sidewalk		☐	☐	Apparent Easements	
Sanitary Sewer	☐		Street Lights		☐	☐	FEMA Flood Hazard Yes* No	
Storm Sewer	☐		Alley		☐	☐	FEMA* Map/Zone	

COMMENTS (Apparent adverse easements, encroachments, special assessments, slide areas, etc.): _____

IMPROVEMENTS

GENERAL DESCRIPTION	EXTERIOR DESCRIPTION	FOUNDATION	BASEMENT	INSULATION
Units	Foundation	Slab	Area Sq. Ft.	Roof ☐
Stories	Exterior Walls	Crawl Space	% Finished	Ceiling ☐
Type (Det./Att.)	Roof Surface	Basement	Ceiling	Walls ☐
Design (Style)	Gutters & Dwnspts.	Sump Pump	Walls	Floor ☐
Existing	Window Type	Dampness	Floor	None ☐
Proposed	Storm Sash	Settlement	Outside Entry	Adequacy ☐
Under Construction	Screens	Infestation		Energy Efficient Items:
Age (Yrs.)	Manufactured House			
Effective Age (Yrs.)				

ROOM LIST

ROOMS	Foyer	Living	Dining	Kitchen	Den	Family Rm.	Rec. Rm.	Bedrooms	# Baths	Laundry	Other	Area Sq. Ft.
Basement												
Level 1												
Level 2												

Finished area **above** grade contains: Rooms;   Bedroom(s);   Bath(s);   Square Feet of Gross Living Area

INTERIOR

SURFACES	Materials/Condition	HEATING	KITCHEN EQUIP.	ATTIC	IMPROVEMENT ANALYSIS	Good	Avg.	Fair	Poor
Floors		Type	Refrigerator ☐	None ☐	Quality of Construction	☐	☐	☐	☐
Walls		Fuel	Range/Oven ☐	Stairs ☐	Condition of Improvements	☐	☐	☐	☐
Trim/Finish		Condition	Disposal ☐	Drop Stair ☐	Room Sizes/Layout	☐	☐	☐	☐
Bath Floor		Adequacy	Dishwasher ☐	Scuttle ☐	Closets and Storage	☐	☐	☐	☐
Bath Wainscot		COOLING	Fan/Hood ☐	Floor ☐	Energy Efficiency	☐	☐	☐	☐
Doors		Central	Compactor ☐	Heated ☐	Plumbing-Adequacy & Condition	☐	☐	☐	☐
		Other	Washer/Dryer ☐	Finished ☐	Electrical-Adequacy & Condition	☐	☐	☐	☐
		Condition	Microwave ☐		Kitchen Cabinets-Adequacy & Cond.	☐	☐	☐	☐
Fireplace(s) #		Adequacy	Intercom ☐		Compatibility to Neighborhood	☐	☐	☐	☐

AUTOS

CAR STORAGE:	Garage ☐	Attached ☐	Adequate ☐	House Entry ☐	Appeal & Marketability	☐	☐	☐	☐
No. Cars	Carport ☐	Detached ☐	Inadequate ☐	Outside Entry ☐	Estimated Remaining Economic Life				Yrs.
Condition	None ☐	Built-In ☐	Electric Door ☐	Basement Entry ☐	Estimated Remaining Physical Life				Yrs.

Additional features: _____

COMMENTS

Depreciation (Physical, functional and external inadequacies, repairs needed, modernization, etc.): _____

General market conditions and prevalence and impact in subject/market area regarding loan discounts, interest buydowns and concessions: _____

reddie Mac Form 70 10/86 12Ch.   AB   Forms and Worms Inc.,® 315 Whitney Ave., New Haven, CT 06511 1(800) 243-4545   Item #130960   Fannie Mae Form 1004 10/86

FIGURE 15.3
Residential Appraisal Report.

(continued)

Valuation Section   **UNIFORM RESIDENTIAL APPRAISAL REPORT**   File No.

Purpose of Appraisal is to estimate Market Value as defined in the Certification & Statement of Limiting Conditions.

COST APPROACH

BUILDING SKETCH (SHOW GROSS LIVING AREA ABOVE GRADE)
If for Freddie Mac or Fannie Mae, show only square foot calculations and cost approach comments in this space

ESTIMATED REPRODUCTION COST - NEW - OF IMPROVEMENTS:

Dwelling _____ Sq. Ft. @ $ _____ = $ _____
_____ Sq. Ft. @ $ _____ = _____
Extras _____ = _____
_____ = _____
Special Energy Efficient Items _____ = _____
Porches, Patios, etc. _____ = _____
Garage/Carport _____ Sq. Ft. @ $ _____ = _____
Total Estimated Cost New .... = $ _____

| | Physical | Functional | External |
Less
Depreciation _____ = $ _____
Depreciated Value of Improvements .... = $ _____
Site Imp. "as is" (driveway, landscaping, etc.) = $ _____
ESTIMATED SITE VALUE .... = $ _____
(If leasehold, show only leasehold value.)
INDICATED VALUE BY COST APPROACH .... = $ _____

(Not Required by Freddie Mac and Fannie Mae)
Does property conform to applicable HUD/VA property standards? ☐ Yes ☐ No
If No, explain: _____

Construction Warranty ☐ Yes ☐ No
Name of Warranty Program _____
Warranty Coverage Expires _____

SALES COMPARISON ANALYSIS

The undersigned has recited three recent sales of properties most similar and proximate to subject and has considered these in the market analysis. The description includes a dollar adjustment, reflecting market reaction to those items of significant variation between the subject and comparable properties. If a significant item in the comparable property is superior to, or more favorable than, the subject property, a minus (−) adjustment is made, thus reducing the indicated value of subject; if a significant item in the comparable is inferior to, or less favorable than, the subject property, a plus (+) adjustment is made, thus increasing the indicated value of the subject.

ITEM	SUBJECT	COMPARABLE NO. 1		COMPARABLE NO. 2		COMPARABLE NO. 3	
Address							
Proximity to Subject							
Sales Price	$	$		$		$	
Price/Gross Liv. Area	$	$		$		$	
Data Source							
VALUE ADJUSTMENTS	DESCRIPTION	DESCRIPTION	+ (−) $ Adjustment	DESCRIPTION	+ (−) $ Adjustment	DESCRIPTION	+ (−) $ Adjustment
Sales or Financing Concessions							
Date of Sale/Time							
Location							
Site/View							
Design and Appeal							
Quality of Construction							
Age							
Condition							
Above Grade Room Count	Total ¦ Bdrms ¦ Baths	Total ¦ Bdrms ¦ Baths		Total ¦ Bdrms ¦ Baths		Total ¦ Bdrms ¦ Baths	
Gross Living Area	Sq. Ft.	Sq. Ft.		Sq. Ft.		Sq. Ft.	
Basement & Finished Rooms Below Grade							
Functional Utility							
Heating/Cooling							
Garage/Carport							
Porches, Patio, Pools, etc.							
Special Energy Efficient Items							
Fireplace(s)							
Other (e.g. kitchen equip., remodeling)							
Net Adj. (total)		☐ + ☐ − $		☐ + ☐ − $		☐ + ☐ − $	
Indicated Value of Subject		$		$		$	

Comments on Sales Comparison: _____

INDICATED VALUE BY SALES COMPARISON APPROACH .... $ _____
INDICATED VALUE BY INCOME APPROACH (If Applicable) Estimated Market Rent $ _____ /Mo. x Gross Rent Multiplier _____ = $ _____
This appraisal is made ☐ "as is" ☐ subject to the repairs, alterations, inspections or conditions listed below ☐ completion per plans and specifications.
Comments and Conditions of Appraisal: _____

Final Reconciliation: _____

RECONCILIATION

This appraisal is based upon the above requirements, the certification, contingent and limiting conditions, and Market Value definition that are stated in
☐ FmHA, HUD &/or VA instructions.
☐ Freddie Mac Form 439 (Rev. 7/86)/Fannie Mae Form 1004B (Rev. 7/86) filed with client _____ 19 _____ ☐ attached.
I (WE) ESTIMATE THE MARKET VALUE, AS DEFINED, OF THE SUBJECT PROPERTY AS OF _____ 19 _____ **to be $** _____
I (We) certify: that to the best of my (our) knowledge and belief the facts and data used herein are true and correct; that I (we) personally inspected the subject property, both inside and out, and have made an exterior inspection of all comparable sales cited in this report; and that I (we) have no undisclosed interest, present or prospective therein.

Appraiser(s) SIGNATURE _____
NAME _____
Review Appraiser SIGNATURE _____
(if applicable) NAME _____
☐ Did ☐ Did Not
Inspect Property

Freddie Mac Form 70 10/86 12Ch. **AB** Forms and Worms Inc.,® 315 Whitney Ave., New Haven, CT 06511 1(800) 243-4545 Item #130960 Fannie Mae Form 1004 10/86

FIGURE 15.3
(Continued).

Seeking value by income derived

Application of the income approach is useful to the person desiring to purchase an investment property. Since risk is involved, the investor will want a greater return than a money market or savings account would bring. The income approach gains importance when the property being appraised is older, and the cost approach is less convincing because of depreciation consideration. First, we will examine the rent multiplier used in the income approach to value.

The gross monthly rent multiplier (GMRM), or often simply stated as the **gross rent multiplier (GRM)**, is used for single-family residential property while the **gross income multiplier (GIM)** is used on commercial and industrial income property.

Single-Family Residence

Using the GRM to determine value

The indicator of value can be obtained from similar rental properties with a figure known as the *gross rent multiplier*. It is calculated by dividing the selling price by the gross monthly income to obtain the gross rent multiplier (GRM).

A brief analysis of the steps used in the income approach for single-family residential property follows.

1. Properties recently sold and rented are used as comparables.
2. The selling price of each property is divided by its gross monthly rent to obtain the GRM.

Selling price ÷ GMR = GRM

Comparables	Date	Price	Income	GRM
1	12-91	$68,000	$575	118.26
2	1-92	71,000	600	118.33
3	2-92	73,500	625	117.60
4	3-92	74,750	650	115.00
Subject	Today	?	615	?

3. Working from the table shown, greater consideration should be given to the examples that are most similar to the subject, and the multiplier would be determined from this information.
4. If the multiplier used is 117.80, we would take the monthly rent from the subject property and multiply it times the GRM; thus 117.80 × $615.00 = $72,447.00.

615.00   gross rent
× 117.80   multiplier
72,447   or 72,400 rounded

This same formula can be used on commercial and industrial income-producing properties by using the gross *annual* income multiplier (GIM). Care must be employed by the appraiser not to use overstated income estimates or the property will have an inflated estimated value. Furthermore, gross income, whether monthly or annual, does not take into account the cost of operating the property nor are allowances for vacancies and rent collection used. The multiplier method of establishing value is a quick means of validating the authenticity of the cost and comparison approaches.

Income-Producing Properties

The income approach, based on the net income produced by a property, is used to determine value following this simple procedure:

Using capitalization method to determine value

1. Estimate the potential gross income (PGI) the property is capable of producing. Subtract from potential gross income for vacancies and rent loss. This gives you effective gross income (EGI).

2. Subtract operating expenses from the effective gross income to arrive at the net operating income (ONI). Once a history of the property is established, a pattern is set, and deriving the property's value becomes easier.

3. Determine which capitalization rate should be used. An overall capitalization rate can be extracted from the data on property recently sold by taking the net income and dividing it by the selling price.

4. Apply the capitalization formula: net income ÷ capitalization rate = value

Capitalization rate provides for the return of the investor's capital and a return on the capital invested (the recapture rate). See Figure 15.4 for an example of the income approach to value.

The simplest method to determine what to pay for a property is to decide what rate of return is desirable and divide the net income by the rate of return. For example, if a building produces $15,000 net per year and the investor wants a 10 percent return, it is feasible to spend $150,000 for the property: $15,000 ÷ 10% (or .1) = $150,000. Other factors must be taken into consideration, which are covered in Chapter 14.

The appraiser needs to analyze the rental history, with past and present rentals serving as guides in estimating future rentals. Comparing what competitive properties are renting for in the area will be another important factor in determining value. Any change in rent anticipation will need to be documented and supported by the appraiser. Not only the quantity of rent but its durability is taken into consideration.

The appraiser will answer the following questions:

1. Is the contract rent high but of short duration?
2. Does the property have long-term, below-the-market rent leases?
3. Is the property managed responsibly so that its value will be maintained?

Potential gross income (PGI) (annual)		$85,500
10 units @ $300 per month × 12 ($36,000)		
15 units @ $275 per month × 12 ($49,500)		
Laundry facility income		500
Annual gross Income		$86,000
Vacancy and rent loss — 5%		4,275
Effective gross income (EGI)		$81,725
Expenses		
Real estate taxes	$7,200	
Insurance	1,100	
Management (resident 6%)	4,900	
Utilities — water, gas, electricity	2,100	
Maintenance and repair	3,200	
Redecorating	1,800	
Replacement (appliances, equipment)	2,600	
Accounting services	700	
Advertising	500	
Total expenses		$24,100
Net operating income (NOI)		$57,625

If the capitalization rate is 12 percent, the indicated value will be:

$$\frac{57,625}{.12} = \$480,208$$

FIGURE 15.4
The income approach to appraisal.

4. What has been the past rental history of the property?
5. If the property is a regional shopping mall:
   a. Is there anchor power by a national chain, such as Penney's or Sears, that will bring customers to the site?
   b. Will the surrounding market support the mall?
   c. What is the household income of the consumers nearby?
6. Is the location premier, marginal, or off the beaten path?

Correlation of Value

Any one of the three mentioned approaches to value may be used to determine the appraisal of the subject property, but they will not necessarily yield the same value. It may be that replacing a structure would cost less than the prevailing market value if the demand were especially great.

In income-producing property, the capitalization approach is usually given the most credence. If the subject is a single-family dwelling, the income approach is generally not used. The use of the cost approach is of value if the home is comparatively new. The market value would probably come closest to the real value of our example property. If the appraisal is to be made on a property for which recent comparison sales are not obtainable, for example, a pickle factory, a library building, or a church, the cost approach will probably carry the greatest weight.

The final step in the appraisal procedure is the written report. The purpose of the appraisal will determine the length and depth of the formal report.

THE APPRAISAL REPORT

Delivery of the report may be by one of four methods: an oral report, a letter, a form appraisal, or a narrative report. The reports may vary in length and type depending on the request from the client. Regardless of the type of report submitted, the appraiser has gathered his information by the same process.

The minimum requirements of any report should include the following:

1. identification of the property
2. purpose of the appraisal
3. date valuation was made
4. data used to support the conclusion
5. statement of any limiting conditions and appraiser assumptions, if any
6. indication of value
7. certification by appraiser
8. signature of appraiser

Appraiser's oral report

The oral report is given verbally by the appraiser, either in person or by telephone, to the person who requested the appraisal. There is no documentation to substantiate the findings, so an oral report is used only when time is of the essence and a quick report is needed.

Appraiser's written report

The letter report is a formal written appraisal in letter form that identifies the property, states the purpose of the appraisal, and briefly summarizes the appraiser's findings. Usage of this simplified form is not encouraged among the professional appraisers since pertinent and crucial facts could be omitted. No data analysis or supporting information is included in the letter report. The appraiser will have made a complete appraisal and will retain this information in his permanent files as support for the report.

The form report is used extensively by appraisers who need a standardized method for their clients or employers. Mortgage lenders and mortgage insurers generally request use of the approved FNMA (Fannie Mae) and FHLMC (Freddie Mac) form, since they often anticipate selling their loans on the secondary market. All the requirements of an FHA and a VA report are on this form, eliminating any problem of missing facts (see Figure 15.3). *Form report*

The form report contains the appropriate boxes to check and blanks to complete. The appraiser has the responsibility to add any additional comments pertinent to the findings. Currently this form is the most popular means of submitting appraisals.

The narrative report permits the appraiser to present the appraisal in summary form. A narrative report can contain a very few pages or a hundred pages. The appraiser must use good judgment in not becoming too elaborate in her writing. Many will begin the report with a one- or two-page synopsis of the findings, enabling the reader to obtain a quick overview of the appraisal. The reader can then proceed through the report for verification and substantiation of the appraiser's opinion of the property's value. The narrative will include the complete steps taken in the analysis used in reaching the conclusion. Included will be neighborhood data and exhibits of the comparable properties used to substantiate the appraisal. An outline of the report would include the following: *Narrative report in summary form*

1. title page
2. letter of transmittal
3. table of contents
4. summary of the facts
5. objectives of the report
6. identification of the property
7. definition of value
8. property rights appraised
9. city data
10. neighborhood data
11. taxes, zoning, and utilities
12. description of the site and its value
13. building description and land improvements
14. analysis and interpretation
15. approaches used to determine the value
16. reconciliation
17. certification
18. conclusion of the value
19. statement of any limiting conditions or contingencies
20. appraiser's qualifications

Some of the professional appraisal societies require a demonstration narrative appraisal prior to acceptance in the organization, and some universities and colleges require a narrative report to be completed by the student who is studying real estate appraisal.

THE PROFESSIONAL APPRAISER

Appraisal is the most specialized division of the real estate business, and becoming an appraiser requires comprehensive training. The farm appraiser's expertise will differ from the residential or commercial appraiser's knowledge. Just as the property *Specialization by appraiser* manager (Chapter 13) specializes, so does the appraiser. The appraiser is rating a property's value, and the importance of accuracy cannot be overstated. The independent fee appraiser is a disinterested third party who follows an orderly process in determining the value of a property. The appraiser certifies that no present or future contemplated interest in the real estate being appraised exists and that the employment or fee is not contingent upon the determined value.

In the early 1980s appraisers came under the scrutiny of the Federal Home Loan Bank because lending institutions held large numbers of defaulted loans on properties that were overvalued. If the owner of a highly leveraged property needed to sell and found the market value to be less than the loan, defaults occurred. Additionally, with the vast number of homeowners refinancing their properties in 1986, when interest rates plunged to a long-time low, lenders were concerned that, with the rush for refinancing and the resultant backlog of appraisals, carelessness could occur.

The National Association of Review Appraisers and Mortgage Underwriters has developed a form to be used in the review of narrative or residential appraisal reports. It is their intent that use of the form will substantially reduce loan loss of financial institutions by calling attention to the strengths and weaknesses of the appraisal report that lenders rely upon when making real estate loans. It is, however, the function of the autonomous reviewer to see that the valuation is based on sound judgment (see Figure 15.5).

In August 1989, Congress passed the **Financial Institutions Reform, Recovery and Enforcement Act (FIRREA)**. Due to the many failed savings and loan institutions, the appraiser came "under the gun" for careless and shoddy appraisals. As a result, Title XI was attached to the FIRREA bill. Title XI provides for the regulation of appraisers in all federally related transactions. With a deadline of January 1, 1992, many states rushed to enact legislation in compliance with the federal requirements. An extension was granted to January, 1993. All appraisals that are federally related must be performed by certified or licensed appraisers. The appraisers are required to meet minimum standards, which include a written report performed in acccordance with appraisal standards.

The Uniform Standards of Professional Appraisal Practice (USPAP)

The set of rules that regulates the preparation of appraisal reports is the Uniform Standards of Professional Appraisal Practice (USPAP). These rules spell out the ethical and technical guidelines with which appraisers must comply when determining an appraisal value for use in a "federally related" transaction. One provision of the USPAP is that the appraiser, when estimating the value of a parcel of real estate, must employ all three approaches to value: comparison, cost and income. USPAP further states that if the appraiser chooses not to consider all three approaches, the appraisal report must state which approach was not considered and why the appraiser feels it does not apply to the subject property. The criteria are as follows:

1–4 Family Residential	**Commercial Property**
$1 million and higher: *Must* use a *certified* appraiser	See below
$250,000–$999,999: *May* use a *licensed* appraiser; a financial institution may presume that residential property is not complex unless the institution has readily available information to the contrary	$250,000 and above: *Must* use a *certified* appraiser

RESIDENTIAL APPRAISAL REVIEW FORM

Lending Institution _____

Lender's Address _____

_____

Name of Borrower _____

Property Address _____

_____

Loan Number _____

Lender's Appraiser _____ Phone _____

Appraiser's Address _____

Appraised Value $ _____ Date _____

Review Appraiser _____ Phone _____

Reviewer's Address _____

_____

Reviewer's Value Opinion $ _____ Varience % _____ $ _____

The reviewer will analyze the appraisal in light of the following questions. In addition, the Reviewer will sum up the results of his or her analysis by completing the "Reviewer's Comments" appearing at the end of each section. Questions that do not apply can be marked N/A.

FORMAT AND PRESENTATION

YES NO
1. Is the appraisal report in conformance with company ☐ ☐
   appraisal requirements?
   Reviewer's Comments _____

LENDER SECTION

YES NO
2. Is the lender section of the report complete and ☐ ☐
   accurate?
   Reviewer's Comments _____

NEIGHBORHOOD SECTION

YES NO
3. Is the neighborhood section of the report complete
   and accurate? ☐ ☐
4. Does the neighborhood section provide the reviewer
   an adequate understanding with respect to locational
   factors, growth rate and economic trends, property
   values, housing supply, marketing time, land use, price
   ranges, convenience to employment and amenities,
   adequacy of utilities and recreational facilities, property compatibility, appearance of properties, detrimental
   conditions and marketability? ☐ ☐
5. Does the appraisal report enable the reviewer to spot
   healthy growth patterns or trends that may indicate a
   deteriorating neighborhood with limited market appeal? ☐ ☐
6. Are comments in the neighborhood section relevant
   and do they give insight into those conditions which
   positively or negatively affect the appraised properties
   value and marketability? ☐ ☐

YES NO
7. Have all fair and poor ratings in the neighborhood
   section been explained? ☐ ☐
8. If marketing time is over six months, has the appraiser
   commented on the reasons for slow market conditions
   in the subject area? ☐ ☐
9. If the market is slow, has the appraiser indicated
   whether or not this has resulted in a decline in values? ☐ ☐
   Reviewer's Comments _____

SITE SECTION

YES NO
10. Is the site section of the appraisal report complete
    and accurate? ☐ ☐
11. Has the appraiser commented on unfavorable site
    factors? ☐ ☐
12. Does the appraiser indicate whether or not the subject
    property meets all the criteria for a desirable lot in the
    area? ☐ ☐
13. Has the appraiser addressed and commented on prob-
    lems relating to poor drainage, flood conditions, adverse
    easements, encroachments or other detrimental factors? ☐ ☐
14. Does the appraiser indicate the subject's zoning and
    whether or not the subject conforms with present zon-
    ing requirements? ☐ ☐

YES NO
15. Has the appraiser accurately indicated the dimensions
    and size of the subject lot? ☐ ☐
16. Does the appraisal report reveal whether or not site
    improvements and services to the site are adequate and
    acceptable in the market place? ☐ ☐
    Reviewer's Comments _____

IMPROVEMENTS SECTION

YES NO
17. Is the improvement section of the report complete and
    accurate? ☐ ☐
18. If the subject property is a condominium, are the project
    improvements and project rating sections complete and
    accurate? ☐ ☐
19. Did the appraiser comment on physical and functional
    inadequacies and indicate whether or not repairs and
    modernization are needed? ☐ ☐
20. Has the appraiser explained fair or poor improvement
    ratings? ☐ ☐
21. Does the appraiser indicate whether or not factors
    receiving poor or fair ratings, adversely affect the proper-
    ty's marketability? ☐ ☐

YES NO
22. Have factors relating to age, condition, quality of con-
    struction, finish and equipment, as well as size and utility
    been properly handled? ☐ ☐
23. Has the appraiser given serious attention to structural
    problems? ☐ ☐
24. Did the appraiser comment on unusual layouts, pecu-
    liar floor plans, inadequate equipment and amenities? ☐ ☐
25. Has the appraiser indicated whether or not factors
    relating to unusual layouts, peculiar floor plans, inade-
    quate equipment and amenities, limit the value and
    market appeal of the subject? ☐ ☐
26. If there is evidence of dampness, termites or settle-
    ment, did the appraiser comment on these factors? ☐ ☐

Review Form No. 2002

FIGURE 15.5
Residential appraisal
review form.

(continued)

IMPROVEMENTS SECTION Continued

YES NO

27. Has the appraiser provided the reviewer with a clear and accurate understanding of the physical and functioning attributes of the subject property?
28. Is the property rating section accurate as well as consistent with other data contained in the report?
29. Has the appraiser presented information on construction features in a manner that gives an accurate and adequate view of the subject property?
30. Has information relating to the improvements been well handled?

YES NO

31. In the reviewer's opinion, is the descriptive section of the appraisal report (page one) acceptable?
    Reviewer's Comments

COST SECTION

YES NO

32. Is the cost section complete and accurate?
33. Are the appraiser's measurements for gross living area correct?
34. Has the appraiser commented on functional and economic obsolescence?
35. In estimating reproduction costs, has the appraiser used cost figures that are appropriate for the local market?
36. Do figures for physical, functional and economic depreciation appear reasonable in light of the subject's age, condition, state of modernization, size and utility, and location?
37. Is the estimate of land value appropriate?

YES NO

38. Has the appraiser used construction cost figures rather than market data to arrive at the subject's market value?
39. Are the appraiser's mathematical calculations accurate?
40. Is the budget analysis section accurate and complete (if condo)?
    Reviewer's Comments

MARKET ANALYSIS SECTION

YES NO

41. Is the market analysis section complete and accurate?
42. Has the appraiser selected his or her comparables from the subject neighborhood?
43. If not, has the appraiser explained why comparables were selected from a different neighborhood?
44. In your opinion, are the comparables really similar with respect to location, site, design and style, quality and amenities, as well as size and utility?
45. Are all of the comparables recent sales of similar properties from the subject neighborhood?
46. If the comparables are over three months old, has the appraiser explained why he or she failed to use recent sales?
47. Are room counts and square foot areas of the subject and comparables similar?
48. Do the sales prices and prices per square foot of the comparables correlate and indicate comparability?
49. Are there large differences in the price per unit and per square foot between the subject and comparable properties?
50. Has the appraiser bracketed his or her sales data (before making adjustments)?
51. Do time adjustments, for date of sale, appear reasonable in light of market trends and current market conditions?
52. Has the appraiser made excessive adjustments (gross adjustment figures that are 25% or more of comparable sales prices and individual line adjustments that are 10% or more of comparable sales prices)?
53. Has the appraiser made numerous large adjustments?
54. Has the appraiser adjusted all three comparables in a reasonable and consistent manner?
55. Does the appraiser make unsupportable or faulty adjustments?
56. Is there missing or inaccurate information in the market analysis section?
57. Are the appraiser's mathematical calculations accurate?
58. Is there a convincing value range with respect to the three adjusted comparables? In brief, are the adjusted value conclusions reasonably similar?
59. Does the appraiser's final value conclusion relate to the adjusted comparables?
60. Has the appraiser selected good market data and handled it well?
61. Has the appraiser commented on the subject's marketability?
62. Does the appraisers marketability information appear to be accurate?

YES NO

63. Does it appear that the appraiser is backing into any or all of the approaches to value?
64. Is there a lack of clarity with respect to the appraiser's reasoning?
65. Can you read the appraisal report, step by step, and arrive at the same conclusion of value as the appraiser?
66. Does the appraiser appear to be an advocate rather than an individual offering an independent and impartial third party opinion of value?
67. Are there missing photographs or photographs that do not adequately show the subject and surrounding properties?
68. Is other illustrative material missing or poorly done?
69. If the appraiser is using computer generated data, are the facts and comments in the report accurate and applicable to the subject and comparable properties?
70. Does it appear that the appraiser is using the computer as a substitute for thinking?
71. Are the appraiser's comments and final reconciliation of value adequate and does the appraisal give insight into the value and marketability of the subject property?
72. Is the appraiser's value conclusion reasonable?
73. Do you wind up with a different value conclusion than the appraiser, based upon data contained within the report?
74. In your opinion, has the appraiser failed to prove his or her case?
75. Does it appear that the subject property has been over appraised?
76. Has the appraiser signed the report and typed his or her name under the signature?
77. Is there a phone number on the report and/or cover letter which would enable the reviewer to contact the appraiser and clarify a questionable appraisal report?
78. Is the valuation section of the report (page two) acceptable?
    Reviewer's Comments

REVIEWER'S SUMMARY

(To be completed by the lender's appraisal, quality control or underwriting department.)

Appraisal Report was: Acceptable ☐   Unacceptable ☐

Recommendations, comments and summary of action taken (if any).

Reviewer's Signature _____   Date of Review _____

Review Form No. 2002

FIGURE 15.5
(Continued).

$100,001–$249,999: *May* use a
licensed appraiser *even if* the
property is complex

$100,001–$249,999; *May* use a
licensed appraiser *even if* the
property is complex

$0–$100,000: No appraisal required;
however, most institutions will
require an appraisal

$0–$100,000: No appraisal required;
however, most institutions will
require an appraisal.

Even before the enactment of FIRREA, 17 states* had already required appraisers to be licensed or certified. Continuing education and minimum standards of performance are criteria sought by the appraisal institutes and societies.

Most states are requiring licensees to have fulfilled the following requirements for state certification:

1. 2,000 hours of appraisal work experience
2. 60 hours of basic appraisal education
3. 15 hours of Uniform Standards of Principles and Practice (USPAP)
4. successfully pass an examination

The appraiser needs to be *state* certified to:

1. appraise federally related commercial transactions of more than $250,000
2. appraise residential properties of more than $1 million
3. appraise complex residential properties of more than $250,000
4. appraise residential properties of more than four units
5. succcessfully pass an examination

For *general* certification the appraiser is required to:

1. complete 1,000 hours of residential experience and 1,000 hours of commercial education
2. complete 150 hours of course work
3. complete 15 hours of the Uniform Standards of Principles and Practices (USPAP)
4. successfully pass an examination
5. if the state has a residential certification available, the course work is reduced to 105 hours

In some areas of the country, lenders are now requesting that appraisers fill out environmental on-site inspection forms. While appraisers already have a responsibility to make note of any condition that could affect the property value through normal research, as they perform the appraisal there is concern over items that cannot readily be observed. Is the appraiser liable to know if there are underground storage tanks? The appraiser needs to inform the client that the appraiser is not an environmental expert and can only observe any existing problems. The appraiser also needs to take care not to report any conclusion about past, present, or future contamination. As more and more responsibility is heaped upon the appraiser, a disclaimer on such issues as environmental hazards and toxic waste should accompany the report.

As professionalism has developed among appraisers, organizations and designations have followed. Rigid appraisal education requirements must be met by appraisers seeking membership and designations in these associations. With local chapters across the country, techniques are taught for appraising urban, rural, and industrial properties.

*The 17 states are Arizona, Colorado, Delaware, Georgia, Indiana, Michigan, Minnesota, Mississippi, Nebraska, Nevada, New Mexico, Oregon, South Carolina, Tennessee, Utah, Virginia, and West Virginia.

Summary

There are three main appraisal techniques: the cost approach, the sales comparison approach, and the income approach. Each of these approaches to the value of real estate is explained in this chapter. The appraiser should always begin by requesting the purpose for the appraisal. Keep in mind that an appraisal is an estimate of value. While this estimate of value can be arrived at by any one of the three approaches, the choice of the method depends on the purpose of the appraisal.

The appraisal procedure is carried out in a sequence of steps, from defining the problem and collecting the data to analyzing the subject property and applying one or more of the three approaches.

Depreciation affects value and is caused by physical depreciation, economic obsolescence, and functional obsolescence. The highest and best use of the property and the various principles involved in creating value are discussed in the chapter.

While there are many more facets involved in the appraisal of real estate, the techniques and definitions presented here should be adequate to introduce you to the field of appraisal. In-depth studies of land and building residual techniques and complete detailed appraisal reports can be found in textbooks written strictly on appraisal.

Discussion Questions

1. How are adjustments for the differences in properties applied by the appraiser?
2. Explain the three approaches to value and describe when each is used.
3. Differentiate between market value and market price.
4. Why is it necessary for the appraiser to know the reason for an appraisal? Isn't value the same regardless of the purpose for the appraisal?
5. Explain the principle of progression and regression.
6. List the sequence of steps an appraiser follows in arriving at the value of a property.

Review Questions

Answers to these questions are found in the Answer Key section at the back of the book.

1. In analyzing a parcel of land to estimate its value, what is the first thing necessary to determine?

   a. the market value
   b. the cost appraisal
   c. the reason for the appraisal
   d. the availability of public transportation

2. Functional obsolescence is due to:

   a. normal wear and tear
   b. poor design or floor plan
   c. poor location
   d. poor upkeep

3. On what type of property would the cost approach be the most accurate?

   a. a 6-month-old residence
   b. an apartment house
   c. an older property with economic obsolescence
   d. a 15-year-old residence

4. The market value of a property is commonly defined as:

   a. the highest and best use of the property
   b. the highest price at which a willing seller will sell and a willing buyer will buy

c. the income the property is annually producing

d. amenities attached to the property

5. The definition of depreciation is:

   a. loss in value

   b. mortgage foreclosures

   c. loss from scarcity of a product

   d. none of the above

6. Physical depreciation is brought about by:

   a. conditions outside the property

   b. functional obsolescence

   c. normal wear and tear

   d. economic conditions

7. Economic obsolescence is related to:

   a. lack of closet space

   b. poor drainage in the yard

   c. faulty heating systems

   d. conditions external to the property

8. A four-bedroom home with one bathroom suffers from:

   a. economic obsolescence

   b. functional obsolescence

   c. physical depreciation

   d. economic depreciation

9. The value of a property CANNOT be lowered by:

   a. a changing neighborhood

   b. economic obsolescence

   c. zoning laws

   d. insurance claims

10. The formula of replacement-cost-less-depreciation-plus-value-of-land is called the:

    a. income approach

    b. market data approach

    c. comparison approach

    d. cost approach

11. The summation or cost approach to value is best used on:

    a. commercial property

    b. service-type buildings

    c. land

    d. older homes

12. The depreciation most difficult to remedy would be:

    a. physical

    b. economic

    c. wear and tear

    d. functional

13. The replacement-cost method of appraising:

    a. tends to set the upper limits of value

    b. tends to set the lower limits of value

    c. is best applied to income property

    d. is best applied to older homes

14. Utilizing a property to its greatest economic advantage is commonly referred to as:

    a. mobilization

    b. economic utility

    c. market value

    d. highest and best use

15. When applying the cost approach to value, the appraiser allows for depreciation:

    a. on land

    b. on improvements

    c. on personal property

    d. on neighboring property

16. Which of the following is NOT a factor to consider when using the comparison approach to value?

    a. date of sale

    b. physical features and amenities

    c. current monthly rent

    d. financing concessions

17. The average home buyer is most concerned with:

    a. floor plan

    b. architectural design

    c. location

    d. tax basis

18. In preparing an appraisal report, the appraiser's first step is to:

    a. collect the data

    b. apply the cost approach

    c. write the appraisal report

    d. define the problem

19. The appraisal approach that is concerned with the

present worth of future benefits of the property is called:

a. capitalization
b. cost approach
c. comparison approach
d. summation approach

20. Functional obsolescence would least likely include:

a. rotting wood
b. poor architecture
c. an outdated kitchen
d. bad design

21. A 25-year-old home is sound and in good condition, but has an outdated bath. The bath is suffering from:

a. normal depreciation
b. physical obsolescence
c. functional obsolescence
d. deterioration

22. When an appraiser measures the area of a house, the appraiser measures:

a. each individual room
b. inside wall measurements, excluding partitions
c. the exterior of home
d. all of the above

23. What value may an appraiser NOT be employed to determine?

a. market value
b. loan value
c. condemnation value
d. past value

24. When an appraiser determines the fair market value of a property, which of the following information should be furnished to the owner who requested the appraisal?

a. a statement revealing how the value was determined
b. data showing recent comparable sales
c. a statement that shows how value was determined using recent comparable values
d. no information goes to owner, only to lender

25. The best definition of an appraisal is:

a. a means of determining depreciation
b. a method to keep values current with reproduction costs
c. a statement of facts that may not necessarily be true
d. an estimate of value

Land Use Controls

16

KEY WORDS

appurtenance
assemblage
building codes
cluster lots
covenants
down zoning
easement
easement in gross
encroachment
homogeneous

license
master plan
nonconforming use
planned unit development (PUD)
plat
police power
variance
zero lot lines
zoning

OVERVIEW

The importance of the wise utilization of our land dates from the beginning of this country's history when the authors of the Constitution determined that the government would need to exercise some control over the use of the land. Title to land was granted by the federal government to individuals, and most titles can be traced back to the original land grant or patent. To encourage settlement, especially of the western territories, land was sold at auction and offered as a bonus to soldiers who served in the Continental Army. Title provided for allodial ownership in fee simple interest, but controls were placed over the use of the land, and today these use restrictions include the addition of private controls. This chapter will cover these controls and restrictions along with the development of a subdivision.

FEDERAL CONTROLS ON LAND USE

From the start, some land was set aside for park areas. In 1872, Congress created the first national park preserve in the world. Yellowstone National Park was followed by 29 other preserves containing mountains, volcanoes, glaciers, and spacious virgin forests. Today all 50 states have established parks within their boundaries as recreational areas for picnicking, hiking, camping, and enjoying nature. With the increased attention to tourism, expanded park facilities welcome and encourage out-of-state visitors. City parks, often with playgrounds and recreational facilities, have been developed for the enjoyment of the residents.

Reserving land for parks

With the growth of our country, many additional federal laws covering the disposition and use of real estate have been enacted. In 1968, the federal government

Regulating interstate land sales

enacted the Interstate Land Sales Disclosure Act, which regulates subdivided land. The U.S. Department of Housing and Urban Development (HUD) requires developers to register interstate land sales with the Office of Interstate Land Sales Registration (OILSR) if the development contains 50 or more units. A property report must be given to a prospective buyer a minimum of three days before a contract to purchase may be entered into. This "cooling-off" period allows the buyer to analyze the wisdom of the decision. This law was implemented to protect people from purchasing land presented as a great opportunity that may in truth be greatly misrepresented.

Controls include the Real Estate Settlement Procedures Act (RESPA), which covers conditions that must be addressed when transferring real estate (see Chapter 8).

In July 1982, Congress passed a law stating that savings and loan institutions do not have to allow mortgages to be assumed upon transfer of title. This superseded law that had been mandated in some states to the contrary. Finally, the Civil Rights Act of 1968 and its amendments in 1989 provide for fair housing throughout the United States (see Chapter 17).

Although all 50 states have control over land within their boundaries, the federal interstate highways, parks, and schools are examples of land under the jurisdiction of the United States government.

STATE AND LOCAL CONTROLS ON LAND USE

Regulating land use in communities

States exercise control over their highways, parks, lakes, water use, and government buildings. Some states have comprehensive plans for orderly development, with special emphasis placed on their natural resources. Through *enabling acts* passed by many states, chartered cities are given the power to regulate land use within their jurisdiction with zoning laws. Zoning regulations give local governments the power to impose controls and restrictions over the private use of land. This power of the government to regulate land use is referred to as **police power** and must be used in the interest of the public. These controls ensure that the growth of a city, whether a large metropolis or an incorporated village, proceeds in a coordinated and harmonious manner. Public land use controls may include the development of a **master plan** for the city, zoning laws, **building codes**, and subdivision regulations.

Creating a master plan

In establishing a comprehensive master plan for land use, a careful study and analysis of existing physical, economic, and social conditions in the community is made. Master planning is needed to meet the ever-changing social and economic requirements of a community. The master plan will consider housing, schools, health care, transportation, and public utilities as the present conditions and the projection of future needs is determined. This plan serves as a guide so that growth will proceed in the manner that best promotes the general welfare of citizens and protects their real estate investments. Decisions are reached and expenditures are decided upon when capital improvements are required. Often changes are foreseen, so proper adjustments must be made. For instance, as our mode of transportation changed, the one-lane dirt road was exchanged for paved streets to accommodate the transition from the horse and carriage to the automobile. Moving traffic to avoid congestion remains one of the most crucial responsibilities of the cities.

The land use planners will survey present land uses and consider the vacant land that lies in the path of possible future development. A projection of future use will be analyzed in considering the hierarchy of rights in real estate. The laws must not only be concerned with the present owner, but with the rights of the community and future generations. Thus, the land use laws proposed by a municipality safeguard and protect the rights of all parties. A county's laws must not be inconsistent with the city government so that an orderly pattern of development may ensue. If the properties in a given area are **homogeneous** or compatible, values will be stable.

Since the desire for land is concentrated around employment areas, land is more in demand in and near large cities. City planning, with a broader outlook to the future, is under constant study by urban governmental agencies, with zoning regulations of extreme importance.

ZONING

Zoning limits the rights of property owners, specifying what is allowable and what specific uses will be prohibited. Zoning restrictions can be traced to early colonial days when the residential areas were separated from industries with the saloons, blacksmith shops, stables, and tanneries placed on the opposite side of the village.

Protection of property rights

The fundamental reasons to have zoning laws are apparent: to protect the interests of the property owner and to achieve an aesthetically pleasing environment in the community. Limiting uses within a zone provides that protection. Imagine how difficult it would be to retain value in your home if an automobile dealership or a saloon could operate next door. Zones place each type of residence, business, and industry in compatible areas.

Today a zoning board or planning commission is appointed to pass and regulate restrictions on land use. A city development plan will view the physical development patterns and establish policies to direct and finance the growth and improvement of the urban environment. It is not unusual for a city to have a strategic plan in place that establishes the general goals for land use that will include economic development, parks and recreation, and transportation. In exercising its police power, the planning board of the local government establishes the zoning ordinances that regulate and control land use.

Zoning falls into four general categories: residential, commercial, industrial, and agricultural. Since it is wise to have homogeneous divisions, each of these four categories is further divided into more specific areas. A typical key to zoning follows, but keep in mind this will vary from city to city.

Zoning categories

1. Residential is represented by R-1 through R-7. R-1 may be the most restrictive, requiring larger lots. Within these classifications the regulations are set as to minimum requirements for the square footage of the lot; minimum lot width; and minimum front, side, and rear setbacks from the perimeter of the property boundaries. Maximum building height and coverage of the lot are other stipulations found in these categories.
2. O-1 is for office uses.
3. C-1 might permit a neighborhood business with C-2 used for community business, C-3 for general business, and C-4 for central business. Again, the size and use will be dictated by the zoning in each of the business categories.
4. I-1 may be used for light industrial, I-2 for heavy industrial, and I-M is for manufacturing use.
5. A represents agricultural.

In each of these areas the zoning laws of the municipality govern the type of structure one can erect and the use to which the property can be adapted. The residential areas are usually buffeted from busy streets by multifamily units with office space following and commercial uses abutting the main streets. The strip of land that separates the areas is referred to as a *buffer zone*.

Buffer zones

Most cities need the use of land to be regulated within a one-to-three mile radius of the city. This right to control is acquired by legislative enactment. As the community spreads, it merges into the rural agricultural areas, and the need for converting the farmland into other uses arises. City dwellers desiring to move into the country may force the conversion of agricultural land into 5- and 10-acre plots.

Changes in Zoning

Change of use

Requests for zoning changes from an existing use to another purpose are generally made with the intention of bringing a higher return to the property. For example, a property in an older residential area now lies in the path of commercial use but, with minor remodeling, can be converted to office or business space. No longer desirable for a residence because of the outside influences, it will lend itself nicely to a new use if the zoning can be changed.

Special use permits are available in some states and allow the conversion of a property to another use. Generally, the person is requesting a use that does not conform to the current zoning of the area. For example, a homeowner requests permission to operate a beauty salon from her home. A special use permit is usually quite restrictive and can only be for the purpose requested. If the owner later decides to open a tailor shop and close the beauty salon, she will have to go through the same procedure of applying for the new use.

A *conditional use* permit would grant a use that would be beneficial to the public, such as a sandwich shop in an industrial tract. Convenience for the employees in the area creates an inducement to permit the use.

Exclusionary zoning requires larger lots, thus excluding people who cannot afford the extra land costs. Restrictions are often placed on agricultural land adjacent to cities requiring the purchase of 5- to 10-acre sites, thus placing it beyond the reach of the people who want the flavor of uncongested, country living.

Inclusionary zoning is the exact opposite as it requires that lower income properties must be included in new housing developments. This eliminates discriminating zoning of properties that tend to limit purchase to the higher income brackets.

Moratorium

Occasionally a community will place a *moratorium* on building, halting the construction of new houses. This has been practiced in areas that want to preserve the mountainsides and natural surroundings and retain the aesthetic beauty that accounts for the popularity of the community. This *zoning freeze* may place a hardship on the person who has purchased a lot with the intention of building at a later date only to discover a building permit is unobtainable.

Zoning ordinances can be changed and rezoning permitted by *amendment*. If it appears another use of the property would be appropriate for the area as it now exists, a zoning amendment allowing the use may be instituted. A residential area may have been infringed upon by commercial use, and changing the ordinance to accommodate the uses now developing in the area would be prudent.

Nonconforming use

A **nonconforming use** of property is a use in violation of present zoning laws but lawful at the time the use was begun. Grandfather rights exist since zoning regulations cannot be retroactive. For example, consider a grocery store built in 1975 on the edge of an undeveloped area. In 1991 a developer plats out the remaining land into large single-family lots. The grocery store is not compatible, so it is now considered a nonconforming use. The grocer is not required to close his business, but another merchant would be prohibited from starting a new store.

Spot zoning

Spot zoning is zoning of isolated properties for activities other than those called for in existing regulations. The law generally does not favor spot zoning since it is inconsistent with the present zoning of the area. A vacant lot at present in an area zoned residential but itself zoned for commercial use would be an example of spot zoning. A change to allow construction of a multi-unit building in a neighborhood of single-family residences is another example of spot zoning.

If an individual owner needs an exception to the zoning ordinance and if the use is not detrimental to the public, a **variance** can be requested. For example, an owner may wish to build a garage but is unable to adhere to the zoning laws because the structure will be 5 feet from the lot line and the regulations in the subdivision call for setbacks of 10 feet from lot lines. In such a case, a variance would probably be granted if the surrounding neighbors have no negative complaint to the variance. The zoning board of appeals can approve variances and grant a waiver when strict adherence of the ordinance produces a hardship to the owner in need of the exception.

Variances

Down zoning occurs when a property is rezoned to a lower use. For example, a property zoned for an apartment building is down zoned to permit only single-family homes. The new uses for these properties do not use the land to its highest and best use for which it was originally zoned. If the down zoning is executed by ordinance, the property owner may be awarded compensation for the loss in property value caused by the new restriction.

Down zoning

Procedure for Rezoning or Variance

In most cities the zoning of property can only be changed by ordinance. Usually a two-tier system exists: the planning board recommends action to the city council, and the city council acts on the ordinance. The planning board members are mayoral-appointed positions, generally selected from a broad employment base. The process will follow a sequence of steps similar to the following:

1. The applicant contacts the planning department for a zoning change.
2. The planning department will inspect the site and make a recommendation.
3. Announcement of a pending hearing will be made in the newspaper.
4. Notification of the petition is sent to surrounding property owners.
5. A public hearing is held, and the applicant presents the request with valid substantiation for the zoning change. Evidence should be presented as to why the change is necessary, that it will be a beneficial use of the property, and not harmful to the surrounding properties.
6. The general public may speak for or against the approval of rezoning.
7. An administration meeting is held, and the request is denied or approved. If denied, the applicant can request an appeal of the denial.
8. The planning board prepares the ordinance.
9. The city council generally holds three meetings (one is a public hearing), and the request is voted upon at the final hearing. If the request is denied and the city council members concur with the planning board, the applicant may appeal the decision to the district court.
10. The rezoning becomes effective.

Changing property use

PRIVATE CONTROL OF LAND USE

As mentioned in the beginning of this chapter, private individuals also have control over real property. It is understood that the property owner must abide by the restrictions placed on the property through the zoning laws and the covenants established when the property was platted.

Deed restrictions

Deed restrictions can determine how a property may be used. You can sell your property "subject to" and place a restriction that prohibits or permits a use, providing it is not inconsistent with the zoning and covenants of the area. **Covenants** are restrictions or agreements that regulate use of property (as discussed later in this chapter). The deed restriction may state that a fence will never be allowed around the property, or a farmer may sell his 80 acres and stipulate that its use always remain agricultural. If the covenants of an area are not adhered to by your neighbor, you may bring suit for loss of value to your property. The covenants may state that no wooden fences can be installed that obscure the view of another owner. So, a neighbor can not install a six-foot fence that blocks your view of the lake.

A *nuisance* complaint would involve loud noises, barking dogs that interrupt sleep, or a lack of property maintenance.

Zoning ensures property owners against nonconforming uses affecting value, and covenants protect each subdivision, but this does not ensure compatibility of neighbors. If covenants are violated, the surrounding neighbors need to band together to ensure conformance and resort to filing suit if the problem is not abated.

Changing Property Uses

Revitalizing downtown areas

Originally the downtown area of a city represented the primary retail and office center. Significant changes have developed in the past 30 years as neighborhood shopping centers and industrial and office parks began to emerge. New emphasis was focused on a changing downtown economy as large retailers abandoned the area for the suburbs, and citizens gravitated to neighborhood shopping centers where parking was adequate and free.

Planning boards across the nation have proposed a variety of land uses to revitalize downtown areas into mixed-use districts. To attract visitors, many cities have established "old town" atmospheres in what were old brick warehouses and industrial plants. New uses have been created with sleek, updated interiors converted into apartments, condominiums, specialty shops, eateries, and entertainment to appeal to downtown employees and visitors. To accommodate the automobile, parking garages have been increased. Many of these downtown areas have riverfronts that attract the tourist trade. Marketing this revitalization has been a major focus of the local chamber of commerce.

The preservation of historic buildings has added to the interesting mix of old and new as the character of the area changed. Tax credits are available to owners for rehabilitating buildings that qualify under the historic guidelines.

Transfer Development Rights (TDRs)

Transfer development rights (TDRs) permit the transfer of a building right to another piece of land. Based on the premise that rights of land use should be equal, it allows the owner of a property, such as a historical landmark, to sell her TDR to an owner down the street and therefore preserve the historical building from demolition. Likewise, an owner of farmland adjacent to the city could sell the TDR to a person located in a district more suitable for construction. This concept promotes the fill-in of urban areas without jeopardizing the right to make a profit for the person owning the farmland. For the most part, TDRs have been used in Chicago and New York in an effort to save historical buildings.

SUBDIVISION DEVELOPMENT

Site Selection

When a subdivider wishes to divide raw land into housing sites, acquisition of the site selection should be made in a location that follows the growth of the area. The location can make the difference between the success or failure of the subdivision. It should be convenient to utilities and employment centers. The general plan should be competitive with and measure up to surrounding developments.

Subdividing raw land

Before the purchase is made, it is critical that the subdivider determines that there is a sufficient demand for new housing in the area. A decision is then made concerning the market that will be targeted. Once the site is selected, the subdivider usually hires an experienced subdivision planner to develop layout concepts in conformance with current styles and trends. Environmental concerns should be considered, along with lot views and street placement.

Sometimes a subdivider will gather together two or more parcels of land to make the whole more valuable. This practice is known as **assemblage**.

The Plat

The preparation of the **plat** will include anticipating any problems and endeavoring to solve them before presenting the plat for approval to the planning board. If it is a large plat, the site will be developed in phases, and the developer may be required to dedicate land for future school or park use. The availability of public utilities will be of prime importance to the subdivider, as well as whether there is easy access to sewer, water, electricity, and gas. Since people inherently resist change, the applicant expects neighborhood opposition to the plan, so the developer should be ready with alternatives and concessions.

The subdivider must submit the proposed plat and the development plans to the city planning department. Subdivision regulations are laws enacted by a local governing body to control the conversion of bare land into building sites. This places legal control over the community's design, thus eliminating the misuse of property and protecting community values, health, and safety. The plat is reviewed by various professionals and city officials, including the planning department, city engineer, health department, utility officials, and the parks and recreation department.

Plat approval

The preliminary plat usually has areas designated for schools and parks and the required number of streets laid out. When the subdivider files the plan, he also files a declaration of covenants and restrictions for the subdivision. In the covenants, the subdivider dedicates these streets to the city (or county, if the area is outside the city limits). In addition, areas must be reserved or dedicated for public use, public utilities must be installed, and lots and blocks must be clearly specified as to size and length. Once approval of the plat is obtained, the subdivider begins construction of the subdivision improvements.

The Engineer's Role

Engineers provide professional services which assist with the development and offer constructive criticism of ideas which may not be fully formed. The engineer may point out a site's physical limitations or such limitations as imposed by governmental regulations. It is the engineer's responsibility to evaluate the proposed development, giving consideration to the atmosphere the developer wants to achieve, the type and styles of buffers from existing or future development, lot sizes, and lot spacing. The cost of public improvements, or infrastructure, is usually a major cost of the site. Reasonably detailed estimates of the cost of streets, sidewalks, utilities, sewers, and streetlights are assembled by the engineer, and any other site-related expenses, such as platting, zoning, subdividing, and grading, are also estimated for the developer. A detailed topographic study is done to determine grading and in-fill needs, boundaries are surveyed, and soil test borings may be made.

Plat certification

The final plat is certified by the engineer and the subdivider and is then recorded. The last task of the engineer is the overseeing of the final grading and seeding and installation and maintenance of erosion control.

Covenants

Protection for property owners

Covenants concerning building lines, setbacks, and side yards must be stipulated in the subdivider's plan. Use restrictions are always for the public good and generally relate to how the land can be best utilized and the sort of construction permissible. These covenants and restrictions will protect the purchaser's investment. The square footage required in a dwelling, the architectural design, whether outbuildings may be constructed, or whether one- or two-car garages are required are examples of restrictions placed in covenants. Restrictive covenants remain in effect for specific time periods—for example, for 10 years, 20 years, or in perpetuity. Local zoning regulations and restrictive covenants filed with the plat plan for a particular subdivision regulate the distance from the perimeter of the property that a building may be erected. Referred to as a *setback*, this applies to front, side, and rear yards.

The Builder's Role

Building permits

The builder reviews three basic documents: the plans and specifications, the site plan, and the elevations and plan views. Upon approval of the plans by the city, a building permit is granted. A survey of the lot is made by a surveyor, and iron stakes are imbedded in the ground at each corner of the lot since it is vital that the boundary lines are accurate before construction commences. The builder will use a transit to stake out the exact location of the house on the lot. Consideration is given to surface drainage, the required slope of the sewer line, and if a view is preferable in one direction as opposed to another. Each phase of the construction, from the initial digging of the foundation to the exterior paint, is carefully monitored by the general contractor. Building permits are required each time a contractor starts to construct a building, thus ensuring compliance with the zoning ordinances and building codes. The city is most concerned that code requirements are met for electrical and sanitary systems and fire and safety standards.

Permits are also required to remodel an existing structure or even to erect a fence. The building must not violate a covenant or deed restriction of the area, or the contractor will be stopped in mid-construction. It is the responsibility of neighboring homeowners to enforce their covenants.

LOT VARIATIONS

New lot variations have become popular in some areas of the country. Greater density can be achieved by clustering homes. **Cluster** house **lots** are usually only half the size of conventional house lots; however, they can provide as much privacy and green space as the normal lots. Instead of breaking up the areas into front, side, and rear yards, the aggregate of all the yards is molded into one open space around the homes, preserving natural features and thus providing less environmental disturbance. With proper design and variance in roof and window placements, visual and noise barriers will exist between the homes, maintaining residential character and privacy. Because the structures are clustered, the developer can pass the savings of fewer sidewalks and utility connections on to the purchasers. There is a perception of safety since through traffic is lessened.

Zero lot line is another concept in lot use whereby single-family homes are built on the lot line, with the owner having an easement, usually five feet, on the neighbor's lot so that access for painting or repairs is available. This saves land since the owner has just one side yard, which is more usable than two small side yards (see Figure 16.1).

Planned Unit Developments

A **planned unit development (PUD)** shares many of the same characteristics as a cluster housing development. PUDs can be small developments planned to accommodate the clustering of houses on smaller lots, or they can be large platted areas, which set aside sites for retail shops, parks, and hiking trails for a total-planned community that includes single-family homes, apartments, and condominiums or cooperatives. A PUD offers a compact community extending many conveniences to its residents.

Smaller lot sizes permitted

The development plan must be platted, detailing the various uses the site will have and the acres involved in each use. A timetable for construction completion of each phase will be stated, and if the development will cause traffic congestion, the applicant may be required to share in the cost of expanding the streets. Design considerations should include adequate parking and landscaping to create privacy.

EASEMENTS

Easements on a section of land are usually outlined in the covenants. Since an easement represents an interest in another's land, the grant must be in writing to conform with the statute of frauds. An **easement** is a right of way through the land of another, referred to as the right of *ingress* and *egress* (entering and leaving) over another's land.

Right of way on another's land

Each easement is classified as either an easement **appurtenance** or an **easement in gross**. An easement appurtenance goes along with the land. Examples of an easement appurtenance include shared driveways and party walls. The two pieces of land must be adjacent and owned by separate individuals for an appurtenant easement to exist. For example, in Figure 16.2, A and B share a common driveway; thus, each has the right to use the adjoining land of the other. Most easement appurtenances are specially written in the deed or by express written contract.

Easement appurtenance

Normal lot line   **Zero lot line**

FIGURE 16.1
Normal and zero lot lines.

FIGURE 16.2
An easement
appurtenance.

An owner of a large section of land splits the property, selling a portion to another. The former owner may reserve the right to use part of the property sold, called an *easement by reservation*. Or, the new owner may have demanded as part of the purchase agreement that he have the right to use of the seller's remaining land, called an *easement by grant*. It is not necessary to be landlocked to have such an easement.

Easement in gross

An easement in gross is personal and generally cannot be assigned to another. Examples would be large billboards or signs erected on another's property, pipelines, utility lines, sewer lines, and power lines (see Figure 16.3). The easement in gross to an individual is limited to the holder's lifetime and does not automatically pass with the land. If a purchaser wants an existing easement in gross to pass with title, it would be necessary to state this in the deed.

Easement in license

Since an easement in gross is for an individual's lifetime, a landowner should issue a **license** if she has any reservations about giving a permanent easement to the other person. A license is revocable at the grantor's option and is not transferable.

Easements of Necessity and Other Easements

An *easement of necessity* arises when there is a special need, as in the case of a land-locked owner. For example, in Figure 16.4, X sold the back portion of her land to Y, and an easement was necessary for Y to get to his land. The *dominant tenant* (Y) receives the easement, and the *servient tenant* (X) gives the easement. Easements granted by one party to another cannot be rescinded by the owner of the land. The land in this example has no other access, and since a purchaser cannot be landlocked, the easement was mandatory.

Dominant & servient tenants

If a servient tenant allows the dominant tenant to remove minerals or soils from the land, it is called *profit a prendre*. These rights may be extended to just the one dominant tenant, or they may be assignable to a future owner of the land.

FIGURE 16.3
Easement in gross.

FIGURE 16.4
Easement of necessity.

An *easement by prescription* is the right acquired through long-term, continuous use of another's property. This use must be in an adverse manner, that is, without the consent of the owner.

Party wall easements exist between two owners when a common wall built on the lot line separates two structures, as in row houses or condominiums. Each owner has the responsibility to maintain his side of the wall, which cannot be removed or changed without approval of both, and each has an easement on the other owner's side. Party wall easements may also exist when a fence separates the boundaries of two properties.

ENCROACHMENT

An **encroachment** exists when one owner's property infringes onto another's land. Examples of common encroachments include fences carelessly erected on neighboring land or driveways and patios extending onto the adjoining property. Tree branches or shrubbery hanging over the property line can create an encroachment.

Since encroachments are generally not covered by title insurance, it is important for a purchaser to have a survey if there is any doubt concerning the accuracy of the boundaries. If the encroachment has existed long enough, an easement by prescription may be in effect or even a claim to the title by adverse possession.

ENVIRONMENTAL CONTROLS

The environment has become a major concern of many Americans. The real estate community and related industries are especially interested in addressing the issue because of their involvement in transferring both existing properties and properties in new developments. Some will remember the Love Canal in New York that resulted in the evacuation of homeowners because of the toxic waste that polluted the ground on which the homes were built. Because of this and other abuses of the environment that have surfaced through the years, Congress has passed laws that endeavor to conserve the environment and protect the welfare of the people.

With the vast amount of properties that transfer ownership annually, our present legislation is holding both past and present owners responsible for hazardous waste removal. Lenders are concerned because of their liability created when they assume title to defaulted properties.

Environmental concerns touch the economic, social, and physical environment and are having an enormous impact on the way that we do business. We are almost daily reminded to save newspaper, cans, and bottles for recycling in an effort to lessen the burden on dump sites. Future pollution through population growth and development can be monitored with effective laws that must be met. Some of the acts that have been mandated in recent years include the following:

- The Air Quality Act of 1967 was amended in 1970 to establish air quality standards and protect the public health and welfare. The act passes the responsibility to the states for control within their boundaries. Automobile fumes contributing to air pollution resulted in emission controls on all vehicles, and on some inner-city roads, diesel-fueled vehicles are banned. The effect on small industries was in many cases disastrous. Costs to meet requirements to curtail fumes discharged from smokestacks generated in the industrial process were prohibitive.

- The National Environment Policy Act (NEPA) was passed by Congress in 1969 to encourage understanding and protection of the environment and to reduce future damage.

- The Flood Control Act as amended in 1969 was passed by Congress due to the devastation of land caused by floods. Private insurance companies found that they could not issue insurance at affordable rates, so the Federal Insurance Agency (FIA) combined with independent agents to offer insurance at rates that were not excessive. To prevent a rash of development in floodplain areas, the FIA offered emergency coverage with curtailments on building in flood zones. The act requires communities to adopt plans to reduce losses in flood-prone areas by building dams and spillways.

- In 1972 Congress passed the Marine Protection Research and Sanctuaries Act to regulate the discharge and dumping of refuse into the offshore areas of the ocean.

- In 1972 noise control legislation became effective due to concern that airports and the flight patterns of jet airplanes near residential subdivisions caused excessive noise. The legislation requires that noise emission standards be developed for products delivered by rail or motor carrier.

- The Coastal Zone Management Act of 1972 offers an incentive program to coastal states that border on the Atlantic, Pacific, and Arctic Oceans, the Great Lakes, and the Gulf of Mexico. The states are required to set regulations on the methods that they will use to protect beaches from erosion, to preserve the wildlife habitats, and to shelter marine life. Once the states meet federal approval, they have jurisdiction over the zones, even those occupied by federal installations. Any development in these zones must obtain a permit from a regional agency resulting in control over buildings which may damage the natural coastline and destroy wildlife habitats.

Protection of wetlands

- In 1972 Congress passed the Clean Water Act and gave the Army Corp of Engineers responsibility for issuing permits regulating the "discharge of dredged or fill material into navigable waters" of the United States. The term *wetlands* was not mentioned; however, any land considered a wetland by the corp and the EPA is to remain protected waters of the U.S. The EPA defines wetlands as "those areas that are inundated or saturated by surface water or groundwater at a frequency and duration sufficient to support, and that under normal circumstances do support, a prevalence of vegetation typically adapted for life in saturated soil conditions." This definition encompasses swamps, marshes, bogs, pine flats, prairie potholds, and even puddles with weeds around them.

Owners cannot develop wetlands

- Some landowners found that when they prepared to develop their land it was labeled a wetland and they could not commence with the development. No compensation is provided to the property owner when land is found to contain a high-quantity wetland.

- Although the idea of protecting wetlands is to retain the natural habitats for wildlife to survive in, many people feel wetlands should be defined based on functional value and that a statewide mapping and classification system needs to be put in place.

- The Safe Drinking Water Act of 1974 set minimum standards for water supply systems to safeguard public drinking water. Chemical pollution was discovered to have seeped into our streams and rivers, and sewage had been released into the waters. According to the Environmental Protection Agency (EPA), as many as 40 million Americans have too much lead in their drinking water. Until it was banned in 1988, lead solder was widely used in plumbing. After a number of years, the lead solder inside the pipes becomes coated with minerals, and the lead stops leaching into the water.

    Lead in drinking water

    Well water should be tested periodically since groundwater can be contaminated if nearby waste disposal systems are not properly treated. A lab certified by the EPA should test for lead content in the water.

- Environmental impact statements prepared by the Environmental Protection Agency (EPA) recognize and analyze the impact developments have on the economic, social, and physical environment. They cover the impact of noise, water, air quality, natural vegetation, and wildlife.

- The Resource and Recovery Act (RCRA) of 1976 placed regulations on the transporting, storage, treatment, and disposal of hazardous wastes and required solid waste materials to be discarded in designated dump sites. The Solid Waste Disposal Act resulted in the EPA monitoring of landfills and disposal sites, although most states and local governments already had the standards in place to which disposal sites must now adhere. This was a direct result of illegal disposal of toxic waste materials that have polluted the groundwater. Although millions of people depend upon septic systems for their waste disposal, FHA, Freddie Mac, and Fannie Mae require that, when available, the municipal system be used.

    Groundwater contamination

- An amendment to the RCRA was passed by Congress in 1984 regulating underground storage tanks. The EPA is concerned that 25 percent of all underground storage tanks are leaking, contaminating the soil and seeping into groundwater. The leaking can contribute to fires and explosions since petroleum products are the most prevalent use of tanks. Since December 1988, all underground storage tanks must be equipped with an EPA leak detector system. When offering property for sale, evidence of storage tanks should be checked, especially in strip shopping centers and abandoned service stations and when the presence of pumps or oil stains are obvious. Any contaminants known or believed to possibly exist must be disclosed and corrected on sale.

    Underground storage tanks

- In 1980 Congress passed the Comprehensive Environmental Response Compensation and Liability Act (CERCLA). Funded with $9 billion (referred to as the Super Fund), this act provides for the organization of programs to set priorities for cleaning up the worst existing hazardous waste sites and requires former and present property owners to pay for toxic waste clean-up regardless if the property is currently owned by them. By the end of 1989, more than 35,000 sites were listed and placed on the EPA's National Priority List (NPL). Top priority was given to 1,215 of these sites for permanent, long-term clean-up programs.

- A growing number of communities are reclaiming landfill sites by a process called landfill reclamation. "Mining" landfills has resulted in providing fuel for waste-burning energy plants and the recycling of materials such as glass, aluminum, and plastic that can be sold, thus creating an extra source of revenue for the community.

The siting of new landfills is severely limited by economic, environmental, regulatory, and social constraints. No one seems to want to live near a landfill, a fact often cited as the NIMBY, "not in my back yard," syndrome.

- HUD has issued warnings to owners, tenants, and purchasers of housing constructed before 1978 regarding the use of lead-based paint. When children play in an area where there are loose paint chips or dust particles containing lead, they may get particles on their hands, put their hands in their mouths, and ingest a dangerous amount of lead. Some states are requiring testing for and removal of lead-based paint at the time a residential property is leased or sold, a process that can carry a tremendous expense for the property owner. It can also result in serious impediment to the remodeling industry.

The provisions of a bill signed by President Bush in October 1992 require a seller or the seller's agent to disclose any known lead hazards as part of an FHA sale or the lease of a property built before 1978. HUD will insure the mortgage on a house even if it has lead-based paint. The purchaser, however, will be responsible for any removal expense as HUD will not remove the contamination. There is no mandatory testing for lead paint, although some states have enacted laws that address disclosure of lead hazards in all real estate transfers.

INDOOR AIR POLLUTION

Asbestos

Three other problem areas that need to be recognized by real estate sales agents are asbestos, radon, and formaldehyde. When rehabilitating existing structures, the asbestos found in many buildings resulted in expensive abatement procedures involved in its removal. Most buildings with asbestos insulation present no problem as long as it is not disturbed by renovation or repairs, for only then does it create a potential hazard to occupants. Current regulations restrict its use in new buildings and require strict adherence to specific guidelines when it is removed or when renovation is being performed on a building.

Radon

Radon is a radioactive gas that is odorless and cannot be seen or tasted. There is evidence that it is a cause of lung cancer, but most radon found in homes is not sufficient to pose a threat to the residents. Purchases of real estate may require that a home be tested to determine the range of radon in the home, although the minimum safe level has not been resolved.

Formaldehyde

Formaldehyde is used as a raw material in the manufacturing of paint, plastic, resins, photographic materials, and building materials, including insulation. Curtains and upholstery textiles are often treated with formaldehyde resins for crease resistance. Formaldehyde creates a colorless, pungent, gas. Emissions ordinarily decrease over a period of time; depending upon the source. The solution to formaldehyde presence may be as simple as opening windows or as complex as utilizing experts to completely remove all insulation.

Summary

While ownership of real estate legally gives one a bundle of rights that extends below the earth's surface and into the sky, the use of land is controlled by various units of government. The federal government maintains jurisdiction over its national parks and freeways. An example of freeway control was the 55 mile per hour speed limit. If states did not enforce the speed law, federal funds to maintain the interstate highways were withdrawn.

The states control their state parks and highways and may adopt regulations to protect the welfare of the public. Similarly, county and city governments establish and enforce regulations over privately owned property under their right of police power.

Many local units of government have planning commissions that study the community's development so that orderly growth will be established. A broad outlook to future development must be considered, and a general master plan laid out for streets, public transportation, park areas, and utility services. Keeping controls over land within a one- to three-mile radius of the city further assists in regulating land use.

The zoning ordinances established by local governments also regulate land use. Plans and specifications must be presented to the planning board before a building permit is issued so that enforcement of the ordinances is ensured.

Private control over land is exercised by subdividers, who establish the covenants and restrictions for their developments. The surrounding owners may enforce these restrictions if a violation occurs.

An easement is a right of way or interest in the land of another. Common easements include shared driveways and party walls. Any protrusion over a property line is an encroachment and can be discovered by survey. Encroachments are not covered by title insurance and should thus be carefully checked by a prospective purchaser.

Environmental controls have made people aware of the need to preserve our natural resources and aid in the preservation of our cities and the welfare of our citizens. The real estate agent must know what to look for on a property, how to clean up environmental problems, and how such problems may affect the value of real estate.

As real estate licensees there is much that we need to be aware of when we assist buyers and sellers in the transfer of real estate. Among our concerns is being alert to hidden defects and circumstances that affect the value of real estate. Many of these concerns may be environmental issues, such as underground storage tanks, radon, asbestos, lead paint, and toxic waste. Being aware of how environmental problems can affect value, we must take a proactive part in the solution.

DISCUSSION QUESTIONS

1. Why is a master plan for a city necessary?
2. Differentiate between platting a subdivision into conventional lots, cluster lots, and zero lot lines.
3. Explain the difference between a nonconforming use and a variance.
4. What is the purpose of a planned unit development? Do you have any in your city?
5. How does an easement in gross differ from an easement appurtenance?
6. Cite environmental issues that may affect property values in your area.

REVIEW QUESTIONS

Answers to these questions are found in the Answer Key section at the back of the book.

1. To the owner of the land it runs across, an easement is:

a. an appurtenance
b. an encumbrance
c. a common interest
d. an attachment

2. Zoning laws are the utilization of a governing body's:

a. police power

b. power of eminent domain

c. escheat

d. license laws

3. A use not in compliance with present zoning, but legal when it was enacted is called a(n):

a. variance

b. spot zoning use

c. nonconforming use

d. encroachment

4. The gathering together of two or more parcels to make the whole more valuable is a(n):

a. easement

b. appurtenance

c. subdivision

d. assemblage

5. If there is a party wall between two lots, which of the following is NOT true?

a. each person must be responsible for its maintenance

b. each person owns a common interest in the wall

c. the neighborhood association will be responsible for any repairs

d. it is placed on the lot line

6. Ingress and egress make reference to:

a. appurtenance

b. an easement

c. subservience

d. police power

7. Which of the following restrict the use of land?

a. townships

b. monuments

c. surveys

d. covenants

8. Communities regulate the use of land by means of:

a. controlling the population

b. exercising zoning laws

c. buying and selling land themselves

d. annexing nearby towns

9. Mr. Jones's good friend, Charlie Smith, lives next door and uses a portion of Jones's land as a driveway. As much as Jones likes his friend, he does not want to grant him the use of the land in perpetuity. Since he wants to retain the privilege of reviewing the situation on a regular basis, Jones should grant his friend:

a. a license

b. an easement

c. an easement appurtenance

d. a permit

10. All of the following are established by the private sector, EXCEPT:

a. building styles

b. restrictive covenants

c. subdivision plats

d. building codes

11. The governmental regulations that most affect the value of real property are:

a. zoning ordinances

b. covenants of deed restrictions

c. laws of escheat

d. Federal Housing Administration regulations

12. The police power of a city is used to enforce all of the following, EXCEPT:

a. building codes

b. zoning restrictions

c. deed restrictions

d. subdivision regulations

13. The government of a municipality holds control over real property through all of the following, EXCEPT:

a. taxation

b. assessments

c. encumbrance

d. eminent domain

14. Which of the following is an example of an easement appurtenance?

a. a shared driveway

b. a power line

c. sewer system

d. view

15. A gas station was built in 1960 in an area that was rezoned to residential in 1990. The gas station constitutes:

a. a variance

b. a nonconforming use

c. spot zoning

d. a violation

16. The separating of two incompatible zoning districts from each other is referred to as:

    a. a variance

    b. a buffer zone

    c. a nonconforming use

    d. a zero lot line concept

17. A building complied with the zoning laws except for the setback. The owners need to request:

    a. spot zoning

    b. a variance

    c. a nonconforming use

    d. a compliance

18. To increase open space and conserve land, a developer will group lots together by:

    a. deed restrictions

    b. placing cul de sacs in the plat

    c. clustering

    d. building apartments

19. The Environmental Protection Agency was created to:

    a. deliver a model building development code

    b. enforce environment laws

    c. provide for nontraditional zoning practices

    d. control growth by the use of building moratoriums

20. The planned unit development (PUD) provides all of the following, EXCEPT:

    a. permitting mixed uses and density

    b. requiring single-family housing lots

    c. allowing for open spaces

    d. offering residents a variety of nearby shops and recreational facilities

21. Which of the following environmental issues should the licensee be concerned with when selling or listing property?

    a. underground storage tanks

    b. lead paint

    c. the presence of radon

    d. all of the above

Federal Fair Housing and License Laws

Chapter 17 covers the federal fair housing laws as they apply to the sale and rental of real property. The Fair Housing Act is explained in detail, since it is important that all people involved in the transfer of real estate abide by this decree.

Chapter 18 gives a general overview of the license law acts that mandate the licensing of people practicing real estate. Each state enacts its own law and rules and regulations, so the reader should be aware that certain information may not apply to every state. The student seeking to become licensed should obtain the state license laws by contacting the department that governs and enacts the law.

PART FOUR

Fair Housing Laws

KEY WORDS

blockbusting
Civil Rights Act of 1866
Civil Rights Act of 1964
Department of Housing and Urban Development (HUD)
Equal Credit Opportunity Act (ECOA)

Fair Housing Act of 1968
Fair Housing Amendment Act of 1988
fair housing laws
panic peddling
redlining
steering

OVERVIEW

Every person engaged in the business of real estate should be familiar with the **fair housing laws** as they relate to the sale and rental of all residential property. Federal, state, and local laws provide for equal opportunity in housing. This is the law of the land, and it is the right of every person in this country to own or rent without regard to race, color, religion, national origin, sex, handicap, or family status.

Real estate salespeople, brokers, and owners must be cognizant of and must put into practice the law that prohibits discrimination. Individuals have a right to purchase or rent housing in any area they desire to live in, as long as they can assume the financial responsibility.

THE CIVIL RIGHTS ACT OF 1866

It is the policy of the United States to provide, within its constitutional limitations, for fair housing throughout the country. Fair housing law dates from the **Civil Rights Act of 1866**, which prohibited discrimination based on race only. This act provided that "all citizens of the United States shall have the same right, in every state and territory, as is enjoyed by white citizens thereof to inherit, purchase, lease, sell, hold, and convey real and personal property."

Equal housing opportunities

THE CIVIL RIGHTS ACT OF 1964

Title VI, the **Civil Rights Act of 1964**, was passed by Congress to prohibit discrimination when a program receives federal financial assistance. The intent of Congress was to ensure that no program utilizing federal financial aid should be tainted by discriminatory acts. The **Department of Housing and Urban Development (HUD)** had set aside funds under sections 235 and 236 respectively to give assistance to low-income citizens in homeownership and low-rent public housing.

THE FAIR HOUSING ACT OF 1968

In June 1968, the United States Supreme Court upheld the 1866 Civil Rights Act in the case of *Jones* v. *Mayer*. The original act proclaimed that all racial discrimination was illegal when selling or renting property; the court extended it to include race, color, religion, and national origin. In the case of *Jones* v. *Mayer*, a black person sued for injunction and other relief with an allegation that the defendant had refused to sell him a home solely on racial grounds. In 1974 sex was added as a protected class.

AMENDMENT TO FAIR HOUSING LAW

Title VIII of the Civil Rights Act of 1968 was changed in two respects when President Reagan signed the **Fair Housing Amendment Act of 1988** in September of that same year. Effective March 12, 1989, the amendment prohibits discrimination based on handicap and familial status, that is, families with children. The act allows certain exemptions for elderly housing. The amendment further alters the procedure of enforcing Title VIII and the penalties that are imposed for a violation.

The **Fair Housing Act of 1968**, under Title VIII of the Civil Rights Act of 1968, prohibits the following acts:

Provisions of fair housing law

1. refusing to sell, rent, negotiate, or deal with any person
2. quoting different terms or conditions for renting or buying housing to persons of different races, colors, religions, or national origins
3. advertising that property is available only to certain races, colors, religions, or national origins
4. not being truthful about the availability of homes for rent or sale
5. **blockbusting**, or inducing owners, for profit, to sell or rent their homes by threatening the movement of minority groups into neighborhoods
6. lenders varying terms or conditions for home loans in an effort to discriminate
7. discriminating in real estate services, multiple listing services, or broker organizations by denying membership or limiting participation

Amendment Act of 1988

The Amendment Act of 1988 additionally prohibits the following:

8. the assessment of higher security deposits to handicapped persons or to families with children
9. the segregation of such persons to particular floors or wings of a building within a complex
10. additionally, such persons must be given access to all services and amenities provided in connection with the building

These laws apply to single-family housing under the following conditions:

1. when single-family housing is privately owned and the owner employs a real estate firm (or any other person who sells or rents)

Application of fair housing law

2. when single-family homes are not privately owned
3. when discriminatory advertising is used for single-family homes
4. when single-family homes are owned by private individuals who own more than three such houses and who, in any two-year period, sell more than one in which the individual was not the most recent resident

These laws apply to multifamily housing under the following conditions:

1. when multifamily dwellings containing five or more rooms or units are rented
2. when multifamily dwellings of four or fewer units or rooms are rented, if none of the units is occupied by the owner of the property

Exemptions to the Fair Housing Act

The law does not affect the sale or rental of single-family houses owned by a private individual if:

When exemptions are applicable

1. The person owns three or fewer houses.
2. A real estate broker is not used.
3. Discriminatory advertising is not used.
4. No more than one house in which the owner was not the most recent resident is sold during any two-year period.
5. Rooms or units in owner-occupied multifamily dwellings for two to four families are rented, and discriminatory advertising is not used.
6. The sale, rental, or occupancy of dwellings that a religious organization owns or operates for other than a commercial purpose is limited to persons of the same religion, if membership in that religion is not restricted on account of race, color, or national origin.
7. The rental or occupancy of lodging that a private club owns or operates for other than a commercial purpose is limited to the club's members. This exemption does not allow discrimination if the reason is race.

Handicapped Persons

Both the mentally and physically handicapped are covered by the 1988 act. Excluded are persons currently using or who are addicted to an illegally controlled substance and those who have been convicted of the manufacture or distribution of illegal drugs. An owner is not required by the act to provide a dwelling to any person whose tenancy poses a direct threat to the health, safety, and property of others.

Housing availability to handicapped

Provisions of the law state that handicapped persons (or families with children) cannot be assessed higher security deposits. Nor can they be segregated in particular sections, floors, or buildings within a development. The availability of all services and amenities provided in connection with the building must be open to them.

Handicapped Accessibility

Reasonable modification to a unit may be made by a handicapped person at the tenant's expense. However, the act permits the property owner to require the tenant to restore the unit, at the tenant's expense, to its original condition. The owner may further require that funds be placed in an escrow account to provide for the restoration.

After March 13, 1991, all new multifamily dwellings of four or more units must be constructed to allow access and use by handicapped persons. In buildings without elevators, only first floor units are covered by this provision.

Families with Children

The 1988 amendment also extends fair housing coverage to families with children under the age of 18. Dwelling owners will abide by local ordinances governing the maximum number of persons who may occupy a unit. HUD felt that such regulations are the province of local and state governments in accordance with the preamble. If no such local ordinance exists, HUD regulations permit property owners to establish reasonable rules governing the number of persons who may occupy a unit, based on the number of sleeping areas or rooms and the overall size of the unit. The act further affords protection to any person who is pregnant or is in the process of securing legal custody of an individual not yet 18 years of age.

Family housing

Elderly Exemptions

Elderly housing   Certain exemptions were made in the 1988 amendment act for elderly housing. The act defines housing for the elderly as:

1. housing provided under any federal or state program that HUD determines as specifically designed and operated to assist elderly persons
2. housing intended for and solely occupied by persons 62 years of age or older
3. housing intended for occupancy by at least one person 55 years of age or older per unit

This type of housing must also provide significant facilities and services to meet the physical and social needs of older persons. The act further states that 80 percent of the units must be occupied by at least one person 55 years of age or older. The policy and procedures and any publications must demonstrate the intent that it is indeed housing for the older person. Housing not occupied in 80 percent of its units by at least one person 55 years or older by September 13, 1988, may qualify for exemption if all vacancies are filled after that date by persons who meet the age requirement.

Enforcement Procedures

The Amendment Act of 1988 provides a new enforcement system that allows all parties the choice of having the case brought before an administrative law judge (ALJ) or a federal district court.

Filing complaints   Under the original Title VIII, single or isolated acts of discrimination were not subject to enforcement by the federal government. The authority invested in HUD was limited to efforts to conciliate disputes, and if these efforts proved unsuccessful the aggrieved individual could file an action in federal court. The Department of Justice's jurisdiction was limited to cases in which a pattern of continuous practice of discrimination was evident. Complaints should be sent to the OEO (Office of Equal Opportunity) at HUD:

> Fair Housing
> Department of Housing and Urban Development
> Washington, D.C. 20410

In addition, complaints can be sent to Fair Housing, in care of the nearest OEO regional office. When filing a complaint, it should be notarized, if possible, and must be sent to OEO within one year of the alleged discriminatory act or the complaint shall be waived. Once a complaint is filed, HUD can pursue the complaint if efforts to resolve it through the conciliation process have not been successful after 100 days. During the 100-day conciliation period, HUD can also seek temporary relief, including temporary restraining orders when such actions are necessary to carry out the intent of the act. The HUD secretary does have the prerogative to file a bias complaint on his own initiative or to begin an investigation of housing practices to determine if a complaint should be filed. (See Figure 17.1.)

If a charge is made by HUD following an investigation of a discrimination complaint, the involved parties have the option of choosing to have HUD file the charge in a U.S. district court, rather than referring the case to an ALJ. HUD will automatically bring the case before an ALJ if no request is made for a jury trial. The plaintiff and the respondent will both have subpoenas. The presentation of evidence must conform to the Federal Rule of Evidence just as it would in a civil action in a U.S. District Court. An ALJ may award compensatory damages, injunctive and other equitable relief, and civil money penalties. A penalty may be levied against the respondent up to a maximum of $10,000 if there is no prior violation; $25,000 if there has been prior violation within the preceding five-year period; and $50,000 if there have been two or more

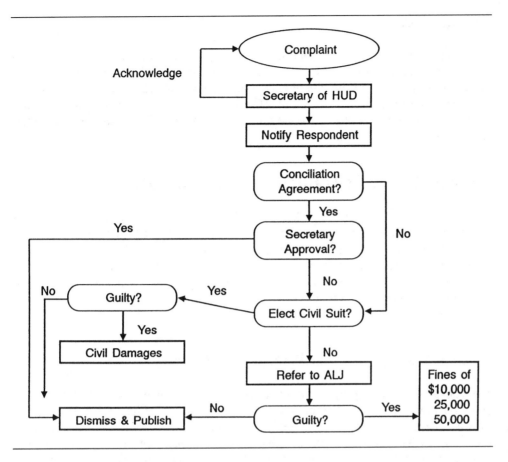

FIGURE 17.1
Fair Housing Amendment Act of 1988 enforcement procedures.

violations within the preceding seven-year period. The fine of $25,000 or $50,000 may be imposed regardless of time limits if the defendant is a single individual rather than a real estate firm engaging in more than one discriminatory housing practice. These maximum civil penalties are not automatic in every situation, and consideration will be given to the nature and circumstances of the violation and past history of the violator.

Once the ALJ's order is issued, HUD must review it within 30 days or the finding becomes final. Either party has the option of obtaining a court review in a federal appeals court in the district where the violation took place. The court could stop the sale or rental of the desired housing to someone else and make it possible for the complainant to buy or rent the desired housing, or it could award damages and court costs or take other appropriate action to benefit the complainant.

It is illegal to coerce, intimidate, threaten, or interfere with a person buying, renting, or selling housing, making a complaint of discrimination, or exercising any such rights in connection with this law.

EQUAL CREDIT OPPORTUNITY ACT (ECOA)

According to the **Equal Credit Opportunity Act**, enacted by Congress in 1975, lenders who make residential real estate loans must not discriminate in fixing the amount, interest, rate duration, terms, or conditions of a loan because of sex, marital status, race, color, religion, national origin, or receipt of income from public assistance. This is not to say that the lender cannot refuse a loan if the borrower is financially unable to meet the commitment.

Lender compliance

REDLINING

The lender must not refuse to make loans in certain neighborhoods; to do so is called **redlining**. Refusal to offer financing in a particular section of the city can lead to the decay of the area. To ensure compliance with the law, the federal government passed the Home Mortgage Disclosure Act in 1975. Large lenders with one or more offices in a particular area are required to issue annual reports on all loans so that if redlining does exist it is easily detectable.

SALESPERSON AND BROKER OBLIGATIONS

Broker and agent compliance

Not only is the salesperson or broker bound by the Civil Rights Act, but if the agent holds membership in the National Association of REALTORS®, she must also abide by Article 10 of the Code of Ethics. Article 10 requires that "the REALTOR® shall not deny equal professional service to any person for reasons of race, creed, sex, or country of national origin. The REALTOR® shall not be a party to any plan or agreement to discriminate against a person or persons on the basis of race, creed, sex, or country of national origin."

BLOCKBUSTING AND PANIC PEDDLING

The salesperson or broker must not induce nonminority homeowners to sell their properties for profit because of the introduction of minorities in or near the neighborhood. This is referred to as *blockbusting* and is prohibited by law. Great care must be taken not to solicit listings on the premise that minority groups are moving into the area, insinuating that property may lessen in value. The salesperson's conduct must be above reproach and not give the impression of **panic peddling.** Intensive door-to-door canvassing in a changing neighborhood or in a neighborhood adjacent to a changing or minority neighborhood would create suspicion.

The agent must affirmatively demonstrate full compliance with the fair housing laws and work in a like manner with all clients so that no accusation of giving less favorable treatment to a minority would occur. This involves servicing customers equally and not ignoring a minority client, submitting offers promptly, and not offering the property on less favorable terms to a minority person.

STEERING

The agent must not try to avoid showing property to minority customers in certain nonintegrated areas. To take them only to minority or changing neighborhoods is referred to as **steering**. Offering a wide range of properties in all areas will alleviate any such complaint. Conversely, the salesperson must show the nonminority customer homes in all neighborhoods to avoid being accused of discouraging a buyer from seeking housing in a minority or changing neighborhood.

EQUAL HOUSING OPPORTUNITY

In 1972, the fair housing law was amended to include the requirement of equal opportunity posters. All real estate firms, model homes, and mortgage lenders must display the Equal Housing Opportunity poster, which states that housing is available equally to all people (see Figure 17.2).

EQUAL HOUSING OPPORTUNITY

We Do Business in Accordance With the Federal Fair Housing Law
(The Fair Housing Amendments Act of 1988)

It Is Illegal to Discriminate Against Any Person Because of Race, Color, Religion, Sex, Handicap, Familial Status, or National Origin

- In the sale or rental of housing or residential lots
- In advertising the sale or rental of housing
- In the financing of housing
- In the provision of real estate brokerage services
- In the appraisal of housing
- Blockbusting is also illegal

Anyone who feels he or she has been discriminated against may file a complaint of housing discrimination with the:	U.S. Department of Housing and Urban Development Assistant Secretary for Fair Housing and Equal Opportunity Washington, D.C. 20410

Previous editions are obsolete   form HUD-928.1 (3-89)

FIGURE 17.2
The Equal Housing Opportunity poster.

RESTRICTIVE COVENANTS

It is further unlawful to place racially restrictive covenants in the transfer, sale, or rental of housing. Many states have enacted legislation that is consistent with the federal fair housing law. Complaints are directed to the state and are handled by the appropriate agency within said state. If an incorporated city has enacted or adopted a resolution equivalent to the state's fair housing law, complaints will be directed to the local agency. If the complaint is not handled with reasonable promptness, the state will regain jurisdiction of the complaint.

The purpose of the federal and state fair housing laws are to:

1. Seek to eliminate and prevent discrimination in places of public accommodation because of race, color, sex, religion, national origin, ancestry, handicap, or family status.
2. Carry through the purpose of this act by conference conciliation and persuasion so that persons may be guaranteed their civil rights and so that good will be fostered.
3. Formulate policies to enforce the purpose of this act and make recommendations to agencies and officers of the state or local subdivisions of government in aid of such policies and purposes.
4. Adopt rules and regulations to carry out the powers granted by this act.
5. Designate one or more members of the commission or the commission staff to conduct investigations of discrimination in race, color, sex, religion, national origin, ancestry, handicap, or family status and to attempt to resolve such complaints by conference, conciliation, and persuasion, and conduct such conciliation

meetings and conferences as deemed necessary to resolve a particular complaint. Such meetings shall be held in the county in which the claim arose.

6. Determine that probable cause exists for crediting the allegations of a complaint.

7. Determine that a complaint cannot be resolved by conference, conciliation, or persuasion. Such a determination is to be made only at a meeting in which a quorum is present.

8. Dismiss complaints when it is determined there is not probable cause to credit the allegations of a complaint.

9. Hold hearings, subpoena witnesses and compel their attendance, administer oaths, take the testimony of any person under oath, and in connection therewith require for examination any papers relating to any matter under investigation or in question before the commission.

10. Issue publications and the results of studies and research that tend to promote good will and minimize or eliminate discrimination because of race, color, sex, religion, national origin, ancestry, handicap, or family status.

THE NAR CODE OF ETHICS

Members of the National Association of REALTORS® are required to follow the NAR Code of Ethics and Standards of Practice, which was adopted in 1913. All brokers and their associated licensees are obligated to follow these guidelines and to conduct themselves in an ethical manner at all times.

SUMMARY

The original Civil Rights Act of 1866 was based on race only, but the spirit of fair housing experienced a breakthrough when the federal Fair Housing Act of 1968 extended the law to include race, color, religion, and national origin. In 1974 an amendment included gender. The amendment signed by President Reagan in September 1988 prohibits discrimination based on handicap and families with children, with exclusions made for housing for the elderly.

Many states have fair housing laws compatible with the federal law. Local organizations, such as a human relations board, are formed in many cities to enforce the laws.

Any person seeking restitution because of discrimination should file a complaint with HUD within one year after the alleged violation occurred. If it appears to be covered by the law, HUD will attempt informal confidential conciliation in an effort to end the discriminatory practice. A person may take a complaint directly to court, but again, the violation must be acted upon within one year's time.

The licensed salesperson and broker must take diligent care to offer all properties to any person seeking housing. The salesperson must not attempt to induce a homeowner to list a house for sale by representing to the owner that minorities are moving into the neighborhood, even when the statement is accurate. Membership in the multiple listing service or in real estate organizations must not be denied to any person because of race, color, religion, national origin, or sex.

The affirmative marketing agreement is a commitment made by many real estate salespeople and brokers to demonstrate their compliance with fair housing laws. Real estate firms are required to display the Equal Housing Opportunity poster in their offices. Anyone engaged in the real estate business must offer to all prospective purchasers equal opportunity to buy the real estate of their choice.

Discussion Questions

1. If you were asked by a prospect to whom you were showing homes if there were any minority families residing in the area, how would you respond?
2. In what instances are there exceptions to the fair housing law?
3. Summarize the two methods of handling a civil complaint.
4. When can property owners be selective to whom they rent or sell their real estate?
5. List the two main provisions of the 1988 amendment to the Fair Housing Act.

Review Questions

Answers to these questions are found in the Answer Key section at the back of the book.

1. The Civil Rights Act of 1866 prohibited discrimination based on:

   a. race, color, religion, and sex
   b. race only
   c. sex only
   d. race, national origin, color, and religion

2. A complaint to the federal Fair Housing Commission must be:

   a. filed within one year after the alleged discrimination
   b. resolved within a 60-day conciliation period
   c. presented only to broker involved
   d. made by an attorney

3. The federal agency that administrates the fair housing law is:

   a. QTE
   b. HUD
   c. FFN
   d. Attorney general

4. In regard to the federal Fair Housing Act, which of the following is NOT true?

   a. the complaint may be reconciled within 18 months
   b. complaints may be sent directly to HUD
   c. parties involved in a discrimination suit may request HUD to file the charge in a U.S. district court
   d. the parties may choose to have the case brought before an administrative law judge

5. The Fair Housing Act prohibits all of the following, EXCEPT:

   a. discrimination in housing because of race
   b. discrimination in housing to the handicapped
   c. the sale of a home in a nonintegrated neighborhood to a black family
   d. failure to rent an apartment in an adult complex to a family with children

6. Which of the following is/are NOT exempt from the Fair Housing Act?

   a. real estate brokers
   b. a religious group that limits rentals of property it owns to members only
   c. the owner of a fourplex who resides in one unit
   d. the homeowner who sells his home without the aid of a real estate firm

7. Under the federal Fair Housing Act, which of the following is NOT considered a discriminatory practice?

   a. refusing to sell a house to a person of a minority race because she is unable to qualify for a loan
   b. advertising a preference to whom you will sell
   c. restricting the rental of a property by religion
   d. refusing to rent a property to a black family because the husband is handicapped

8. The federal Fair Housing Act does NOT apply to which of the following?

   a. denying a person the right to buy a home because of his national origin
   b. a discriminatory restrictive provision in a deed
   c. denying lessees with pets a lease
   d. denying a person the right to buy a home because of her sex

9. Under the housing discrimination laws, which of the following is NOT an illegal act?

a. requiring a security deposit from a handicapped person

b. refusing to show property to a person based on sex

c. limiting a purchaser's choice by steering

d. a lender refusing to place a loan on a property in a deteriorating neighborhood

10. Ms. Loring asked A-1 Realty to lease her home for four months while she was in Europe on vacation. She specified she preferred only white tenants. Under the Fair Housing Act, her preference is:

a. illegal

b. legal, since Ms. Loring is the owner-occupant

c. legal upon acceptance of the lease agreement

d. legal if the broker obtains the request in writing

11. Ms. Gomez and her three children went to Ace Realty to find a residence for rent. The firm assigned her to Mr. Alvarez in accordance with their policy of matching their client's race and interests as closely as possible. During the course of viewing property, Ms. Gomez asked to see an apartment in a white middle-class neighborhood that she had seen advertised in a newspaper. Mr. Alvarez said the apartment was rented, when in fact it was not. Under the Fair Housing Act:

a. Mr. Alvarez committed illegal steering

b. Mr. Alvarez acted in his customer's best interest

c. it was legal, since it is approved office practice

d. it was illegal, because Ms. Gomez is a single parent

12. The provisions covered in the Fair Housing Amendment Act of 1988 include:

a. discrimination based on handicap

b. the assessment of higher security deposits to families with children

c. the segregation of families with children to particular sections of an apartment complex

d. all of the above

13. This symbol represents:

a. HUD

b. fair housing

c. equal housing opportunity

d. FHA

14. A nonprofit religious sect bought property and developed condominiums that they sold back to their church members exclusively. According to the Fair Housing Act, this was:

a. illegal, because a religious sect cannot build condominiums

b. illegal, because it is discriminatory

c. legal, because a religious sect is not subject to law

d. legal, because a religious sect is allowed to sell property exclusively to its members

License Law

OVERVIEW

The real estate field is of great interest to everyone. Many would like to be involved. Private individuals acting in their own behalf find this very rewarding when buying, selling, and investing. In time they feel that they can offer their expertise to others and charge a fee for this service. However, this cannot be done before first obtaining a real estate license.

All 50 states have enacted legislation requiring the licensing of real estate salespeople and brokers. At this time there is no uniform **license law** covering the states, but basically their content is quite similar. The license law and the rules and regulations adopted by each individual state are for the express purpose of protecting the public. To further protect citizens from unscrupulous or incompetent practitioners, the law prescribes the standards and qualifications for licensing. This has elevated the standards of the real estate profession and protects licensees from unfair competition.

Mandatory education continues to be of primary concern to licensing officials in the belief that specified knowledge will better qualify the licensee to serve the public. Most states are now requiring completion of certified real estate courses prior to application to take the licensing examination. Many states require continuous education after becoming licensed, so the licensee keeps abreast of new laws and practices.

WHO NEEDS A LICENSE?

While the laws vary from state to state, the majority of states require that anyone who negotiates or attempts to negotiate the business of selling, listing, purchasing, exchanging, renting, leasing, managing, optioning, or auctioning real estate for a fee, commission, or other valuable compensation must be licensed.

Exceptions

Those persons who are generally exempt from needing a license include the following:

1. an owner or lessor of real estate
2. an attorney-in-fact (someone given power of attorney by the property owner)
3. an attorney-at-law in the performance of her duty as such attorney-at-law
4. a receiver or trustee in bankruptcy
5. the administrator or executor of a deceased estate
6. a court-appointed guardian
7. an officer or employee of a federal or state agency
8. in many states, resident managers of apartment complexes or persons employed by an owner to lease or manage the owner's property

Keep in mind that these exceptions do not permit a person to act in the capacity of a real estate firm without a license.

TYPES OF LICENSES

Broker and salesperson

There are generally two types of licenses issued: that of a real estate **salesperson** and that of a real estate **broker**. The broker is also called the **agent**. The agent is the personal representative of the principal, usually the seller. A broker's license permits the individual to set up a real estate office and to hire other brokers and salespeople to work for the broker. An **associate broker** is an individual who holds a broker's license but who has elected to work for another broker in preference to owning and operating a firm. A salesperson is always required to be in the employ of a broker, and all money that comes into the salesperson's possession must be given to the broker for placement into the broker's **trust account** (an account for all money belonging to others). The broker is considered by law to be legally responsible for all the actions of the salespeople. The broker may set up her business using her own name, for example, Jane A. Smith, or may transact business under a trade name such as A-1 Real Estate Company. If the broker purchases a franchise, the broker will need to disclose the business name (whether it is Jane A. Smith or A-1 Real Estate Company) along with the franchise name. The broker may further elect to form a partnership or corporation with another broker or brokers. In most states all *active* members of the partnership or corporation must be licensed to conduct the business of a real estate agent.

If branch offices are opened, a broker or associate broker generally must be in charge of each branch office. Again, this is to provide adequate supervision for the sales associates. Since the broker is responsible for the actions of the salesperson, the broker will supervise and guide the salesperson's performance so that the firm is properly and lawfully represented. The salesperson will list and sell property in the name of the broker, and all advertising will be under the broker's business name.

LICENSING EXAMS

Competency tests

To obtain the license of salesperson or broker, the person must pass a written or computerized examination designed to test real estate knowledge and competency to transact the duties of a real estate salesperson or broker. The state **real estate commission** or regulatory agency examination is given at stated times throughout the year. Failure to pass the written examination is grounds for denial of a license. However, applicants will be given another opportunity to pass the exam.

In the past, individual states prepared their own exams for evaluating the applicant's ability to conduct the business of real estate salesperson or broker. This placed the burden of writing, preparing, and grading the exam upon the state's real estate governing body.

While approximately one-third of the states still adheres to that form of testing, many states now subscribe to exams prepared by testing services. These services prepare a uniform test generally consisting of 80 to 100 questions applicable to all the states and a minimum of 30 questions relating to the individual state's licensing laws. In addition to the license law questions, the uniform test covers the basic fundamentals of the principles and practices of real estate.

The California multistate examination is presently utilized by several other states. A significant factor of this testing procedure is that the states adhering to the exam require that the licensee need only take the license law portion in a subscribing state if she desires to obtain a license in that state. Some states permit a licensee from another state to obtain a license in a new state of residence without further examination.

Exams differ for the salesperson and broker. A more comprehensive understanding is required from the broker. Since the broker can go into business alone, it is necessary that he understand closing procedures and the fundamentals of operating a real estate business.

REQUIREMENTS OF APPLICANTS

The minimum age requirement for license applicants is generally between 18 and 21 years with a high school diploma or its equivalent. Other prerequisites may vary also. Many states require one to three years' practical experience as a salesperson prior to applying for a broker's license. Nebraska accepts 18 college credit hours or 180 classroom hours in accredited real estate courses in lieu of practical experience, while Arizona requires the equivalent of 12 classroom hours of continued education annually. Throughout the country, education requirements are constantly increasing to better ensure the public of being represented by qualified sales representatives.

Minimum age and education

COMMISSIONS

Since the salesperson generally works as an independent contractor, the sales agent is considered self-employed and as such is responsible for social security and federal and state withholding tax payments. This requires the salesperson to file quarterly estimates of income earned. The broker does not offer fringe benefits such as accident and health insurance or retirement plans for self-employed persons. Based on IRS rulings, to do so would destroy independent contract status. The salesperson would be considered an employee of the broker.

Compensation for services

The salesperson generally earns a percentage of the commission paid to the real estate firm. Assuming the earned commission is 7 percent on a $50,000 property and further assuming that the real estate firm pays the listing salesperson 30 percent of the commission and the selling salesperson another 30 percent, each agent would earn $1,050.

Percentages paid to sales associates on listing and sales are not uniform. The broker in this situation retained 40 percent, or $1,400, to cover the expenses of maintaining an office, paying salaries to the office staff (such as secretaries, receptionists, and bookkeepers), advertising, signs, materials, rents, management fees, and other fixed and miscellaneous expenses.

Many contract variations exist between employing brokers and sales associates. In some instances, the sales agent may receive 100 percent of the commission but will share in the office expenses, paying a percentage of the rent, utilities, secretarial costs, and so on. Under the 100 percent plan, the cost of advertising listings and purchasing signs would be the salesperson's expense. While 100 percent commission may sound alluring, sales agents must make payments on their share of the expenses even during months when they do not make any sales.

Commissions charged by brokerage firms vary; there is no set fee. Since the listing agreement constitutes a contract between the real estate firm and the property owner, they both determine the fee. Should a salesperson leave a company, generally the real estate firm retains the listings.

LICENSE FEES

The licensee pays a fee for the issuance of her license plus an annual renewal fee. In some states the renewal fee is paid for a two- or three-year period. This license remains in force unless revoked or suspended for just cause. Since a license is a privilege, committing an infraction of the license law is cause for **revocation** or **suspension**. For states that require continuing education courses, proof of completing the required hours must be submitted before the license will be renewed.

NONRESIDENT LICENSES

Reciprocal license

The right of reciprocity is in effect among many states. A nonresident may apply for a **reciprocal license** upon showing proof of being presently licensed and engaged in business in the state of residence. A nonresident salesperson must be employed by a broker holding a nonresident license. In some states the salesperson must further sign a designation in writing that appoints the director of the real estate commission or regulatory agency to act as his licensee agent in the event that judicial or legal process is served upon the agent. This has the same effect as if it were served upon the licensee.

Fees for reciprocal licenses vary but are generally higher than for resident licenses. This license permits the recipient to go to the other state and conduct business. However, should the licensee move to that state permanently, it would be necessary to meet the requirements of that state to work as a salesperson or broker.

GOVERNING BODIES

Regulatory agencies

The real estate commission or regulatory body enforces the license laws, which are statutes that have been passed by the state legislature. Rules and regulations consistent with the law are promulgated by the state real estate commission or governing body. The licensee is further bound by rules of the local, state, and National Association of REALTORS® boards if the broker is a member of that organization. The state governing body generally consists of licensees actively engaged in the real estate industry and unlicensed people that represent the public. A director is employed to keep records of all official acts of the governing body, conduct licensing exams, issue and renew licenses, hold educational seminars for licensees, and transact any other duties the agency may require. The governing body has the full power to regulate the issuance of licenses and to revoke or suspend licenses for just cause.

TRUST ACCOUNTS

Brokers must set up a trust account in a depository located in the state where they are doing business. Most states require that all money coming into their possession that belongs to others must be put in the designated non-interest-bearing trust account. Some states, however, require that the earnest money be placed in an interest-bearing checking account. This would include earnest money deposits, money advanced by a buyer or seller for payment of expenses in connection with a closing, the balance received from the buyer at the time of closing, rent deposits, and other trust funds. This account is subject to inspection by the real estate governing body and, if found to be in an "unsound" condition, would be cause for revoking or suspending the broker's license. Because of the large sums of money involved, real estate commissions are extremely sensitive in the area of trust accounts and require strict adherence to balanced accounts.

A trust account is shielded from any creditors of the broker. In the event of the broker's bankruptcy or if a judgment is entered against a broker, the trust account is immune from creditor's claims because the funds are held in a fiduciary capacity by the broker. This protection makes it mandatory that the broker not mix or commingle personal funds in the account.

EARNEST DEPOSITS

Upon receipt of an accepted contract, the broker puts the **earnest money** deposit in her trust account, where it remains until the transaction is consummated or terminated. If the sale was a cooperating broker's listing, the broker issues a check to the cooperating broker's trust account since the listing company closes the sale. In states where closing of the sale is done exclusively by escrow companies, the broker transfers the earnest deposit and purchase agreement into the possession of the escrow agent.

GUARANTY FUNDS (RECOVERY FUND)

Some states establish a special fund secured through licensing fees to compensate individuals who may incur financial losses from a licensee's negligent or illegal act. Usually this fund is tapped only after the financially insured party has pursued all legal action for recovery through the courts. If judgment liens then cannot be collected, an award from the fund may be issued for part or all of the loss. This is another effort to assure the public that the law is protective of their interests.

ADVERTISING

All advertising by those in the real estate business must be in the name of the firm and clearly indicate that it is indeed a real estate company. This does not preclude the advertisement from carrying a salesperson's name and telephone number. No advertisement may simply give a box number or telephone number implying that the ad is being placed by a private party. This is considered a "blind ad" and is prohibited in most states.

Newspaper ads

While the broker may "puff" the goods, the ad must not intentionally misrepresent the property or the terms under which it may be purchased. "Puffing" the goods refers to using terms to attractively describe the property, such as "treed lot with lovely view." While it must have a reasonable number of trees to qualify as "treed," it would be easy for the purchasers to ascertain for themselves whether the property has a lovely view. Advertising must not be directed to or against any particular race, color, religion, national origin, sex, handicap, or families with children. When advertising property, the licensee must comply with Regulation Z of the Truth-in-Lending Act. If any mention of credit terms is made beyond the annual percentage rate (APR) and the price of the property, all of the terms must be disclosed.

UNFAIR TRADE PRACTICES

Required professionalism

Licenses are granted only to persons who bear a good reputation for honesty and integrity. If a broker, associate broker, or salesperson commits an infraction of the license law, the real estate commission will investigate the actions of the licensee and has the power to suspend or revoke the license or **censure** the licensee. The following are some of the unfair trade practices that result in such action.

1. Discrimination regarding the offering for sale or rent of real property because of race, color, national origin, ethnic group, sex, handicap, or families.
2. The use of misleading or inaccurate advertising.
3. All money coming into the possession of the licensee must be accounted for and placed in the broker's trust account unless the parties having an interest in the funds (seller and purchaser, in the case of a purchase contract) agree otherwise in writing. Placing the money directly into the broker's business or personal account is prohibited since it would constitute the commingling of funds.
4. Accepting, giving, or charging any undisclosed commission, rebate, or direct profit on expenditures made for a principal.
5. The salesperson or associate broker places her license with one broker and must never attempt to represent another broker or accept a commission from another broker unless the employing broker has given consent.
6. The licensee must disclose whether any personal interest is held in a property, for a licensee cannot act in a dual capacity as agent and principal without revealing this to all parties concerned.
7. Guaranteeing to the purchaser future profits from the resale of the real property.
8. In many states, written consent from the owners is needed before placing a "For Sale" sign on the property.
9. Offering property for sale on terms other than those authorized by the owner or the owner's representative.
10. Inducing a party to break a contract for the purpose of substituting a new contract with another principal.
11. If an owner has an exclusive right-to-sell listing contract, all offers to purchase, including those obtained by other agents, must be presented to the owner through the listing agent.
12. Paying a fee or compensation to an unlicensed person.
13. Most states require a fixed expiration date in a listing contract and require that a copy be left with the seller.
14. A copy of the accepted purchase agreement must be given to the seller and the purchaser.
15. When closing a transaction, a completed copy of the settlement statement showing all the receipts and disbursements must be given to both sellers and purchasers.
16. Failure to reduce an offer to writing when a prospective purchaser requests the same.
17. All written offers to the owners must be presented promptly for their acceptance or refusal. It is not the licensee's discretion to decide whether an offer would be acceptable or not to the owners. Nor can offers be held waiting for another offer to be written.

Disciplinary Action

While the preceding license law violations vary from state to state, the basic necessity for ethical conduct appears in all the state license laws. When it appears to the real estate commission that a licensee is in violation of a license law, or upon receiving a sworn complaint in writing against a real estate broker or salesperson, the commission will investigate the actions of the licensee. If the investigation reveals no violation, the complaint will be dismissed. Should they determine justification for the complaint, a date will be set for a hearing. If the licensee is found guilty of an unfair trade practice, the license will be revoked or suspended or the licensee will be censured.

Penalties for disregarding license law

If the salesperson is declared guilty of a violation of the license law, the broker's license may also be in jeopardy if the broker is guilty of not properly supervising the actions of the agent. If the broker's license is suspended or revoked, all the licenses of the salespeople under the broker's supervision are suspended until they place their licenses with another broker.

OUT-OF-STATE SUBDIVISIONS

To further protect purchasers, many states have strict regulations regarding the selling of lands within their state when such land is located in another state or is of a promotional nature. Under the Interstate Land Sales Full Disclosure Act, the real estate commission requires from the applicant a full disclosure of the area of real estate being offered for sale. A recorded plat of the area, an audited financial statement, and copies of the instrument used to obtain title to the land must be submitted. The real estate commission may request a personal inspection of the property at the applicant's expense. If the purchaser has not seen the land prior to said purchase, the contract will allow the purchaser an unconditional right of refund on all payments made if the real estate is inspected within a period of not more than 4 months. The contract may be rescinded within 14 days if the purchaser has not seen the land.

Interstate land sales

The **subdivider** will need to show proof in the form of performance bonds or other security that any promised public improvements to the property can be provided.

UNLICENSED PERSONS

When an unlicensed person acts in the capacity of a licensee and does not fall under the exceptions to the state's law, the real estate regulatory agency will bring this fact to the attention of the attorney general. Prosecution will be recommended and an injunction order to cease filed against the violator in the district court in the county where such violation occurred.

SUMMARY

Considering that the purchase of real estate is the largest investment that the average person ever makes, it is understandable that all states have laws that govern the actions of the licensed salesperson and broker.

Educational requirements are mandatory in most states prior to licensing, and many states also require continuing education. Since the financing of real estate has changed dramatically in the past few years, it is imperative that the salesperson keep abreast of these changes. Compulsory education is a means of giving added assurance of the licensee's competence to transact business.

The salesperson or broker who belongs to the National Association of REALTORS® is further bound by a code of ethics to uphold fair practices and use diligence in preparing to conduct business as a licensee.

Anyone who conducts the business of listing, selling, exchanging, purchasing, renting, leasing, optioning, or managing real estate for a fee, commission, or other valuable compensation must be licensed. This license is a privilege that can be rescinded if the licensee commits an infraction of the license law. Although there are differences in the laws among various states, license law is intended to protect the consumer from unfair real estate practices.

DISCUSSION QUESTIONS

1. What is the basic purpose for license laws?
2. In what instance may a broker act for more than one party in a transaction?
3. Explain the procedure that the regulatory agency of your state follows when a licensee is accused of committing an infraction of the license law.
4. What are the requirements in your state for obtaining a salesperson's license?
5. Why is it necessary for a broker to maintain a separate trust account? Is this requirement ever waived in your state?
6. Under what circumstances may a person be refused a license?
7. Explain the differences between censure, suspension, and revocation.
8. What are the advantages of holding a broker's license as opposed to a salesperson's license?
9. Do you feel that continuing education is necessary for the licensee? Why or why not?

REVIEW QUESTIONS

Answers to these questions are found in the Answer Key section at the back of the book.

1. Which of the following are violations of real estate license laws?

   a. placing a "For Sale" sign on property without the written permission of the owner
   b. purchasing property as an undisclosed principal
   c. failure to submit a written offer to an owner
   d. all of the above

2. Which of the following is true concerning a listing contract?

   a. a copy must be left with the sellers
   b. the listing contract must not contain an expiration date
   c. buyers must be given a copy
   d. no listing can exceed 120 days

3. When a real estate broker advertises in the local newspaper, the advertisement must:

   a. always state the price of the house
   b. give the address of the house
   c. contain the broker's telephone number and business address
   d. contain the brokerage firm's name

4. If a salesperson mishandles funds:

   a. the salesperson's license may be revoked
   b. the employing broker will not be held responsible
   c. the salesperson will have 90 days to deposit funds in the trust account
   d. the local police department will fine the licensee

5. Jill Kingston has obtained a listing on a property for $89,350, and upon showing the property to a prospective buyer, she received an offer of $88,500. A salesperson from another firm shows the property and brings Jill an offer of $88,000. As Jill leaves the

office to present the offers to the sellers an agent from her office hands her an offer of $89,000. How should Jill present the offers to the sellers?

   a. Jill will present her offer first and if the sellers do not accept it she will present the offer for $89,000 since it is the highest offer

   b. since Jill is the listing agent, she has the right to present her offer and if accepted, need not discuss the other offers

   c. Jill must present all of the offers

   d. only the highest offer should be presented unless one of the other offers contains more favorable terms

6. A broker may place an earnest deposit:

   a. in his personal account if the money is designated as to whom is purchasing the property

   b. in the company's business account

   c. in the firm's trust account

   d. with the real estate commission

7. A broker may lose her license if she fails to:

   a. give a completed copy of the closing statement to the buyer and the seller

   b. file a copy of the closing statement with the recorder's office

   c. send a facsimile of the seller's closing statement to the purchasers

   d. retain a copy of the statements in the office files for six weeks

8. A salaried employee selling tracts of land for a land developer:

   a. must be licensed

   b. must receive a commission on the sales he makes

   c. does not need a license

   d. would need a broker's license

9. A real estate salesperson can:

   a. work independently

   b. open and operate a real estate firm

   c. manage a branch office for her employing broker

   d. list, sell, and lease real property

10. Real estate law is intended to:

   a. protect the public

   b. ensure that the salesperson will be paid a commission

   c. set commission rates

   d. foster good relations between brokers and salespersons

11. Which of the following people must be licensed to transact the business of real estate?

   a. court appointed guardians

   b. real estate secretaries

   c. the executor of an estate

   d. an owner of four income-producing properties

12. A real estate licensee may NOT:

   a. work on a part-time basis

   b. lease property listed with the firm

   c. sell commercial property

   d. pay a finder's fee to a neighbor

13. A license may be revoked upon proof of:

   a. charging more than the usual rate of commission

   b. refusal to accept a listing

   c. not advertising on a weekly basis

   d. steering customers away from an urban neighborhood

14. A broker's license may be revoked under which of the following circumstances?

   a. withholding earnest money when the purchaser is rightfully entitled to return of same

   b. dividing or splitting commissions with another broker

   c. dismissing a salesperson that is not producing listings or sales

   d. sending referral fees to a licensed broker in another state

15. Which of the following is NOT an infraction of the license law?

   a. failure to submit to an owner, before her acceptance, all formal written offers received on the property

   b. quoting a price other than that stipulated by the owner because the original asking price was unrealistic

   c. informing a prospective purchaser of a latent defect in the property

   d. paying a referral fee to a neighbor

16. A salesperson in a real estate transaction may NOT accept compensation in the form of:

   a. a percentage of the listing price

b. a percentage based on a sliding scale

c. a flat fee

d. a direct payment without his broker's knowledge

17. A broker fails to renew his license by the due date, but he did send it in two months later. In the interim a sale was negotiated, but the seller refused to pay the commission as agreed in the contract. Regarding this situation:

    a. the broker is not entitled to a commission

    b. the seller must pay the commission since it was agreed to in the listing contract

    c. if the broker pursues the issue and brings court action he will receive the commission

    d. the commission is due the broker since the property was listed prior to the license lapsing

18. A broker would be censured for commingling funds if she deposited earnest money in anything other than:

    a. her general real estate account

    b. her personal account, because the portion of money was due her

    c. a separate checking account designated as a trust account

    d. a separate savings account designated as a trust account

19. Which of the following is NOT a violation of license law?

    a. failure to offer property to a minority

    b. accepting an undisclosed rebate on an expenditure made for a principal

    c. quoting a price other than that stipulated by the seller

    d. showing properties to four different people in a single day

20. If a salesperson is working as an independent contractor, he is considered self-employed. Under these circumstances, the broker's responsibilities would include:

    a. withholding social security tax from the commission paid to the salesperson

    b. offering a retirement plan to the salesperson

    c. supervising the salesperson

    d. opening an IRA account for the salesperson

21. A salesperson in a real estate transaction may accept compensation from:

    a. the seller

    b. the real estate commission

    c. the buyer

    d. the employing broker

22. A license may be revoked upon proof of:

    a. charging more than the usual rate of commission

    b. refusal to accept a listing

    c. inducing a party to withdraw from a contract

    d. not advertising a property frequently

23. According to the license laws in most states, which of the following is true of a listing agreement?

    a. the listing must contain a termination date

    b. the contract must show the listing in effect until the property is sold

    c. it must be shown to any prospective purchaser

    d. all copies are retained by the real estate firm

24. A salesperson/broker ratio of commission will be determined by:

    a. the real estate commission or regulatory agency of the state

    b. the federal Fair Trade Commission

    c. statute of frauds

    d. contractual agreement

25. An agent must disclose to a potential buyer all, EXCEPT:

    a. that the property is in a flood zone

    b. any existing liens

    c. that the seller is financially stressed and anxious to sell

    d. that the home has a septic system and is not on public sewer

Basic Tools

Chapter 19 covers the various mathematical problems encountered in real estate transactions. Examples in computing square footage, interest earned, profit and loss, taxes and commissions, ratio and proportion, and loan amortization are provided in this chapter.

PART FIVE

Real Estate Math

OVERVIEW

Salespeople and brokers must have an understanding of the basic mathematical principles involved in the real estate transaction. While we covered the ad valorem tax structure on real property in Chapter 15, the amortization of a loan in Chapter 9, and the proration of costs in the settlement procedure in Chapter 10, it is necessary to further elaborate on the math involved in real estate transactions.

It is necessary to correctly measure the area (square footage) of a house or a parcel of land when the sales representative lists the property. Commercial land is generally priced per square foot, so the exact amount of square footage must be determined by the agent. A contractor may price a plan by square footage. An appraiser determines value by the square footage when using the cost approach to value. Cubic footage may be important to the purchaser of a commercial building or to the contractor pouring a driveway or patio.

A general review of the approach used in percentage problems is important when fractions or percentages of a tract of land are being divided. Many of the areas of arithmetic covered in this chapter involve percentages. For example, an inflationary market results in rapidly increasing property values, so the techniques used to evaluate percentages of appreciation must be understood. If the property depreciates, the resulting loss in value must also be calculated. To an investor, the past history of the value increase on a particular piece of property is very important.

Another area of mathematics important to real estate involves taxation. Since all real estate is subject to taxation, understanding the tax structure as expressed in dollars or mill levy is further explained in this chapter.

When analyzing the worth of a subdivided property, it is of value to both buyer and seller to determine the proportionate amount being sold. If a segment of a property is being taken under the right of eminent domain, the owner will want to know the proportion taken to determine the value of the land he is losing. Ratio problems concerning scales are also analyzed in this chapter since house plans are drawn to scale.

Determining the capitalization of an income-producing property is a prime concern of the investor, since the investor will want to know the rate of return on the investment.

Amortization is the liquidation of a loan by making monthly payments. This chapter explains how to determine the loan payment or to find the rate when you know the interest and principal payment. Discount problems when interest points are charged on a new loan are also included in this chapter. The differences among simple, add-on, and compound interest are explained.

When a property is sold, the financial responsibility of taxes, insurance, interest, and rents is divided (prorated) between the purchaser and seller. This is a bookkeeping procedure that the real estate agent should understand.

And last, the sales agent will be interested in computing commission problems. The split commission between real estate firms, broker-agent arrangement concerning commissions, and sliding-scale commission problems are presented in this chapter.

MEASUREMENT PROBLEMS

Let's review the following basic elements of arithmetic: The measurement of land and areas—square footage, cubic feet, acreages—are all of importance to the real estate salesperson. The following lists show the equivalents of various types of measures.

Linear measure
12 inches = 1 foot
36 inches = 3 feet or 1 yard

Square measure
144 square inches = 1 square foot
9 square feet = 1 square yard

Cubic measure
1 cubic foot = 1,728 cubic inches
27 cubic feet = 1 cubic yard

Surveyor's measure
link = 7.92 inches
chain = 66 feet or 4 rods
rod = 16½ feet or 1 perch
mile = 5,280 feet
acre = 43,560 square feet, 4,840 square yards, or 160 square rods
section = 640 acres

Circular measure
60 seconds ($''$) = 1 minute ($'$)
60 minutes ($'$) = 1 degree ($°$)
90 degrees ($°$) = 1 quadrant
360 degrees ($°$) = a circle

Square Footage and Yardage

Area problems   To find the square footage of a square or rectangular area, multiply the lengths of the two sides together.

area = length $\times$ width

By drawing the basic formula in a circle, the math procedure is simple to determine: just blot out the element you are looking for. Thus, if you have the total square footage and are looking for the width, divide the area by the length to obtain the width.

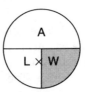

EXAMPLE: A room measures 18 feet long and 12 feet wide. Find the area.

A = 18$'$ (L) $\times$ 12$'$ (W)
A = 216 square feet

EXAMPLE: Compute the square footage of the house shown in the diagram.

Square off the diagram as shown:

A = 40′ × 28′   =   1,120 square feet
B = 2′ × 10′   =   20 square feet
C = 20′ × 10′   =   200 square feet
Total area   =   1,340 square feet

EXAMPLE: To find the square yards, divide the square feet by 9 (there are 9 square feet in a square yard).

216 square feet divided by 9 equals 24 square yards.

EXAMPLE: Find the *square yards* of carpet needed to cover a 15-foot × 18-foot room.

15′ × 18′ = 270 square feet
270 square feet ÷ 9 = 30 square yards

To find the *area of a triangle*, multiply the base by the height and divide by two.

area = half the base × the altitude

The altitude is the distance from the base of the triangle to its peak, as shown here by the dotted line. Line CD is the base and line AB the altitude.

EXAMPLE: A triangular lot has a base of 200 feet and an altitude of 150 feet. Find the area.

A = half the base × the altitude
$A = \dfrac{200}{2} \times 150$
A = 100 × 150
A = 15,000 square feet

EXAMPLE: To compute the square feet in the diagram, add the 2 widths, 40′ + 50′ = 90′. Then divide by 2: 90′ ÷ 2 = 45′.

Now multiply by the length: 45′ × 80′ = 3,600 square feet.

Note: An angle marked by an arc and "90°" is a right angle.

Cubic Footage and Yardage

To find the cubic footage of an area, multiply the length by the width by the height: L × W × H = cubic feet.

EXAMPLE: A 20-foot × 12-foot room has a height of 8 feet. Compute the cubic footage.

L (20′) × W (12′) × H (8′) = 1,920 cubic feet

EXAMPLE: If a driveway measures 60 feet long by 8 feet wide and is 3 inches deep, what is the cubic footage (3″ equals ¼ of a foot)?

$60' \times 8' \times \frac{1}{4}' = 120$ cubic feet

To find the *cubic yards*, divide the cubic feet by 27 (there are 27 cubic feet in a cubic yard).

EXAMPLE: A driveway 54 feet long by 15 feet and 4 inches deep will be poured at a cost of $30 per cubic yard of concrete. Find the cost.

$54' \times 15' \times \frac{1}{3}' = 270$ cubic feet

270 cubic feet ÷ 27 = 10 cubic yards
10 × $30 = $300

Linear Footage

Linear feet, sometimes referred to as running feet, are the measure of the distance from one point to another.

EXAMPLE: A lot 100 feet wide by 150 feet deep is to be fenced on all 4 sides. How much fencing is needed?

100′ + 100′ + 150′ + 150′ = 500 feet

EXAMPLE: A lot 65 feet wide by 80 feet deep will be fenced on both sides and the rear. How many linear feet of fencing is needed?

65′ + 80′ + 80′ = 225 feet

PERCENTAGES AND FRACTIONS

Decimals and percentages   It is necessary for salespeople and brokers to understand the conversion of decimals to percentages. Remember that the whole of anything is 100 percent. Anything less than the whole is a part or percentage of the whole. For example, think of $1.00 as being the whole and 50 cents as a part—in decimal form, .50. When converting a decimal to percentage, move the decimal point two places to the right and add the percentage symbol (%). Thus, you would write .50 as 50%. Another way to think of this is ⁵⁰⁄₁₀₀.

Remember, to change a percent to a decimal, move the decimal point two places to the left: 50% = .50. To change a decimal to a percent, move the decimal point two places to the right: .05 = 5%, .108 = 10.8%, 1.00 = 100%.

To change the percent to a common fraction, express it as hundredths and reduce:

$$50\% = \frac{50}{100} = \frac{1}{2} \qquad 75\% = \frac{75}{100} = \frac{3}{4}$$

To change a fraction to a percentage, express it in hundredths and then as a percentage:

$$\frac{1}{2} = \frac{50}{100} = .50, \text{ or } 50\% \qquad \frac{3}{4} = \frac{75}{100} = .75 \text{ or } 75\%$$

Fractions must have common denominators before you can add or subtract them:

$$\frac{1}{3} = \frac{4}{12}$$
$$\frac{2}{4} = \frac{6}{12}$$
$$\overline{\phantom{\frac{2}{4} = \frac{6}{12}}}$$
$$\frac{10}{12} \text{ or } \frac{5}{6}$$

As the example shows, ⅓ and ¾ have a common denominator of 12. When they are added together, the answer ¹⁰/₁₂, which is reduced to ⅚.

In multiplying fractions, the numerators are multiplied and the denominators are multiplied. For example, when multiplying the following fractions:

$$3\frac{1}{3} \times \frac{1}{2} =$$

Change 3⅓ to an improper fraction and multiply numerators and denominators:

$$\frac{10}{3} \times \frac{1}{2} = \frac{10}{6} \text{ or } \frac{5}{3} = 1\frac{2}{3}$$

To divide a fraction, the divisor is inverted and then multiplied:

$$\frac{2}{3} \div \frac{4}{5} =$$
$$\frac{2}{3} \times \frac{5}{4} = \frac{10}{12} = \frac{5}{6}$$

PROFIT AND LOSS

As we learned in the chapter on appraisal, depreciation is loss from any cause, whether it is physical deterioration, functional obsolescence, or economic obsolescence. If a property *depreciates* in value, it has simply lost value. If it *appreciates* in value, it has gained in value and is now worth more.

Appreciation and depreciation

We begin with the original value of a building as 100 percent. If the useful life of a building is 50 years, it will depreciate ¹⁄₅₀, or 2 percent, a year. Thus, if a property depreciates 2 percent a year for 8 years, it has a 16 percent loss in value.

We subtract this loss from 100 percent:

$$100\% - 16\% = 84\%$$

If the property is now worth, say, $16,800, this represents 84 percent of its original value. To determine its original value, we divide:

$$\$16,800 \div 84\% = \$20,000 \text{ (original value)}$$

When appreciation occurs, it represents a gain in value. Assuming a property at present valued at $23,000 had appreciated 3 percent a year for the last 5 years, it would have gained 15 percent in value. Its present value would thus be 115 percent of the original value.

$$\$23,000 \div 115\% = \$20,000 \text{ (original value)}$$

EXAMPLE: If a property sold for $12,100, gaining a 10 percent profit for the owner, what was the original cost of the property?

100% (cost) + 10% (profit) = 110% (selling price)
$12,100 ÷ 110 = $11,000 (original cost of property)

Here we divided the selling price by its percentage to determine the original cost.

EXAMPLE: A $40,000 house appreciates in value at the rate of 2.5 percent each succeeding year. What is the value of the house at the end of the second year?

$40,000 × 2.5% = $1,000 (appreciation the first year)
$40,000 + $1,000 = $41,000
$41,000 × 2.5% = $1,025 (appreciation the second year)
$41,000 + $1,025 = $42,025 (value after the second year)

The wording "each succeeding year" indicates compound interest; that is, the interest is added to the new balance at the end of each year.

EXAMPLE: A $30,000 house appreciates 5 percent each year for 5 years. What is its present value? (In this problem we need only multiply the 5 years by 5 percent, for a total of 25 percent appreciation.)

25% × $30,000 = $7,500
$30,000 + $7,500 = $37,500 (present value)

If we know the value of a house was $20,000 ten years ago and that it depreciated 2 percent a year, we can find the present value by multiplying:

10 years × 2% = 20% (total depreciation)
The present value of the house is 80% (100% − 20% = 80%)
$20,000 × 80% = $16,000 (present value)

EXAMPLE: A-1 Construction Company built a home in a new subdivision. It was sold 6 months after completion for $48,500, which represented a depreciation (loss) of 3 percent. What was the original asking price?

$48,500 ÷ 97% = $50,000 (asking price)

EXAMPLE: A duplex depreciates 3 percent for 5 years. If the building originally cost $20,000, compute the present value of the duplex.

3% × 5 years = 15% (total depreciation)
$20,000 × 15% = $3,000
$20,000 − $3,000 = $17,000 (present value)

EXAMPLE: Mr. Loser sells his house for $27,000, which represents a 10 percent loss over the price he originally paid for it. What did he pay for the house?

100% − 10% = 90%
$27,000 ÷ 90% = $30,000

TAXATION PROBLEMS

The property tax structure is an ad valorem (*according to value*) tax. This value is determined by a tax assessor, who appraises the value of each piece of property. An assessment roll is prepared that gives a description of the property, its assessed valuation, and the owner's name.

The tax rate is referred to either as *mill levy* or in *dollars*. In determining the taxation of a property, the assessed value is acquired by taking the percentage of the real value the taxes are based on; then the mill levy is multiplied by the assessed value. A mill represents ¹⁄₁₀ of 1 cent and is written as .001. Thus, 83 mills would be written as .083, and 6.5 mills would be written as .0065.

EXAMPLE: A property valued at $35,000 is assessed at 40 percent of its value. The mill levy is 83. Compute the annual tax.   *Taxation by mill levy*

$35,000 (value of property) × 40% (percentage taxed) = $14,000 (assessed value)
$14,000 × .083 (mill levy) = $1,162 (annual taxes)

EXAMPLE: If the assessed valuation is $20,000 and the tax rate is $4.00 per $100 of value, compute the annual tax.   *Taxation by dollars*

The $4.00 per hundred indicates that the $20,000 assessed valuation must be divided by 100.

$20,000 ÷ 100 = $200
$200 × $4 = $800 (tax)

RATIO AND PROPORTION

Ratio problems involve comparisons of 2 related numbers. A house plan or map is "scaled" so that 1 inch or a fraction of an inch equals a number of feet. The ratios must always be equal or in proportion.   *Comparing ratios*

EXAMPLE: What is the scale of a house plan if a room 16 feet × 28 feet is shown on the scale as 4 inches × 7 inches?

$$\frac{4}{16} = \frac{1}{4} \quad \frac{7}{28} = \frac{1}{4} \quad \text{Scale is } \frac{1}{4}'' = 1'$$

EXAMPLE: What is the actual measurement of a property 6 inches in length by 8 inches wide if the scale is $\frac{1}{8}$ inch = 1 foot?

If the scale is $\frac{1}{8}''$ to $1'$, $1'' = 8'$

$6 \times 8 = 48$
$8 \times 8 = 64$
The measurement is $48' \times 64'$.

EXAMPLE: In 9 months, a salesperson sells property to 1 out of every 5 prospective purchasers. How many sales would she make in 3 months if she showed property to 150 people? (Since the months involved are of no significance, we disregard the time element.)

$$\frac{5}{1} = \frac{150}{X}$$
$$\frac{150}{X} \times \frac{1}{5} = \frac{150}{5X}$$
$$\frac{150}{5} = X$$
$$X = 30 \text{ sales}$$

EXAMPLE: How many acres are there in plot A if plot B contains 25 acres?   *Proportion problems*

$$\frac{900}{X} = \frac{1,350}{25}$$
$$\frac{900}{X} \times \frac{25}{1,350} = \frac{22,500}{1,350} = 16\frac{2}{3} \text{ acres}$$

EXAMPLE: If the ratio of a salesperson's commission to that of his broker is 4:6, what amount does the salesperson earn from a $3,000 commission?

4 + 6 = 10 parts
100% ÷ 10 = 10%
4 × 10% = 40% and 6 × 10% = 60%
40% of $3,000 = $1,200

CAPITALIZATION AND OTHER FINANCE PROBLEMS

To solve income problems, use the formula P = R × B (principal equals rate × base). This is similar to using A = L × W in finding the square footage of an area.

P = principal (sum due)
R = rate (interest)
B = base (amount of value)
Use a circle and blot out the one unknown.

EXAMPLE: $140 is 3½% of what amount?

principal ÷ interest rate = amount or base
$$\frac{\$140 \ (P)}{.035 \ (R)} = B$$
$140 ÷ .035 = $4,000
Always *divide* to find the base or rate.

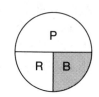

EXAMPLE: If the quarterly interest payments are $150 on a $12,000 loan, what is the annual interest rate?

$150 × 4 (4 quarters in a year) = $600

$$\frac{\$600 \ (P)}{\$12,000 \ (B)} = R$$

$600 ÷ $12,000 = 5%

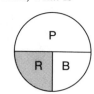

To determine the percentage, divide the *income* by the *investment*. (This is usually the larger number into the smaller.)

*Determining value
income property*

EXAMPLE: Compute the value of a property that has a net income of $5,480 and that returns 8 percent annually on the investment.

$$\frac{\$5,480 \ (P)}{.08 \ (R)} = B$$

$5,480 ÷ .08 = $68,500

Interest into return equals investment.

In this example, we divided the percentage rate *into* the net return to determine the value of the property.

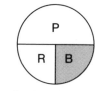

EXAMPLE: A buyer obtains a 75 percent loan on a house with a value of $28,000. What is the interest percentage if the interest payments are $140 monthly?

75% × $28,000 = $21,000 loan
$140 × 12 months = $1,680 annual interest
$$\frac{\$1,680 \ (P)}{\$21,000 \ (B)} = R$$
$1,680 ÷ $21,000 = 8% interest

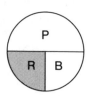

EXAMPLE: If an investment valued at $350,000 returns 12 percent annually, what is
the amount of income produced?

$350,000 (B) × 12% (R) = $42,000

EXAMPLE: If the capitalization rate on a building that produces $20,000 annual
income is 10 percent, find the estimated value of the structure.

$$\frac{\$20,000\ (P)}{.10\ (R)} = B$$
$20,000 ÷ .10 = $200,000

EXAMPLE: Compute the value if the same building had a
capitalization rate of 5 percent.

$$\frac{\$20,000\ (P)}{.05\ (R)} = B$$
$20,000 ÷ .05 = $400,000

In using the capitalization approach, remember that the *higher* the cap rate, the
lower the appraised value.

LOAN PAYMENTS

The buyer's foremost concern when purchasing a home is what the monthly loan commitment will be. The amount borrowed will be amortized over a period of years in
equal payments, a portion of which will be interest, with the remainder applied toward
the principal payment to gradually reduce the loan.

EXAMPLE: Ms. Morley purchases a home with a $45,000 mortgage at 9¾ percent   *Amortization problems*
interest. If the monthly payments are $387.70, what amount is applied
against the principal after the first payment?

$45,000 × .0975 = $4,387.50 annual interest
$4,387.50 ÷ 12 months = $365.63 first month's interest
$387.70 − $365.63 = $22.07 against principal

The $22.07 is deducted from the principal amount of $45,000 so that the
second month begins with the remaining balance of $44,977.93.

To determine the total monthly payment if the interest is in addition to
the stated principal payment, we compute the interest and add it to the
principal payment.

EXAMPLE: Mr. Winslow negotiates for a $30,000 loan with $200 monthly payments
plus 9 percent interest.

$30,000 × .09 = $2,700 ÷ 12 months = $225 interest per month.
$200 principal payment + $225 interest payment = $425 principal and
interest.

If the loan amount is unknown, but the interest payment and rate of
interest are given, we compute the amount as follows:

EXAMPLE: The semiannual interest payments are $400 with interest of 5 percent
annually.

$400 × 2 = $800 annual interest ÷ .05 = $16,000 loan amount

Simple Interest

When we do not have the money to make a purchase, we borrow and pay interest, but all interest is not the same.

Simple interest is what is paid for most real estate loans. Payments are made on the unpaid balance, that is, on the amount still owed.

The formula is:

Interest = Principal × Rate × Time

EXAMPLE: The interest paid on a $20,000 loan at 8 percent repayable in 5 years is:

I = PRT
I = $20,000 × 0.08 × 5 years = $8,000
I = $8,000

Add-on Interest

Some lenders, especially when financing second mortgages or household items, will calculate interest on the total amount of the loan for the complete time of the loan. The interest amount is added to the principal owed for repayment over the term of the loan before calculating the monthly payments. Note how much this method increases simple interest.

EXAMPLE: $20,000 × .08 × 5 years = $8,000

The $8,000 interest is added to the total principal amount owed before the payments are calculated. $20,000 + $8,000 = $28,000

The $28,000 is divided by the total number of payments (12 × 5 = 60 payments).
$28,000 divided by 60 = $446.67

The first payment is the same as a simple interest payment. However, the second and subsequent payments are not because the interest is still being charged on the portion of the principal that has been repaid.

Compound Interest

To calculate compound interest, we add interest onto interest.

EXAMPLE: $500.00 × 10% for 1 year = $50 interest earned.

Now add the $50 to the $500, and we begin the next year with $550.00.
$550 × 10% = $55.00 interest earned the second year.

More Interest Problems

EXAMPLE: Mr. Jones wanted to remodel his business. He obtained a loan for $4,300 at 6 percent interest. He paid it off in 8 months. What amount of interest did he pay?

$4,300 × .06 = $258 interest for year
$258 ÷ 12 months = $21.50 per month
$21.50 × 8 months = $172 interest paid

EXAMPLE: A buyer purchases a home for $50,000. She takes out a 25-year loan for 75 percent of the purchase price. Assuming that her mortgage payments are equal and the interest payment is ¾ percent of the principal each month, what would be the amount of her first monthly payment?

$50,000 × .75 = $37,500 loan
25 years × 12 months = 300 months
$37,500 ÷ 300 months = $125 principal per month
¾% × 12 months = 9% interest per year
$37,500 × .09 = $3,375 ÷ 12 months = $281.25 interest
$125 + $281.25 = $406.25 principal and interest

EXAMPLE: Jane Jones obtains an FHA loan on a $56,000 home. The down payment scale is 3 percent of the first $25,000 and 5 percent of the balance. There is a loan fee of 2 points that the buyer is to pay. What amount should Ms. Jones bring to the closing?

3% of $25,000 = $ 750 $56,000
5% of $31,000 = $1,550   − $ 2,300 down payment
                $2,300 $53,700 loan

Two points would be .02 of the loan ($53,700) = $1,074

$2,300 + $1,074 = $3,374

EXAMPLE: How much less are the monthly payments on a $36,000 home than on a $40,000 home if a 75 percent loan is obtained at $8.70 a month per $1,000 of value?

$40,000 − $36,000 = $4,000 × 75% = $3,000
$3 (thousands) × $8.70 = $26.10

EXAMPLE: Ms. Randall purchases a home for $58,000 and puts 10 percent down. The 20-year loan is to be repaid with a constant principal payment, and interest will be charged at the rate of ¾ percent per month. Compute the amount of the first month's payment.

$58,000 − $5,800 (10% down) = $52,200 loan
20 years × 12 months = 240 months
52,200 ÷ 240 = $217.50 principal per month
¾% × 12 months = 9% × $52,200 = $4,698 ÷ 12 = $391.50
interest per month
$217.50 + $391.50 = $609 principal and interest

DISCOUNT PROBLEMS

A discount is an amount charged by the lender in excess of the closing costs to equalize or increase the lender's yield. In addition to the interest rate, a percentage is charged on the *amount loaned* to the borrower. The effective yield to the loan company becomes greater when these discount points are charged. A "point" is really 1 percent of the amount of the loan. If 1 point is charged on a $20,000 loan, the lender collects 1 percent of $20,000, or $200. If 2½ points are charged, the fee would be $500.

Discount points

EXAMPLE: Mr. Corkle purchases a $55,000 home using FHA financing. He is required to put 3 percent down on the first $25,000 loaned with 5 percent on the balance of the purchase price. The lender is charging 3½ discount points. Compute the discount points that will be paid.

$25,000 × .97 = $24,250
$30,000 × .95 =   28,500
                $52,750 loan amount

$52,750 × .035 = $1,846.25 discount points

PRORATIONS

Dividing expenses
by prorating

Prorating means *dividing expenses* between buyer and seller. The person who uses must pay her share for the time used. In prorating, one must analyze the period of time involved and multiply it by the rate. Real estate prorating at the time of closing a sale may commonly include taxes, rents, insurance, or interest charges.

EXAMPLE: Mr. Howard sells his home July 1, with closing and possession set for July 15. Since Ms. Stucky is assuming the loan, she has also decided to assume the insurance policy, which was paid March 1 for 1 year in the amount of $156. What amount will appear as a credit on Mr. Howard's closing statement?

March 1 to July 15 = 4½ months. (This represents the amount of insurance used by Mr. Howard, leaving 7½ months *unused*.)

$156 divided by 12 months = $13 monthly
$13 × 7½ months = $97.50 (amount due to Mr. Howard)

EXAMPLE: The mortgage being assumed by Ms. Stucky is in the amount of $15,000 at 8 percent interest. The interest has been paid to June 1. Mr. Howard is liable for the interest to the date of closing. Compute the amount he owes.

$15,000 × .08 = $1,200 ÷ 12 months = $100 for June, plus $50 for half of July
Total = $150

EXAMPLE: I. M. Lloyd sold her home November 15 with possession set for December 5. Mr. Wiley will assume the 3-year insurance policy, which became effective July 15 of last year in the amount of $396. The annual taxes of $982.80 were paid by the owner for the first half of the year; the second half year's taxes are due and payable. What amounts are payable and by whom?

1. *Insurance*

   July 15 (last year) to December 5 = 1 year, 4 months, 20 days *used* (16 months and 20 days *used* or 19 months and 10 days *not used*)

   $396 ÷ 36 months = $11 per month × 19 months = $209
   $11 ÷ 30 days = $.366 per day × 10 days = $3.67
   $209 + $3.67 = $212.67 (insurance paid for and not used will be refunded to Ms. Lloyd)

2. *Taxes*

   $982.80 ÷ 12 months = $81.90 per month
   July 1 to December 5 = 5 months, 5 days taxes due
   $81.90 × 5 = $409.50
   $81.90 ÷ 30 days = $2.73 per day
   $2.73 × 5 days = $13.65 + $409.50 = $423.15 (taxes due from seller)
   $2.73 × 25 days = $68.25 (taxes due from buyer to complete year)
   $212.67 insurance prorate due to I. M. Lloyd
   $423.15 taxes due from Ms. Lloyd
   $68.25 taxes due from Mr. Wiley

COMMISSIONS

In the real estate business a salesperson normally is paid on a commission basis. Instead of receiving a fixed salary, the salesperson is paid a percentage or proportion of the real estate he sells or lists. This straight commission earning is received only if the salesperson produces. The real estate firm, of course, must retain a portion for its fixed expenses.

Earnings of real estate agents

EXAMPLE: If a property sells for $20,000 and a broker's commission is 6 percent, the broker's commission would be:

$20,000 \times 6\% = \$1,200$ commission

EXAMPLE: If a salesperson receives 35 percent of a total commission from his broker, what is the broker's share if the property sold for $23,000 and the commission was on a 6 percent basis?

$23,000 \times .06 = \$1,380$ (total commission)
$100\% - 35\% = 65\%$ (broker's share)
$1,380 \times 65\% = \$897$ (broker's portion)

EXAMPLE: Tom Lyons earns 6 percent on the first $50,000 of a $160,000 sale. If the total commission is $7,400, what percentage was paid on the remainder?

$50,000 \times .06 = \$3,000$
$7,400 - \$3,000 = \$4,400$
$160,000 - \$50,000 = \$110,000$
So: $4,400 =$ what % of $110,000?
$4,400$ (P) $\div \$110,000$ (B) $= .04 = 4\%$ (R)

EXAMPLE: Mr. Jones, a real estate broker, leases a property to Ms. Whitney for 5 years. Mr. Jones will receive a 5 percent commission. The rent will be $300 per month for the first year, with a $50-a-month increase each succeeding year. What is Mr. Jones's commission?

$300 @ 12$ months $= \$\ \ 3,600$
$350 @ 12$ months $= \$\ \ 4,200$
$400 @ 12$ months $= \$\ \ 4,800$
$450 @ 12$ months $= \$\ \ 5,400$
$500 @ 12$ months $= \underline{\$\ \ 6,000}$
$\qquad\qquad\qquad\quad \$24,000 \ \times .05 = \$1,200$ commission

---

REVIEW QUESTIONS

Answers to these questions are found on pages 347–348 in the Answer Key section.

1. Find the square footage of the diagram, excluding the small area indicated in the lower right hand corner:

   170'

   a. 30,000 sq. ft.
   b. 33,600 sq. ft.
   c. 33,800 sq. ft.
   d. 34,000 sq. ft.

   200'   180'
   150'

2. If a house depreciates at the rate of 2.5 percent per year for 10 years and has a present value of $12,500, what was the original value of the house?

   a. $14,000
   b. $16,666
   c. $17,000
   d. $18,000

3. An $11,000 house is assessed at 30 percent of its original cost. The school tax on the property is 12 mills. What was the approximate yearly tax (rounded off to the nearest dollar)?

   a. $40
   b. $396

c. $400

d. $600

4. A house is appraised for $25,000 and shows an assessed value of $20,000. If taxes on it are $300 yearly, what would the tax be on a house appraising at $45,000 with an assessed value of $40,000?

a. $150

b. $500

c. $600

d. $700

5. Mr. Lewis is working for Ms. Morris on a 50/50 basis. Mr. Lewis sells 360 acres at $150 an acre; another firm, ABC Realty, has the listing and splits on a 50/50 basis with Ms. Morris's firm. The commission rate is 5 percent on the first $25,000, 2.5 percent on the next $20,000 and 1 percent on the balance. How much does Mr. Lewis earn?

a. $230

b. $460

c. $920

d. $1,840

6. What portion of the whole piece of land is lot A?

a. $\dfrac{1}{30}$

b. $\dfrac{3}{60}$

c. $\dfrac{2}{15}$

d. $\dfrac{2}{9}$

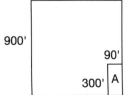

7. Find the actual measurement of a property shown as 5¾ inches long and 4½ inches wide if the scale is ⅛ inch = 1 foot:

a. 12′ × 9′

b. 24′ × 18′

c. 36′ × 32′

d. 46′ × 36′

8. A house sale is closed on July 15. The taxes of $546 for the calendar year have been paid. The fire insurance premium of $102 for the calendar year has also been paid. What is the total prepaid portion that the buyer will owe back to the seller?

a. $54

b. $297

c. $351

d. $425

9. Shelly Ford pays her taxes of $660 for the calendar year. She sells her property and closes on June 15. What is the remaining prepaid portion due back to her?

a. $302.50

b. $330.00

c. $357.50

d. $412.50

10. An apartment house has 10 units renting at $275 a month and 12 units at $250 a month. Expenses are $6,789 annually. The vacancy factor is 15 percent annually. If you desire to make 10 percent return on your investment, approximately what should you pay for the property?

a. $62,100

b. $518,610

c. $585,000

d. $612,100

11. Carol Reed purchases a $62,000 property on which she obtains an 80 percent loan. She pays 4 discount points, and the attorney's fees and miscellaneous costs amount to $2,500. How much money should she bring to the closing?

a. $1,984

b. $12,400

c. $14,900

d. $16,884

12. What was the selling price of a property if Jerry Brown paid $350 for taxes due, has a $12,500 mortgage, paid a 6 percent broker commission, and netted $7,000 on the sale?

a. $13,621.00

b. $15,500.00

c. $21,041.00

d. $21,117.02

13. A building that cost $300,000 to construct 10 years ago has depreciated 25 percent. The land cost $51,000. Find the current appraised value:

a. $263,250

b. $265,000

c. $276,000

d. $351,000

14. Mr. Leonard owns a lot measuring 80 feet × 120 feet. The city puts in a new street in front and to the side of his house and assesses him 6 cents a square foot based on the area of this lot. His costs are:

a. $48.00

b. $57.60

c. $480.00

d. $576.00

15. If the transfer taxes are payable at the rate of 55 cents per $500 or part thereof, compute the grantor's cost on a $49,750 sale:

a. $27.36

b. $53.90

c. $54.55

d. $55.00

16. Ms. Dale buys a $20,000 property. She puts $1,000 down with the balance to be repaid over 20 years at 12 percent interest. Her monthly payments are $209.38. What is the amount of interest paid in the second month's payment?

a. $75.44

b. $85.79

c. $189.06

d. $190.00

17. What is the approximate amount of interest paid on the loan in problem 16 at its maturity?

a. $19,000

b. $31,200

c. $45,400

d. $66,100

18. The gross annual income for each of 5 apartments is $145 per month. The building is 90 percent occupied. The caretaker is paid 5 percent of the gross, and the total yearly maintenance is $1,400. Find the monthly net income of the apartments:

a. $391.20

b. $503.21

c. $620.00

d. $6,038.51

19. James Stole manages an office building with leases of $60,000 per year. His management agreement is for 7 years, with fees as follows: 7 percent the first year, 5 percent the second and third years, and 3 percent the remaining years. Find the total management fee the broker would receive:

a. $9,000

b. $12,000

c. $14,400

d. $17,400

20. Find the annual percentage rate of net return of an $88,000 investment if the weekly gross income is $225 and the monthly expenses are $370:

a. 7%

b. 8.25%

c. 10%

d. 12.5%

21. Ms. Carlson owns a 110-acre orchard that yields an average net profit of $13,000. If she sells the land and invests the money at 5 percent, what price per acre must she sell for to match her present earnings?

a. $236.36

b. $2,250.00

c. $2,363.64

d. $21,500.50

22. A building worth $430,000 rents for $1,500 a month. What is the rate of capitalization?

a. 4%

b. 8%

c. 9%

d. 23.75%

23. An office building earns $850,000 a year; expenses run 35 percent of that amount. If the property is capitalized at 12 percent, what is its approximate value?

a. $297,500

b. $552,500

c. $4,604,000

d. $6,630,000

24. Mr. Jay buys a home and obtains a $20,000 loan on which monthly payments will be $7.50 per $1,000. Annual taxes are $360; a 3-year fire insurance policy cost $54. What was the first payment, including taxes and insurance?

a. $181.50

b. $193.50

c. $216.50

d. $280.00

25. A map is drawn to scale and marked 13.5 inches $\times$ 16.5 inches. In reality that area equals 108 feet $\times$ 132 feet. What is the scale?

a. $\frac{1}{8}'' = 1'$

b. $\frac{1}{4}'' = 1'$

c. $\frac{3}{8}'' = 1'$

d. $8'' = 1'$

26. A salesperson receives 8 percent of the first $90,000 he sells each month and 2 percent of the excess above that amount. In August, he made sales of $42,000, $48,000, $36,500, and $55,600. If he had been paid a flat 6 percent commission, how much more or less would he have made?

   a. less than $500 more
   b. less than $600 more
   c. less than $5,000 more
   d. more than $5,000

27. Ms. Randall's $85,000 condominium is assessed at 35 percent of value. The tax rate is $2.70 per $100 of value. If the tax increases $.35 per $100, her new tax will be:

   a. $699.13
   b. $750.00
   c. $907.38
   d. $9,073.80

28. A house is currently worth 50 percent of its original value. The land, however, has appreciated in 5 years from $60,000 to its present value of $96,000. Find the average annual rate of appreciation of the land over the 5-year period:

   a. 6.25%

b. 12%

c. 16%

d. 63%

29. Now that you are entering the real estate profession, you purchase a new four-door automobile costing $9,200. Your accountant advises that you deduct $2,300 as depreciation this year. What percentage are you deducting?

   a. 4%
   b. 12%
   c. 12.5%
   d. 25%

30. The diagram contains:

   a. 5,600 sq. ft.
   b. 6,800 sq. ft.
   c. 8,000 sq. ft.
   d. 8,500 sq. ft.

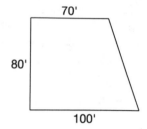

31. This type of interest is paid on the amount of principal that is still owed:

   a. simple
   b. complex
   c. compound
   d. add-on

Practice Examination

This examination is to test your knowledge of the material you have studied and to prepare you for the licensing exam if you are pursuing becoming a licensed real estate salesperson or broker. Since many states adhere to a standardized multiple choice test given by a testing service, the following 100 questions are an example of what you may expect.

Answers can be found on pages 348–349 in the Answer Key section.

PART ONE: REAL ESTATE

1. Which of the following conditions least affects our real estate markets?

   a. interest rates
   b. economic conditions of a given region
   c. supply and demand
   d. foreign market conditions

2. Which of the following conditions does NOT stimulate the purchase of homes?

   a. employment
   b. desire for a larger home
   c. rising interest rates
   d. environment

3. If property is abandoned by its owner, the state's power to claim possession of the property is known as:

   a. escheat
   b. police power
   c. eminent domain
   d. taxation

4. Which of the following is NOT considered real property?

   a. minerals
   b. firewood
   c. air rights
   d. growing trees

5. The process whereby the government takes property for the public good by the right of eminent domain is the act of:

   a. escheat
   b. reversion
   c. accretion
   d. condemnation

6. Riparian rights apply to:

   a. a reversionary interest owned in a life estate
   b. land bordering a moving body of water
   c. land under cultivation
   d. property taken by means of eminent domain

7. Possession of real property that is hostile to the true owner's title is called:

   a. tenancy at sufferance
   b. reversion
   c. adverse possession
   d. police power

8. The gradual loss of land through water and wind is called:

   a. percolation
   b. riparian
   c. alluvion
   d. erosion

9. The term *fructus industriales* or emblements would describe which of the following?

   a. trade fixtures
   b. annual crops

c. trees and bushes

d. air rights

10. The suggestion that an individual has an ownership interest in a property when this is not the case causes a condition referred to as:

a. reversionary interest

b. color of title

c. escheat

d. eminent domain

11. Land is considered immobile because:

a. of its fixed geographic location

b. it is real property

c. it is nonhomogeneous

d. it is indestructible

12. The metes and bounds method of surveying is based primarily upon:

a. survey lines that run east and west

b. survey lines that run north and south

c. a map of a subdivision

d. a point of beginning

13. The N½ of the SW¼ of the NE¼ of a section in a government rectangular survey township contains:

a. 160 acres

b. 80 acres

c. 20 acres

d. 10 acres

14. The system of land ownership in the United States is referred to as:

a. the feudal system

b. the allodial system

c. writ of passage

d. allotment

15. The largest unit of measurement in the rectangular survey method is known as a:

a. check

b. township

c. section

d. lot and block

16. All of the following are true facts, EXCEPT:

a. the lot and block method of land description is employed when subdividing land into building lots

b. the rectangular government survey uses meridians and base lines

c. townships are divided into 48 sections

d. a check contains 16 townships

17. Which of the following forms of a quitclaim deed is used when a property owner conveys street rights to the county or jurisdiction within which the property lies?

a. cession

b. warranty

c. executor's deed

d. gift deed

18. To give notice by recording an instrument is referred to as:

a. constructive notice

b. actual notice

c. verbal notice

d. written notice

19. Michael has a lifetime estate in 823 S. Maple. Kent will inherit the property upon Michael's death. Kent's interest is:

a. possessory

b. a leasehold interest

c. a reversionary interest

d. an easement

20. A type of deed that warrants the title against defects only during the time since the present owner has held title is called a:

a. quitclaim deed

b. special warranty

c. general warranty

d. bargain and sale

21. Which of the following statements does NOT apply to joint tenancy?

a. all owners must acquire title at the same time

b. all owners have equal right to possession

c. the right of survivorship exists

d. owners hold separate title in the same estate

22. Which of the following is an example of a freehold estate?

a. reversion

b. fee determinable

c. estate for years

d. tenancy at will

23. A life tenant may do all of the following, EXCEPT:

    a. lease the property to another individual
    b. pay taxes on the property
    c. bequeath her interest
    d. sell her interest

24. A form of ownership with the right of survivorship is known as:

    a. joint tenancy
    b. tenancy in common
    c. estate of inheritance
    d. partnerships

25. Rights of survivorship do not exist in this ownership:

    a. joint tenancy
    b. dower
    c. tenancy in common
    d. tenancy by the entirety

PART TWO: THE ORDERLY PROCESS OF A SALE

26. Which of the following elements does NOT need to be present to have a valid and enforceable contract?

    a. legality of object
    b. legal capacity of parties
    c. consideration
    d. an assignment clause

27. While viewing homes with her agent, a buyer asks if the drapes will remain in a particular house. Although the listing does not include the drapes, the agent explains that they can be written into the contract. The buyer submits an offer for the house, and it is accepted by the seller as written. Upon taking possession of the house, the buyer discovers the drapes are gone. The agent confirms that although they had discussed asking for them while viewing the property, the item had not been put into the contract. The rule that forbids the admittance of any prior oral or written evidence to vary or add to the terms of a written instrument is the:

    a. statute of frauds
    b. rule of specific performance

    c. dual contract rule
    d. parol evidence rule

28. The contracts most commonly used in real estate transactions include all of the following, EXCEPT:

    a. listing contracts
    b. purchase contracts
    c. mortgages
    d. abstracts

29. Broker A has listed a property, and one of her salespersons, Agent A, is showing the property to a potential buyer. Agent A informs the prospect that the sellers are due to move out of state and are anxious to sell, and thus will be willing to lower their asking price. Which of the following is a true statement in reference to this situation?

    a. if the seller has not agreed to disclosure of this information, Agent A has breached his fiduciary obligation to the seller
    b. this is a case of dual agency
    c. since the prospective buyer is a close friend of Agent A, he may bend the rules a little without breaching his responsibilities
    d. all three are true statements

30. Owners hire real estate firms to sell their property for all of the following reasons, EXCEPT:

    a. brokers financially qualify customers in advance
    b. the salesperson may purchase the property and later resell it
    c. the salesperson keeps current on available financing
    d. the salesperson is aware of market conditions and market values

31. A contract providing for payment of a commission regardless of who sells the property is a(n):

    a. net listing
    b. open listing
    c. exclusive agency
    d. exclusive right to sell

32. A listing contract must contain all of the following, EXCEPT:

    a. the signatures of all parties named
    b. the agreed-upon commission
    c. nondiscrimination wording
    d. proration of closing costs

33. An agent who has the power of attorney to act for a principal in all lawful transactions concerning the principal is called:

    a. a general agent
    b. an implied agent
    c. a special agent
    d. a universal agent

34. Under what circumstances does a dual agency exist?

    a. an agent is employed by a home buyer
    b. an agent sells a property listed by the broker for whom he works
    c. an agent shows property listed by another broker
    d. a salesperson represents both buyer and seller by prior written agreement

35. A broker can accept a commission from both the buyer and the seller in some states under which of the following circumstances?

    a. upon full disclosure and consent of all parties
    b. if the broker feels he has represented both equally in the transaction
    c. providing the commission is not excessive
    d. if the listing broker is also the selling broker

36. If a buyer is concerned about the condition of the furnace in a house that she is considering purchasing, the buyer could:

    a. obtain an inspection from a qualified service
    b. purchase a buyer warranty policy
    c. have the seller purchase a buyer warranty policy
    d. any of the above

37. Fannie Mae can best be described as:

    a. purchaser of loans in the secondary market
    b. an agency that insures private mortgages
    c. a regulatory agency that governs the interest rates charged on government loans
    d. a lender in the primary market

38. The definition that best describes the term *hypothecate* is:

    a. to lend money below current market rates
    b. to retain possession but pledge as security
    c. the transfer of funds from one bank to another to obtain higher interest rates
    d. to consolidate a borrower's debts

39. This act requires the lender to provide the borrower with a good faith estimate of all costs associated with closing:

    a. RESPA
    b. FNMA
    c. APR
    d. EOC

40. Which of the following loans is insured by the government?

    a. FHA
    b. VA
    c. farm loans
    d. PMI

41. A lender will make a loan on real estate based on a percentage of the property's value. This is called:

    a. the resale value
    b. the loan-to-value ratio
    c. liquidation value
    d. market value

42. *Disintermediation* defines the process whereby:

    a. depositors withdraw their funds from the savings and loans to invest them directly in corporate bonds, government securities, etc.
    b. the secondary mortgage market buys loans from the primary lender
    c. government agencies interfere in the business of making loans
    d. ceilings on loans are eliminated

43. A lien that is attached to a particular property is known as a:

    a. judgment in personam
    b. judgment in rem
    c. tort
    d. lis pendens

44. Which of the following encumbrances is placed on real property by someone other than the owner?

    a. transfer development right
    b. easement
    c. mortgage lien
    d. license

45. The processs of amortization is best described as:

    a. reduction of debt on a payment plan

b. mortgaging with a land contract

c. assignment of a mortgage

d. the paying on a construction loan

46. Which of the following mortgages offers reduced payments for the first few years because a portion of the interest has been prepaid for the buyer?

   a. adjustable rate mortgage (ARM)

   b. buydown mortgage

   c. growing equity mortgage (GEM)

   d. land contract

47. In which of the following mortgages is the final payment substantially larger than the previous monthly payments?

   a. blanket mortgage

   b. package mortgage

   c. balloon mortgage

   d. second mortgage

48. Which of the following statements is true regarding delinquent property taxes?

   a. they become a lien against the property

   b. a lien is placed against all personal property of the debtor

   c. a federal tax lien is placed against the property

   d. they are taxed as a special assessment

49. A painting contractor paints two properties for a customer but is only paid for painting one. Which of the following is NOT true regarding a lien the contractor files?

   a. the lien will be a mechanic's lien

   b. the lien is created by statute

   c. the lien can only be placed on the one property

   d. the lien can be filed against both properties

50. Which of the following items is prorated at the time of closing?

   a. the earnest deposit

   b. proceeds from the sale

   c. the mortgage

   d. property taxes

51. Which of the following would NOT be charged to the buyer's closing statement?

   a. the purchase price

   b. the recording of the deed

   c. the new mortgage loan

d. property taxes

52. A property owner is insured against a forged title or defects in the title by:

   a. an appraisal

   b. title insurance policy

   c. examination of the abstract

   d. homeowner's insurance

PART THREE: OTHER ASPECTS OF REAL ESTATE OWNERSHIP

53. Rules for governing the operation of a condominium development are set by:

   a. zoning laws

   b. each owner sets his own rules

   c. the development's homeowners' association

   d. local ordinance

54. Legislation governing a condominium development is referred to as:

   a. a horizontal property act

   b. a free cooperative act

   c. a vertical property act

   d. deeded restrictions

55. Disadvantages of condominium ownership could include:

   a. density

   b. limited private outdoor space

   c. limited parking area

   d. all of the above

56. Which of the following is the type of ownership that gives a proprietary lease?

   a. cooperative

   b. condominium

   c. time-share

   d. exchange programs

57. All of the following statements are true, EXCEPT:

   a. cooperative owners will hold shares or stock

   b. condominium owners acquire fee simple title

   c. conversion changes the use of a property

   d. a condo owner owns the common areas with other owners in joint tenancy

58. This lease provides for the payment of rent and certain costs involved in the operation and maintenance of the property:

    a. percentage lease
    b. net lease
    c. graduated lease
    d. gross lease

59. The mutual agreement between the lessee and the lessor to cancel a lease is termed:

    a. detainer
    b. notice to quit
    c. surrender and acceptance
    d. gross lease

60. Jones leases space for his bakery in a 10-year-old mall. A new shopping center is being built one mile away, so Jones decides not to renew his present lease, which expires June 10, because he feels his business will increase at the new location. The new location will be ready June 15, so Jones keeps a key so that he can remove the trade fixture at that time to the new location. Can Jones legally do this?

    a. yes, trade fixtures are property of the tenant
    b. yes, because he automatically has 30 days to remove them
    c. no, once fixtures are attached they become the property of the landlord
    d. no, trade fixtures must be removed before the lease expires

61. The instrument that transfers the right to possess property but does not convey ownership is:

    a. a lien
    b. a mortgage
    c. a lease
    d. a deed

62. A percentage lease may be used for all of the following, EXCEPT:

    a. a sporting goods store
    b. a specialty shop
    c. a 10-unit apartment building
    d. a computer sales store

63. Which of the following does NOT have an insurable interest in the real estate?

    a. life tenant
    b. mortgagee

    c. trustee
    d. property manager

64. A property manager will generally perform which of the following functions?

    a. offer lower rental rates to preferred tenants
    b. invest the owner's profits in new buildings
    c. advertise available space
    d. make long-term decisions on capital improvements

65. The shopping center that offers a broad mix of shops, including several nationally recognized stores such as Sears and Penney's, is referred to as a(n):

    a. strip center
    b. regional center
    c. neighborhood shopping center
    d. industrial park

66. Which of the following is NOT an advantage to investing in real estate?

    a. liquidity
    b. appreciation
    c. equity build-up
    d. leverage

67. Many investors use the financial practice of leverage to:

    a. shelter their income
    b. guarantee a positive cash flow
    c. reduce their equity investment
    d. increase their equity investment

68. The Real Estate Investment Trust (REIT) offers which of the following?

    I. real estate ownership through indirect participation
    II. shares in real property can be purchased by small investors
    III. control by all of the investors

    a. I only
    b. II only
    c. I and II
    d. I, II, and III

69. Concerns of investors include all, EXCEPT:

    a. the risk involved in the project
    b. tax considerations

c. whether inflation will erode the growth potential

d. building equity

70. Which of the following type(s) of depreciation is curable?

a. physical obsolescence

b. economic obsolescence

c. functional obsolescence

d. a and c

71. Functional obsolescence is primarily the result of:

a. wearing out of the building and its components

b. changing requirements of buyers

c. changes in surrounding properties

d. decreased demand

72. An appraisal report may be in the form of all, EXCEPT:

a. an oral report

b. a letter

c. a narrative

d. a video report

73. The appraisal process used to establish the potential return on an investment is:

a. the comparison approach

b. the income approach

c. the cost approach

d. summation

74. The purpose for an appraisal may include all of the following, EXCEPT:

a. to determine the market value of the property

b. for insurance purposes

c. for loan value

d. to determine regional value

75. The term *ad valorem* means:

a. ability to repay a debt

b. appraisal to determine value

c. according to value

d. insured against disaster

76. In the preparation of a market value analysis it is important that the appraiser use which of the following?

a. the income approach

b. adjustments for differences in the properties

c. the quantity survey method

d. the cost approach

77. According to the principle of conformity:

a. value increases if a property is overimproved for the area

b. values tend to rise if a neighborhood is homogeneous

c. value is created by anticipation

d. supply and demand dictate new home starts

78. In August 1989 Congress passed the Financial Institutions Reform, Recovery and Enforcement Act (FIRREA). Title XI of the bill requires:

a. appraisers to meet minimum standards of performance

b. that a certified appraiser be used to appraise single- to fourplex-family residences of $1 million value and higher

c. that all federally related appraisals must be performed by a certified or licensed appraiser

d. all of the above

79. Which of the following is a use that existed prior to current zoning regulations and is not consistent with the present zoning?

a. a nonconforming use

b. a variance

c. spot zoning

d. a special use

80. Mrs. White gives her neighbor, Mr. Redding, a written easement to cross her property and records the document. Mrs. White later sells her property but fails to tell the buyer about the easement rights. What happens to the easement?

a. the sale invalidates the easement

b. the easement is owned by Mrs. White

c. a new easement needs to be written and recorded

d. the easement goes with the land

81. Which of the following would NOT be a violation of a zoning ordinance?

a. a house is built closer to the lot line than covenants allow to meet the special needs of the occupant

b. the building does not meet the minimum square footage

c. a house is occupied after the occupancy permit is issued

d. a duplex is built in an area zoned for single family homes

82. The roof of a building protrudes over a public alley. This is an example of:

a. an easement
b. an encroachment
c. escheat
d. adverse possession

83. In 1984 an amendment to the Comprehensive Environmental Response, Compensation, and Liability Act (CERCLA) was passed:

a. to set minimum standards for safe drinking water
b. to remove asbestos from buildings
c. to regulate underground storage tanks
d. to regulate the disposal of solid waste in designated dump sites

84. Down zoning occurs when:

a. a property is rezoned to a lower use
b. a property is rezoned to a higher use
c. spot zoning is given
d. raw land is developed into homesites

85. All of the following are true of a planned unit development (PUD), EXCEPT:

a. it may have characteristics of cluster housing
b. it may provide for mixed uses
c. it has common areas
d. it is used only for apartment houses

PART FOUR: FEDERAL FAIR HOUSING AND LICENSE LAWS

86. Discouraging a prospective buyer from looking for housing in a particular area is considered:

a. redlining
b. blockbusting
c. steering
d. reprisal

87. A lender refuses to make a loan for a purchaser because the home is located in a certain neighborhood. This is an example of:

a. steering
b. redlining
c. blockbusting
d. legitimate procedure

88. Exemptions to the fair housing law include all of the following, EXCEPT:

a. discriminatory advertising is not used
b. a religious group sells retirement homes in a subdivision they developed only for their members
c. the rental of lodging that a private club owns and operates for other than commercial purposes
d. the rental of an apartment to a family with children

89. A broker lists a home on January 5 and on January 7 learns the taxes are three years delinquent and the property is scheduled to be sold at a sheriff sale. On January 20 the house is destroyed by fire. On January 30 the owner declares bankruptcy. When was the listing voided?

a. January 5
b. January 7
c. January 20
d. January 30

90. An agent must disclose to a potential buyer all, EXCEPT:

a. that the property is in a flood zone
b. that the home has a septic system and is not on public sewer
c. that the seller must sell quickly
d. that the air conditioner is not working

91. The primary reason for license law is:

a. to protect the public
b. to arbitrate commissions
c. to protect the brokers
d. to encourage continuing education programs for salespersons

92. Which of the following laws requires lenders to inform buyers and sellers of all fees and charges?

a. the Fair Housing Act
b. the Equal Credit Opportunity Act
c. the Real Estate Settlement Procedures Act
d. the Truth-in-Lending Act (Regulation Z)

93. Which of the following would NOT be an infraction of the license laws of most states?

a. intentionally using misleading advertising

b. acting as agent and undisclosed principal

c. acting for more than one party without the knowledge of both parties

d. all would be infractions

PART FIVE: BASIC TOOLS

94. A house cost $77,000. Gross rents are $525 per month, with a net return to the owner of $450 per month. What is the gross rent multiplier?

a. .07

b. .075

c. .08

d. 146.7

95. Mr. Tice obtains a $65,000 loan on his home. The principal and interest payments are based on a factor of $8.54 per $1,000. The loan is for 30 years at 9 percent. How much does Mr. Tice pay in total interest over the life of the loan?

a. $55,510

b. $66,612

c. $134,836

d. $199,836

96. A broker has a four-year contract to manage a rental unit for an investor. She is to receive 50 percent of the first month's rent and 5 percent of each remaining month. The rent is $600 per month. Over the term of the contract the broker earns:

a. $1,410

b. $1,440

c. $1,710

d. $2,880

97. A two-story house measures 48' × 25' and cost $70.00 per square foot to build. What is the construction cost of the house?

a. $84,000

b. $96,000

c. $168,000

d. $230,000

98. Mrs. Charlesworth purchases a home for $90,000. She paid $4,000 as earnest deposit and is obtaining an 80 percent loan. Costs include $250 for title insurance, $360 for homeowner insurance, recording fees of $60, and a tax prorate fee of $430. Mrs. Charlesworth will need to bring a check to closing in the amount of:

a. $14,679

b. $15,100

c. $19,100

d. $22,200

99. Three members of a partnership are investing $300,000 in a $1 million venture. If partner A invests $150,000 and partner B invests $100,000, what is the equity position of the third party?

a. ⅙

b. ¼

c. ⅓

d. ½

100. Susie Quinn lists her home for $170,000 with A-1 Realty. She agrees to pay a 6 percent commission on the gross sales price. The property sells for 15 percent below her asking price. The selling broker and the listing broker split the commission evenly; thus, selling broker Doe Realty receives 50 percent of the commission. He gives 20 percent to his salesperson for assisting him with the sale. Doe retains for himself:

a. $867

b. $950

c. $3,468

d. $4,335

Glossary

A

abandonment   Terminating rights and title to property.

abstract (of title)   A publicly available summary of the title changes on a specific property, beginning with the original land grant.

abstractor   A title searcher and preparer of abstracts.

acceleration clause   The clause in a mortgage that allows the lender to advance the time when the entire sum owed is due and payable.

accession   An addition to real estate acquired by accretion of land through soil deposits; acquiring fixtures by a tenant.

accretion   Addition to the land through natural causes, usually by a change in water flow.

acknowledgment   The act of going before an authorized officer or notary public and declaring a legal document to be one's voluntary act and deed.

acre   A parcel of land that measures 43,560 square feet, or 208.71 feet square.

actual eviction   The lessee is evicted by the lessor for failure to live up to the terms of the lease.

actual notice   Notice given; knowledge of a condition.

addendum   Additions to a contract that become a part of the document; sometimes referred to as "riders" to a contract.

adjustable rate mortgage (ARM)   The interest rate for a mortgage will be renegotiated at set times to adjust to current interest rates.

adjusted basis   The reduction or increase of the original basis of a property caused by expenses or improvement to the property.

administrator   Person appointed by the court to settle the estate of one who died without leaving a will.

ad valorem tax   An assessment on real property according to its market value.

adverse possession   Rightful owner loses land to occupant who has taken possession in a hostile, distinct, continuous, visible, and actual way for the statutory period.

affidavit   A written statement sworn to under oath.

agency   The legal relationship between principal and agent with the agent representing the principal in transactions with third parties.

agency by ratification   The express affirmation or implication whereby a principal agrees to be obligated by the acts of another who contends to act as an agent even though not employed as an agent for the principal.

agent   One who is authorized to represent another; the employee of the principal, that is, the broker.

agreement of sale   A written agreement between buyer and seller for the purchase and sale of real estate. The owner retains title until the sale is consummated.

air lot   A unit of space individually owned in a high-rise condominium.

air rights   The right to use or occupy air space above a designated property.

alienation   The transfer of real property from one person to another.

alienation clause (due on sale)   Permits lender to call balance of mortgage upon sale.

allodial system   The system of landownership that permits individuals to own land in fee simple title; used in the United States.

alluvion   Land gained along the shore of a waterway due to accretion.

amenities   Attractive features of a property that add to the pleasure of homeownership.

American Land Title Association (ALTA)   A national association of title insurance companies, abstractors, and attorneys specializing in real estate law.

amortization   The liquidation of a financial debt on the installment basis; equal payments are made over a period of time.

annexation   Attaching one object to another such as a city incorporating land near its legal boundaries.

annual percentage rate (APR)   The effective interest rate that must be revealed under the Truth-in-Lending Act, which includes the loan origination fee and the discount points.

annuity   A series of periodic payments; for example, money received in a long-term lease.

anticipation   The principle used in appraising stating that values may change which affect the future of a property, either to its detriment or advantage.

antitrust laws   Federal laws created to promote fair trade practices in the marketplace; prohibits price-fixing.

appraisal   An estimate of value made after analysis of the facts and data.

appreciation   The increased value of property due to economic or related causes, whether temporary or permanent.

appurtenance   Rights that pass with the title to real property, such as an easement over an adjoining land.

assemblage   Gathering together two or more parcels of land to make the whole more valuable.

assessed valuation   Value placed upon real estate for taxation purposes.

assessment   A charge against real property by a unit of government, as a tax levy or a special assessment.

assessor   A public official who evaluates property for the purpose of taxation.

assessor's map book   Prepared for county records from plats the developer of the land files with the county.

assignee   The person to whom an interest has been assigned, as in the sale of a mortgage.

assignment   The transfer of interests, rights, and title, as in the assignment of a mortgage, deed, lease, or option.

assignment of lease   Lessee transfers all rights held under the terms of the lease to another.

assignment of rent   The clause in a mortgage that permits the lender to collect rents directly from a tenant upon default of mortgage payments by mortgagor.

assignor   The person who makes an assignment to the assignee.

associate broker   An individual who holds a broker license but who works for another broker.

assumption of mortgage   The obligation of a purchaser to be personally liable for payment of an existing note secured by the mortgage she assumes.

attachment   Legal seizure of property to force payment of a debt.

attorney in fact   A person who has power of attorney for another, allowing him to execute legal documents.

attorney's opinion of title   An attorney examines the abstract of title and gives an opinion certifying the condition of the title.

avulsion   Loss of land due to sudden change in the flow of water.

B

balloon payment   A final payment on a note that is larger than previous payments and that repays the full debt.

bargain-and-sale deed   A deed that conveys property and in which warranties are implied by the grantor.

base and meridian   Imaginary lines used by surveyors in locating and establishing the boundaries of lands; used in the rectangular survey system.

baseline   One of the imaginary lines used in the U.S. government survey system. These lines act as points of beginning for land descriptions, running east-west and intersecting with the meridians that run north-south.

basis   The initial cost of the property; the financial interest of the owner.

before-and-after method   An appraisal technique used when a part of the property has been condemned, as under the right of eminent domain.

bench mark   Identification symbols on a permanent marker used in measuring land elevations.

beneficiary   A person designated to receive a benefit, as in a trust deed, the lender.

bequeath   To transfer personal property by will.

bequest   A gift of personal property by will.

biannual   Semiannual; twice a year.

biennial   Taking place once every two years.

bilateral contract   A contract involving promise on the part of both parties, as in a purchase agreement.

bill of sale   A written document that transfers title to personal property.

binder   A commitment; the temporary means to insure one's interest; or an agreement that covers a down payment on the purchase of real estate.

blanket mortgage   A single mortgage that covers two or more properties.

blend mortgage   The merging of a new mortgage with an existing loan, averaging the interest rate of both loans.

blockbusting   Inducing an owner, for profit, to sell or rent residential property by threatening the movement of a minority group into the neighborhood.

blue sky laws   State and federal laws that regulate the registration and sale of securities.

bond   A written obligation given as security on a mortgage.

breach of contract   A violation of the terms and conditions set forth in the contract.

broker   A person licensed to transact real estate negotiations for another.

brokerage   The occupation carried out by a broker; the bringing together of two parties in a real estate transaction.

buffer zone   A corridor of land that separates two unrelated land uses, such as residential from commercial.

building code   A group of ordinances that legislate building construction within a community; the controls provide for the health and safety of the public.

building line   The distance from the perimeter of a property within which no structure may be built; a setback.

building restrictions   Limit property use and outline size of structures as set forth in the deed covenants.

bulk transfer law   *See* Uniform Commercial Code.

bundle of rights The legal rights an owner of real estate acquires, such as the right of possession, use, enjoyment; including the right to sell, will, and mortgage.

business cycles Shifts in the economy ranging from prosperity to recession and back again.

buydown A cash payment to a lender that creates lower monthly mortgage payments for a period of time for the buyer.

buyer agency The buyer hires a real estate agent to represent his interests.

buyer brokerage An agency relationship between a buyer and a broker.

bylaws The rules and regulations of a condominium association that outline the covenants, restrictions, and conditions of the regime.

C

capacity of parties All parties must be legally capable of entering into a contract.

capitalization The process of converting future income into present capital value.

capitalization rate The rate of interest considered a reasonable return on an investment; the sum of interest rate and recapture rate.

cash flow The cash income or return on an investment after all expenses are met.

caveat emptor Let the buyer beware; the buyer examines the property and buys at her own risk.

censure To reprimand or express disapproval of the actions of a licensee.

census report A survey taken every 10 years in the United States to determine the population.

certificate of no defense An instrument executed by the mortgagor to the assignee upon the sale of the mortgage, revealing the amount owed. Also known as declaration of no set off and estoppel certificate.

certificate of title A written opinion by an attorney or title company that certifies the condition of the title.

Certified Property Manager (CPM) A designation awarded to candidates who fulfill requirements as outlined by the National Institute of Real Estate Management.

cession deed Given by a subdivider when he dedicates the streets in the subdivision to a governing body.

chain A unit of measurement used in land surveying—66 feet.

chain of title A record of the past owners of a property, beginning with the original land grant.

chattel Personal property, movable in nature.

check A measurement of land; 24 miles square containing 16 townships.

cite To quote as authority; refer to; to summon; to notify a person of legal proceedings against her and require her appearance in court.

Civil Rights Act of 1866 A federal law that prohibits racial discrimination in the sale or rental of real estate.

Civil Rights Act of 1964 The Federal Fair Housing law that expanded upon the 1866 Civil Rights Act by prohibiting discrimination based on race, color, religion, and national origin.

client Hires another to represent him.

closing Finalization of a sale, signing and transferring the title, and distributing the money.

closing costs An accounting of costs and credits to buyer and seller upon finalization of a sale.

closing statement A final settlement statement that lists the debits and credits of purchaser and seller; discloses all funds received and those necessary to close the sale.

cloud on title A claim or interest revealed by a title search that may affect the title.

cluster lots These lots are placed more closely together and are typically smaller than standard lots to allow room for open space in the development, referred to as "common areas."

codicil An addition to a will that may alter the provisions of the will.

co-insurance The insurer and the insured share the insurance risk; calculated on the policy amount and the percent of the actual insured value.

collateral Security given on debt.

color of title A title that appears to be good but upon the title search is found to be defective; indicates another may have some rights of ownership.

commingling Unauthorized mixing of personal funds with the funds of a client.

commission The fee earned by a real estate broker for services rendered in negotiating a real estate transaction.

common elements Land that is jointly used by all residents of an area, as in a condominium regime. Includes such items as pools, walkways, elevators, and clubhouses.

common law An unwritten law derived from general usage.

community property Property acquired by either the husband or wife during their marriage.

comparable market analysis The evaluating of recent sales of properties that are comparable to the subject property in an attempt to place a market value on the subject property.

comparison approach An appraisal method that compares the subject property to similar properties recently sold.

complainant A person who brings a complaint against another.

compound interest Interest computed on the original sum plus accrued interest.

concurrent ownership Property held by two or more parties, as in joint tenancy or tenancy in common.

condemnation The legal right under eminent domain to take private property for public use with just compensation to the owner.

condemnee The person whose property has been condemned (as by right of eminent domain).

condominium Individual ownership of a single unit in a multiunit structure or group of buildings, with joint ownership of common elements.

consideration The price or substance that induces a contract, the value one party is giving another; their mutual exchange of promises.

constant-payment mortgage A mortgage with the reduction of the loan in fixed monthly payments, a portion applying to repayment of principal and a portion to interest.

construction loan Interim financing used during construction of the building.

constructive eviction The breach of a covenant in a lease whereby the landlord failed to live up to terms of the lease.

constructive notice Legal notice given.

consummate Conclude; bring to completion, as in the finalization of a sale.

contract An agreement between competent parties to perform a legal act.

contribution The appraisal principle that states that the value of a component part is justified by what it adds to the overall value of the property, minus any costs.

conventional loan A loan that is not government-insured or guaranteed. The lender generally requires a larger down payment.

conveyance Written instrument used to transfer real estate.

cooperative Ownership of shares or stock in a corporation for which the owner obtains a proprietary lease.

co-ownership Two or more parties own an undivided interest in the same property.

corporation An entity created by law that holds the rights and privileges of a natural person.

corporeal Tangible real or personal property, as buildings and fences.

correction deed Corrects an error that has occurred in a deed, such as the misspelling of a name.

correction lines Placed by surveyors at 24-mile intervals to compensate for the earth's curvature.

correlation of value The appraiser's final step in reconciling the value by analyzing the three approaches to arrive at an estimate of value.

cost approach A method of appraisal based on replacement cost minus depreciation plus land value.

counteroffer An offer made after the original offer was rejected.

covenant Agreement or restriction found in real estate documents that regulates the use of real property.

credit Asset; something of worth or value; an amount given to a buyer or a seller on a closing statement.

credit report Relates the credit history of a borrower, a necessary step for the lender to verify the credit worthiness of the borrower since it reveals past performance in paying debts.

cul de sac A road with one outlet, usually ending in a circle.

curtesy The right of a husband to his wife's estate upon her death.

customer Purchaser of commodity; is not represented by an agent unless expressly stated.

D

datum The spot where the surveyor begins measurement of a specific parcel.

debenture An unsecured note given as evidence of a debt, secured only by the reputation of the maker.

debits Costs, charges against a seller or buyer in closing a sale.

declaration The document (master deed) that establishes the condominium regime and defines the individual units within the association.

dedication Real property given to the public by an individual, as land for a park.

deed A written instrument that transfers ownership of real property.

deed of reconveyance Transfers legal title from the trustee to the trustor upon payment in full of the debt.

deed of trust Deed that secures repayment of a debt, held by a trustee until the note is paid.

deed restriction Limits or restricts the use of real property.

default Failure to meet an obligation, as defaulting on mortgage.

defeasance clause The clause in a mortgage that allows the mortgagor the right to redeem her property upon payment of her obligation.

deficiency judgment Judgment against a debtor for the amount due the lender when the sale price is less than the funds received from a foreclosure sale.

demise The conveyance of an estate under lease.

Department of Housing and Urban Development. *See* HUD.

deposit   Earnest money tendered in conjunction with an offer to purchase real property.

depreciation   Loss of value from any cause; an expense deduction taken when depreciating the value of an income-producing investment for income tax purposes.

descent   Property of an intestate passes to heirs by descent.

developer   An individual who adds to the value of land by erecting improvements upon the land.

devise   A gift of real estate by will.

devisee   The person to whom a gift of real estate is given by will.

director's deed   Issued when a public agency sells surplus land.

direct reduction mortgage   A set amount of the principal is paid at stated periods. Payments will vary since the interest will be less with each payment.

disclosure statement   A written statement required under the Truth in Lending Act that the lender issuing the loan must give to the borrower.

discount points   A percentage charged by the lender to increase the yield of the loan. Each point represents 1 percent of the loan amount.

discrimination   The act of making a distinction in favor or against an individual on the basis of that individual's characteristics.

disintermediation   Funds that leave the savings and loans to go to the higher yielding markets.

distraint   Legal seizure of goods when rent is in arrears.

doctrine of prior appropriation   The first owner or user has the right to divert water for his use.

document   Formal certificate confirming facts or relaying instructions.

dominant estate   An estate that enjoys the rights of an easement through an adjoining estate known as the servient.

donee   A person who receives a gift.

donor   A person who makes a gift.

dower   The right of a wife in her husband's estate at the time of his death.

down zoning   The process of the local government reducing the allowable density for a tract of land, such as from office to apartment.

dual agency   The representation of a third party by an agent already in a principal-agent alliance, thereby creating two principals.

dual contract   Two contracts written with different terms and financing in an attempt to obtain a larger loan; a fraudulent practice.

durability   An economic characteristic of land that considers improvements made to land that are not as durable as the land.

duress   Unlawful constraint; insisting someone perform against his will.

E

earnest money   A deposit made by the purchaser at the time the purchase agreement is written to bind the contract.

easement   Interest in another's land, as a right of way.

easement appurtenance   An easement that runs with the land, such as a shared driveway.

easement by prescription   Rights to the land of another gained through continuous use.

easement in gross   An easement that does not run with the land and is personal in nature.

easement of necessity   Created by law when a landlocked party needs access to her property.

economic base   The stable base necessary for a community to grow and prosper; created by a diversity of resources, goods, and services supplied.

economic life   The period over which a property may be profitably utilized.

economic obsolescence   A loss in value caused by conditions external to the property and over which the owner has little or no control, such as a deteriorating neighborhood.

economic rent   The base rent justifiably payable in the open market.

egress   Exit; the right to leave a tract of land.

emblements   Crops that are produced annually through labor and industry; also referred to as *fructus industriales.*

eminent domain   Right of the government to take private property for public use upon just payment to the owner.

employee   A person hired by and who takes directions from another. The employee status requires the employer to withhold social security and income taxes from the employee's salary.

encroachment   The act of trespassing or intruding upon the domain of another, such as tree branches.

encumbrance   An interest in real property that diminishes value, such as a lien or mortgage.

environmental controls   Laws passed and supervised by the Environmental Protection Act (EPA) and other agencies for the care and protection of our environment.

Environmental Protection Agency (EPA)   An agency that recognizes and analyzes the impact that developments have upon the economic, social, and physical environment.

Equal Credit Opportunity Act (ECOA)   Prohibits lenders from discrimination on the basis of race, color, religion, national origin, sex, or marital status.

equitable interest   The difference between the value of the property and the amount owed.

equitable title   The right the purchaser has to obtain absolute title to a property as in a land contract or an accepted purchase agreement.

equity   The value of real property above the indebtedness.

equity of redemption   The right of an owner to reclaim property before it is sold in a mortgage foreclosure.

erosion   The gradual wearing away of land from natural causes.

errors and omission insurance   Insures for errors, mistakes, or liabilities in the practice of real estate.

escalator clause   The clause in a lease or mortgage allowing the holder to vary the interest rate.

escheat   Right of the sovereign state to succeed to the property of an intestate without heirs.

escrow agreement   An agreement held by a disinterested third party until terms and conditions of the instrument are met.

escrow closing   The closing of a sale by means of a third party not involved in the sale, such as a title company or an attorney.

estate   Rights in property and possessions; quantity of ownership.

estate at sufferance   A tenant who remains in possession after expiration of the lease; referred to as a holdover tenant.

estate at will   *See* tenancy at will.

estate for years   A leasehold interest extending for a definite period of time.

estate of inheritance   Permits owner of real property to distribute his estate by will.

estate from period to period   *See* periodic tenancy.

estoppel certificate   *See* certificate of no defense.

et al.   A term meaning "and others."

et ux   A term meaning "and wife."

eviction   Legal proceedings to recover possession of leased premises.

examination of title   Title opinion based on the abstract or title search.

exclusive agency   A listing that gives one brokerage firm the exclusive right to sell while the owner retains permission to sell without paying a commission.

exclusive right to sell   A listing that gives the brokerage firm the sole right to sell the property during the term of the agreement.

executed contract   The conditions of the contract have been completed.

execution   Dispossession of property; the terms of a contract have been completed.

executor   A male named in a will to carry out the terms of the will.

executor's deed   Issued by the executor of an estate; carries no warranties.

executory contract   A contract not completed, such as a purchase agreement.

executrix   A female named in a will to carry out the terms of the will.

expressed contract   Either oral or written, especially states obligations of parties and contract terms.

ex rel   A term meaning "examination relating to."

external obsolescence   Conditions that reduce the value of the property caused by forces outside of the property.

F

Fair Credit Reporting Act   Borrowers may see a summary of a report on their credit, and if errors are found, the borrower has a right to correct them.

Fair Housing Act of 1968   *See* Civil Rights Act of 1968.

Fair Housing Amendment Act of 1988   Prohibits discrimination based on handicap and familial status.

fair housing laws   Laws relating to the sale and rental of housing, ensuring equal opportunity for all people.

Federal Fair Housing Act of 1986   This law prohibits discrimination in the sale or rental of housing based on race, color, religion, national origin, or sex.

Federal Home Loan Mortgage Corporation (FHLMC)   Controlled by the Federal Home Loan Bank Board, the FHLMC was created to buy conventional mortgages from savings and loan institutions.

Federal Housing Administration (FHA)   A government agency that insures approved loans; created to provide homes with modest down payments.

Federal National Mortgage Association (FNMA)   Created to purchase loans from qualified lenders. It is the leader in the secondary mortgage market in defining standards for underwriting loans and appraising one- to four-family residential properties.

Federal Reserve Board   Its directors control the actual amount of money in circulation, thus determining the amount of money available to our economy.

fee   *See* fee simple.

fee conditional   A fee simple estate subject to the happening or nonhappening of a stated condition.

fee determinable   An estate in fee simple for a certain period of time, after which it reverts to the grantor or to his estate.

fee simple   The greatest and most complete interest in land, with absolute ownership in real property.

fee simple defeasible   Limits title holder to conditions as set forth by grantor.

fee simple to a condition subsequent   A defeasible (title), recognizable by words "but if".

fee tail   Specially named heirs are to inherit the estate. If such heirs are not available, the estate reverts to the grantor or to her heirs.

feudal system System whereby the governing body of the land retains ownership of real property.

fiduciary Involving confidence and trust, as in the relationship between agent and principal.

Financial Institutions Reform, Recovery and Enforcement Act (FIRREA) Title IX of this act provides for the regulation of appraisers in all federally related transactions.

finder's fee A fee paid to an individual for bringing together the parties to a transaction.

fixture Personal property that becomes real when permanently affixed to real property, such as a light fixture, oven and range, or bookcase.

foreclosure The legal process by which the mortgagee cuts out the equity of the defaulting mortgagor.

forfeiture Giving up something of value due to failure to perform (delinquent taxes or failure to make mortgage payments both constitute forfeiture).

fraud A statement made with the intention to deceive.

free enterprise Economic system that provides an open market that allows all people to participate, creating competition and a favorable business climate.

freehold estate An estate in real estate that conveys fee simple title, granting the maximum interests for an indefinite period.

front foot Measurement applied to the width of a lot at the street frontage. Residential lots are often priced by the front foot.

functional obsolescence A loss in value due to poor design or age that outmodes an improvement, such as a poor floor plan, outdated electrical wiring, or inadequate closet space.

G

gain A profit received from the sale of an asset; the difference between the adjusted basis and the net selling price.

general agency Authorized by the principal to transact all affairs for the principal.

general liens Liens that can be attached to all the property of the debtor.

general warranty deed A deed giving fee simple title; grantors guarantee title through themselves, their heirs, and their predecessors.

Government National Mortgage Association (GNMA) Dubbed "Ginnie Mae" and operated by HUD, this agency produces reduced interest rates for low-income purchasers and participates in the secondary mortgage market.

government survey system *See* rectangular survey system.

graduated lease A lease providing for a stipulated rent for an initial period, with increases or decreases at stated intervals.

graduated payment plan (GPM) Monthly payments begin at a lower than normal rate with increases periodically as the borrower's income increases.

Graduate REALTORS® Institute (GRI) A professional designation earned upon completion of prescribed courses of study offered through real estate boards.

grandfather rights A clause permitting continued use of a property that does not conform to present zoning; referred to as a nonconforming right.

grant The transfer of title to real property.

grant deed The grantor warrants the validity of the deed and guarantees that interest in the property has not been paid to another.

grantee The purchaser of real estate.

grantor The seller who conveys interest in real property.

gross income multiplier (GIM) A formula used to establish value of income property. Divide the sale price by the gross annual income of comparable properties to determine the multiplier.

gross lease A straight lease; the lessee pays only rent to the owner, as in an apartment lease.

gross national product (GNP) The value of all goods and services used and produced in this country.

gross rent multiplier Using comparable sales that are divided by the monthly rent and multiplying this factor by the actual rent of the subject property to arrive at a rough estimate of the property's market value.

ground lease Rent on unimproved land.

ground rent Earnings from unimproved land.

groundwater The water beneath the earth's surface.

growing equity mortgage (GEM) The monthly payment increases annually, with the increase applying to the principal.

guarantor The person giving a guarantee.

guardian The person appointed by the court to administer the affairs of a minor or other legally incapable persons.

guardian's deed Conveys title to the estate of a minor or other persons under guardianship.

H

habendum clause The "to have and hold" clause, which defines or limits the quantity of the estate the grantor is deeding to the grantee.

heir The person who may succeed or inherit real property even if there is no will.

heirs and assigns The term used in deeds and wills to provide that the recipient receives a fee simple estate in lands.

hereditament Inheritable property, real or personal.

highest and best use As determined at the time of appraisal, the use that will produce the greatest net return over a given period of time.

holdover tenant   A lessee who remains in possession of the premises after termination of the lease.

holographic will   An entirely handwritten will that is not witnessed but is signed by the testator.

home buyer's insurance   Insurance that covers a property owner against loss due to various hazards. The coverage depends upon type of policy purchased.

home equity loan   A line of credit using the equity in a home as collateral from which the homeowner may draw capital that is taken on a prearranged basis.

homeowners' association   Composed of property owners in a condominium regime; administrates the affairs of the common elements and facilities and carries out the rules that control the project.

homeowners' insurance   Insurance to cover major perils to the property; required by lenders as protection for the loan placed on the property and desired by the homeowner as protection on the investment.

homestead   An estate in land occupied as a residence; in some states a portion of the homestead is exempt from creditor's claims.

home warranty insurance   Offers the buyer coverage on the component parts of a house. Usually insures major appliances, electrical, plumbing, heating, and air conditioning.

homogeneous   Compatible; land use is regulated by zoning to create homogeneity and stabilize values.

Horizontal Property Act   Legislation that permits the creation of condominiums.

HUD   Federal Department of Housing and Urban Development. Involved in housing activities, such as rehabilitation loans, urban renewal, subsidy programs, and public housing. HUD has jurisdiction over FHA and GNMA.

hypothecate   To give as security, as when pledging a mortgage.

I

immobility   Incapable of being moved, fixed in location; an important physical characteristic of land.

implied contract   The act constitutes agreement to a contract.

improvement   Something that has been attached "on" the land such as a building or "to" the land such as a sidewalk or paved street thus adding value to the land.

inchoate   Incomplete; not finished, such as a wife's right to her husband's estate under dower rights.

income approach   An appraisal method whereby the net income of an income-producing property is divided by the capitalization rate to determine the property's value.

incorporeal rights   Intangible interest in real property, such as an easement.

indemnification   Reimbursement of loss.

indenture   A binding agreement in writing, such as a deed.

independent contractor   Individual employed but paid only upon production; no salary or normal fringe benefits are paid by the employer.

indestructible   A physical characteristic of land describing that land as a permanent commodity that cannot be destroyed.

index lease   Provides for rent adjustments that conform to changes in a price index.

industrial parks   Land zoned expressly for use by manufacturing and industrial plants.

inflation   A decline in the purchasing power of money, causing the price of a commodity to rise.

ingress   The right to enter land.

inheritance tax   A tax imposed by the state on the heirs to the property of a decedent.

in lieu of   Instead of; in place of.

installment sale   A means of selling real estate and postponing the capital gains tax by extending the payment over several years and paying the taxes on a pro-rata basis.

instrument   A written document capable of being recorded.

intangible property   Property that is not visible, such as the "good will" of a business.

interest   A percentage charged for the use of a principal sum.

interim financing   Temporary financing, such as a construction loan.

intestate   Person who dies without leaving a will.

involuntary lien   A lien placed against a property without the owner's consent, such as taxes, special assessments, mechanics' liens, or federal tax liens.

irrevocable   Unalterable; not changeable.

J

joint tenancy   Ownership by two or more persons with rights of survivorship.

joint venture   The operation of a single business by two or more people in an effort to raise capital and spread the risk; sometimes referred to as a general partnership.

judgment   A court decree to determine a settlement.

judgment lien   A charge upon the lands of a debtor resulting from a court decree.

junior mortgage   A mortgage subordinate to an existing or subsequent lien.

K

key lot   A lot that has one side adjoining the rear of another lot, usually on a corner. Key lots are valued for their locations.

L

laches A delay in asserting one's legal rights, causing forfeiture of these rights.

land contract Seller finances purchaser and retains title; purchaser obtains equitable title.

landmark A monument or marker that establishes a certain spot, such as the boundary of a property.

latent defect A material defect that is hidden from view, such as defective plumbing.

lawful object The contract itself must be for a lawful purpose.

lease A contract giving the lessee (tenant) the right to use property owned by the lessor (landlord) for a stated period of time and for a specific purpose.

leasehold The interest a lessee has in a lease.

lease option A clause in a lease that affords the lessee first right to purchase the property.

lease purchase Agreement between a lessee and lessor whereby a portion of the rent applies to the purchase price.

legal description The description of property boundaries recognized by law.

legal life estate An interest in real estate created by law such as dower, curtesy, and homestead rights.

lessee The tenant or person given use of a property under a lease contract.

less than freehold estate *See* nonfreehold estate.

lessor The owner of property leased to another. Holder has leasehold rights in real property.

leverage The investor takes the largest loan possible for the longest period of time with the smallest down payment; the use of other people's money (OPM) to finance the bulk of an investment.

license A personal privilege or right that is nontransferable.

license law Authority given through the laws enacted by the state to regulate the actions of salespeople and brokers.

lien A charge or claim against a debtor's property.

lien theory Deed of trust is a security for the debt, with the trustor the title holder.

lien waiver An affidavit signed by the sellers attesting to the fact that there are no unpaid debts against the property.

life estate An interest in real estate limited to the lifetime of the life tenant.

life tenant The holder of a life estate; ceases to exist upon death of the holder.

limited common area Common elements that are for the exclusive use of certain residents, such as parking stalls and storage units.

limited partnership A group of passive investors with a sponsor or general partner who manages the investment portfolio.

link In land measurements, a link equals 7.9 inches.

liquidity Being able to convert a product into cash in a minimum time frame for a value close to its actual worth.

lis pendens Notice of a suit pending that could affect ownership of land.

listing contract The contract between the broker and the principal to negotiate the sale of the principal's property.

littoral rights Rights of a landowner who borders a lake to use the water.

livery of seizin Transfer of possession.

loan commitment A loan approval by the lender of the loan.

loan-to-value ratio (LTV) The ratio of a mortgage to the appraised value of a property.

lot A plot of land with fixed boundaries.

lot and block number system Location of lots within a subdivision.

M

majority The age at which a person is legally entitled to handle her affairs.

management budget A financial plan prepared by the manager that includes an annual budget for operating the property.

management contract A contract detailing responsibilities of the owner and the manager of a property.

marginal land Land that barely repays the cost of production.

marketable title A title without defect.

market price The price paid for a property.

market value The highest price for which the willing seller will sell and the willing buyer will buy.

master deed The deed that is recorded and is the principal document that conveys ownership of the overall condominium regime.

master plan A comprehensive plan to develop a community's future expansion; serves as a guideline for principal expenditures.

mechanic's lien The right of a contractor to place a lien against property for work completed but not paid for.

meeting of minds An agreement on specified subject matter, such as a seller accepting the offer of a buyer.

meridian Used in the government rectangular survey system; lines that run north and south across the country.

metes and bounds Measurements and boundaries that describe a property.

mile A measurement of distance; 5,280 feet.

mill levy A tax rate expressed in one tenth of one cent per one dollar of assessed valuation.

minor A person not of legal age.

misrepresentation A misstatement of a material fact that was relied upon by an innocent party.

monument A stone or fixed object used to establish a land boundary.

monument survey Description of a property in terms of natural and artificial boundaries.

moratorium The legal period of delay for meeting a financial obligation.

mortgage The pledge that secures the lender's investment and that accompanies the note.

mortgage-backed security (MBS) Securities sold to investors that are "backed" by a mortgage, thus creating more funds available to lenders for loans.

mortgage banker Originates mortgages and subsequently sells the loans to long-term investors through the secondary mortgage market; retains servicing of the loans.

mortgage broker Person or firm acting as an intermediary between borrower and lender; does not service the loan.

mortgage correspondent Agent for a lender who places a loan for a borrower.

mortgagee The lender or holder of the mortgage.

mortgagee in possession The mortgagee becomes in possession of a property when the mortgagor defaults on the note, permitting the lender to collect rents from tenant.

mortgage lender Lending institution that makes and services mortgage loans.

mortgagor The debtor or borrower; the owner of property that is used as security for a mortgage.

multiple listing service (MLS) A group of brokers that pools listings and cooperates to sell any listing of a member firm.

N

National Association of REALTORS® (NAR) A national trade organization that promotes fair and ethical practices among its members. All members are entitled to use the trademark REALTOR®.

negative amortization The monthly payment is less than needed to reduce the mortgage debt and thus results in an increase in the original indebtedness.

negative cash flow Occurs when an investment yields less than the expenses, causing a negative cash return to the investor.

negotiable instrument A promissory note that, upon meeting certain legal requirements, may be circulated freely in commerce.

negotiate To arrange for or to transact business, such as negotiating the sale of a property.

neighborhood shopping center Several buildings grouped together with 15 or more retail bays; easily accessible to the nearby neighborhood.

net lease A lease whereby the lessee assumes some or all of the expenses normally paid by the owner.

net listing Property listing at an agreed-upon net price that the seller wishes to receive with any excess going to the agent as commission.

nonconforming use A use in violation of present zoning laws but permitted because the usage was in effect before the law. The user is said to have "grandfather rights."

nonfreehold estate Also known as less than freehold estates, the holder has a leasehold interest under the terms of the lease.

nonfungible Cannot substitute one parcel of real property for another; no two are alike.

nonhomogeneous Characteristic of real property; no two parcels are alike.

notary public Lawfully authorized official who attests to and certifies documents by his hand and official seal.

note A written promise to pay a certain sum of money within a specified time.

notice to quit A notice to a tenant to vacate the premises.

novation The substitution of a new contract for an existing contract, or new parties to an obligation.

O

obsolescence Lessening in value due to functional, economic, or physical conditions.

offer and acceptance A promise by the purchaser to complete the terms of the contract upon acceptance by the seller.

offeree Owner of property.

offeror Buyer who "offers" to purchase.

office parks Development of a parcel of land for office buildings, usually in suburban areas.

open-end mortgage A mortgage that allows the mortgagor to borrow additional funds and extend the amount of the loan without changing the terms of the mortgage.

open listing A nonexclusive listing, generally oral, available for sale to any number of brokers with a commission paid to the selling firm.

open mortgage A mortgage overdue and up for payment.

opinion of title A legal opinion to determine if title is clear and marketable.

option The right to buy within a specified time.

option clause A clause that grants the right to buy for a limited time.

ordinance A city or county legislative enactment, such as a zoning law.

origination fee A finance charge made by the lending institution to the borrower that covers costs of preparing the loan.

ostensible agency An agency that occurs through the dependence of information from a third party.

owner's association Composed of property owners who group together to administrate the affairs of the neighborhood.

ownership The right to possess and use property to the exclusion of all others.

ownership cycle The sequence of home purchases made by individuals to meet their evolving needs and desires.

P

package mortgage A mortgage that especially designates all personal property included in the sale.

panic peddling Creating unrest in a neighborhood by placing fear in the minds of property owners that the introduction of minorities in or near the area will lessen property values.

parol evidence rule Oral evidence; not in writing and cannot change the terms of the written document.

partition A court action for legal division of real estate by owners in order to sever their ownership.

partnership Two or more parties join together in an enterprise.

party wall A common partition between adjoining properties for use by both parties.

passive income Income derived solely from an investment of money in an enterprise that is managed by another, such as a limited partnership.

patent A land grant by the U.S. government to an individual.

patent defect A material defect that can be seen upon inspection.

percentage lease A lease whereby the lessee pays a flat sum plus a percentage of the volume of business transacted on the premises.

percolating water Underground water that is sufficient enough to be tapped for a well.

periodic tenancy A lease that continues from period to period with no set termination date.

personal property Movable items not affixed to real property, such as chattels.

personalty Chattel; personal property not permanently affixed to the real property.

physical depreciation Caused by normal wear and tear through use and the action of the natural elements.

PITI The principal, interest, taxes, and insurance paid in monthly installments on an amortized loan.

planned unit development (PUD) Community planned to allow better use of land.

plat A map of a certain area of land.

plat book A public record of information concerning land.

pledge Security held by the lender until a debt is paid off.

plottage The assembling of several parcels of land into one ownership.

point of beginning (POB) The starting point used in the metes and bounds description. It is marked at one corner of the property, and the description must return to this point of beginning.

points *See* discount points.

police power Right of the government to pass legislation protecting the safety and welfare of the public.

positive cash flow An investment produces a net return over and above expenses.

power of attorney A written instrument authorizing one person to act for another.

prepaids Items paid in advance, such as taxes and insurance that are paid monthly with the principal and interest payment.

prepayment clause A mortgage clause stating the penalty for payment of the mortgage before the actual due date.

prescription Rights in property acquired through continuous use.

principal The property owner who employs an agent to sell her property; also denotes money as the principal amount on a loan.

principal meridian A survey line running due north and south, as established by the rectangular system of survey.

prior appropriation A water use acknowledged in many western states that is based on the scarcity of water and allows the first owner to have priority over all subsequent owners.

private mortgage insurance (PMI) Insurance on conventional loans that require less than a 20 percent down payment.

profit a prendre The right to remove something for profit from another's land such as minerals, oil, or timber.

promissory note The note signed by the mortgagor that promises repayment of the debt.

property Owner's interest and rights in his property to the exclusion of all others; the land and anything permanently attached, such as buildings, fences, and fixtures.

property management A specialized branch of the real estate business that involves overseeing leasing, managing, and maintenance of another's property.

proprietary lease The right to occupy a cooperative unit by the shareholder.

prorations The dividing of expenses and credits between buyer and seller.

prospectus Preliminary information on an enterprise that is required by the SEC to be given, in advance, to prospective purchasers of securities.

public records   Publicly available notice of matter concerning land.

public trustee   A disinterested third party who serves as an escrow agent under the terms of an agreement.

purchase agreement   An offer to purchase that becomes a binding contract when accepted by the owner of the property.

purchase-money mortgage   A mortgage carried by the seller to secure an unpaid balance of the purchase price.

Q

qualified fee   A fee simple estate with limitations set by the grantor.

quantity survey method   The totaling of all the component parts in the construction plus adding labor costs to arrive at an exact cost of the total project.

quiet enjoyment   The right to use property without disruption by the grantor or the landlord.

quiet title action   Action in court to either establish title or to remove a cloud on a title.

quitclaim deed   A deed containing no warranties, in which the grantor relinquishes any claims or rights she may have.

quit notice   Notice given to a tenant to vacate the premises.

quorum   The minimum number of members needed at any official meeting in order to conduct business (usually more than half).

R

range   Used in the government rectangular survey system; comprises a strip of land every six miles east and west of the principal meridian.

real estate   Land and all improvements that are "on" or permanently attached and any improvements "to" the land, such as sidewalks and sewers.

real estate commission   The regulatory body that governs the actions of licensees.

Real Estate Investment Trust (REIT)   Individuals pool their funds to purchase shares in large investment properties.

Real Estate Settlement Procedures Act (RESPA)   An act passed by Congress in 1974 that requires lenders to provide full disclosure of closing costs to buyer and seller when the loan is federally related.

real property   All the rights and privileges the owner of real estate possesses; the "bundle of rights" one has.

Realtist   A member of a group of real estate brokers whose organization is made up of minority brokers.

REALTOR®   A coined trade name that refers to members who belong to the National Association of REALTORS®.

reappraisal lease   A clause in a long-term lease that requires periodic appraisals to determine the economic rent.

receiver   Recipient; a person appointed under a statute to wind up a business.

reciprocal license   The ability of a licensee to obtain a license in another state, depending on that state's requirements.

recission   To revert to the original conditions.

recordation   The act of giving public notice by recording a legal document.

rectangular system   The government method of surveying land based on imaginary lines of longitude running north and south called meridians and east-west latitude lines called base lines.

redemption   The act of repurchasing real property after the mortgage is in default.

redlining   The refusal of lenders to make mortgage loans in specific neighborhoods.

reduction certificate   A document showing the balance due on a mortgage at the time the transaction is closed.

reformation   Action taken to correct a mistake in a deed or other instrument.

regional center   A large complex housing several national retail stores with a broad mix of shops that draw customers from a great distance.

Regulation Z   Implements the truth-in-lending law through the Federal Reserve Board.

reliction   The gradual increase of land due to receding waters.

remainder estate   What is left from a life estate.

remainderman   The person who receives an estate after the termination of a life estate.

rent   The cost of using the real estate of another; the tenant pays rent to the landlord.

replacement cost   The present cost of reconstructing a new building having the same utility value as the old.

reproduction cost   The present cost of reproducing an exact replica of the old building.

rescind   Revoke, annul, or cancel (as a contract).

reserves   Funds impounded by the lender to pay for taxes and insurance when they become due.

resident manager   Person employed to manage an apartment complex and who lives on the premises.

residential property management   The business of managing the residential property of others.

residual   Remainder, as the residual value of land after the economic life of the building is over.

Resolution Trust Corporation (RTC)   A federal agency formed to liquidate insolvent savings and loans and banks.

respondent   A person against whom a complaint is made.

restrictive covenant   A condition limiting the use of land, as stated in a deed.

reverse annuity mortgage   The homeowner receives income from the equity in the home.

reversion A future interest in real estate created by a grantor that provides for the property to revert to the grantor upon expiration of the interest.

reversionary interest The future interest that reverts to a grantor or his heirs.

revocation The rescinding of a contract; such as a buyer nullifying an offer to purchase. Also, the power of a real estate commission to take away a license for failure to conform to the license laws of that state.

right of first refusal Gives a person first opportunity to buy or lease.

right of redemption The period within which a debtor may redeem his property after default.

right of survivorship The legal right to obtain ownership of the decedent's property provided for in joint tenancy and tenancy in the entirety.

right of way An easement through the land of another.

riparian rights Rights of a landowner to use waters of an adjacent stream or lake.

rollover mortgage A renegotiable mortgage that calls for changes in interest rate at set intervals.

S

sale-leaseback The owner sells her property with the stipulation that she may lease it back from the new owner.

sales comparison approach *See* comparison approach.

salesperson One who is licensed by a state to render services authorized by a broker who holds a salesperson's license.

salvage value The value that remains after the useful life is exhausted, usually 5 to 10 percent of the property's depreciable basis.

sandwich lease A leasehold interest involving a lessor, lessee, and sublessee.

satisfaction piece An instrument that is recorded to announce payment of the debt; a mortgage release.

Savings Association Insurance Fund (SAIF) Replaces the FSLIC fund that became insolvent due to failed thrifts. Insures savings of insured depositors' funds.

scarcity In short supply in comparison to demand.

sea level Zero feet in altitude; base from which altitude measurements begin.

secondary mortgage market The sale of existing mortgages by the primary lender to the secondary mortgage market lenders, thus affording greater liquidity of mortgages.

second mortgage A mortgage second in priority to a first mortgage; pledges the owner's equity in the property.

section division of land; 640 acres or one square mile.

Securities and Exchange Commission (SEC) Established to monitor the sale of securities.

security deposit Lessor requires a deposit that is refundable at expiration of the lease if the property has not been damaged.

servient estate An estate that includes an easement existing in favor of the dominant estate.

setback The distance that zoning regulations require a structure to be located from the front, rear, and side property lines.

settlement closing The broker prorates and adjusts the credits and costs for the buyer and seller upon closing the transaction.

severable Capable of being divided.

severalty Sole ownership by one person.

shared appreciation mortgage (SAM) The mortgagee participates in any appreciation of the property in exchange for a fixed, below-market interest rate.

sheriff's deed Transfers property sold at a public sale; usually the result of a foreclosure.

simple interest Interest paid on the declining balance of a loan; thus the interest payments lower as the principal amount is paid off.

site The location of a particular parcel of land.

situs The location or site of a real property; value is partially based on a property's situs.

sky lease A lease with the right to occupy the space of another above the leased real estate.

special agent Usually limited to transacting a single business affair, such as the relationship between a brokerage firm and a principal.

special assessment A tax levied against property for the cost of a public improvement.

special warranty deed A deed wherein grantors guarantee title through themselves and their heirs but not their predecessors.

specific agency Agent is given right to act for principal for one express purpose.

specific lien Affects only the property that it is placed against.

specific performance A remedy in a court of equity to carry out the terms of a contract.

spot zoning Land use in violation of a zoning ordinance, differing from current usage of surrounding property.

statute A law passed by the legislative body of government.

statute of frauds State laws that require certain contracts to be in writing in order to be enforceable.

steering Limiting the choice of buyers or renters of housing by channeling them to certain neighborhoods.

strawman Person who purchases for another unidentified buyer; used when confidentiality is important.

strip center A building consisting of a number of units (bays) conveniently located near main arteries.

subagent An agent who may assist the appointed agent in the performance of an assignment; often created in the multiple listing services used by real estate brokers.

subdivider A person who divides undeveloped land into smaller lots for the purpose of development.

subdivision A parcel of land subdivided into individual lots.

sublet Lessee retains lease but rents a portion of the premises to a sublessee.

subordination clause Clause found in a mortgage or lease that states the rights of the holder are secondary to any existing or subsequent encumbrance.

subpoena A legal summons requiring court appearance to give testimony.

subrogation Substituting one person for another regarding a claim, as in a loan assumption.

subsurface right The right to use the land beneath the surface of the earth, such as for mining or digging a well.

summons Notification to appear in court.

surety Legal liability for another's debt.

surface right The right to use the surface of the land.

surrender and acceptance The cancellation of a lease by mutual consent of the lessee and lessor.

survey The precise measuring of the boundaries of a property from which the legal description is derived.

suspension Placing a license on temporary retention, thus forbidding the licensee to perform the services of a salesperson or broker.

syndication A group of people who pool their funds to invest in a common enterprise.

T

tacking The legal right that permits a person to add or "tack" their time of possession on to a past claimant's adverse possession right.

tax assessment A levy against property to pay for a public improvement that benefits the real estate.

tax deed Real property sold at a public sale due to delinquent taxes.

tax free exchange A method of deferring capital gains taxes by exchanging one property for another.

tax participation clause A lease clause whereby the tenant assumes a proportionate share of an increase in property taxes.

tax sale The sale of property for nonpayment of taxes.

tax shelter A phrase used to describe advantages of real estate investments, such as deductions for taxes, interest, and depreciation, resulting in the postponement, reduction, or elimination of income tax.

temporary buydown A mortgage differential allowance program that allows the seller to place funds with the lender to reduce the borrower's payments for the first two to three years.

tenancy at sufferance The tenant remains in possession of the leased premises after expiration of the lease.

tenancy at will Use of the property at the will of the landlord. Either party can terminate the lease at any time since there is no set termination date.

tenancy by the entireties Ownership by husband and wife with both spouses sharing an equal, undivided interest in the whole property.

tenancy for years A leasehold estate that grants the lessee use for a specified period of time.

tenancy in common An interest in real estate held by two or more persons each having equal rights of possession but without right of survivorship.

tenant The lessee; a person given the right to use real estate owned by another.

tender To fulfill; to offer to perform as the terms of a contract state.

term mortgage Short duration loans that are not amortized and are used for brief periods of time, such as construction loans.

testate A person who dies leaving a will that designates the distribution of his estate.

testator A person who leaves a will or who has died testate.

time-share Joint ownership of a single unit by several purchasers that gives use for a specified time.

title Evidence of ownership in real estate.

title insurance Insures the holder of the policy against defects in the title.

title search An examination of public records to establish ownership of real estate and to determine condition of the title.

title theory Mortgagee has legal title to the property; as with a trust deed, the mortgagor acquires equitable title.

Torrens System The system of land registration whereby a certificate of title is issued.

tort An actionable wrong, a violation of a legal right.

townhouse A form of construction generally in a clustered group which is usually two stories with common walls between the units.

township A parcel of land that contains 36 sections and that is 6 miles square.

trade fixture Personal property that has been affixed to leased property by a tenant who uses it in his business.

transfer tax A charge levied by some states upon real estate when it is sold; based on the property value.

trust account A non-interest-bearing account in which the real estate broker places all money entrusted to her by or on behalf of the principal and the customer.

trust deed   A deed held in trust by a third party until the obligation is paid; it is used to mortgage land, or to place a lien upon it.

trustee   A third party to a trust deed: the one who holds the trust deed.

trustor   The owner of the property under a trust deed.

truth-in-lending law   A federal law requiring disclosure of costs involved in obtaining a loan.

U

underwriter   The person who reviews a loan application and makes recommendation to the loan committee concerning the risk and desirability of making the loan.

unenforceable contract   A contract that may appear valid but is unenforceable in a court of law.

Uniform Commercial Code (UCC)   Requires the recording of personal property that is sold for a price in excess of $500 so that the creditor may file a financial statement and reclaim the property if the debtor defaults.

Uniform Landlord/Tenant Act   Regulates the landlord-tenant relationship on residential leases.

unilateral contract   A promise on the part of one party to perform a specific act according to the contract, as in an option or a listing contract.

unit conversions   The converting of apartments to condominium units.

United States government land survey   Also known as a rectangular land survey; a method of land description.

unit-in-place cost approach method   An appraisal technique that calculates the cost of all the component parts to be used in the construction to arrive at the value.

universal agency   Empowered to perform any act that can be lawfully authorized to an agent; usually established by power of authority.

Upfront Mortgage Insurance Premium (UFMIP)   A mortgage insurance premium paid at the time an FHA loan is originated.

useful life   The economic life of an improvement; period of time over which it can be profitably utilized.

usury   The act of charging in excess of the legal interest rate.

V

vacation license   A right to occupy a unit in a condominium regime for a specified period of time without fee title; prepaid lodging.

valid contract   A contract that complies with the law and is legally sufficient and enforceable.

VA loans   Guaranteed by the Department of Veterans Affairs and available for veterans who qualify under the law.

valuation   The estimated worth of a property.

variable rate mortgage   Allows the lender to increase or decrease the interest rate within the perimeters set down in the mortgage rate.

variance   Permission given to an individual to use land in a way that varies from current zoning laws when compliance with the zoning ordinance would create an undue hardship.

vendee   The purchaser of real property who receives equity title under the terms of a land contract.

vendor   The seller of real property who retains title in his name under terms of a land contract.

verify   To substantiate under oath.

vested   With an interest in; owned as a right in real property.

voidable contract   A contract that can be terminated even though it appears valid, such as a contract with a minor that can be rescinded by the minor.

void contract   A contract entered into for illegal purposes.

W

waiver   The voluntary surrender of rights or claims.

warranty deed   The grantor guarantees that the title is good, free and clear of all liens and encumbrances.

words of conveyance   Words in a deed that expressly grant the title to the grantee.

wraparound mortgage   Lenders refinance a property by lending an amount more than the existing mortgage, leaving the first mortgage in place. The complete package is considered as one loan, with the mortgagee of the wrap paying the obligation to the first mortgage.

Z

zero lot line   The placing of a structure on the lot line without being required to have a setback from the perimeter of the property.

zoning   The regulation over the use of land within a specific municipality.

Answer Key

CHAPTER 2
1. a
2. d
3. b
4. b
5. c
6. d
7. d
8. d
9. d
10. a
11. b
12. d
13. c
14. a
15. b
16. b
17. d
18. c
19. c
20. d

CHAPTER 3
1. d
2. c
3. d
4. a
5. d
6. c
7. c
8. a
9. c
10. a   T10N, R2W
    b   T10N, R1E
    c   T8N, R2W
    d   T8N, R1E
11. b
12. d
13. a   40 acres
    b   10 acres
    c   20 acres
    d   80 acres
14. b
15. c
16. b
17. a
18. b

CHAPTER 4
1. b
2. b
3. d
4. c
5. d
6. c
7. b
8. a
9. b
10. c
11. c
12. b
13. b
14. a
15. d
16. d
17. d
18. b
19. a
20. a
21. c
22. c
23. b
24. d

CHAPTER 5
1. d
2. c
3. a
4. a
5. c
6. b
7. a
8. c
9. c
10. b
11. d
12. a
13. b
14. d
15. c

CHAPTER 6
1. a
2. a
3. b
4. b
5. a
6. b
7. b
8. b
9. a
10. c
11. a
12. a
13. a
14. b
15. b
16. a
17. c
18. d
19. c
20. a
21. d
22. b
23. b
24. b
25. b

CHAPTER 7
1. c
2. c
3. d
4. c
5. c
6. a
7. b
8. b
9. d
10. a
11. a
12. a
13. d
14. b
15. a
16. d
17. b
18. a
19. c
20. d
21. c

CHAPTER 8

1. c
2. d
3. b
4. d
5. c
6. c
7. a
8. c
9. d
10. b
11. b
12. a
13. b
14. c
15. a
16. d
17. c
18. a
19. b
20. c
21. d
22. a

CHAPTER 9

1. c
2. a
3. a
4. b
5. c
6. b
7. b
8. a
9. a
10. d
11. b
$90,000 × .20 down payment = $18,000
$90,000 − $18,000 = $72,000 loan
$72,000 × 7% = $5,040 annual interest
$5,040 ÷ 12 months = $420.00 interest paid
12. b
20 years × 12 monthly payments = 240 payments
$558.72 × 240 = $134,092.80 principal and interest

$134,092.80 − $72,000.00 = $62,092.80 interest
13. b
14. b
15. c
16. c
17. c
18. d
19. c
20. b
21. b
$45,000 × 8% = $3,600 annual interest
$3,600 ÷ 12 months = $300 interest
$330.30 − $300 = $30.30 against principal reduction
$45,000 − $30.30 = $44,969.70
22. b
23. a
24. a
25. b

CHAPTER 10

1. b
2. a
3. c
4. c
5. b
6. a
7. a
8. d
9. d
10. c
11. a
12. a
13. a
14. d
15. a
16. c
17. b
18. c
19. a
20. b

CHAPTER 11

1. b
2. a
3. a
4. b
5. a
6. d
7. d
8. b
9. b
10. c
11. d
12. d
13. c
14. a
15. b
16. c

CHAPTER 12

1. a
2. b
3. d
4. b
5. a
6. c
7. b
8. d
9. b
10. c
11. c
12. a
13. c
14. d
15. d
16. c
17. c
18. a
19. a
20. a

CHAPTER 13

1. d
2. b
3. d
4. a
5. d
6. c
7. b
8. b
9. b
10. d

Answer to Closing Statement

BUYER

	Debit	Credit
Purchase price	$90,695.00	
Loan		$72,600.00
Insurance policy	350.00	
Loan discount	726.00	
Tax prorate 8/10-12/31 4 mos, 20 days	513.33	
Record deed	6.00	
Title insurance	430.00	
Balance due		$20,120.33
Total	$92,720.33	$92,720.33

SELLER

	Debit	Credit
Selling price		$90,695.00
Loan balance	$58,548.00	
Discount point 1%	726.00	
Tax prorate		513.33
Mortgage release	7.00	
Commission	6,348.65	
Proceeds due to seller	$25,578.68	
Total	$91,208.33	$91,208.33

CHAPTER 14

1. c
2. b
3. d
4. c
5. c
6. d
7. b
8. b
9. c
10. a
11. a
12. c
13. d
14. c
15. a
16. b
17. d
18. b

CHAPTER 15

1. c
2. b
3. a
4. b
5. a
6. c
7. d
8. b
9. d
10. d
11. b
12. b
13. a
14. d
15. b
16. c
17. c
18. d
19. a
20. a
21. c
22. c
23. d
24. c
25. d

CHAPTER 16

1. b
2. a
3. c
4. d
5. c
6. b
7. d
8. b
9. a
10. d
11. a
12. c
13. c
14. a
15. b
16. b
17. b
18. c
19. b
20. b
21. d

CHAPTER 17

1. b
2. a
3. b
4. a
5. c
6. a
7. a
8. c
9. a
10. a
11. a
12. d
13. c
14. d

CHAPTER 18

1. d
2. a
3. d
4. a
5. c
6. c
7. a
8. a
9. d
10. a
11. b
12. d
13. d
14. a
15. c
16. d
17. a
18. c
19. d
20. c
21. d
22. c
23. a
24. d
25. c

CHAPTER 19

1. c $200' \times 170' = 34,000$ sq. ft.
$20 \times 20 = 400$ sq. ft. $\div 2 = 200$ sq. ft.
$34,000$ sq. ft. $- 200$ sq. ft. $= 33,800$ sq. ft.

2. b $2.5 \times 10 = 25\%$ depreciation
$100\% - 25\% = 75\%$
$12,500 \div .75 = \$16,666$

3. a $\$11,000 \times .30 = \$3,300$
$\$3,300 \times .012$ mills $= \$39.60$
(*approximate* tax is \$40.00)

4. c $\$300 \div 20,000 = .015$ mill levy
$\$40,000 \times .015 = \$600$

5. b 360 acres $\times \$150 = \$54,000$
$\$25,000 \times .05 = \$1,250$
$\$20,000 \times .025 = \$500$
$9,000 \times .01 = \$90$
Total commission $= \$1,840$
Half to Morris's firm $= \$920$
Half of \$920 to Mr. Lewis $= \$460$

6. a $900' \times 900' = 810,000$ sq. ft.

$300 \times 90 = 27,000$ sq. ft.
$810,000 \div 27,000 = \frac{1}{30}$

7. d 1 foot $= \frac{1}{8}$, or 8 ft. $= 1$ inch
$8 \times 5\frac{3}{4} = 46$
$8 \times 4\frac{1}{2} = 36$
area $= 46 \times 36$

8. b   July 15 through December 31 $= 5\frac{1}{2}$
months unused $\$546 + \$102 = \$648$
$\div 12$ months $= \$54$ per month $\$54 \times$
$5\frac{1}{2}$ months $= \$297$

9. c   June 15 through December 31 $= 6\frac{1}{2}$
months unused $660 \div 12 = \$55$ month
$\times 6\frac{1}{2}$ months $= \$357.50$

10. b $\$275 \times 10 = \$2,750$ per month $\times 12$
months $= \$33,000$ annual rent
$\$250 \times 12 = \$3,000$ per month $\times 12$
months $= \$36,000$ annual rent
$\$33,000 + \$36,000 = \$69,000 \times 15\%$
vacancy $= \$10,350$
$\$69,000 - \$10,350 = \$58,650 - \$6,789$
(expenses) $= \$51,861$

$51,861 ÷ 10% = $518,610

11. d $62,000 × .80 = $49,600 loan × .04 =
$1,984.00 (discount points)
$1,984.00 + $2,500 = $4,484
$62,000 − $49,600 = $12,400 down
payment plus $4,484 = $16,884 total

12. d $350 + $12,500 + $7,000 = $19,850 ÷
.94 = $21,117.02

13. c 25% depreciation × $300,000 =
$75,000
$300,000 − $75,000 = $225,000 +
$51,000 = $276,000

14. d 120′ × 80′ = 9,600 sq. ft. × .06 =
$576.00

15. d $50,000 × 1.10 = $55.00

16. c 19,000 × .12 = 2,280 ÷ = $190.00
interest per month
$209.38 − $190 = $19.38 toward princi-
pal
19,000 − 19.38 = 18,980.62 × 12 =
$2,268.74 ÷ 12 mos. = $189.06

17. b 20 years × 12 = 240 months × $209.38
= $50,251.20 − $19,000 =
$31,251.20

18. b $145 × 5 apartments = $725 monthly
$725 × 12 months = $8,700 × 90% =
$7,830 × .05 = $391.50
$1,400 (expenses) + $391.50 =
$1,791.50 total expenses
$7,830 (gross income) − $1,791.50 =
$6,038.50 (yearly income)
$6,038.50 ÷ 12 months = $503.21

19. d 7% of 60,000 = 4,200
5% of 60,000 = 3,000 × 2 years =
6,000
3% of 60,000 = 1,800 × 4 years =
7,200
4,200 + 6,000 + 7,200 = $17,400

20. b $225 × 52 weeks = $11,700
$370 × 12 months = $4,440
$11,700 − $4,440 = $7,260 net income
$7,260 ÷ 88,000 = .0825 = 8¼%

21. c $13,000 = 5% of what?
$13,000 ÷ 5% = $260,000 ÷ 110 acres
= $2,363.64

22. a $1,500 × 12 = 18,000 ÷ 430,000 =
4%

23. c $850,000 × .35 = $297,500
$850,000 − $297,500 = $552,500
$552,500 ÷ 12% = $4,604.17

24. a $7.50 × 20 = $150 payment
$360 ÷ 12 months = $30 taxes
$54 ÷ 36 months = $1.50 insurance
$150 + $30 + $1.50 = $181.50

25. a 108 ÷ 13.50 = 8
132 ÷ 16.50 = 8
1 ÷ 8 = ⅛; therefore ⅛″ = 1′

26. c $42,000 + $48,000 + $36,500 +
$55,600 = $182,100
$90,000 × 8% = $7,200

$182,100 − $90,000 = $92,100 × 2%
= $1,842
$1,842 + $7,200 = $9,042 commission
$182,100 × 6% = $10,926 − $9,042 =
$1,884 difference

27. c $85,000 × .35 = $29,750 assessed value
$29,750 ÷ 100 = $297.50
$297.50 × 3.05 (2.70 + .35) = $907.38

28. b $96,000 − $60,000 = $36,000 ÷ 5
years = $7,200 per year
$7,200 ÷ $60,000 = 12%

29. d $2,300 ÷ $9,200 = 25%

30. b 70′ × 80′ = 5,600 sq. ft.
30′ × 80′ = 2,400 ÷ 2 = 1,200 sq. ft.
5,600 + 1,200 = 6,800 sq. ft.

31. a

PRACTICE EXAMINATION

1. d
2. c
3. a
4. b
5. d
6. b
7. c
8. d
9. b
10. b
11. a
12. d
13. c
14. b
15. a
16. c
17. a
18. a
19. c
20. b
21. d
22. b
23. c
24. a
25. c
26. d
27. d
28. d
29. a
30. b
31. d
32. d
33. d
34. d
35. a
36. d
37. a
38. b
39. a
40. a
41. b

42. a
43. b
44. c
45. a
46. b
47. c
48. a
49. c
50. d
51. c
52. b
53. c
54. a
55. d
56. a
57. d
58. b
59. c
60. d
61. c
62. c
63. d
64. c
65. b
66. a
67. c
68. c
69. d
70. d
71. b
72. d
73. b
74. d
75. c
76. b
77. b
78. d
79. a
80. d
81. c

82. b
83. c
84. a
85. d
86. c
87. b
88. d
89. c
90. c
91. a
92. c
93. d
94. d $77,000 \div \$525 = 146.67$
95. c $\$65 \times \$8.54 = \$555.10$ per month payments on P & I
    $\$555.10 \times 360$ months $= \$199,836$
    $\$199,836 - \$65,000$ loan $= \$134,836$
96. c 12 months $\times$ 4 years $= 48$ months $\times$ $\$600 = \$28,800$
    $\$28,800 \times .05 = \$1,440 + \$300$ (half first mo. rent)
    $\$1,740$ total commission earned
97. c $48' \times 25' = 1,200$ sq. ft. $\times$ 2 stories $= 2,400$ sq. ft.
    $2,400$ sq. ft. $\times \$70 = \$168,000$
98. b $\$90,000 \times .80 = \$72,000$ loan, $\$18,000$ down payment due
    $\$18,000 + \$250 + \$360 + \$60 + \$430 = \$19,100 - \$4,000$ earnest deposit $= \$15,100$
99. a $\$150,000 + \$100,000 = \$250,000$
    $\$50,000 = $ 3rd parties share
    $\$50,000 \div \$300,000 = \frac{1}{6}$
100. c $\$170,000 \times 85\% = \$144,500$ sale price
    $\times .06 = \$8,670$
    $\frac{1}{2}$ of $\$8,670 = \$4,335$. 20% of $\$4,335 = \$867$
    $\$4,335 - \$867 = \$3,468$ for Joe Doe

Index